A-Z DORSET

GW00420180

CONTENTS

REFERENCE

Primary Route	A35	Airport	✈
Proposed		Car Park (Selected)	P
A Road	A352	Church or Chapel	†
Proposed		Cycleway (Selected)	⚲
B Road	B3143	Fire Station	■
Dual Carriageway		Hospital	H
One-way Street		House Numbers (A & B Roads only)	21 40
Traffic flow on A Roads is also indicated by a heavy line on the driver's left		Information Centre	i
Restricted Access		National Grid Reference	³05
Pedestrianized Road		Park & Ride	Norden P+
Track / Footpath		Police Station	▲
Residential Walkway		Post Office	★
		Toilet: without facilities for the Disabled	▽
Railway	Station / Heritage Station / Level Crossing / Tunnel	with facilities for the Disabled	▽
		Viewpoint	※ ✳
Built-up Area	BARNS ROAD	Educational Establishment	
Beach		Hospital or Hospice	
Local Authority Boundary		Industrial Building	
National Park Boundary		Leisure or Recreational Facility	
Posttown Boundary		Place of Interest	
Postcode Boundary (within Posttown)		Public Building	
		Shopping Centre or Market	
Map Continuation	74 / Large Scale Centres 120 / Road Map Pages 122	Other Selected Buildings	

SCALE

Map Pages 4-119	Map Pages 120-121
1:16,896 3¾ inches (9.52 cm) to 1 mile 5.9cm to 1km	1:8,448 7½ inches (19.05 cm) to 1 mile 11.8cm to 1km
0 ¼ ½ Mile	0 ⅛ ¼ Mile
0 250 500 Metres	0 100 200 300 400 Metres

Copyright of Geographers' A-Z Map Company Limited

Fairfield Road, Borough Green, Sevenoaks, Kent TN15 8PP
Telephone: 01732 781000 (Enquiries & Trade Sales)
01732 783422 (Retail Sales)
www.a-zmaps.co.uk
Copyright © Geographers' A-Z Map Co. Ltd.

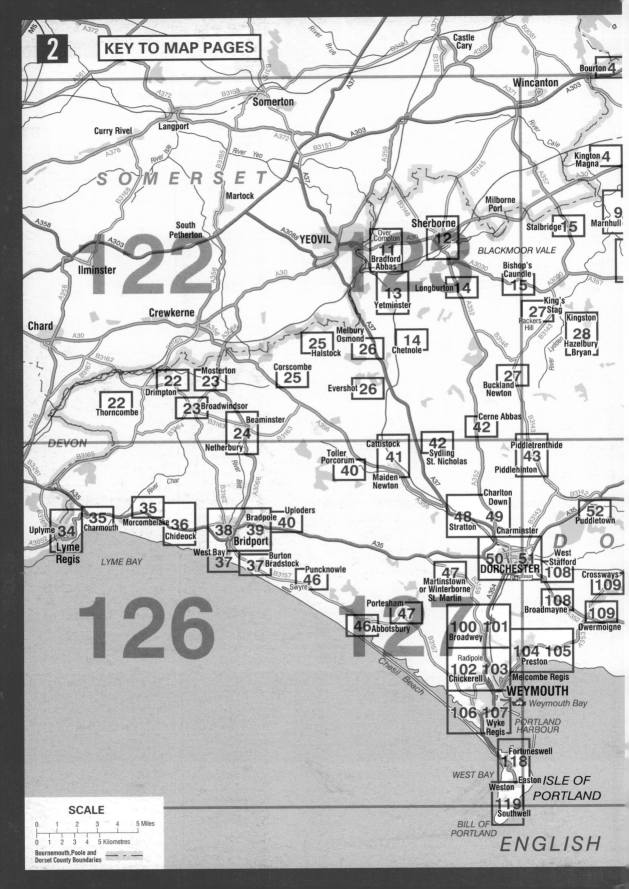

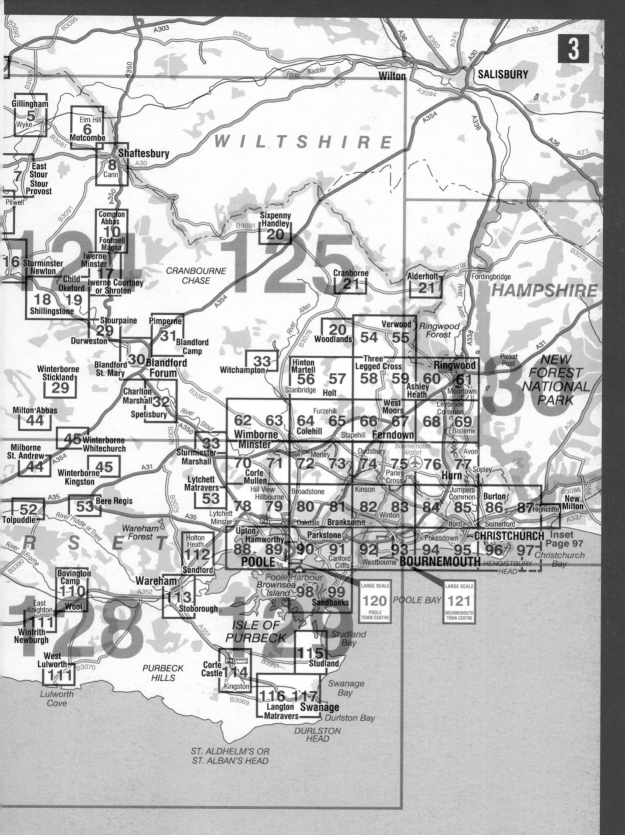

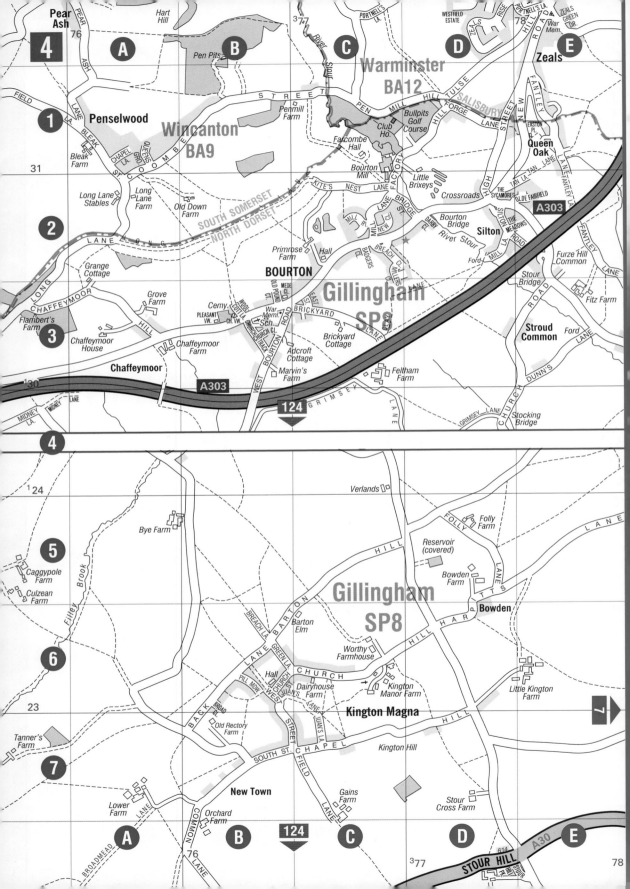

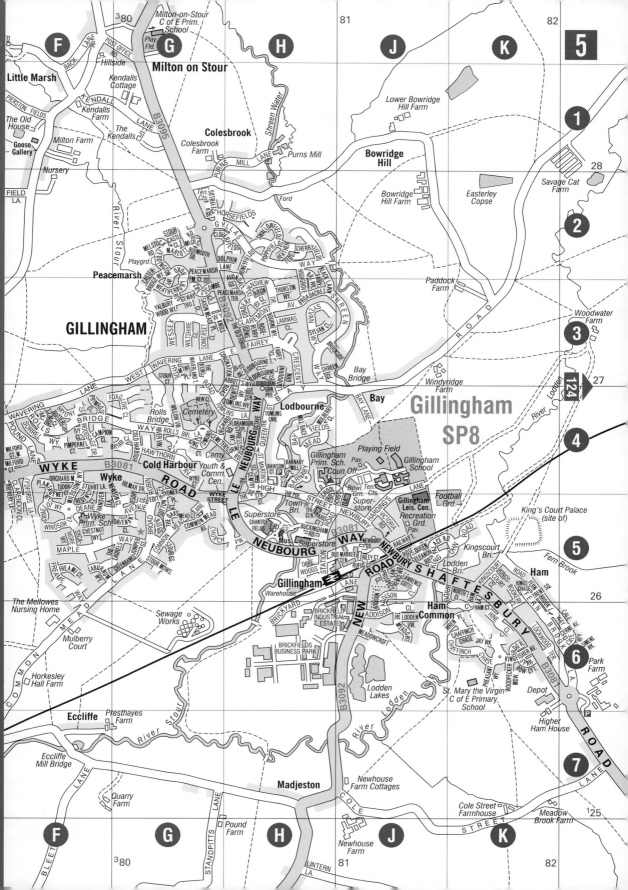

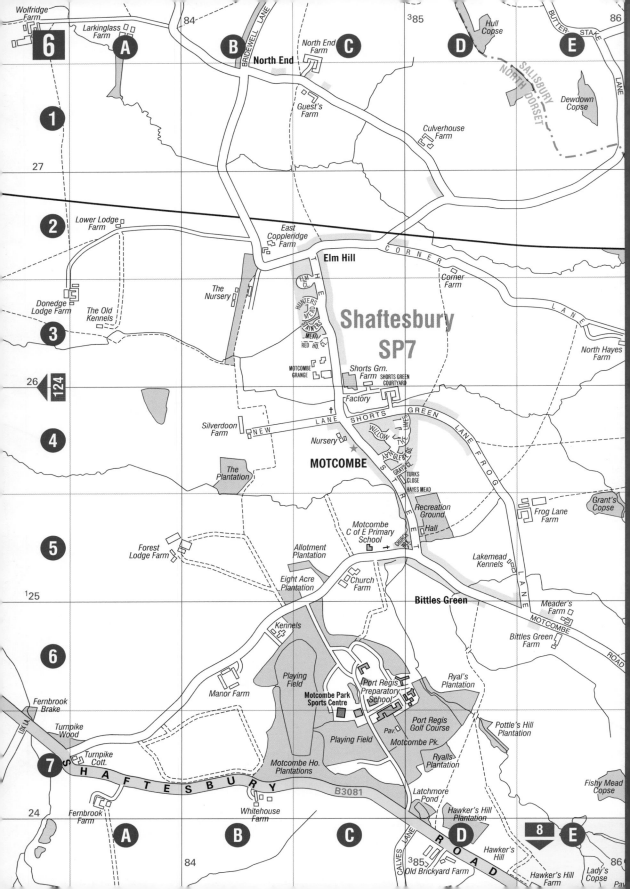

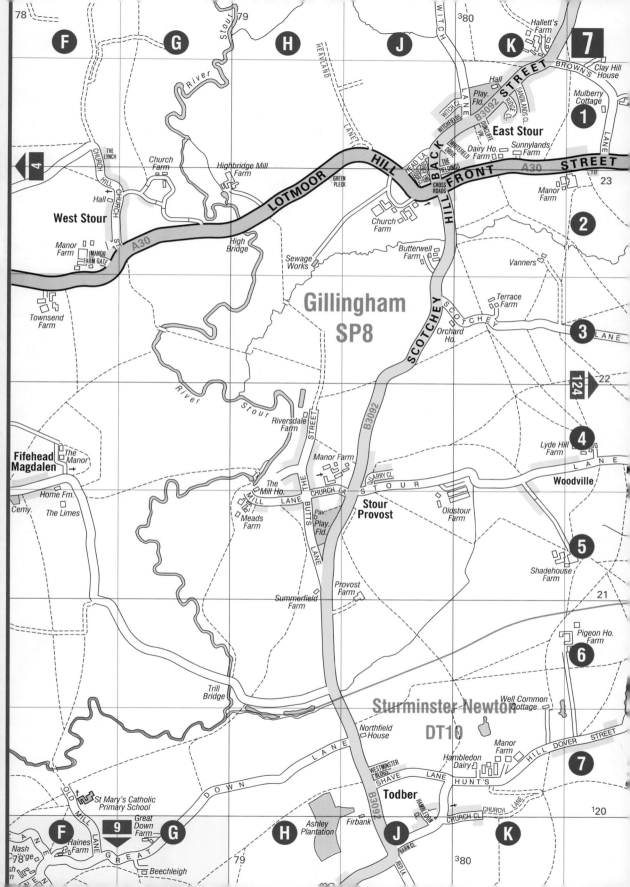

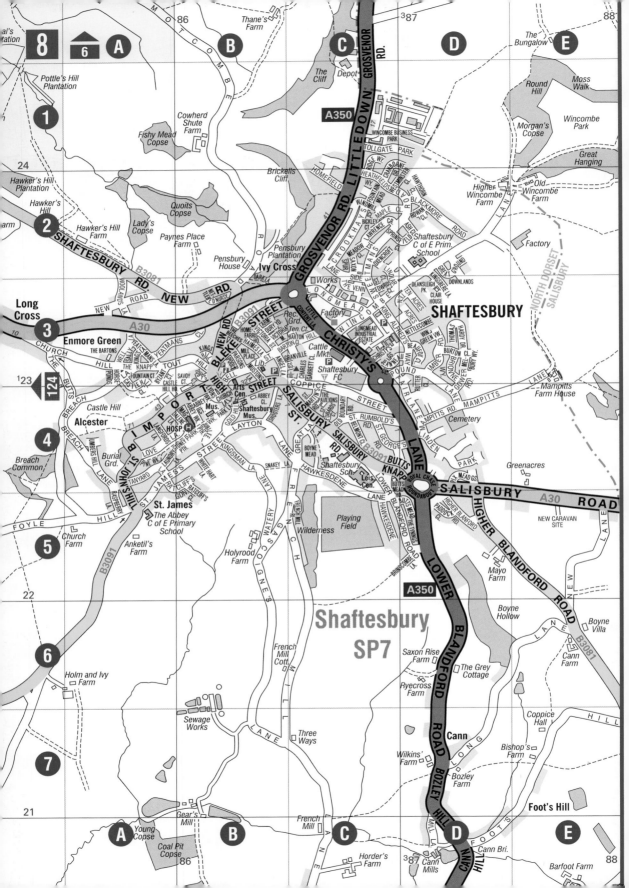

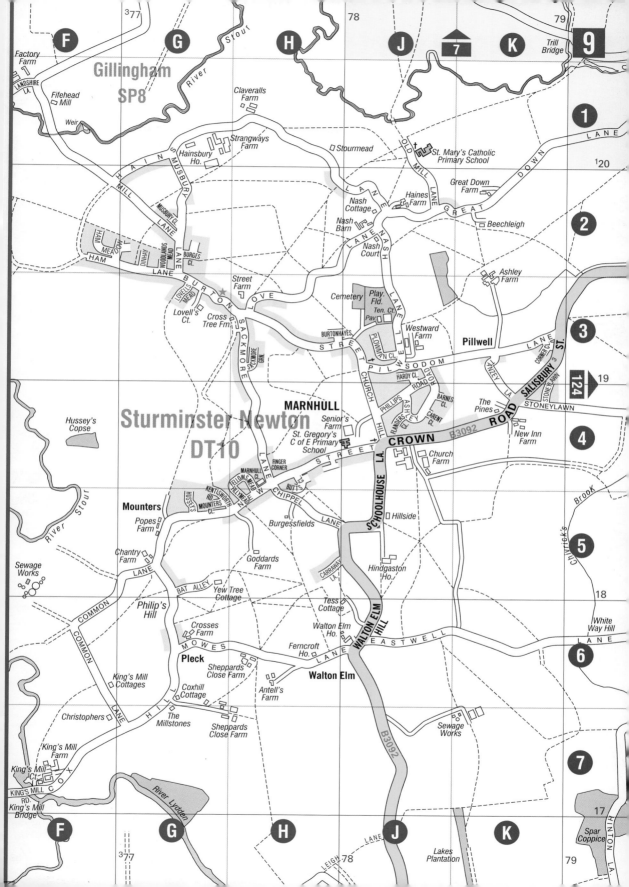

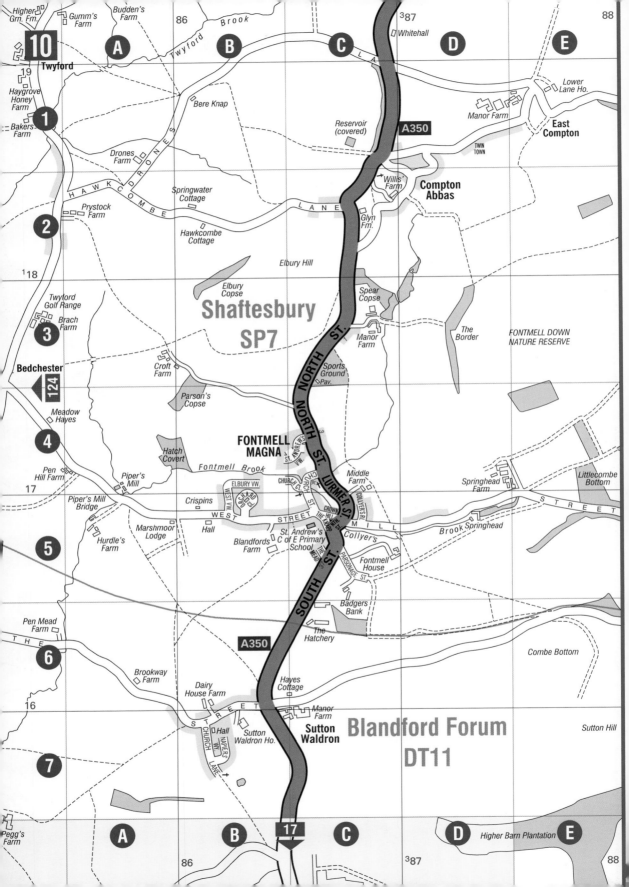

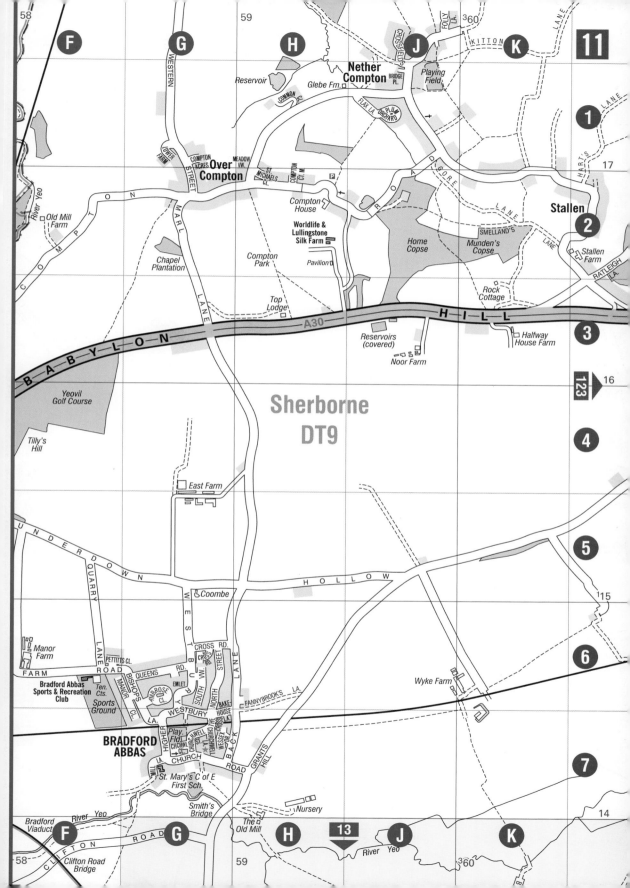

FOLLY LA.
360
KITTON
LANE
LANE

1

Nether
Compton
Reservoir
Glebe Fm.
BRIDGE PL.
CROSSFIELDS
Playing
Field

17

WESTERN
COMMON
FLAX LA.
ORCHARD PL.

OVER FARM
COMPTON ACRES
LOWER STREET
Over
Compton
MEADOW VW.
ST. MICHAELS CL.
COMPTON CL. M.
ROAD
GORE

Stallen

2

River Yeo
Old Mill
Farm
Compton
House
Worldlife &
Lullingstone
Silk Farm
Home
Copse
Munden's
Copse
SMELLAND'S
LANE
RATLEIGH LA.
Stallen
Farm

COMPTON
MARL
LANE
Chapel
Plantation
Compton
Park
Pavilion
Rock
Cottage

Top
Lodge
A30
BABYLON
HILL
Reservoirs
(covered)
Noor Farm
Halfway
House Farm

3

123
16

Yeovil
Golf Course
Sherborne
DT9

4

Tilly's
Hill
East Farm

5

115

UNDERDOWN
QUARRY
LANE
WEST STREET
Coombe
HOLLOW

6

Manor
Farm
FARM ROAD
PETTITS CL.
BISHOPS
QUEENS
MANOR CL.
AMBROSE CL.
EMLET
CROSS RD.
CROSS RD.
SOUTH VW.
NORTH ST.
LANE
WESSEX CROSS RD.
FANNYBROOK'S LA.
Wyke Farm

Bradford Abbas
Sports & Recreation
Club
Ten.
Cts.
Sports
Ground
WESTBURY
BAKE
HOUSE LA.
BACK

7

BRADFORD
ABBAS
HIGHER LA.
CHURCH
WELL
CL.
CHCH.
ST.
PLAY. FLD.
TINNEYBURROW
THE
WESSEX
CHURCH ROAD
GRANTS HILL
MILL LA.
St. Mary's C of E
First Sch.
Nursery

14

Bradford
Viaduct
River Yeo
Smith's
Bridge
The
Old Mill
River Yeo

CLIFTON ROAD
Clifton Road
Bridge

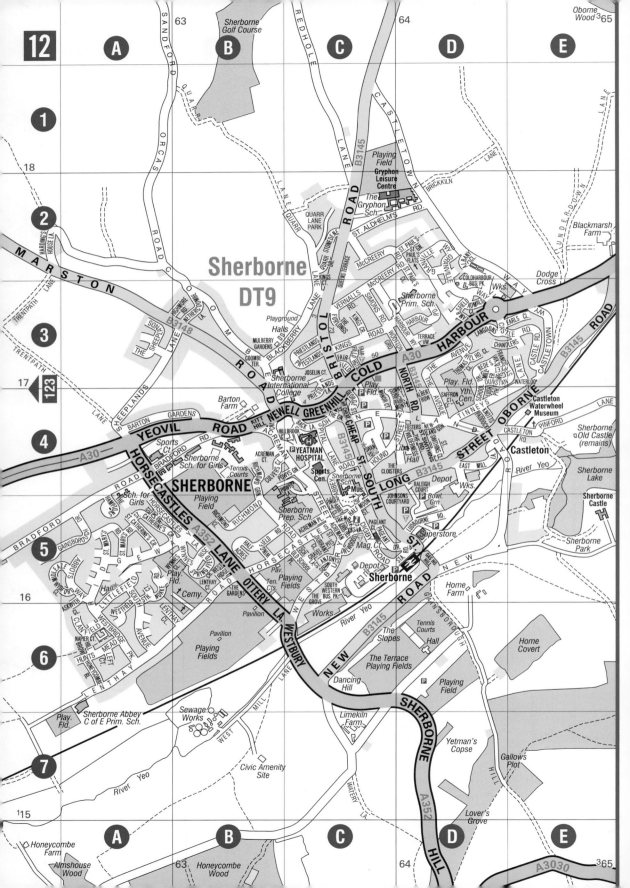

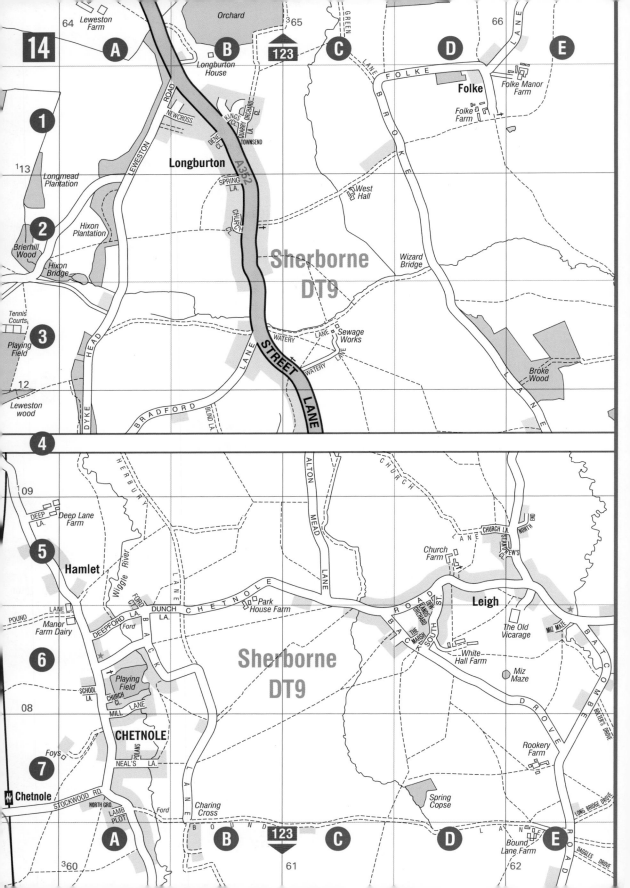

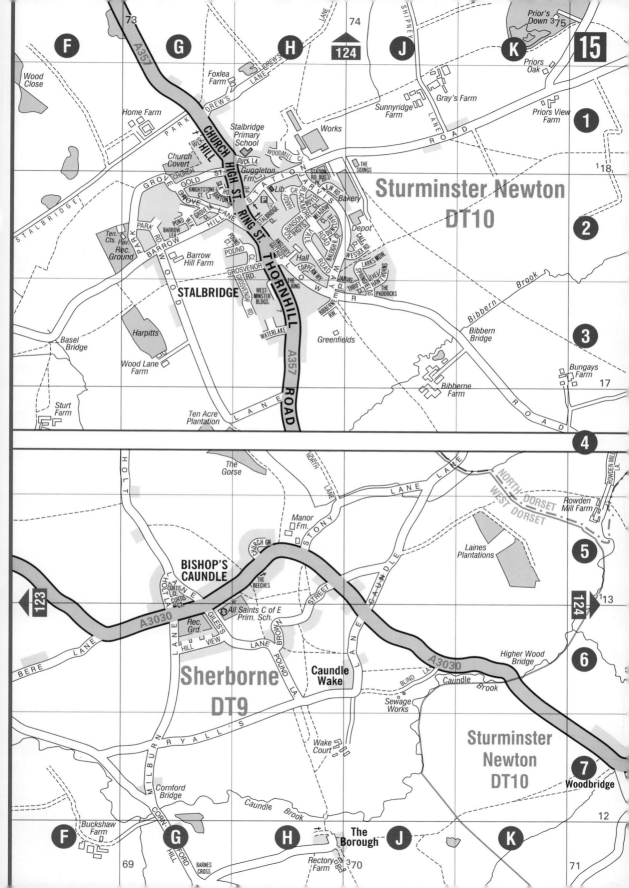

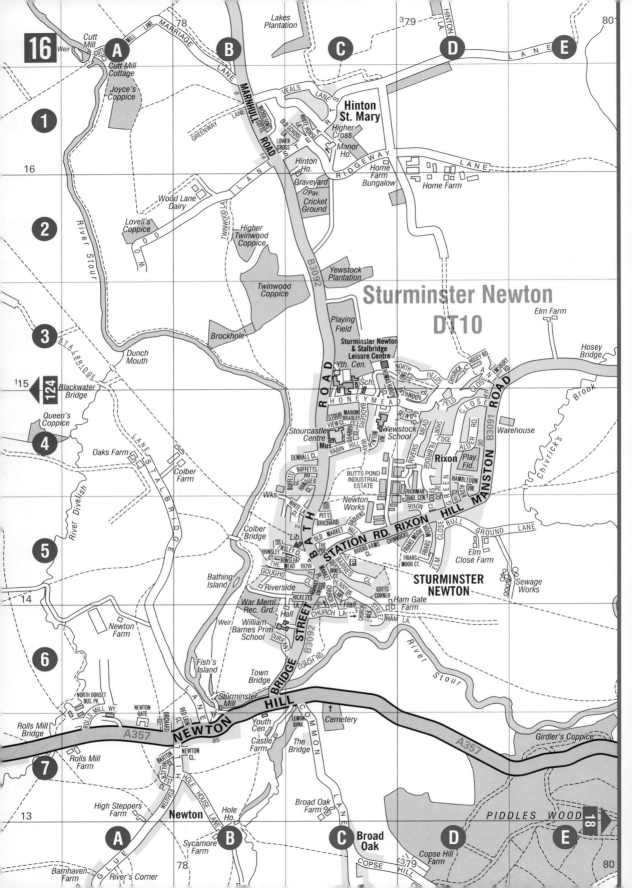

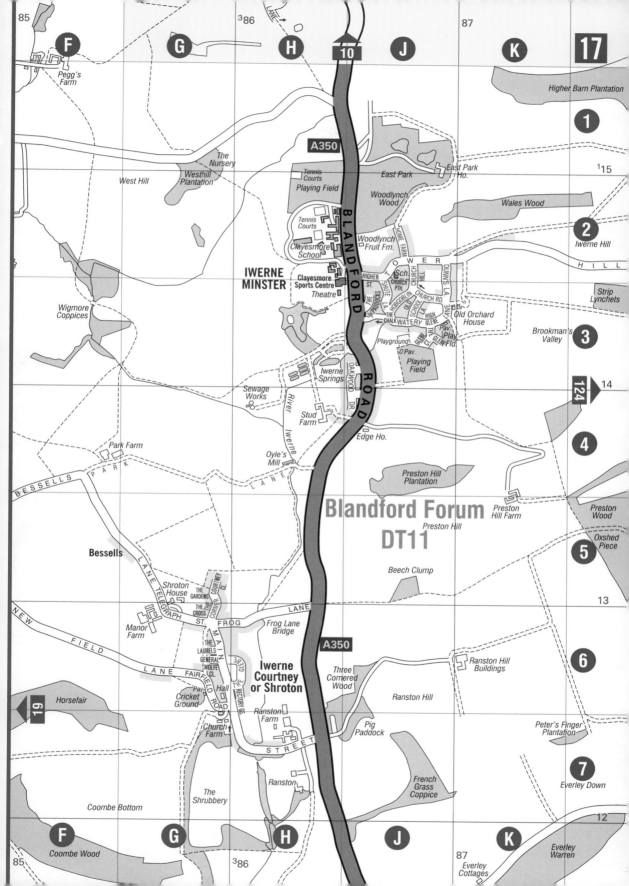

Pegg's Farm

Higher Barn Plantation

1

The Nursery

A350

Westhill Plantation

West Hill

East Park

East Park Ho.

15

Woodlynch Wood

Wales Wood

2

Tennis Courts
Playing Field

Iwerne Hill

HILL

Tennis Courts

Woodlynch Fruit Fm.

HOME FARM

IWERNE MINSTER

Clayesmore School

Clayesmore Sports Centre
Theatre

THE PADDOCKS

HIGHER ST.

CHUTE LA.

Sch.

CHURCH PTH.

LOWER

DUNN'S LA.

Strip Lynchets

NOBCARLIN

SCHOOL LA.

CHILD LA.

CHURCH RD.

BLANDFORD ROAD

THE CHALK

WATERY

HIGH

Old Orchard House

Brookman's Valley

3

GLEBE CT.

THE GLEBE

Pav.
Play Fld

Playground

Pav.

Playing Field

Iwerne Springs

124

14

OAKWOOD DR.

Wigmore Coppices

Sewage Works

River Iwerne

Stud Farm

Edge Ho.

4

Park Farm

Oyle's Mill

Preston Hill Plantation

Preston Hill Farm

Preston Wood

BESSELLS

PARK

Blandford Forum
DT11

Preston Hill

Oxshed Piece

5

13

Bessells

LANE

Beech Clump

Shroton House

THE GARDENS

THE CROSS

CORNER CL.

THE CROSS CL.

TELEGRAPH ST.

FROG

LANE

Frog Lane Bridge

A350

Ranston Hill Buildings

6

Manor Farm

MAIN

THE LAURELS

GENERAL WOLFE CL.

Iwerne Courtney
or Shroton

Three Cornered Wood

Ranston Hill

19

Horsefair

NEW

FIELD

LANE

FAIRFIELD ROAD

Cricket Ground

Pav.

Hall

RECTORY GDS.

A350

Ranston Farm

Pig Paddock

Peter's Finger Plantation

Church Farm

Ranston

STREET

French Grass Coppice

7

Everley Down

The Shrubbery

Coombe Bottom

Coombe Wood

85

386

87

Everley Cottages

Everley Warren

12

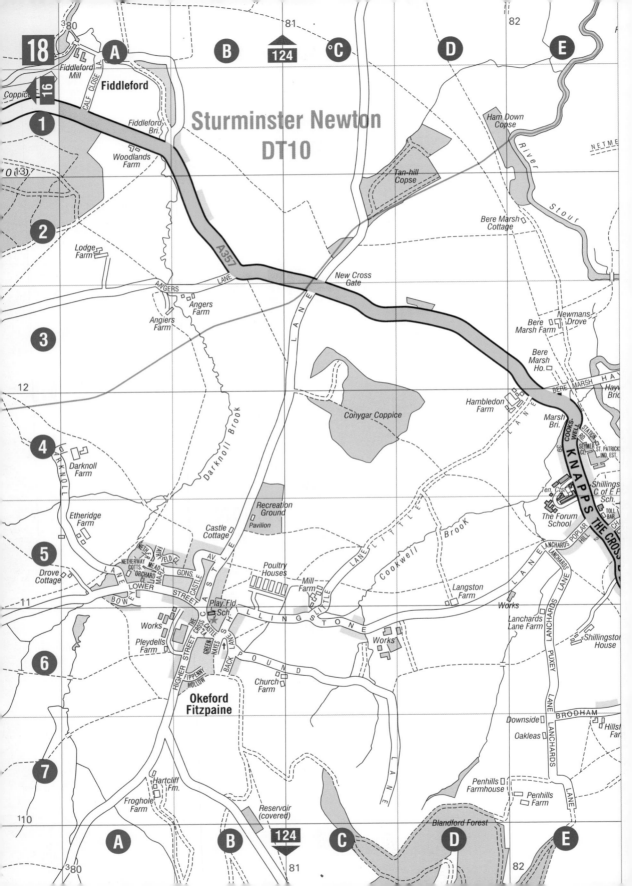

Sturminster Newton DT10

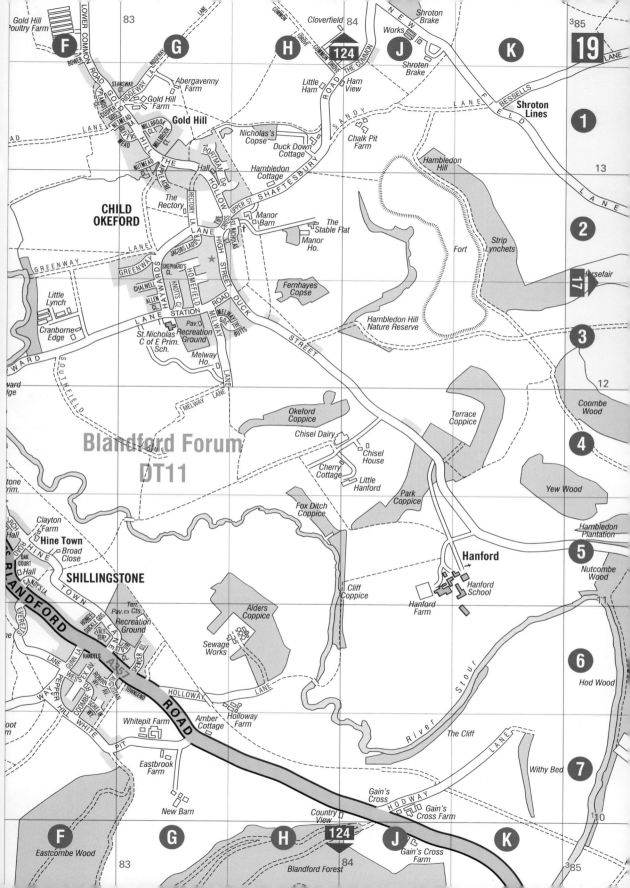

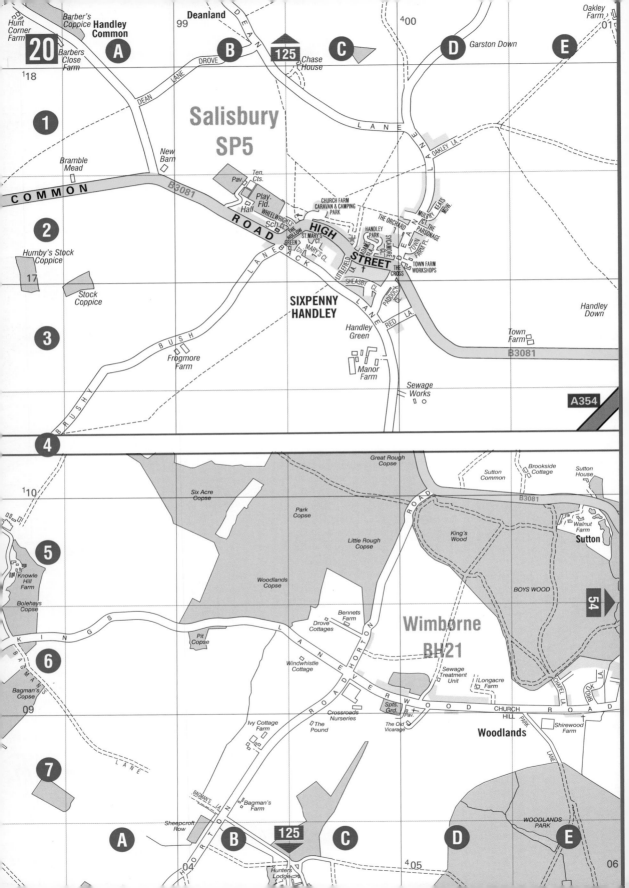

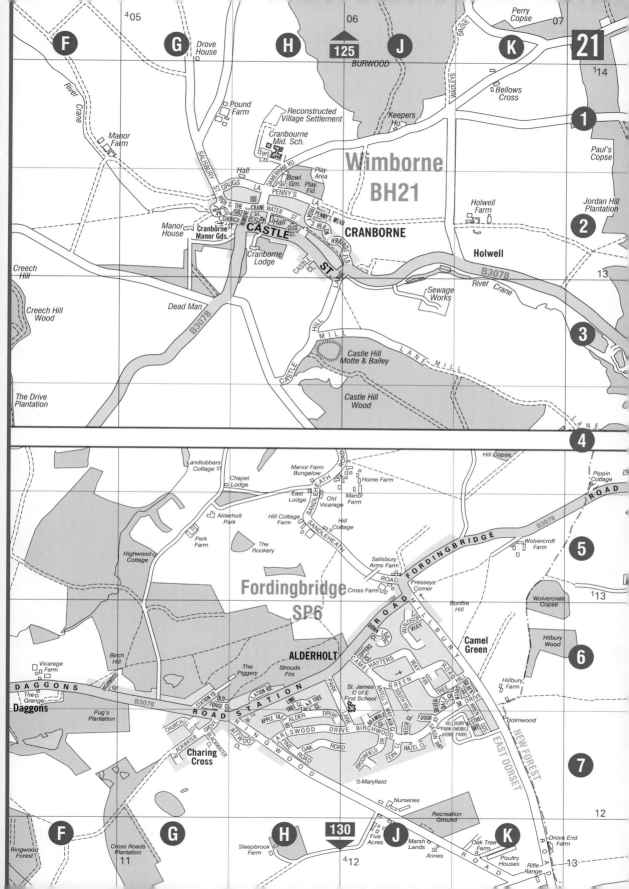

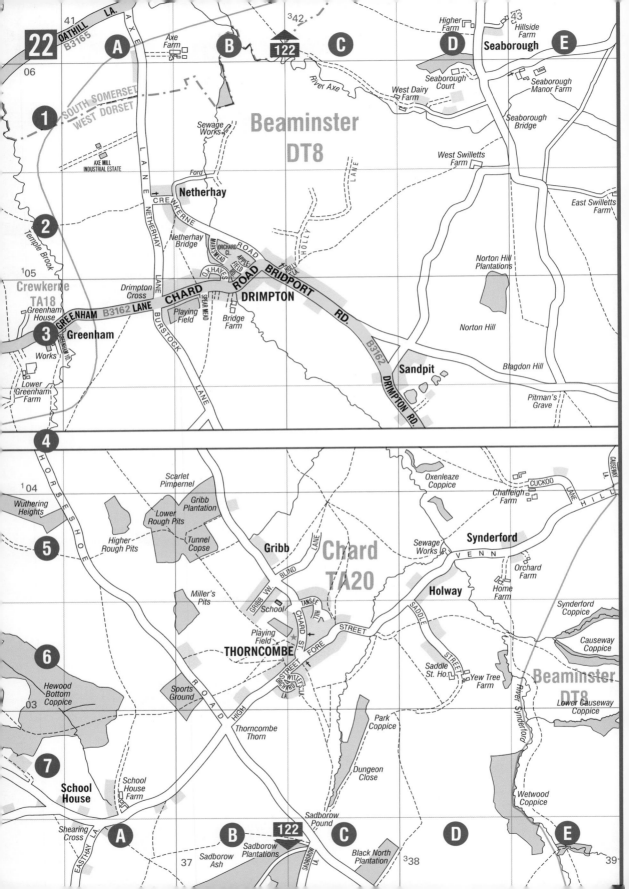

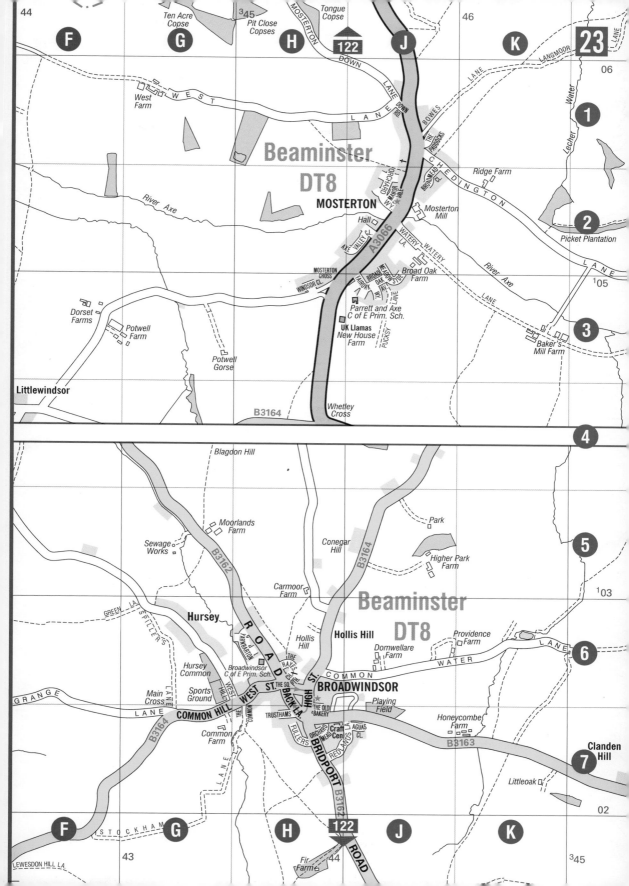

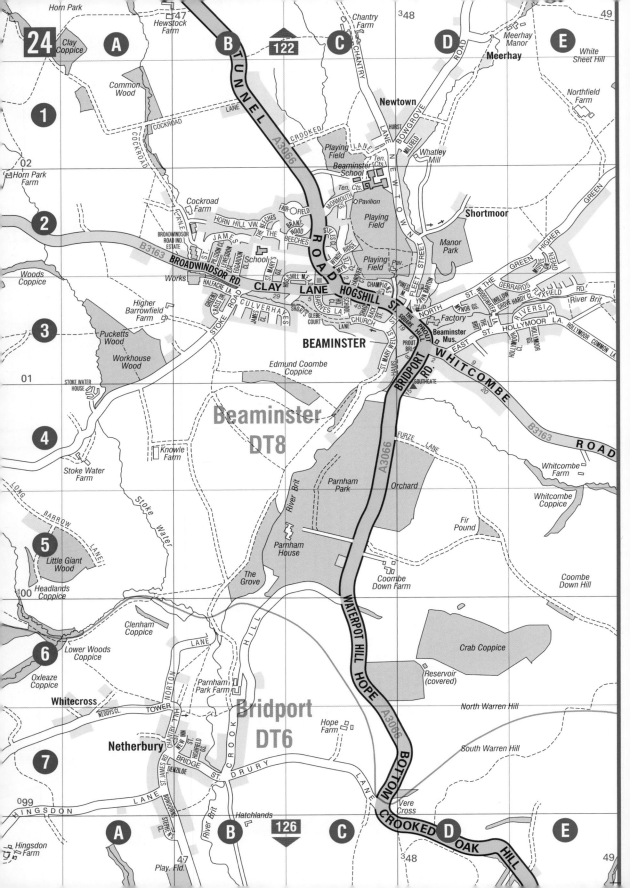

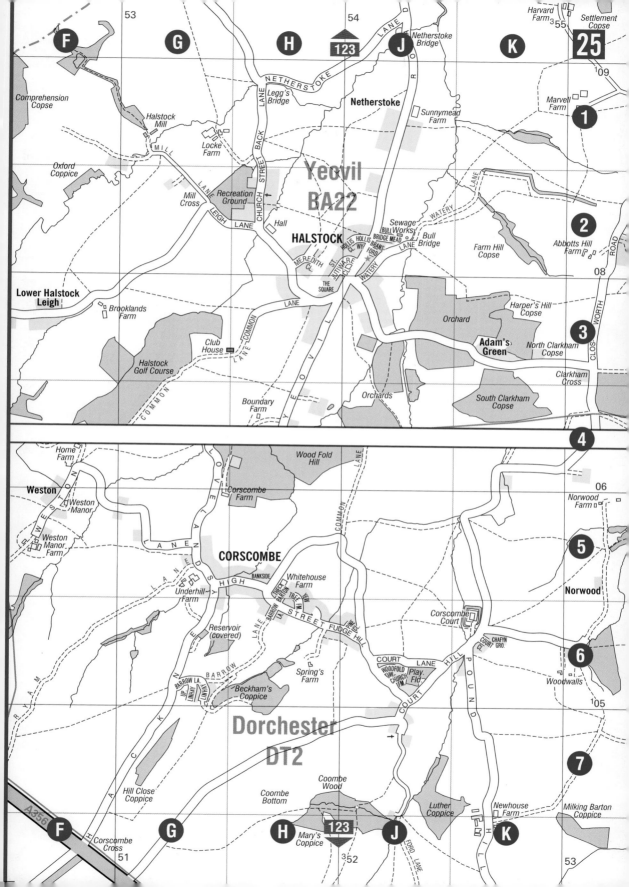

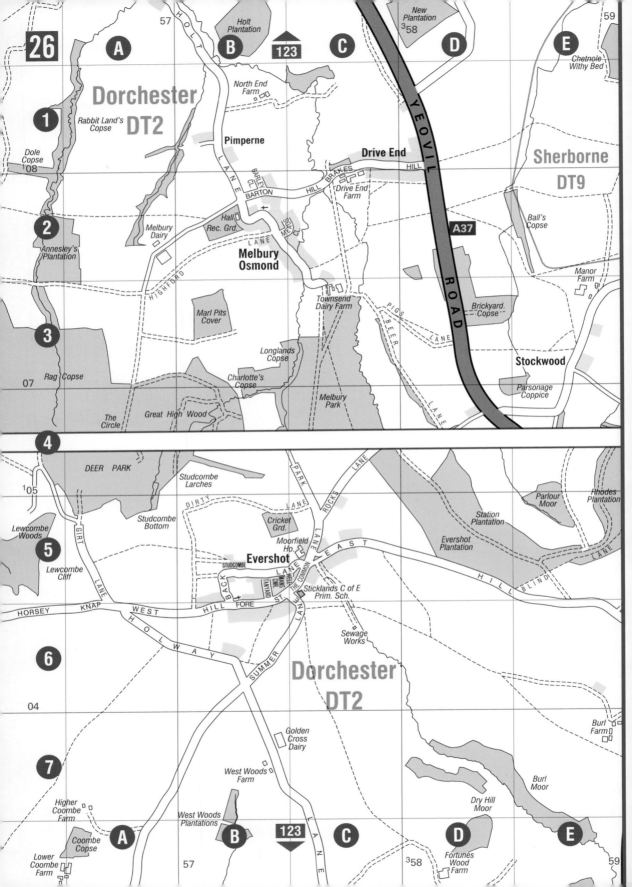

26

57   58   59

Holt Plantation

New Plantation

Chetnole Withy Bed

Dorchester DT2

Rabbit Land's Copse

North End Farm

Pimperne

Drive End

Sherborne DT9

Dole Copse 08

Barley Cl.
BARTON
Melbury Dairy
Hall
Rec. Grd.
BRAKES
Drive End Farm

HILL

YEOVIL

Ball's Copse

Annesley's Plantation

Melbury Osmond

MEAD CL.

A37

ROAD

Manor Farm

HIGHFORD

Townsend Dairy Farm

PIGS LANE

Brickyard Copse

Marl Pits Cover

BEER LANE

Rag Copse

Longlands Copse

Stockwood

07

Charlotte's Copse

LANE

Parsonage Coppice

The Circle

Great High Wood

Melbury Park

4

DEER PARK

Studcombe Larches

PARK LANE

LANE

Parlour Moor

Rhodes Plantation

05

DIRTY

Studcombe Bottom

Cricket Grd.

ROCKS LANE

Station Plantation

Lewcombe Woods

Moorfield Ho.

Evershot

STUDCOMBE

Evershot Plantation

HILL

BLIND LANE

5

GIRT LANE

Lewcombe Cliff

LANE

NEW LANE
MANS CNR.
TANYARD

BACK

FORE

THE COMMON

Sticklands C of E Prim. Sch.

EAST

HORSEY KNAP

WEST

HILL

ST.

6

HOLWAY

SUMMER LANE

Sewage Works

Dorchester DT2

Burl Farm

04

Golden Cross Dairy

7

West Woods Farm

Burl Moor

Higher Coombe Farm

West Woods Plantations

Dry Hill Moor

Coombe Copse

Fortunes Wood Farm

Lower Coombe Farm

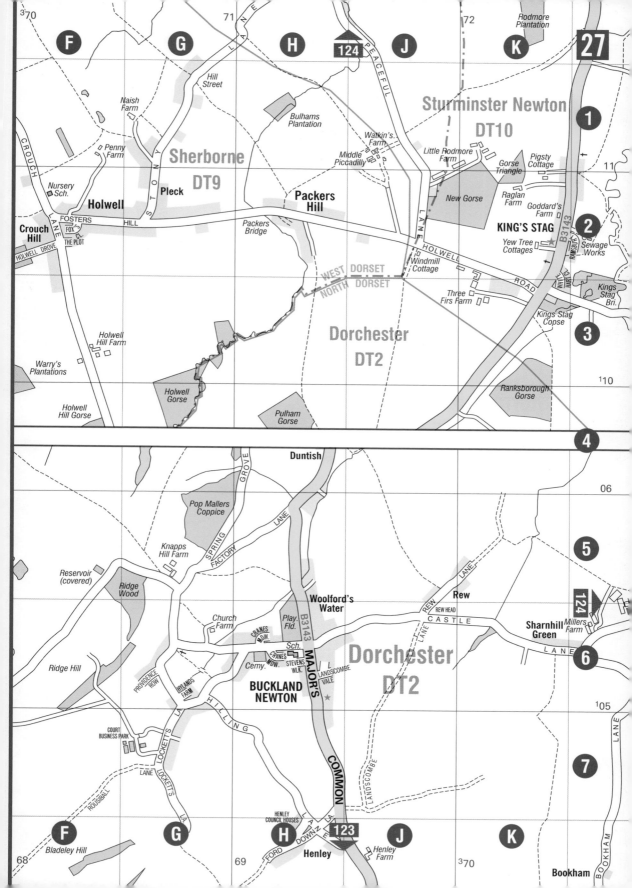

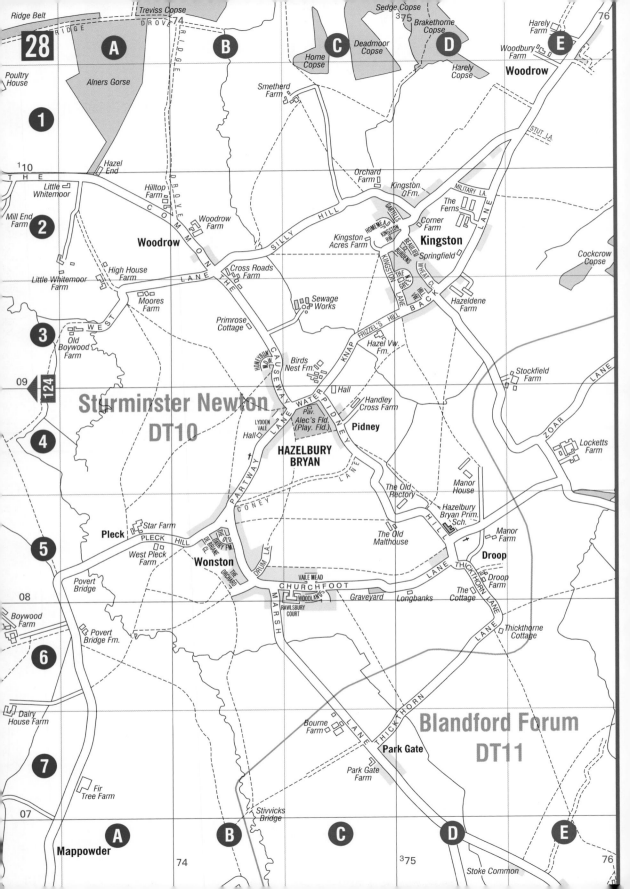

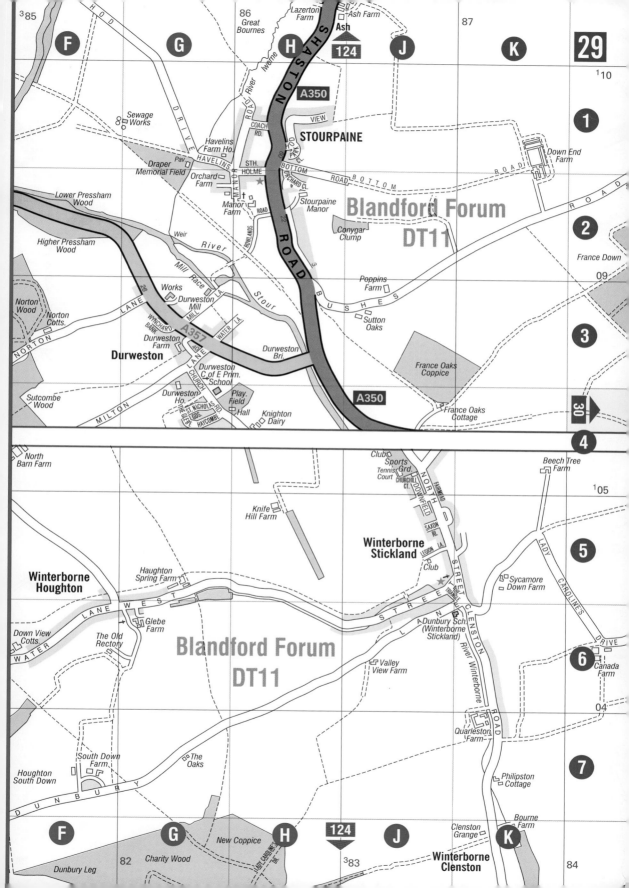

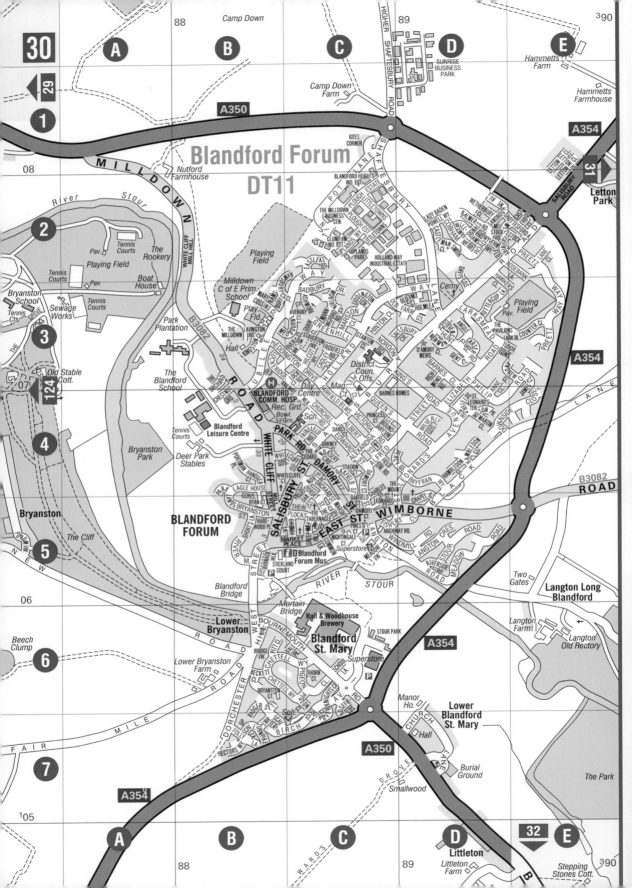

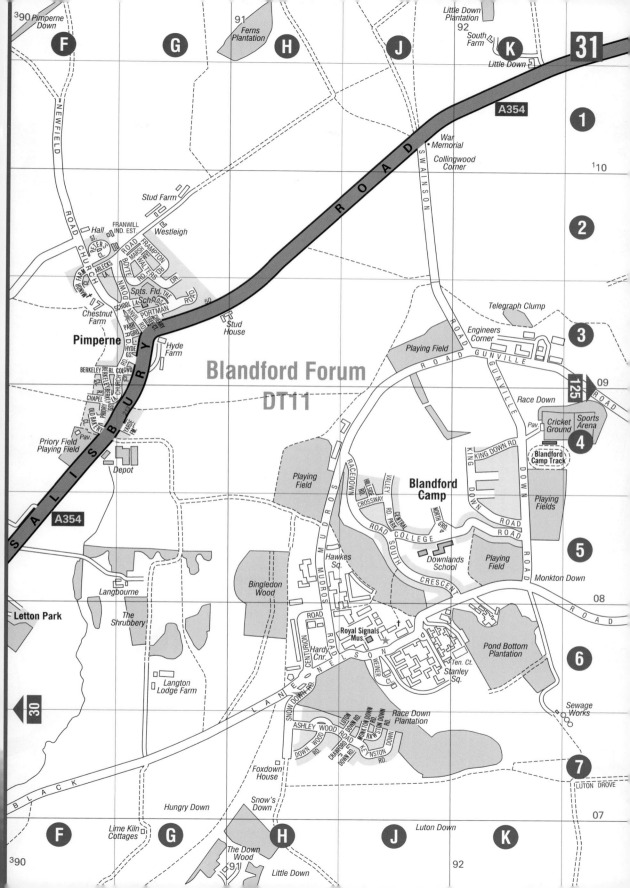

Blandford Forum
DT11

Pimperne

Blandford Camp

Letton Park

F   G   H   J   K

A354

1

¹10

2

3

125   09

4

5

08

6

30

7

07

F   G   H   J   K

Pimperne Down

Ferns Plantation

Little Down Plantation

South Farm

Little Down

War Memorial

Collingwood Corner

Stud Farm

Westleigh

FRANWILL IND. EST.

Hall

Chestnut Farm

Stud House

Hyde Farm

Telegraph Clump

Engineers Corner

Playing Field

Race Down

Cricket Ground

Sports Arena

Blandford Camp Track

Pav.

Priory Field Playing Field

Depot

Playing Field

KING DOWN RD.

Playing Fields

Monkton Down

Langbourne

The Shrubbery

Bingledon Wood

Hawkes Sq.

Downlands School

Playing Field

Pond Bottom Plantation

Langton Lodge Farm

Royal Signals Mus.

Hardy Cnr.

Stanley Sq.

Ten. Ct.

Sewage Works

Foxdown House

Race Down Plantation

Hungry Down

Snow's Down

The Down Wood

Little Down

Lime Kiln Cottages

Luton Down

LUTON DROVE

NEWFIELD

ROAD

CHURCH

SALISBURY

A354

BLACK LANE

SWAINSON ROAD

ROAD

GUNVILLE ROAD

KING DOWN ROAD

COLLEGE ROAD

CRESCENT

ROAD

MUDROS ROAD

RACEDOWN RD.

CROSSWAY

HILLSIDE RD.

VALLEY RD.

CENTRAL RD.

PARK RD.

SOUTH

NORTH GRD.

CENTURION ROAD

SNOW DOWN RD.

ASHLEY WOOD DOWN RD.

LUTON DOWN RD.

MONKTON DOWN RD.

CRANFORD DOWN RD.

KEYNSTON RD.

NMOD WILLS RW.

WEINER

390   91   92

390   91   92

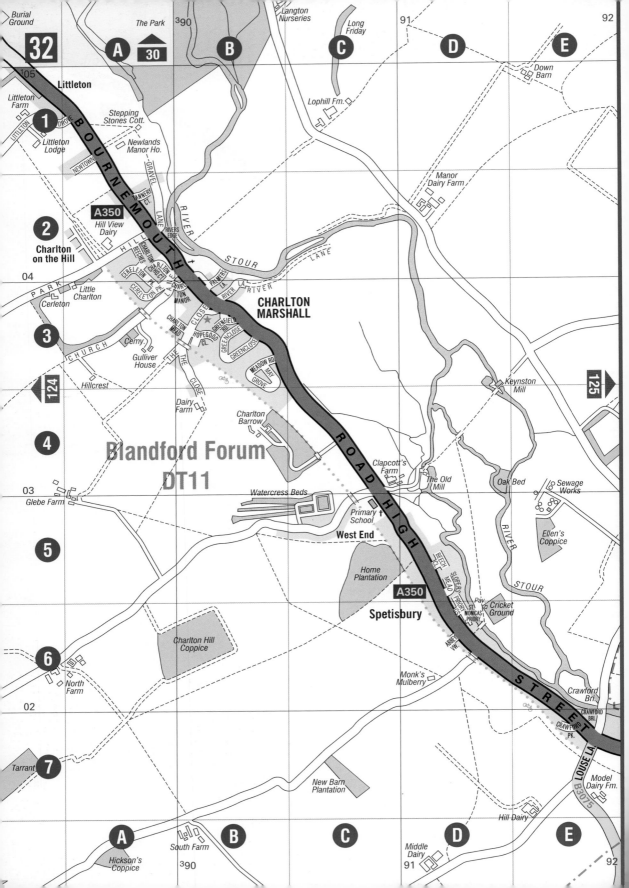

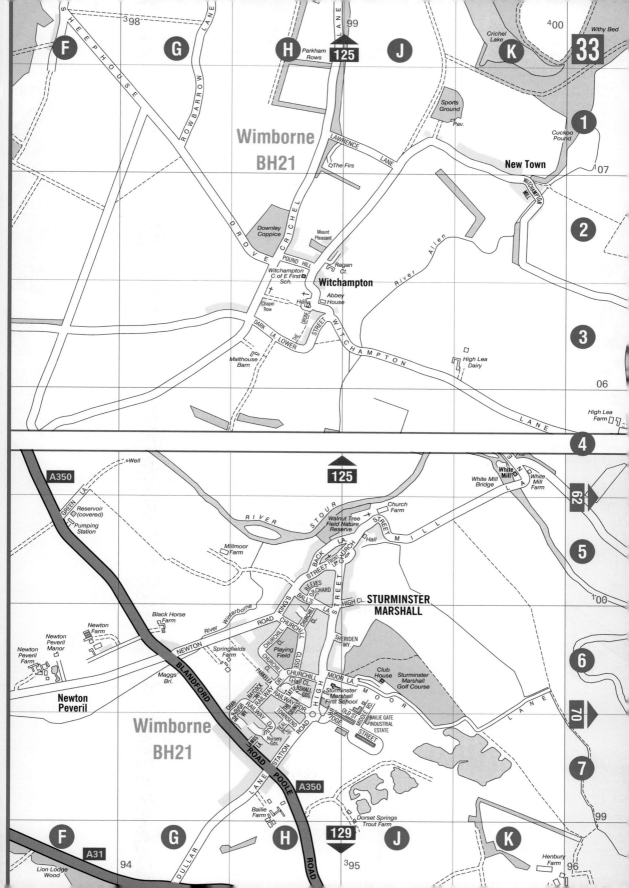

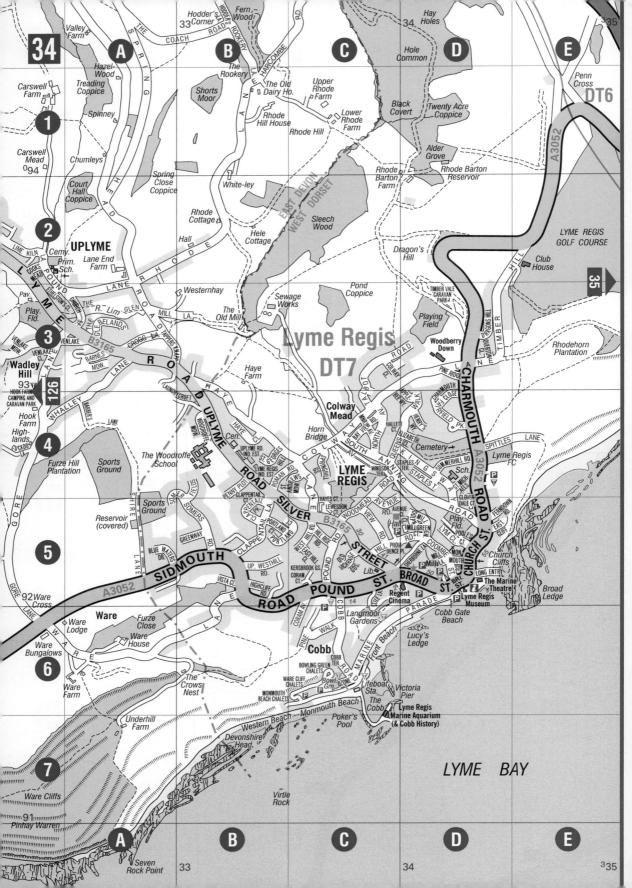

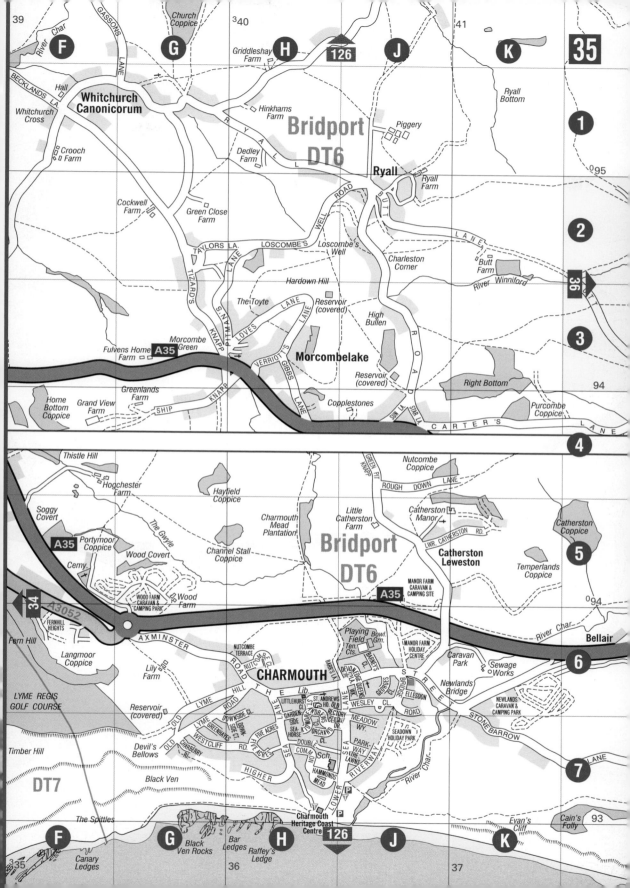

39 · River Char · F

GASSONS LANE

Church Coppice · G

³40

Griddleshay Farm · H

126 · J

K · 35

Ryall Bottom

BECKLANDS LA.

Hall

Whitchurch Canonicorum

Whitchurch Cross

Hinkhams Farm

Bridport DT6

Piggery

Crooch Farm

Dedley Farm

Ryall

Ryall Farm

095

1

Cockwell Farm

Green Close Farm

RYALL ROAD

WELL ROAD

Loscombe's Well

Charleston Corner

Butt Farm

LANE

SOUTH LANE

River Winniford

2

TAYLORS LA.

LOSCOMBE'S

TIZARD'S LANE

PITMAN'S KNAPP

The Toyte

Hardown Hill

Reservoir (covered)

High Bullen

36

Fulvens Home Farm · A35

Morcombe Green

LOVES LANE

ROAD

3

94

VERRIOTTS LANE

GIBBS LANE

Morcombelake

Reservoir (covered)

Right Bottom

Purcombe Coppice

Home Bottom Coppice

Grand View Farm

Greenlands Farm

SHIP KNAPP

Copplestones

SUN LA.

STAR LA.

CARTER'S LANE

4

Thistle Hill

Hayfield Coppice

Nutcombe Coppice

ROUGH DOWN LANE

GREEN PIT KNAPP

Catherston Manor

Hoggchester Farm

Soggy Covert

Charmouth Mead Plantation

Little Catherston Farm

Catherston Coppice

A35

Portymoor Coppice

The Gwyle

Bridport DT6

LWR. CATHERSTON RD.

Catherston Leweston

5

Wood Covert

Channel Stall Coppice

Temperlands Coppice

Cemy.

WOOD FARM CARAVAN & CAMPING PARK

Wood Farm

MANOR FARM CARAVAN & CAMPING SITE

A35

34 · A3052

FERNHILL HEIGHTS

River Char

Bellair

Fern Hill

AXMINSTER ROAD

Langmoor Coppice

Lily Farm

THE STREET

Playing Field

Ten. Cts.

Bowl. Grn.

MANOR FARM HOLIDAY CENTRE

Caravan Park

Sewage Works

6

LYME REGIS GOLF COURSE

Reservoir (covered)

THE STREET

BARNEY'S

DEVON EDGE

QUEENS

OLD

GEORGES

BRIDGE

Newlands Bridge

NEWLANDS CARAVAN & CAMPING PARK

CHARMOUTH

NUTCOMBE TERRACE

NUTCOMBE

Lib.

St. ANDREWS

ELLESDON

STONEBARROW LANE

LYME ROAD

OLD LYME HILL

THE STREET

Littlehurst

ST. ANDREWS DR.

RECTORY CL.

WESLEY CL.

ELLESDON ROAD

DOWNSIDE CL.

GARDEN SIDE

SEA-HORSE

ORCHARD CL.

MEADOW WY.

Timber Hill

GREENHAYES

WESTCLIFF RD.

FIVE ACRES

DOWN

FIVE ACRES

DOUBLE COMM.

SEA LANE

PARK-WAY

THE LAWNS

SEADOWN HOLIDAY PARK

RIVERWAY

River Char

7

CHARBERRY RI.

Devil's Bellows

Sch.

HAMMONDS MEAD

LOWER SEA LANE

Evan's Cliff

Cain's Folly

93

DT7

Black Ven

HIGHER

P

P

Charmouth Heritage Coast Centre

126

The Spittles

F · ³35 · Canary Ledges

G · Black Ven Rocks

Bar Ledges

Raffey's Ledge

H · 36

J · 37

K

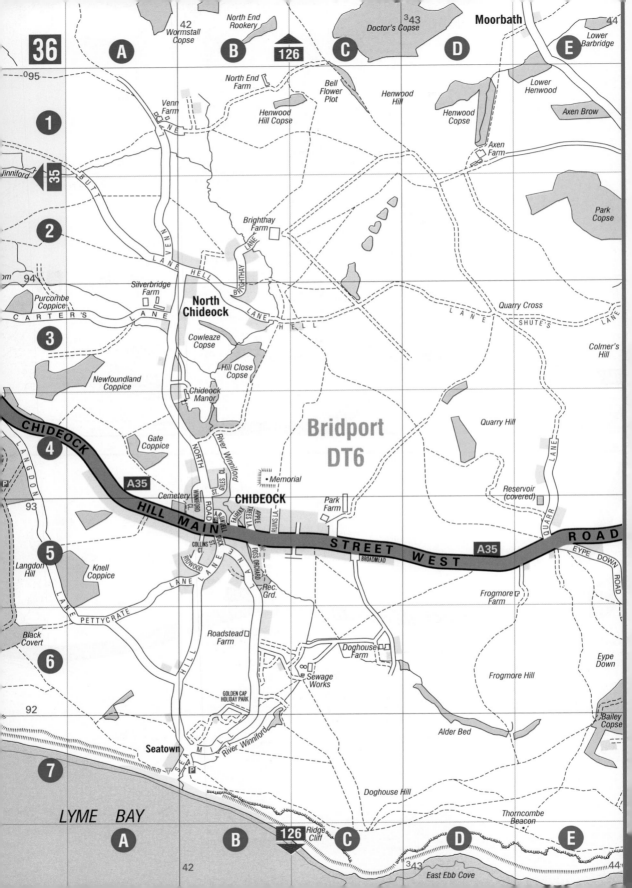

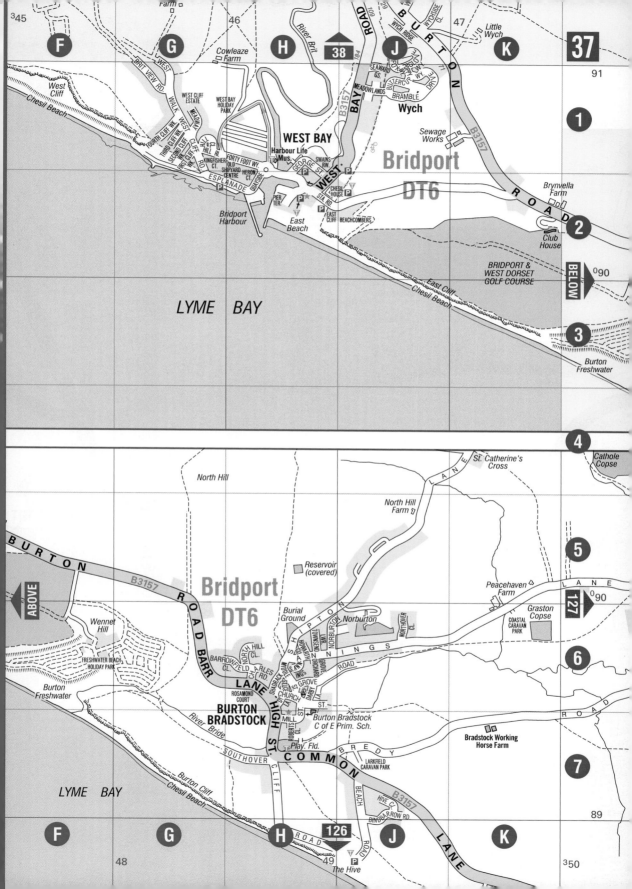

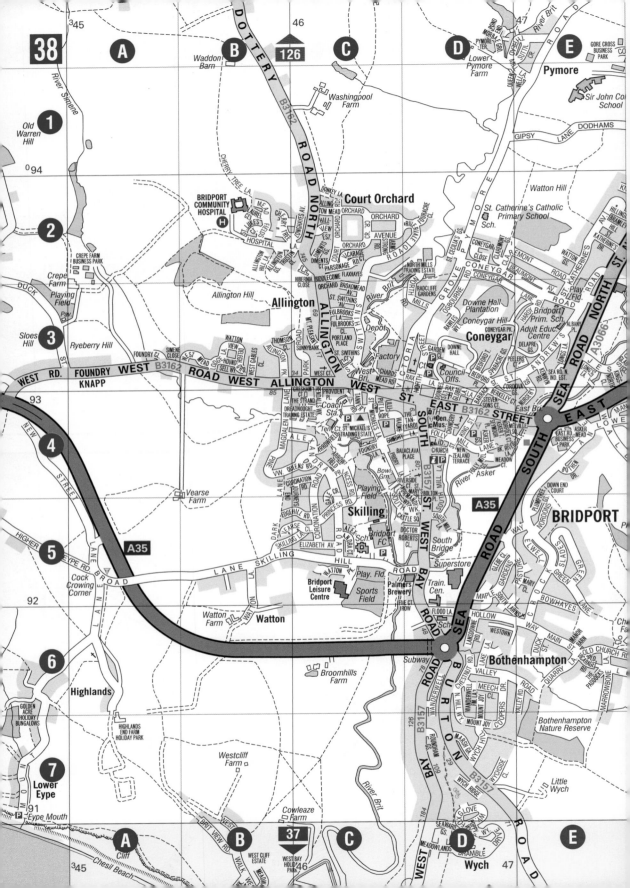

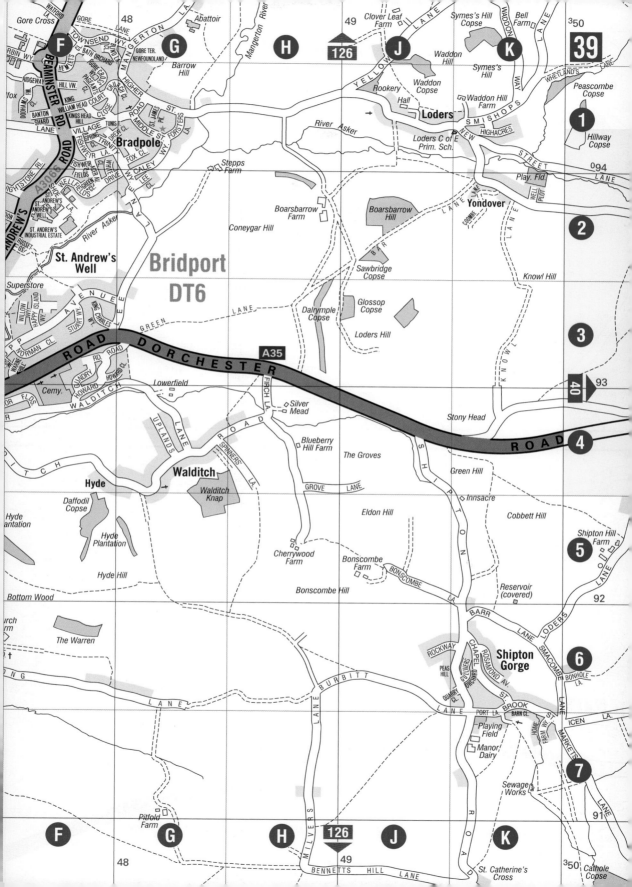

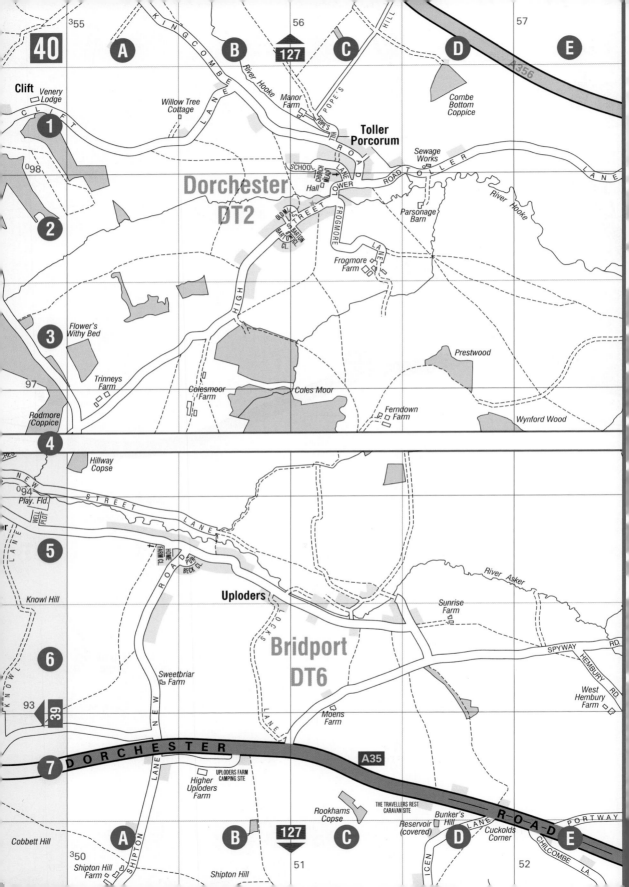

40

KINGCOMBE LANE

River Hooke

127

POPES HILL ROAD

Clift

Venery Lodge

Willow Tree Cottage

Manor Farm

Toller Porcorum

Combe Bottom Coppice

A356

1

098

CLIFT

SCHOOL

CHURCH MEAD

Hall

Sewage Works

TOLLER LANE

Parsonage Barn

River Hooke

Dorchester DT2

2

OLD MILL
ST BURTON
BARTON CL.

TOWER

STREET

FROGMORE LANE

Frogmore Farm

3

HIGH

97

Flower's Withy Bed

Prestwood

Trinneys Farm

Colesmoor Farm

Coles Moor

Ferndown Farm

Wynford Wood

Rodmore Coppice

4

Hillway Copse

NEW STREET LANE

094

Play. Fld.

WELL PLOT

LANE

FARM ROAD
HIGH

PURBECK CL.

Uploders

River Asker

Sunrise Farm

5

Knowl Hill

Bridport DT6

KNOWL

6

Sweetbriar Farm

NEW

93

39

NEW LANE

Moens Farm

SPYWAY RD.

HEMBURY RD.

West Hembury Farm

7

DORCHESTER

A35

Higher Uploders Farm

UPLODERS FARM CAMPING SITE

ROAD

PORTWAY

Rookhams Copse

THE TRAVELLERS REST CARAVAN SITE

Bunker's Hill

Reservoir (covered)

ICEN LANE

Cuckolds Corner

CHILCOMBE LA.

Cobbett Hill

SHIPTON

Shipton Hill Farm

Shipton Hill

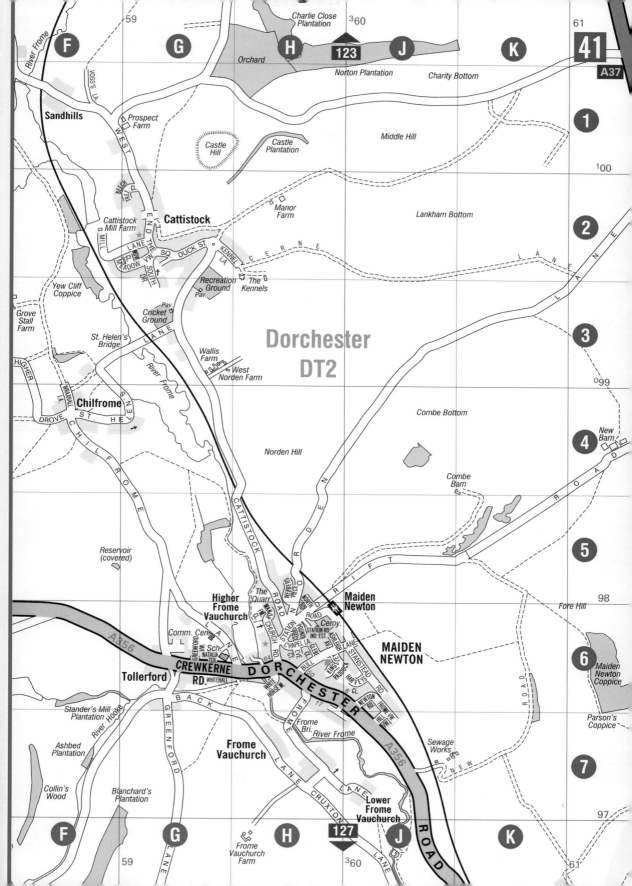

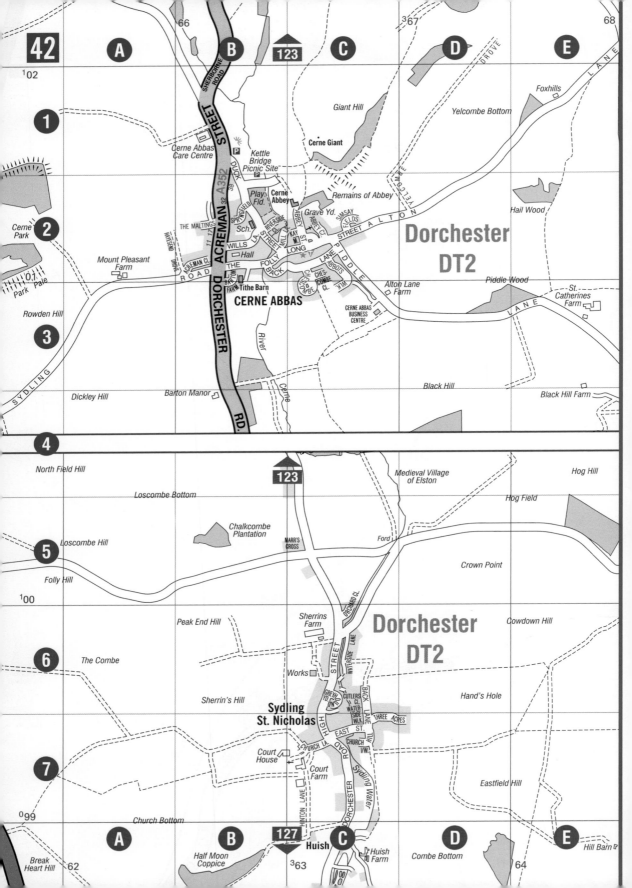

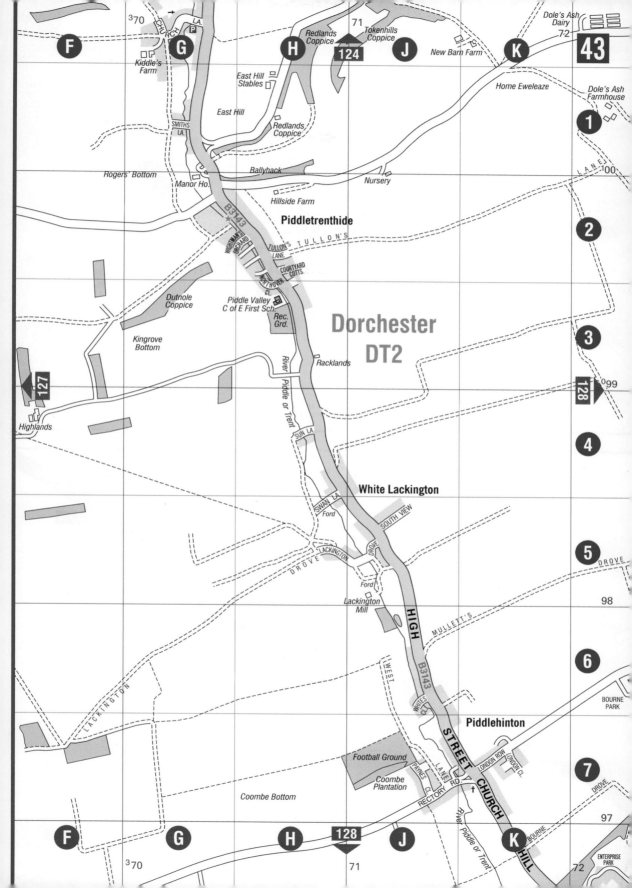

F G H 124 J K

Dole's Ash Dairy

71 Redlands Coppice Tokenhills Coppice

New Barn Farm

72

Kiddle's Farm

Home Eweleaze

Dole's Ash Farmhouse

East Hill Stables

LANE 00

East Hill

Redlands Coppice

1

SMITHS LA.

Rogers' Bottom

Ballyhack

Nursery

Manor Ho.

Hillside Farm

2

B3143

Piddletrenthide

WIGHTMAN'S ORCHARD

ZULLON'S LANE   TULLON'S LANE

NORTH OVER CL.

COURTYARD COTTS.

Dorchester DT2

3

Dutnole Coppice

Piddle Valley C of E First Sch.

Rec. Grd.

128 099

127

Kingrove Bottom

River Piddle or Trent

Racklands

Highlands

SUN LA.

4

White Lackington

SWAN LA.
Ford

SOUTH VIEW

5 DROVE

DROVE

DROVE LACKINGTON

Ford

DROVE

98

Lackington Mill

LACKINGTON

HIGH

MULLETT'S

6

BOURNE PARK

B3143

Piddlehinton

WEST

Football Ground

WHITE'S

LONDON ROW

LONDON CL.

7

Coombe Plantation

PAINES CL.

STREET

CHURCH

RECTORY RD.

†

Coombe Bottom

River Piddle or Trent

BOURNE

97

ENTERPRISE PARK

F 70   G   H 128 J   K HILL   72

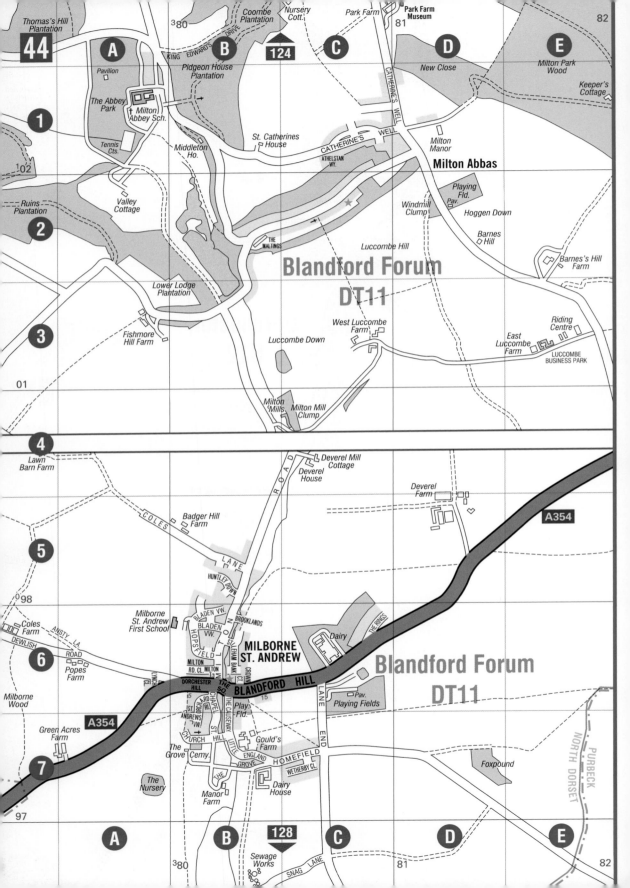

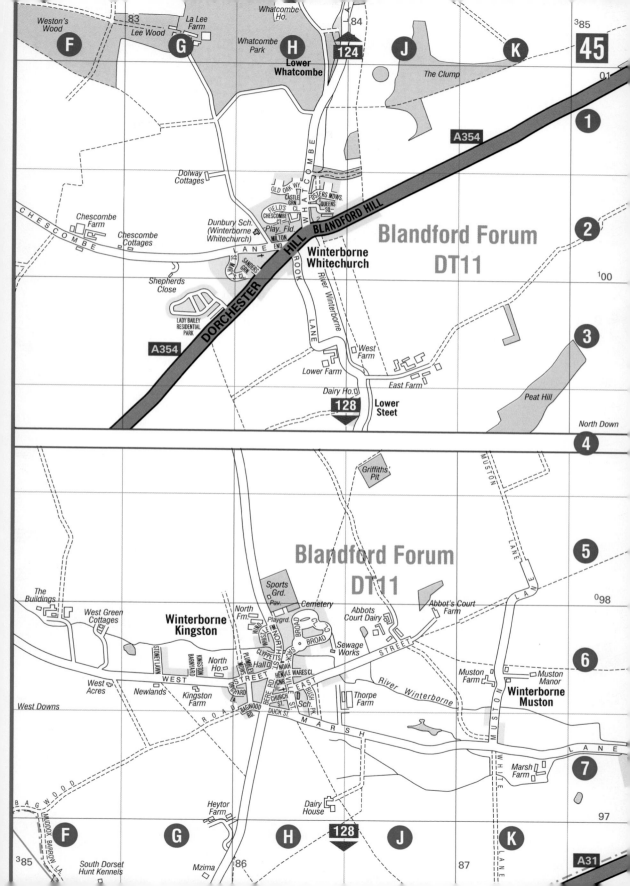

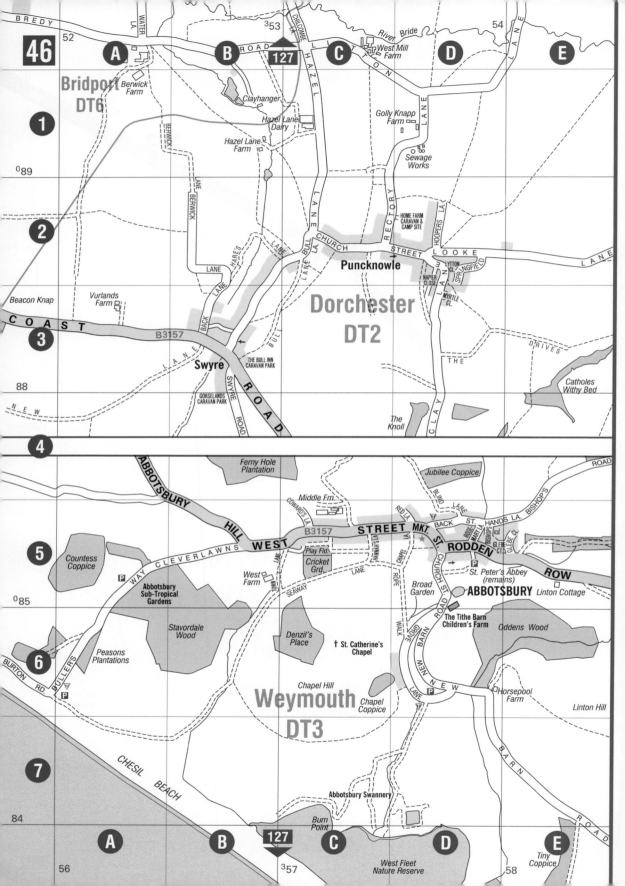

46

52   WATER LA.   353   CHILCOMBE   54

BREDY

A   **B**   Broad   **C**   **D**   **E**

127

1   Bridport   Berwick   Clayhanger   River Bride   West Mill Farm
DT6   Farm   Golly Knapp Farm

89   Hazel Lane Dairy

Hazel Lane Farm   Sewage Works

BERWICK LANE   HAZEL LANE   LYTTON LANE   HOOPERS LA.   LOOKE LANE

2   HOME FARM CARAVAN & CAMP SITE

LANE   YARES LANE   BACK LANE   LANE   BULL LA.   CHURCH LANE   Puncknowle   RECTORY STREET   LYTTON CL.   SPRINGFIELD   NAPIER CLOSE   MYRTLE CL.

Beacon Knap   Vurlands Farm   **Dorchester DT2**

3   COAST   B3157   Swyre   THE DRIVES

88   SWYRE ROAD   THE BULL INN CARAVAN PARK   The Knoll   CLAY   Catholes Withy Bed

NEW   GORSELANDS CARAVAN PARK   BULL   ROAD

4

ABBOTSBURY HILL   Ferny Hole Plantation   Jubilee Coppice   ROAD

Middle Fm.   BLIND LANE   BISHOPS ROAD

5   Countess Coppice   WEST   B3157   STREET   MKT ST.   RODDEN   HANDS LA.   ROW
WAY   CLEVERLAWNS   West Farm   Play Fld.   Cricket Grd.   BACK   ROSES ST.   MARTLE   BISHOPS CL.   GLEBE CL.   St. Peter's Abbey (remains)   Linton Cottage
85   Abbotsbury Sub-Tropical Gardens   CHURCH ST.   CHAPEL LANE   ROPE   ABBOTSBURY
P   SEAWAY   WALK   Broad Garden   The Tithe Barn Children's Farm

Stavordale Wood   Denzil's Place   † St. Catherine's Chapel   GROVE   Oddens Wood

6   Peasons Plantations   NEW BARN LANE   Horsepool Farm   Linton Hill
BURTON RD.   BULLERS   P   Chapel Hill   Chapel Coppice   P   NEW   BARN ROAD
P   **Weymouth DT3**

7   CHESIL BEACH   Abbotsbury Swannery   Tiny Coppice

84   Bum Point   West Fleet Nature Reserve

A   **B**   127   **C**   **D**   **E**

56   357   58

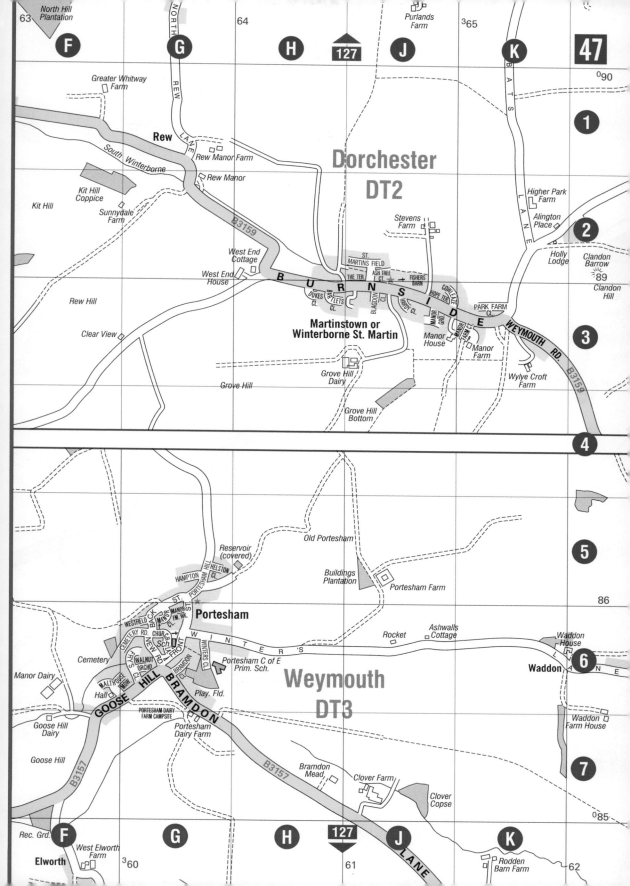

North Hill Plantation
63
F
G
64
H
127
J
K
47
090

Greater Whitway Farm
Rew
South Winterborne
Rew Manor Farm
Rew Manor
B3159
Kit Hill Coppice
Kit Hill
Sunnydale Farm
West End Cottage
West End House
Rew Hill
Clear View

Dorchester
DT2

Higher Park Farm
Alington Place
Holly Lodge
Clandon Barrow
⌂89
Clandon Hill

Stevens Farm

ST. MARTINS FIELD
THE TER.
ASH TREE CT.
FISHERS BARN
BURNSIDE
DUKES CL.
BARTLETS CL.
BLAGDON CL.
HARDY CL.
HOPE TER.
COURTLEAZE
MANOR GRO.
MANOR FARM CL.
PARK FARM CL.
WEYMOUTH RD.
B3159

Martinstown or Winterborne St. Martin

Manor House
Manor Farm
Wylye Croft Farm

Grove Hill Dairy
Grove Hill

Grove Hill Bottom

1
2
3
4

Purlands Farm
365

Reservoir (covered)
Old Portesham
HAMPTON HILL
HELSTON CL.
PORTESHAM HILL

Buildings Plantation
Portesham Farm

86

WESTFIELD
CEMETERY RD.
ST.
BACK
MANOR
CL.
CHUR.
FM. WK.
MANOR CL.
Sch.
Portesham
NEW RD.
FRONT
WINTER'S
WINTERS CL.
FRYS CL.
WALNUT
ORCHD.
BRAMDON CL.
Portesham C of E Prim. Sch.

Rocket
Ashwalls Cottage
Waddon House
Waddon

Weymouth
DT3

Cemetery
Manor Dairy
MALTHOUSE MDW.
Hall
GOOSE HILL
BRAMDON
Play. Fld.

Goose Hill Dairy
Goose Hill
PORTESHAM DAIRY FARM CAMPSITE
Portesham Dairy Farm
B3157

Waddon Farm House

Bramdon Mead
Clover Farm
Clover Copse

5
6
7

085

Rec. Grd.
F
West Elworth Farm
Elworth
360
G
H
127
J
LANE
K
Rodden Barn Farm
62

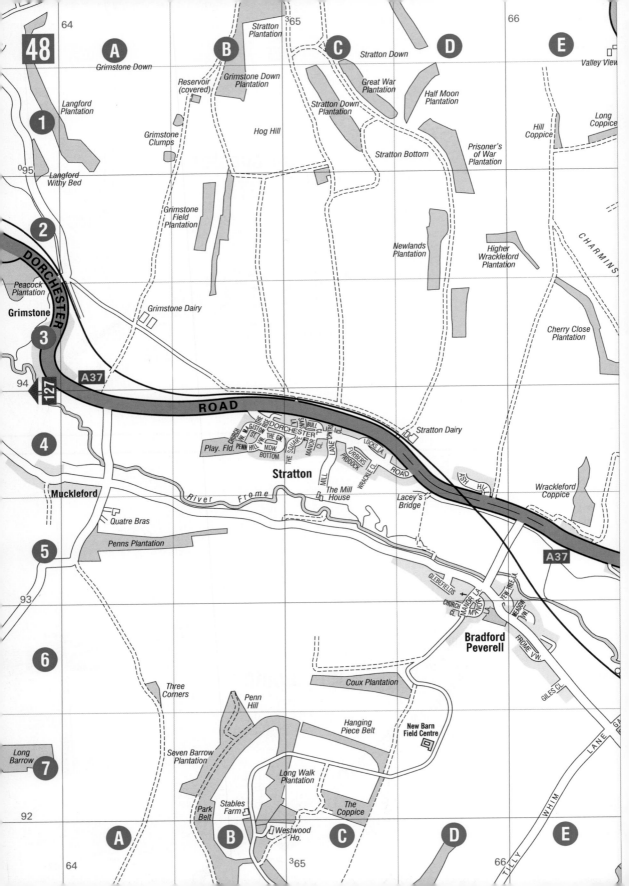

48

64   365   66

A   B   C   D   E

Grimstone Down

Stratton
Plantation

Reservoir
(covered)

Grimstone Down
Plantation

Stratton Down

Valley View

1

Langford
Plantation

Grimstone
Clumps

Hog Hill

Great War
Plantation

Half Moon
Plantation

Hill
Coppice

Long
Coppice

095

Langford
Withy Bed

Stratton Down
Plantation

Stratton Bottom

Prisoner's
of War
Plantation

2

Grimstone
Field
Plantation

DORCHESTER

CHARMINS

Peacock
Plantation

Newlands
Plantation

Higher
Wrackleford
Plantation

Grimstone

3

Grimstone Dairy

Cherry Close
Plantation

94

127

A37

ROAD

DORCHESTER

Stratton Dairy

Play. Fld.

THE
GN

BULL

4

CHURCH ST.
EGISTON VW.
PENN HILL

THE SQUARE
THE GN

MANOR
CL.

LOCKS LA.

Muckleford

BOTTOM

MDW.

LANE
ORCHD.

PARKS
CL.

Stratton

MILL

The Mill
House

URBERS
PADDOCK

WRACKLE CL.

ROAD

ASH HL.

Wrackleford
Coppice

River   Frome

Lacey's
Bridge

Quatre Bras

5

Penns Plantation

A37

93

GLEBEFIELDS

YEW TREE LA.

6

CHURCH
CL.

MANOR LA.
MANOR

MEADOW
VW.

**Bradford
Peverell**

FROME VW.

Three
Corners

Coux Plantation

New Barn
Field Centre

GILES CL.

Long
Barrow

7

Penn
Hill

Hanging
Piece Belt

Seven Barrow
Plantation

Long Walk
Plantation

Stables
Farm

The Coppice

WHIM   LANE

TILLY

92   365   66

A   B   C   D   E

64

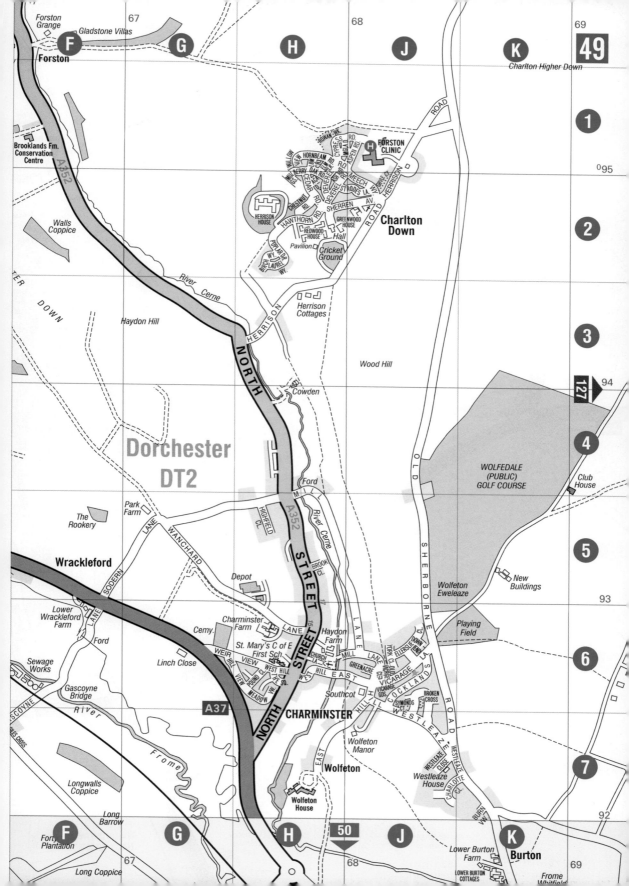

67 68 69

Forston Grange
Gladstone Villas

Forston

Charlton Higher Down

1

Brooklands Fm.
Conservation
Centre

⁰95

A352

HORNBEAM
WILLOW
NEW
BERRY
OAK RI.
CEDAR
CHESTNUT
ROMAN PK.
CYPRESS
OPEN LA.
RD.
HER

**FORSTON
CLINIC**

H

HERRISON
HOUSE

HAWTHORN RD.
POPLAR DR.
BIRCH
LAUREL WY.
REDWOOD
HOUSE
Pavilion
Hall
SHERREN
GREENWOOD
HOUSE
MEECH WY.
DEVEREL RD.
STRODE'S LA.
AV.

HERRISON ROAD

**Charlton
Down**

2

Walls
Coppice

Cricket
Ground

River Cerne

Herrison
Cottages

ER DOWN

Haydon Hill

HERRISON

NORTH

Wood Hill

3

127 ► 94

Cowden

**Dorchester
DT2**

SHERBORNE

OLD ROAD

**WOLFEDALE
(PUBLIC)
GOLF COURSE**

Club
House

4

Ford

A352

River Cerne

5

The
Rookery

Park
Farm

HIGHFIELD CL.

LANE

WANCHARD

BROOK CL.

New
Buildings

Wolfeton
Eweleaze

Wrackleford

SODERN LANE

Depot

Charminster
Farm

Cemy.

Linch Close

STREET

MILL LANE

Playing
Field

93

Lower
Wrackleford
Farm

Ford

Sewage
Works

Gascoyne
Bridge

River Frome

A37

St. Mary's C of E
First Sch.

WEIR HILL VIEW

POUND
WEST HILL
MEADOW WY.
HILL EAST
VIEW SQ.

CHURCH
Haydon
Farm
MILL LANE

GREENACRE

YORK RD.
ELLERSLIE DOWN
VICARAGE CL.
GDNS.
VICARAGE
SYMONDS
CT.
COCKLANDS
BROKEN
CROSS

NORTH

CHARMINSTER

Southcot

WESTLEAZE

Wolfeton

EAST HILL

Wolfeton
Manor

WESTLEAZE
CLOSE

Westleaze
House

CHARLOTTE CL.

BURN VW.

6

7

92

Longwalls
Coppice

Long
Barrow

F

Fort
Plantation

G

**Wolfeton
House**

H

50 ▽

J

Lower Burton
Farm

K

Burton

LOWER BURTON
COTTAGES

Long Coppice

67 68 69

Frome Whitfield

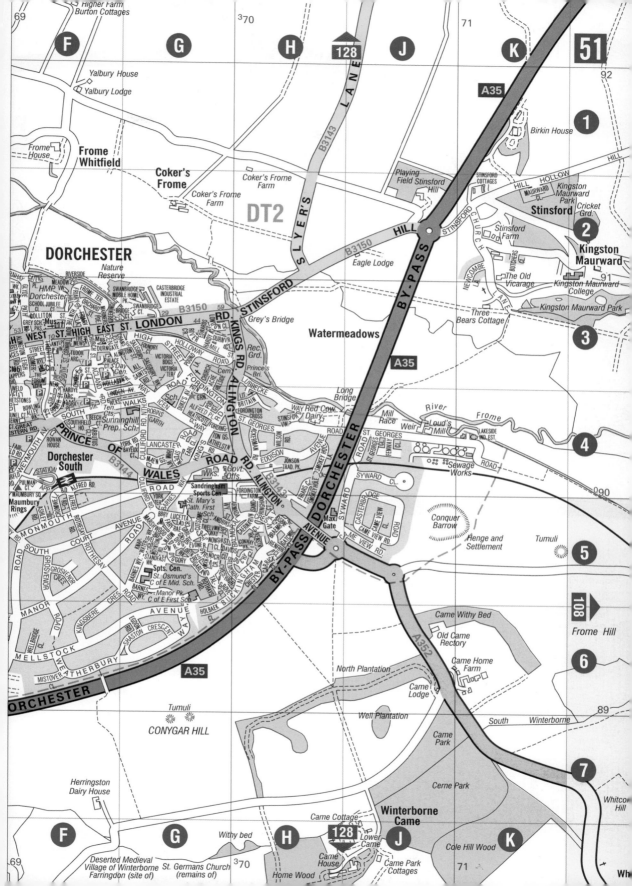

51

Higher Farm
Burton Cottages

F G H **128** J K **51**

A35

92

Yalbury House
Yalbury Lodge

Birkin House **1**

Frome
House

Frome
Whitfield

Coker's
Frome

Coker's Frome
Farm

Coker's Frome
Farm

Playing
Field Stinsford
Hill

Stinsford
Cottages

HILL HOLLOW

Stinsford
Hill

MAURWARD

Kingston
Maurward
Park

Stinsford

Cricket
Grd.

2

DT2

Eagle Lodge

The Old
Vicarage

Stinsford
Farm

Kingston
Maurward

B3150

B3143

SLYER'S

STINSFORD

HILL

BY-PASS

STINSFORD

NEWCOMBE LA.

CHURCH

BUTCHERS CL.

Kingston Maurward
College

91

Kingston Maurward Park

DORCHESTER

Nature
Reserve

RIVERSIDE

SWANBRIDGE
MOBILE HOME
PK.

CASTERBRIDGE
INDUSTRIAL
ESTATE

Grey's Bridge

B3150

59

Watermeadows

Three
Bears Cottage

A35

3

WEST ST HIGH EAST ST. LONDON RD.

KINGS RD.

ALINGTON RD.

Rec.
Grd.

Prince's
Bri.

Long
Bridge

Way Red Cow
Dairy

Fordington
Cross

Stinsford
VW.

River Frome

Mill
Race

Loud's
Mill

Weir

LAKESIDE
IND. EST.

4

090

PRINCE OF WALES ROAD

B3144

Dorchester
South

STATION

PULMAN

ALFRED RD.

Maumbury
Rings

MONMOUTH

CULLIFORD RD.

ROAD RD. ALINGTON

Govt.
Offs.

Sandringham
Sports Cen.

St. Mary's
Cath. First

Fordington
FARM

FRIARS CL.

Maxi
Gate

ST. GEORGES

CASTERBRIDGE

SYWARD

Sewage
Works

DORCHESTER

AVENUE

SYWARD
CL.

CAME VIEW CL.

CAME VIEW RD.

Conquer
Barrow

Henge and
Settlement

Tumuli

5

BY-PASS

A35

AVENUE

ROAD

Spts. Cen.

St. Osmund's
C of E Mid. Sch.

Manor Pk.
C of E First Sch.

St. Osmund's

HOLBAEK

BUCKINGHAM WAY

CRESCENT

North Plantation

Came Withy Bed

Old Came
Rectory

Came Home
Farm

108

Frome Hill

6

MANOR
ROAD

MELLBRIDGE
CL.

KINGSBERE

SHASTON CRESCENT

AVENUE

MISTOVER
CL.

ATHERBURY

A35

Tumuli

CONYGAR HILL

Came
Lodge

Well Plantation

Came
Park

South Winterborne

89

DORCHESTER

Herringston
Dairy House

Came Cottage

**Winterborne
Came**

Cerne Park

Came Park
Cottages

Cole Hill Wood

Whitcom
Hill

7

F G H **128** J K

69

Deserted Medieval
Village of Winterborne
Farringdon (site of)

370

St. Germans Church
(remains of)

Withy bed

Lower
Came

Came
House

Home Wood

71

Wh

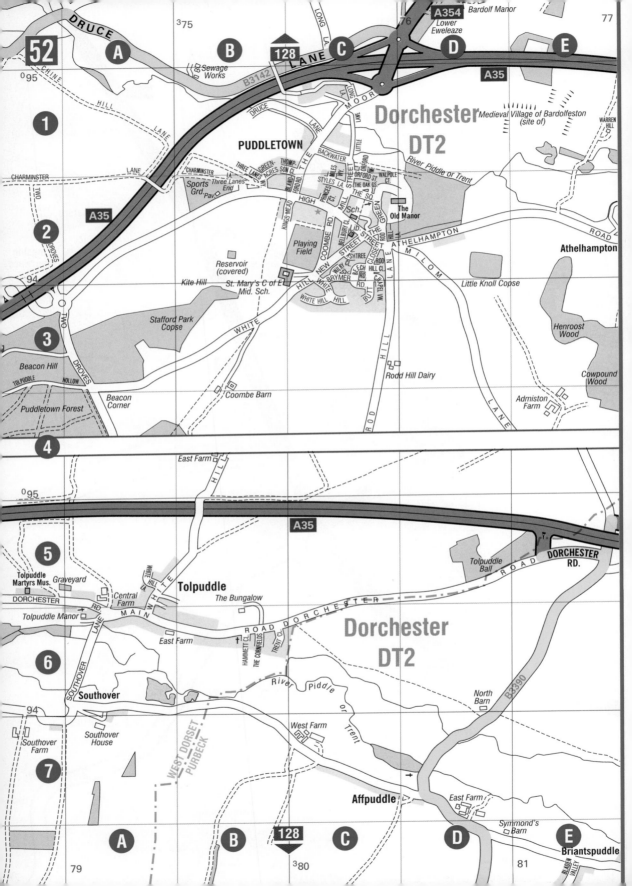

52

DRUCE

A

B

C

128

D

A354
Bardolf Manor
Lower Eweleaze

E

A35

375

76

77

CHINE

095

HILL

CHARMINSTER

LANE

LANE

TWO

094

DROVES

A35

A35

1

2

3

Sewage Works

B3142

DRUCE LANE

THOMP SON CL

THREE LANES GREEN ACRES CL

CHARMINSTER LA

Three Lanes End

Sports Grd.

Pav.

ISLAND

FORD RD

Reservoir (covered)

Kite Hill

St. Mary's C of E Mid. Sch.

Stafford Park Copse

Beacon Hill

HOLLOW

Beacon Corner

TOLPUDDLE

Puddletown Forest

Coombe Barn

KINGS MEAD

HIGH

Playing Field

NEW COOMBE RD.

HILL

WHITE HILL

WHITE HILL HILL

PUDDLETOWN

MILES LA

PRINCES CT.

STYLES LA

WILBY CL

BRYMER RD.

BUTT CL

BEECH RD.

BELBURY CL

MILL STREET

THE BACKWATER

LITTLE STREET

ORFORD ST.

THE SQ.

THE OAK GS.

Sch.

LID.

THE GREEN

WALPOLE CT.

THE

ROD

HILL CL.

HILL CL.

CLOSE

WM. BARNE

The Old Manor

ATHELHAMPTON

MILOM

ROAD

ROD

HILL

LANE

Rodd Hill Dairy

Dorchester DT2

Medieval Village of Bardolfeston (site of)

WARREN HILL

River Piddle or Trent

Little Knoll Copse

Athelhampton

Henroost Wood

Cowpound Wood

Admiston Farm

LANE

4

East Farm

HILL

095

A35

5

6

7

Tolpuddle Martyrs Mus.

Graveyard

DORCHESTER

Tolpuddle Manor

Central Farm

WHITE HILL

Tolpuddle

East Farm

The Bungalow

MAIN

RD

SOUTHOVER

LANE

WHITE

ROAD

HAMMETT CL.

THE CORNFIELDS

TRENT CL.

DORCHESTER ROAD

Southover

094

Southover Farm

Southover House

WEST DORSET

PURBECK

River Piddle or Trent

West Farm

Tolpuddle Ball

ROAD

DORCHESTER RD.

Dorchester DT2

North Barn

B3390

Affpuddle

East Farm

Symmond's Barn

Briantspuddle

BLADEN VALLEY

A

B

128

C

D

E

79

380

81

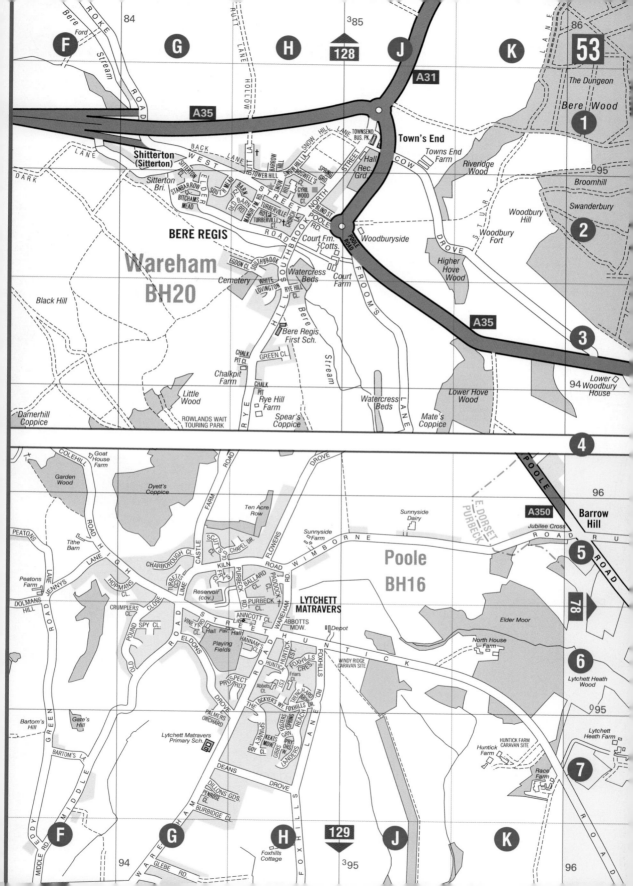

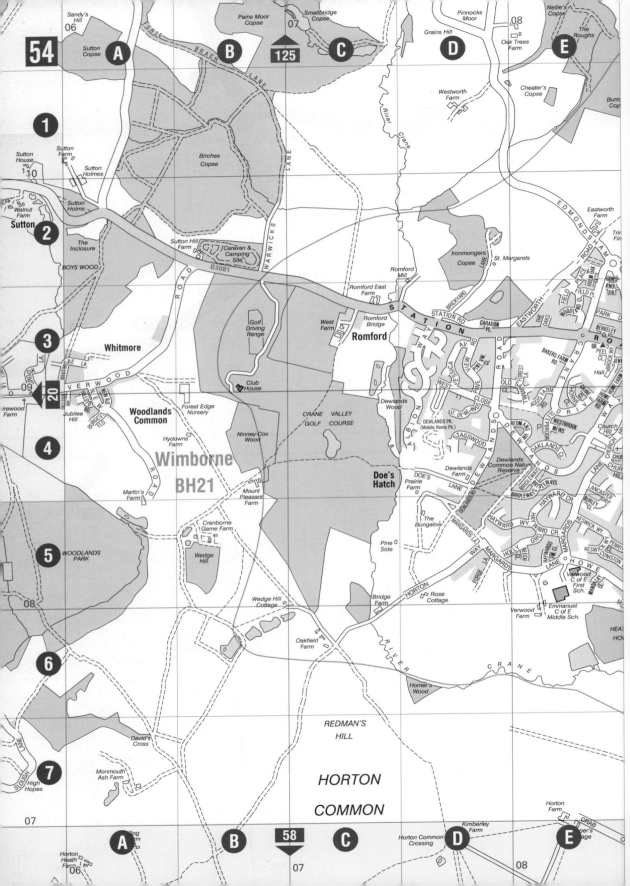

125

Pistle Hill

Burrows Farm

Mount Ararat

Fire Tower

1

10

BOVERIDGE

HEATH

Bailey's Plantation

2

Stephen's Castle

WILD CHURCH BOTTOM

Stephen's Castle Nature Reserve

ity C of E st School

Forest Lodge

3

Hillside First School

Moorside Cottage

130   09

MOORLANDS

Bowl. Grn.
Pav.
Fayrewood Ct. Rec. Grd Hall

Town Council Offs.
Liby.

Hillside First School

Moorside Cottage

Starlight

STRATHMORE

Noon Cott.

NOON

Noon Hill Cott.

Noon Hill Farm

RINGWOOD FOREST

4

HOWARD RD.

Bugden's Copse Nature Reserve

VERWOOD

Verwood Leisure Cen.

Superstore

HEATHLANDS CL.

SHARD CL.

Crescent Rd.

Works

RAYMOND RD.

VERWOOD IND. EST.

Black Hill Works

Verwood BH31

SOUTHERNHAY

HUNTERS CL.

EAST DORSET

NEW FOREST

5

Woodcote

Little Cranebrook

Playing Field

Ebblake

08

EBBLAKE ENTERPRISE PARK

THE FORELLE CEN.

Cemetery

Ebblake Bridge

6

St. Michael's Cott.

Cranebrook Manor

Potterne Hill Nature Reserve

Oakleigh

EBBLAKE INDUSTRIAL ESTATE

Ebblake Ho.

Ebblake Stream

Verwood Manor Farm

The Bungalow

Aqueduct (Disused)

POTTERNE

Poultry House

Potterne Park Playing Field

Potterne Farm

Games Ct.

POTTERNE WOOD

Ringwood

BH24

7

Rock Vale

Foster's Wood

Potterne Poultry Farm

Poultry Houses

CRANE

07

Cottage Farm

nglish arm

⁴10 MOORS VALLEY COUNTRY PARK

Crane Lake

ORCHARD

Crab Orchard Farm

WAY

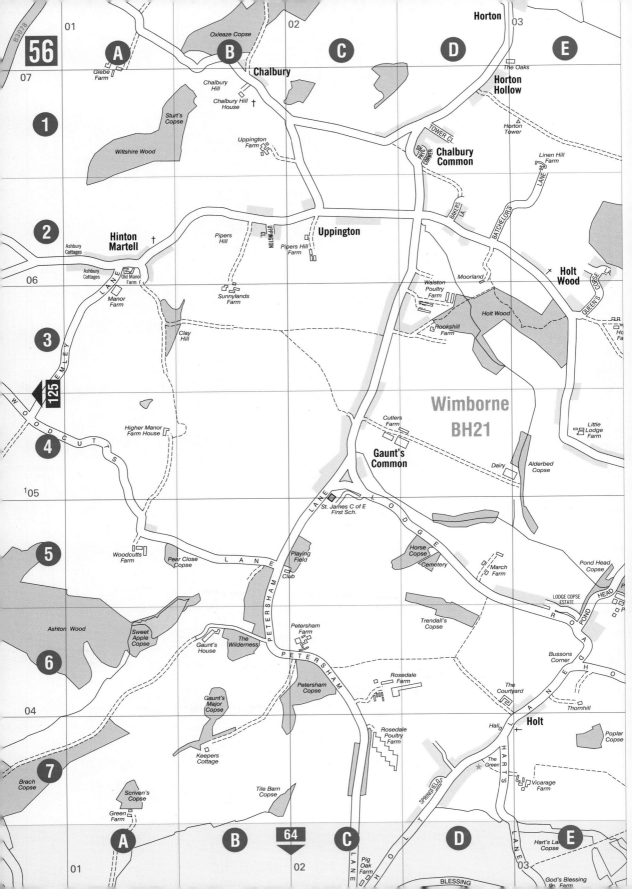

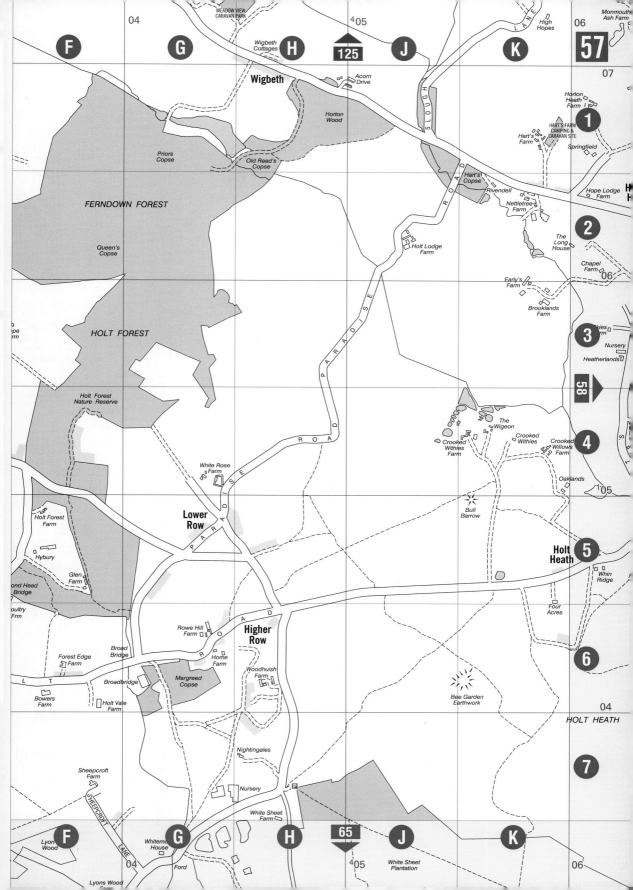

F   **G**   **H**   125   **J**   **K**

04   405   06   07

MEADOW VIEW
CARAVAN PARK

Wigbeth Cottages

High
Hopes

Monmouth
Ash Farm

Acorn
Drive

Wigbeth

Horton
Wood

SLOUGH

Horton
Heath
Farm

HART'S FARM
CAMPING &
CARAVAN SITE

1

Hart's
Farm

Springfield

Priors
Copse

Old Read's
Copse

ROAD

Hart's
Copse

Rivendell

Nettletree
Farm

Hope Lodge
Farm

FERNDOWN FOREST

2

The
Long
House

Chapel
Farm

06

Queen's
Copse

Holt Lodge
Farm

Early's
Farm

Brooklands
Farm

PARADISE

3

...kies
...rm

Nursery

Heatherlands

HOLT FOREST

58

Holt Forest
Nature Reserve

The
Wigeon

Crooked
Withies

Crooked
Willows
Farm

4

ROAD

Crooked
Withies
Farm

Oaklands

05

White Rose
Farm

Bull
Barrow

**Lower
Row**

Holt Forest
Farm

**Holt
Heath**

5

PARADISE

Hybury

Glen
Farm

Whin
Ridge

...nd Head
Bridge

Four
Acres

...oultry
...rm

Rowe Hill
Farm

**Higher
Row**

6

Broad
Bridge

ROAD

Home
Farm

Woodhuish
Farm

Forest Edge
Farm

Broadbridge

Margreed
Copse

04

Bowers
Farm

Holt Vale
Farm

Bee Garden
Earthwork

HOLT HEATH

7

Nightingales

Sheepcroft
Farm

Nursery

F   **G**   **H**   65   **J**   **K**

SHEEPCROFT LANE

Lyon
Wood

Whitemo...
House

Ford

White Sheet
Farm

White Sheet
Plantation

Lyons Wood

04   405   06

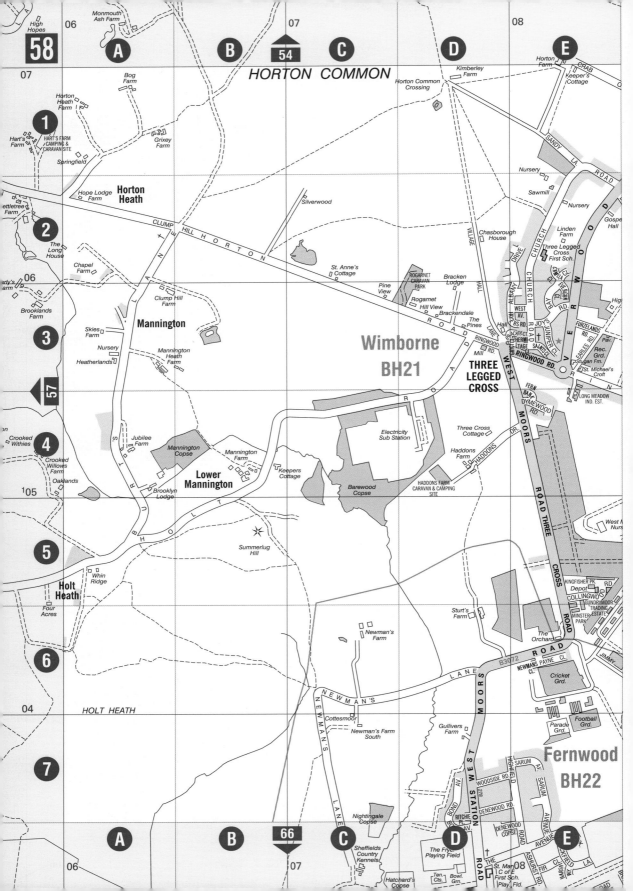

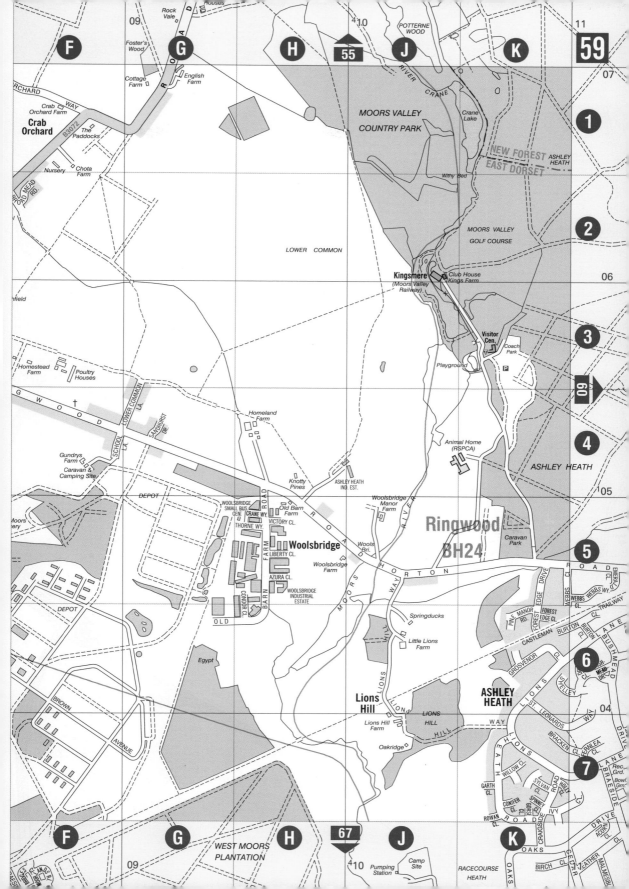

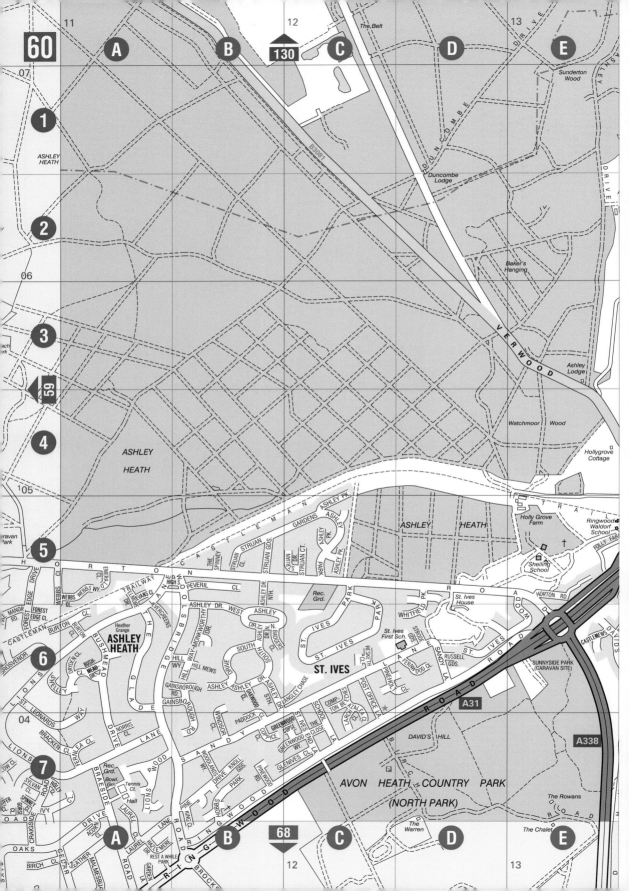

60

A   B   130   C   D   E

11   12   13

07

The Belt

Sunderton Wood

1

ASHLEY HEATH

Duncombe Lodge

2

06

Baker's Hanging

3

VERWOOD

Ashley Lodge

59

4

ASHLEY HEATH

Watchmoor Wood

Hollygrove Cottage

05

ASHLEY PK. GARDENS

ASHLEY HEATH

Holly Grove Farm

Ringwood Waldorf School

Folly Farm

5

THE SPINNEY   STRUAN CL.   STRUAN GDS.   STRUAN CT.   STRUAN DR.

ASHLEY PARK

Rec. Grd.

Sheiling School

EMERY CL.   WEBBS WY.   WEBBS CL.   EVANS CL.   PEVERIL CL.

ASHLEY DR. WEST   ASHLEY DR. NTH.

ST. IVES PARK

St. Ives House

HORTON RD.

6

FOREST EDGE DRIVE   FOREST EDGE CL.

BURTON CL.   BURTON

Heather Grange

ASHLEY HEATH

MONKWORTHY DR.   ASHLEY DR.

ASHLEY DR. SOUTH

ST. IVES

St. Ives First Sch.

WHITFIELD

STRODE GDNS.

RUSSELL GDS.

SANDY LA.

HESKETH CL.   FERNWOOD CL.

CASTLEMAN   GROSVENOR

BUSHMEAD

GAINSBOROUGH RD.

ST. IVES STH.

PINEHOLT CL.

SHELLEY CL.   DRYDEN CL.   BUSH CL.   MEAD DR.

THE GLADE

LANGLEY CHASE

COMPTON BECCHES

LARCH CL.   LARCH CL.

POST OFFICE LA.

ST. IVES ROAD

A31

SUNNYSIDE PARK (CARAVAN SITE)

CASTLEMEWS

DAVID'S

04

LIONS

ST. LEONARDS WAY

BRACKEN CL.   FERNLEA CL.

NORRIS CL.

WOOD LANE

PADDOCK

WINDSOR CL.

GREENWOOD COPSE   COPPICE

ST. IVES CLOSE   THE

GREENWOOD WY.

DAVID'S HILL

A338

7

SYLVAN CL.   SPINNEY   IVY

HOLLY CL.

ROAD

BRAESIDE

Rec. Grd.

Bowl. Grn.   Tennis Ct.

Hall

WOODLANDS DRIVE

KNOLL GDS.

PINEWOOD RD.

GLENIVES CL.

AVON HEATH COUNTRY PARK (NORTH PARK)

The Warren

The Rowans

The Chalet

HEIFER   BIRCH CL.   CEDAR

OAKS

LAUREL DR.   HAZEL   LAUREL DR.

HEATHER GARDEN CL.

REST A WHILE PARK

DRIVE

RINGWOOD ROAD

BROCKS

PINE LANE   HOBBS RD.   KING CL.

A   B   68   C   D   E

12   13

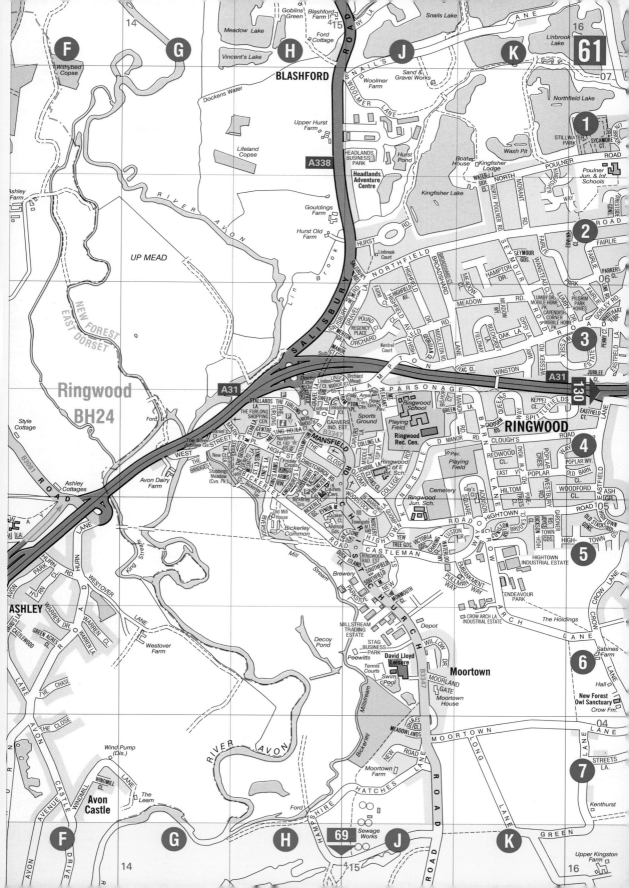

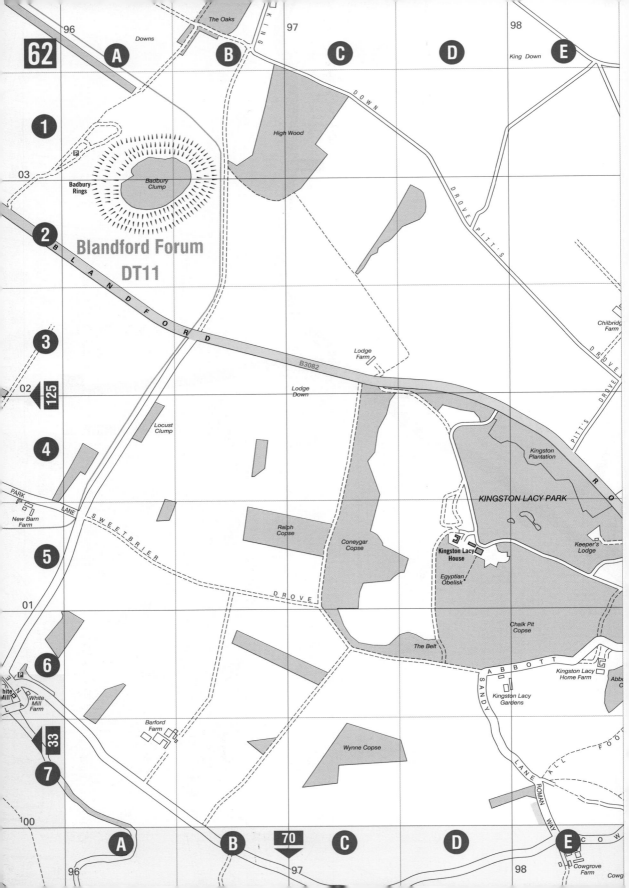

62

96   97   98

A   B   C   D   E

Downs

The Oaks

King Down

1

03

High Wood

Badbury Rings   Badbury Clump

**Blandford Forum
DT11**

2

DROVE
PITT'S

BLANDFORD

3

Lodge Farm

B3082

Chilbridge Farm

02   125

Lodge Down

DROVE

4

Locust Clump

Kingston Plantation

PARK

LANE

New Barn Farm

SWEETBRIER

Ralph Copse

KINGSTON LACY PARK

Keeper's Lodge

5

DROVE

Coneygar Copse

Kingston Lacy House

Egyptian Obelisk

PITT'S ROAD

01

Chalk Pit Copse

6

White Mill

White Mill Farm

The Belt

ABBOTT

SANDY

Kingston Lacy Home Farm   Abb

Kingston Lacy Gardens

33

Barford Farm

Wynne Copse

LANE

ALL FOO

ROMAN WAY

7

100

A   B   70   C   D   E   COW

96   97   98   Cowgrove Farm   Cowg

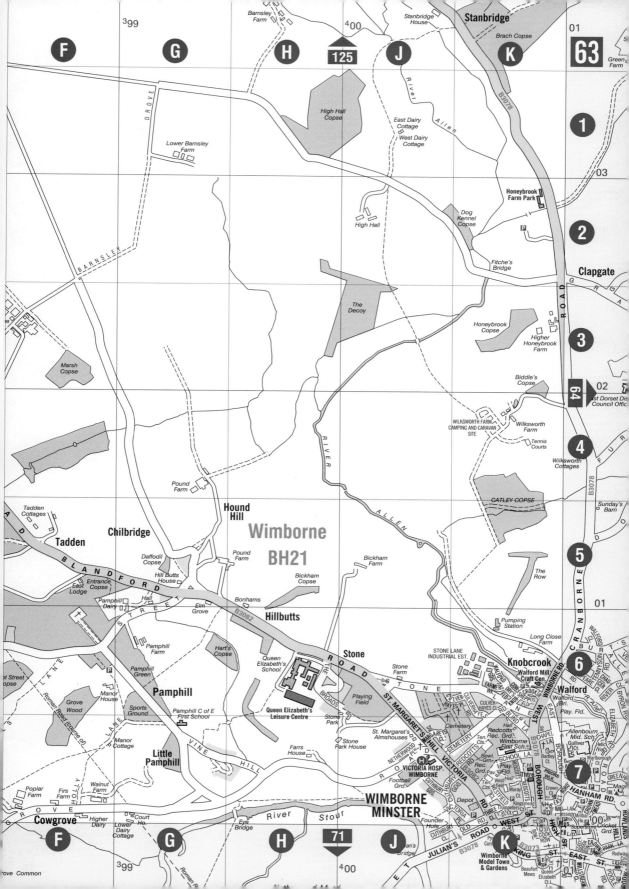

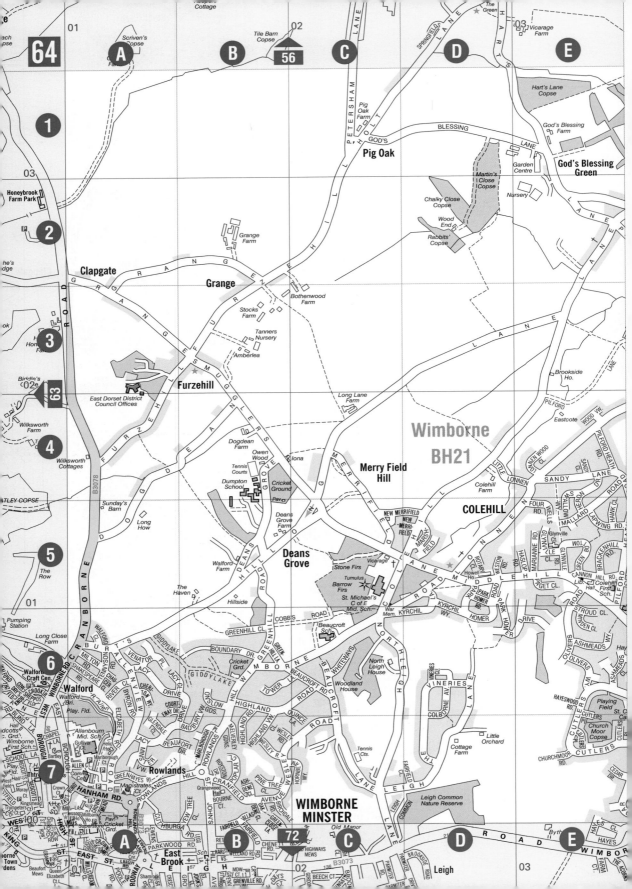

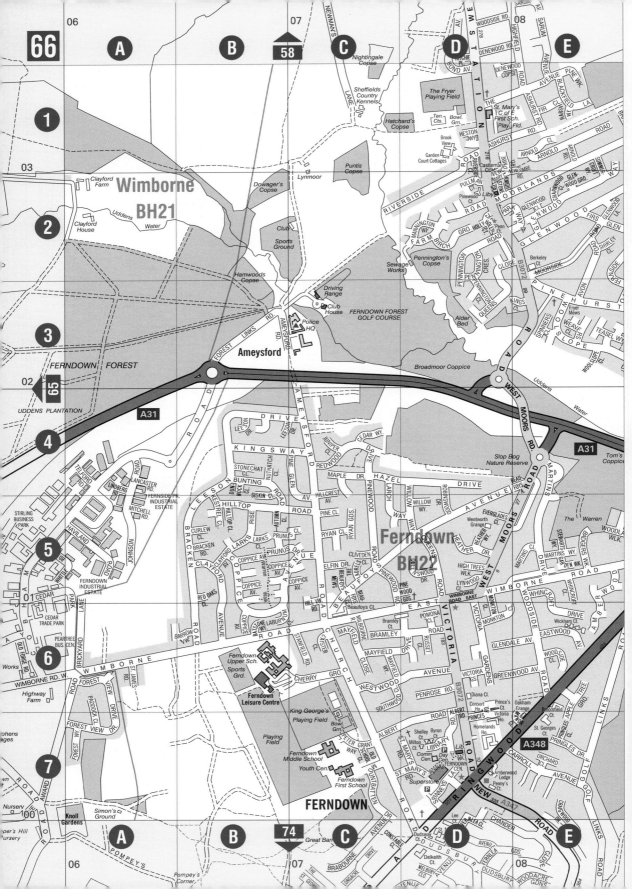

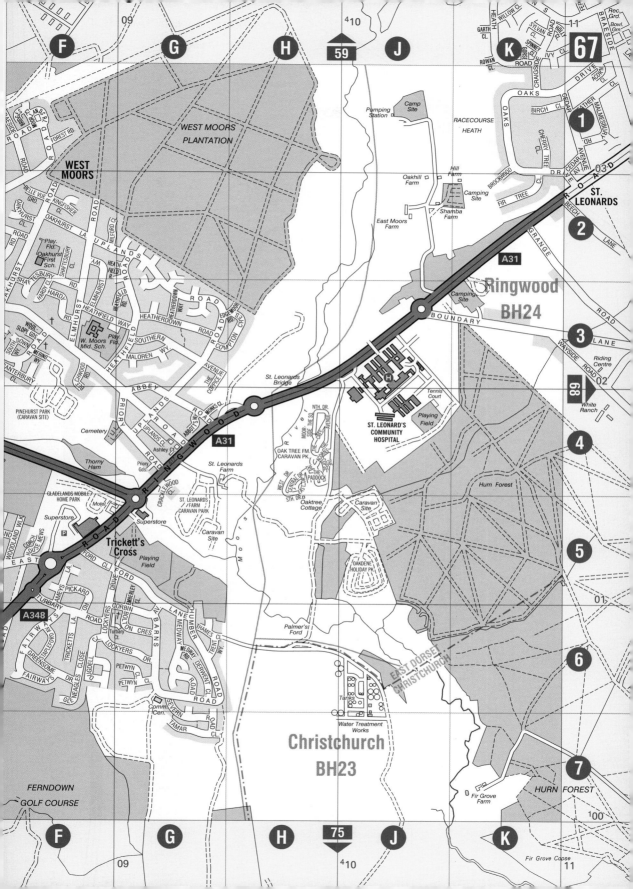

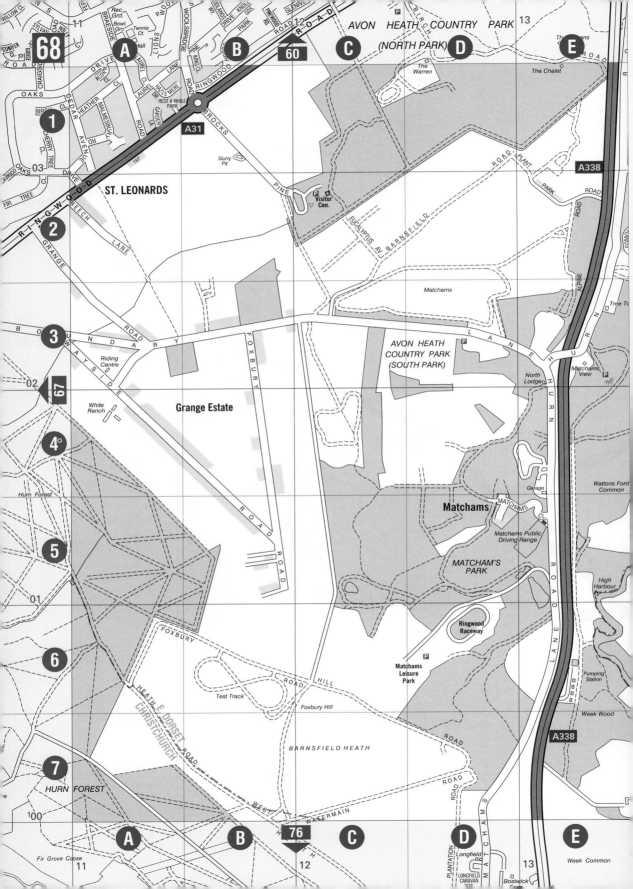

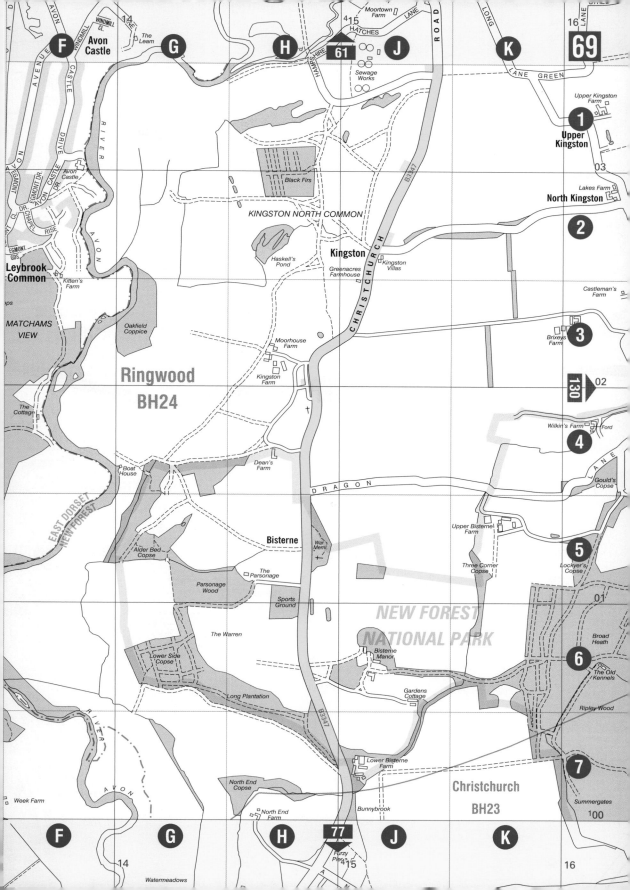

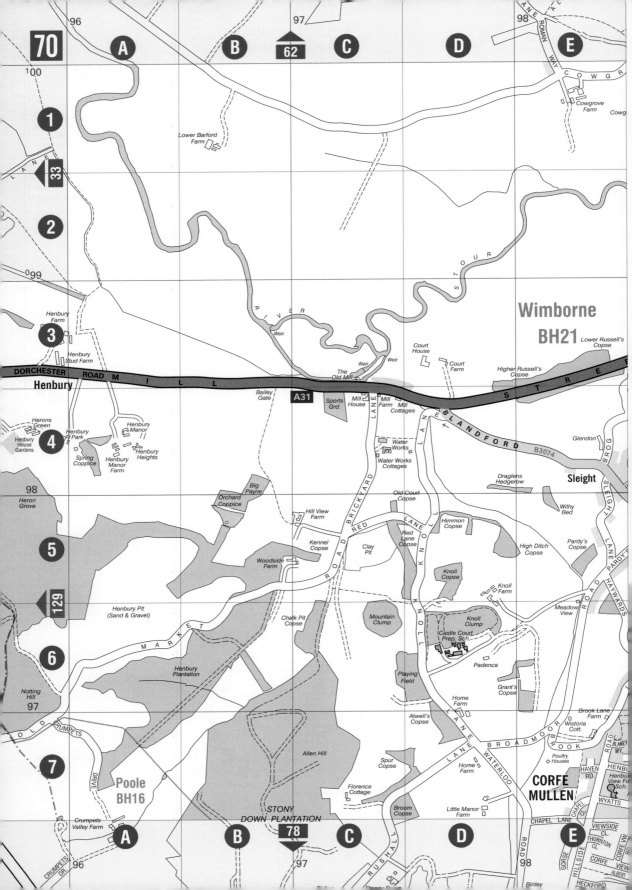

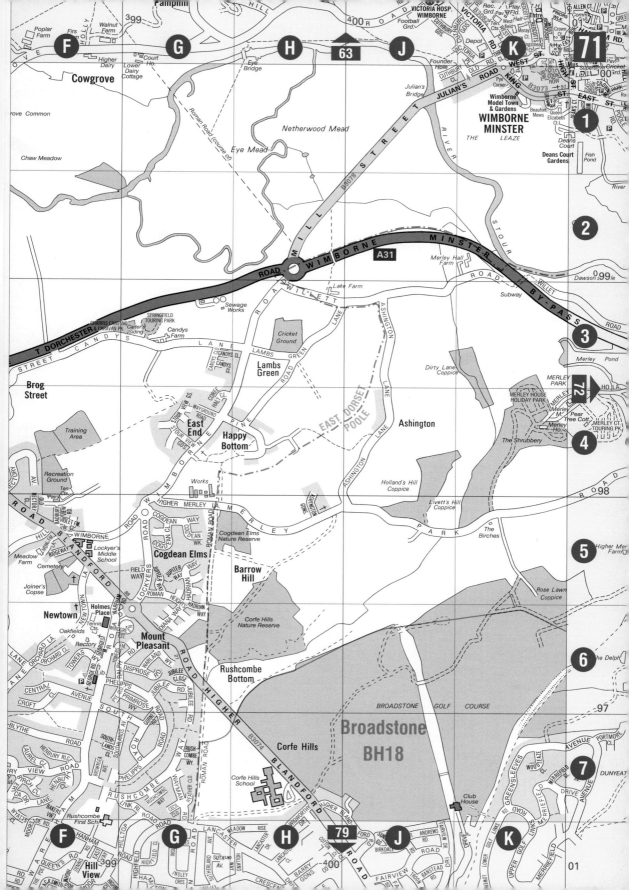

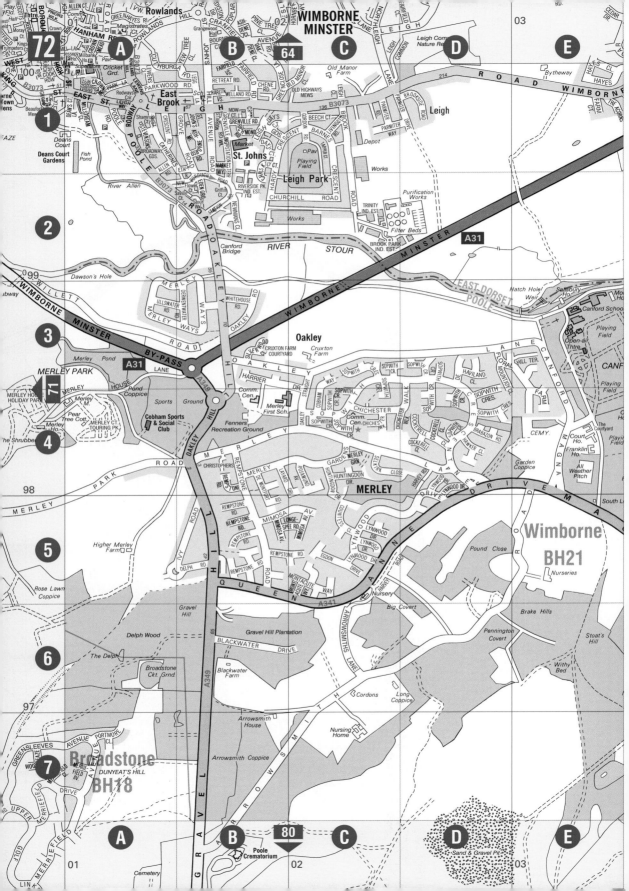

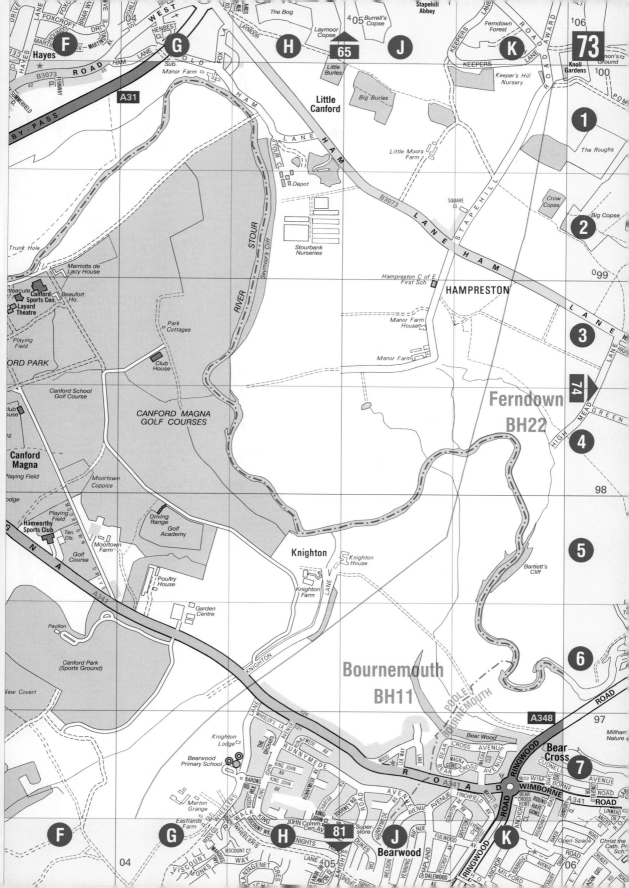

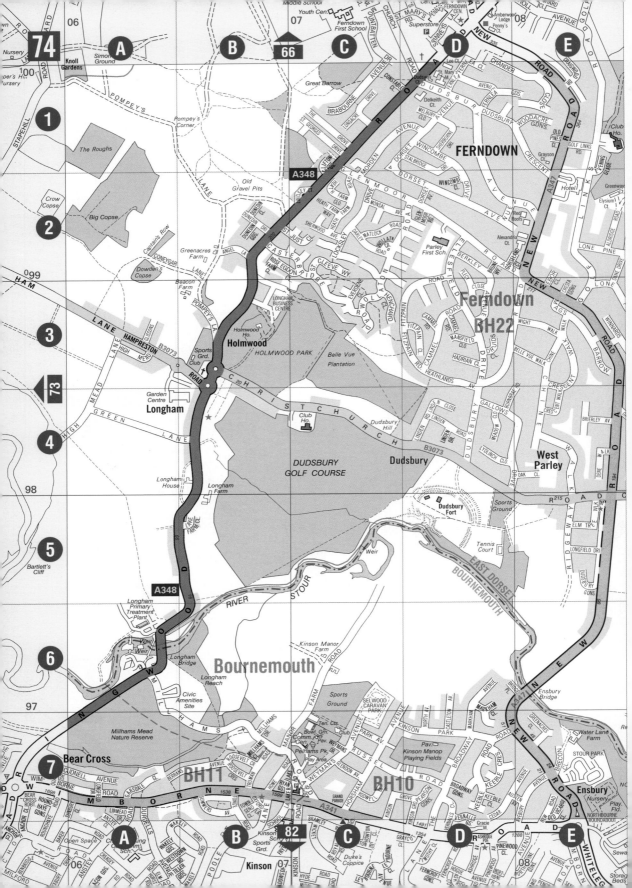

F G H J K

67

Fir Grove Farm

HURN FOREST

100

FERNDOWN GOLF COURSE

Ringwood BH24

Fir Grove Copse

Moors River

1

Gibbet Firs

Parley Common

East Parley Common

2

PINE END
BIRCH
PINE WALK
SPENDLY CR.
LONE PINE MOBILE HOMES Park
SKELA ALLUNLODGE
FAR WORLEY
PINE

99

DRIVE

Ralph's Barrow

LONE PINE WY.

Christchurch BH23

3

CLOSE

EAST DORSET
CHRISTCHURCH
CHRISTCHURCH
ROAD

AVENUE
OAK
HIGHMOOR CL.
WALK

Parley Wood

Works

Works

WAY

76

Ford

Works

Works

ENTERPRISE
ENTERPRISE

NORTH WEST INDUSTRIAL AREA

4

Playing Field Club

Equestrian Centre

Heathfield Farm

Sports Ground

Rugby Ground

AVIATION PARK WEST

Works

98

PARLEY
CLOSE
CHRISTCHURCH

Rec. Grd. Hall

CROOKS RD.

The Oaks

Cricket Ground

Ten. Cts.

Bournemouth Sports Club

CHAPEL LANE

Refuse Plant

Parley Cross

CHRISTCHURCH
LANE

328

BARRACK ROAD

Barnes's Farm

Nursery

Portfield School

Sports Ground

GATE
ENTERPRISE WY.

BOURNEMOUTH AIRPORT

5

B3073 ROAD PARLEY LANE CHAPEL

East Parley

Day Centre

Wood Town Farm

PARLEY

B3073

PARLEY GOLF COURSE

MERRITOWN LANE

Alice in Wonderland Family Park

6

Merritown

Bramble's Farm

New Cottages

Club House

Driving Range

Merritown Copse

97

PARLEY
GREEN

White Cottages

LANE

Tudor Cottage

Bounds Farm

Parley Green

Mead Cottage

Parley Court Farm

PARLEY

RIVER STOUR

CHURCH

Victory

Church Farm

Lake

Bournemouth BH8

7

RIVER

STOUR

NORTHBOURNE MEADOWS

BH9

Sewage Works

Berry Hill

Sewage Works
Vernold's Coppice
Stour Valley Nature Reserve

F G H J K

83

Erlin Farm

The Wilderness

Berry Hill

MUSCLIFF

09

410

11

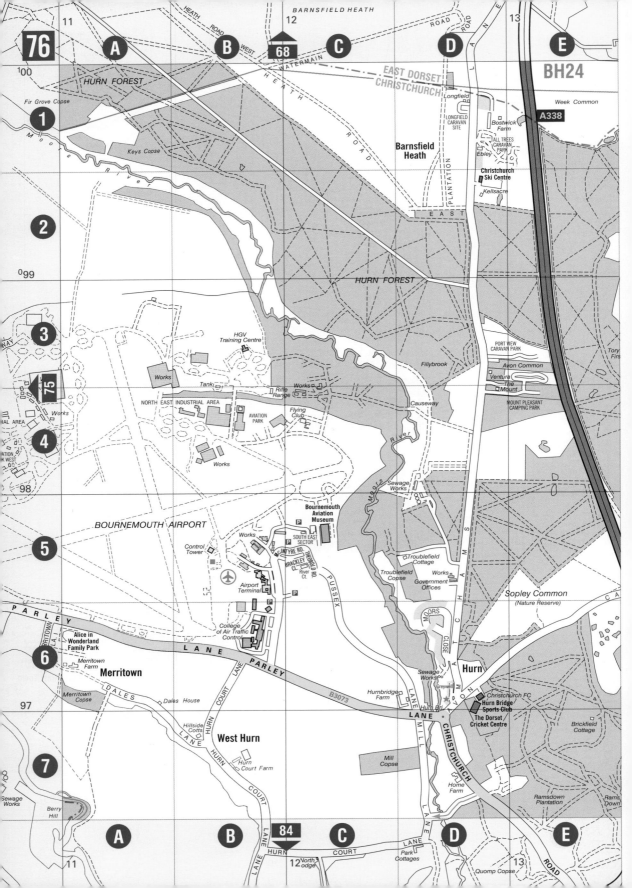

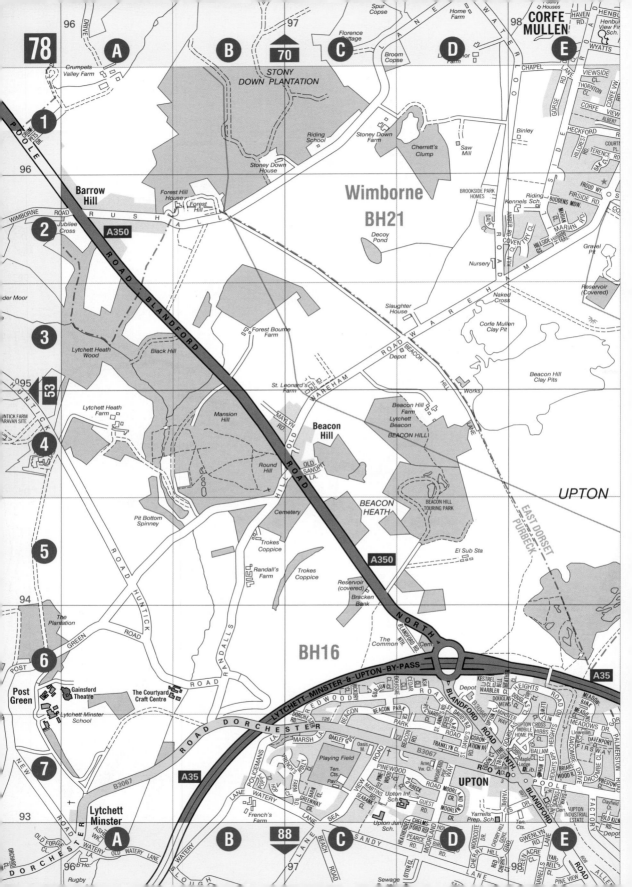

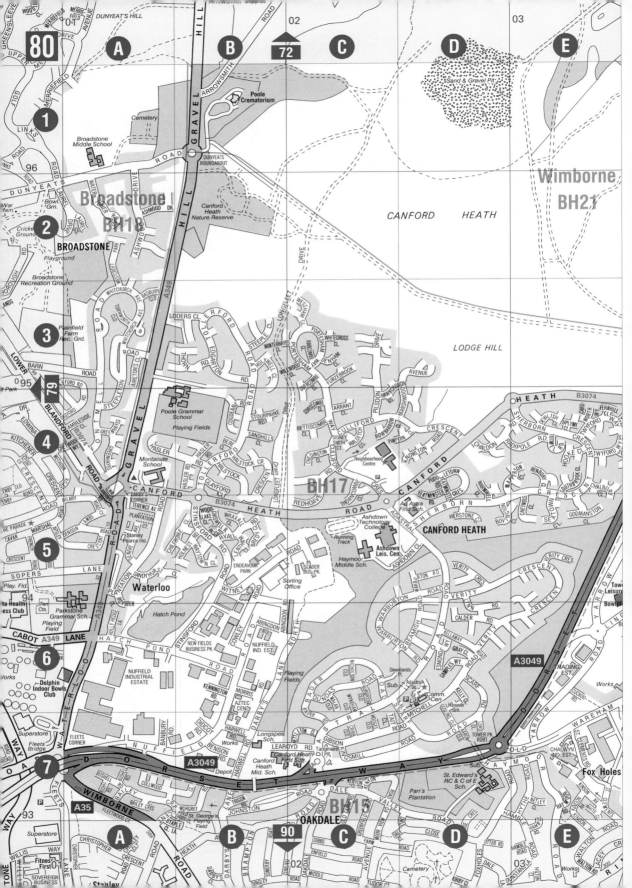

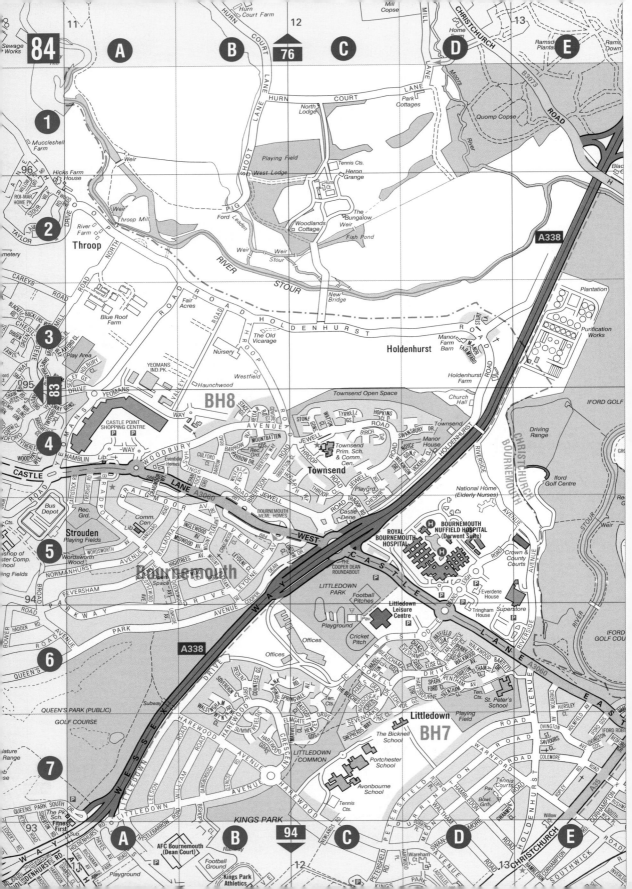

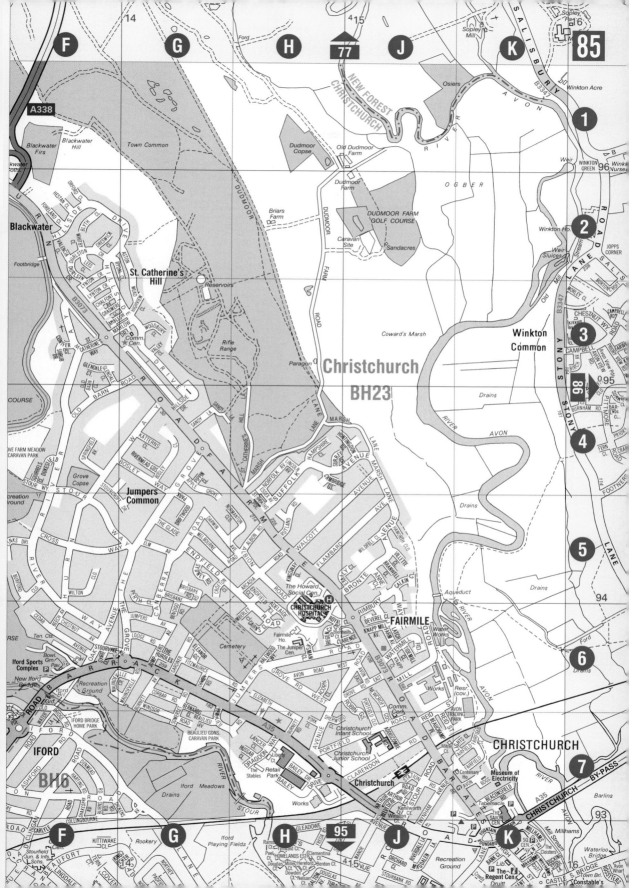

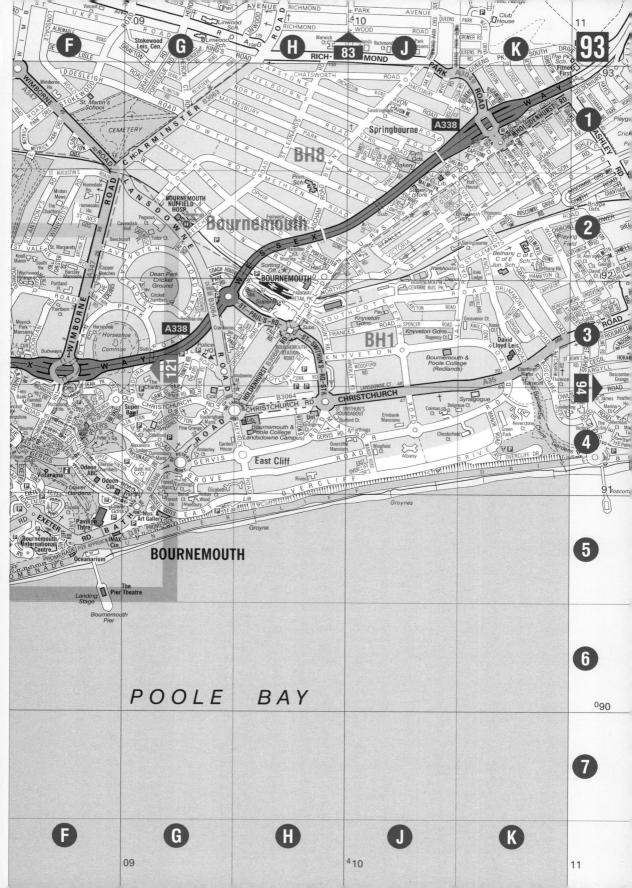

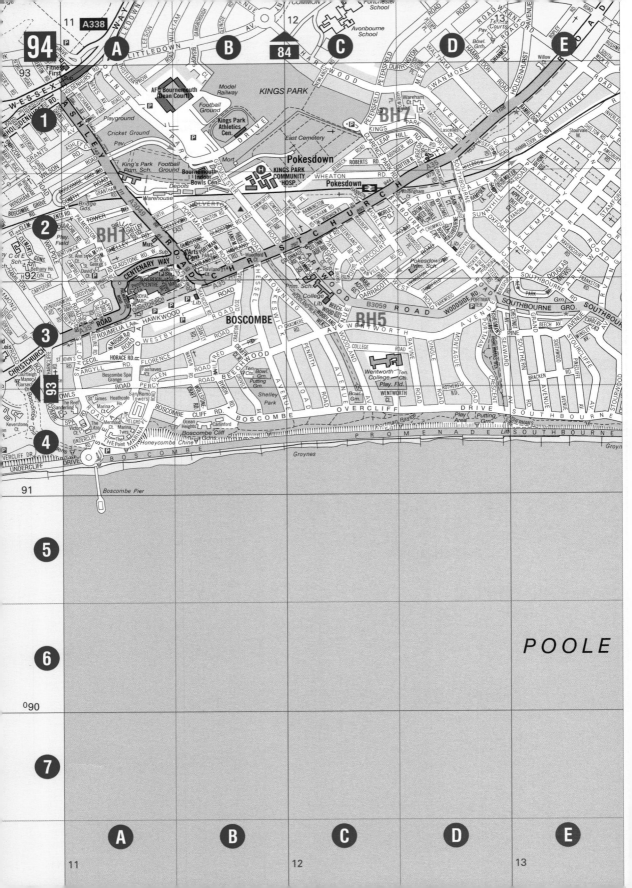

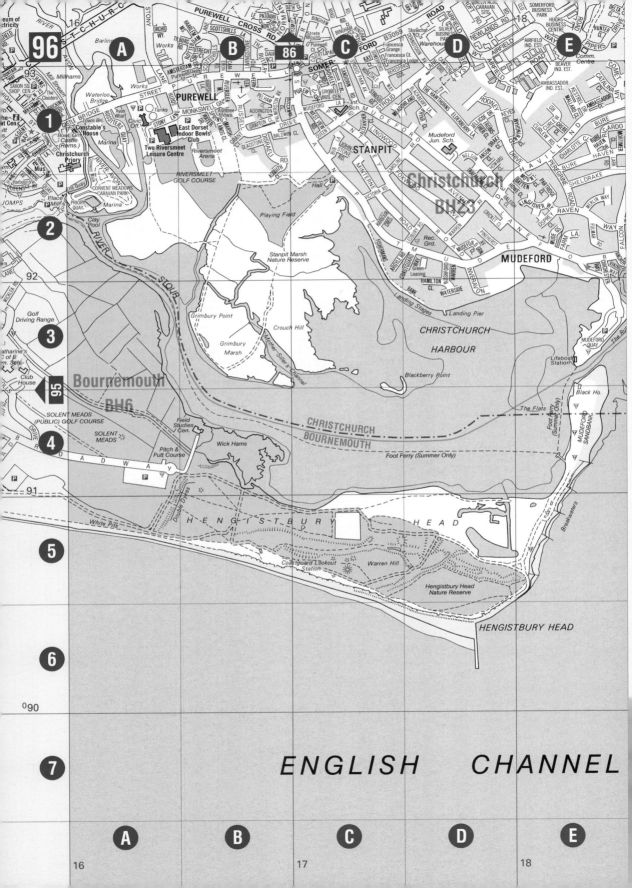

F **G** **H** 87 **J** **K** 97

HIGHCLIFFE CASTLE GOLF COURSE 4 20 HM 21 CLIFF

Highcliffe Castle

93

FRIARS CLIFF

Steamer Point Woodland
Steamer Lodge
HM Coastguard Training Cen.
Vis. Cen.

Groynes

1

130

2

CHRISTCHURCH   BAY

92

SANDHILLS CARAVAN PARK

3

INSET

Meetinghouse Plantation

Castlefield Copse

95

Walkford

4

Chewton Glen Fm

Chewton Common

Christchurch BH23

CHRISTCHURCH NEW FOREST

5

Hotel

94

130

Chewton Common

Highcliffe St. Mark Primary School

87

CHEWTON COMMON

HIGHCLIFFE

Mt. Flats

Chewton Common

The Weirs

Chewton Farm Estate

CHRISTCHURCH RD.

6

COBBS HOLIDAY PK

BUCEHAYES

THE MEADOW
NAISH HOLIDAY VILLAGE

FIELD PLACE

Highcliffe Cnr.
The Farthings

Comm. Centre 314

THE LAWNS

New Milton BH25

7

Rec. Grd.

Recreation Ground

Bay View
Island View
Smugglers

Lob's Hole

HIGH CLIFF

93

F **G** **H** **J** **K**

4 19   4 21   **CHRISTCHURCH**   22   **BAY**

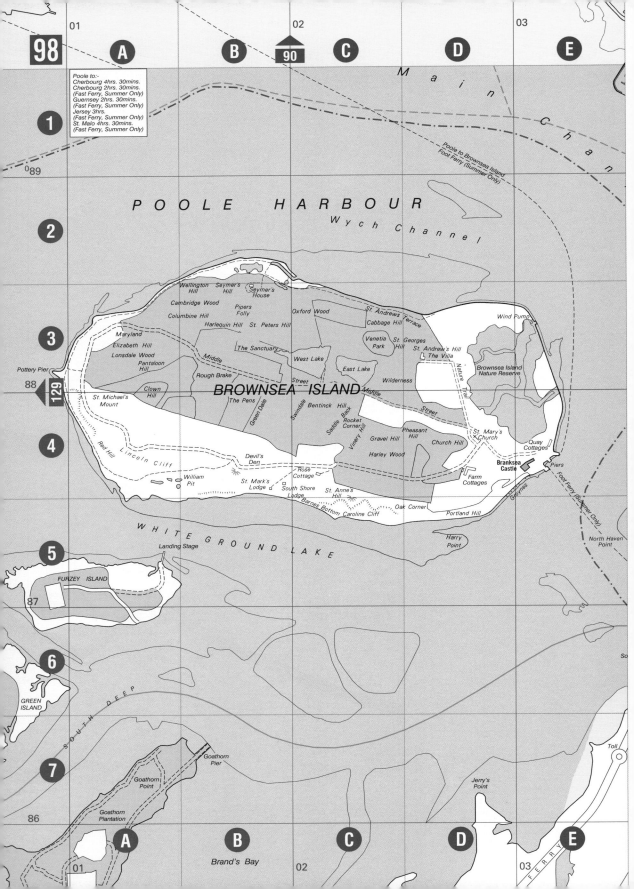

A   B   90   C   D   E

01   02   03

Poole to:-
Cherbourg 4hrs. 30mins.
Cherbourg 2hrs. 30mins.
(Fast Ferry, Summer Only)
Guernsey 2hrs. 30mins.
(Fast Ferry, Summer Only)
Jersey 3hrs.
(Fast Ferry, Summer Only)
St. Malo 4hrs. 30mins.
(Fast Ferry, Summer Only)

1

M a i n   C h a n

Poole to Brownsea Island
Foot Ferry (Summer Only)

89

2

P O O L E   H A R B O U R

Wych Channel

3

Wellington Hill
Seymer's Hill
Seymer's House
Cambridge Wood
Columbine Hill
Pipers Folly
Oxford Wood
St Andrews Terrace
Cabbage Hill
Wind Pump
Harlequin Hill
St. Peters Hill
Maryland
Venetia Park
St Georges Hill
St. Andrew's Hill
The Villa
Elizabeth Hill
The Sanctuary
Lonsdale Wood
Pantaloon Hill
Middle
West Lake
East Lake
Brownsea Island Nature Reserve
Rough Brake
Wilderness
Nature Trail

Pottery Pier
88
129
St. Michael's Mount
Clown Hill
Street
BROWNSEA   ISLAND
Middle
Street
The Pens
Green Dale
Swindale
Bentinck Hill
Saddle Back
Rocket Corner
Vinery Hill
Pheasant Hill
Church Hill
St. Mary's Church
Quay Cottages

4

Red Hill
Lincoln Cliff
Devil's Den
William Pit
St. Mark's Lodge
Rose Cottage
South Shore Lodge
Barnes Bottom
St. Anne's Hill
Caroline Cliff
Oak Corner
Gravel Hill
Harley Wood
Portland Hill
Farm Cottages
Branksea Castle
Piers
Groynes
Foot Ferry (Summer Only)

5

Landing Stage
FURZEY   ISLAND
87

W H I T E   G R O U N D   L A K E

Harry Point
North Haven Point

6

GREEN ISLAND

S O U T H   D E E P

7

Goathorn Pier
Goathorn Point
Jerry's Point
Toll

Goathorn Plantation

86

A   B   C   D   E

01   Brand's Bay   02   03   FERRY

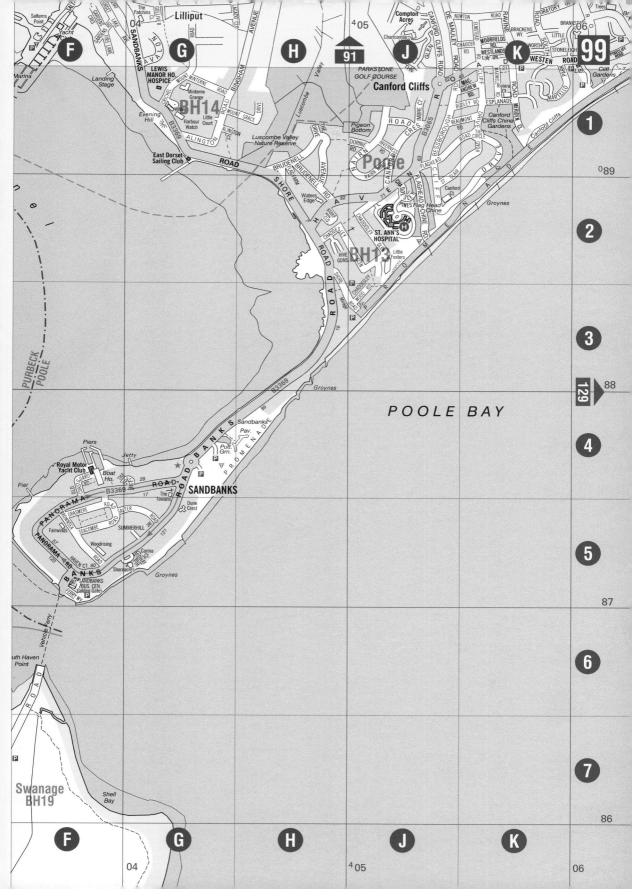

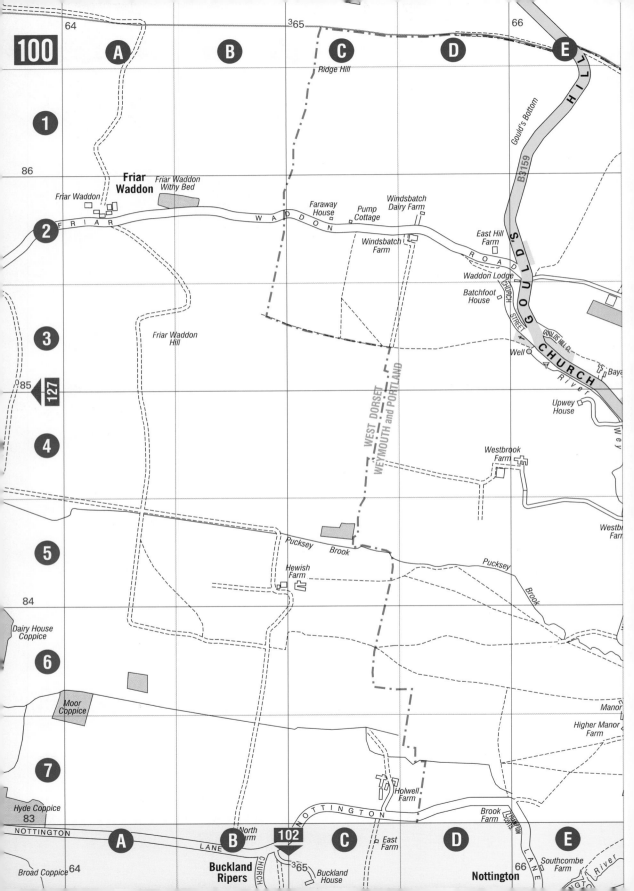

100

A   B   C   D   E

64   365   66

1

86

Friar Waddon
Friar Waddon   Friar Waddon Withy Bed
Friar Waddon

2   FRIAR   WADDON   Faraway House   Pump Cottage   Windsbatch Dairy Farm   ROAD   East Hill Farm   GOULD'S HILL   Gould's Bottom   B3159
Windsbatch Farm   Waddon Lodge
Batchfoot House   CHURCH   GOULD'S HILL CL.

3   Friar Waddon Hill   Well   CHURCH   Baya
River
Upwey House

085
◄ 127   85   WEST DORSET   Wey

4   WEYMOUTH and PORTLAND   Westbrook Farm   Westbr Farr

5   Pucksey   Brook   Pucksey   Brook
Hewish Farm

84

Dairy House Coppice

6   Manor

Moor Coppice   Higher Manor Farm

7

Hyde Coppice   Holwell Farm   Brook Farm
83   North Farm   Southcombe Farm
NOTTINGTON   A   LANE   B   102   C   East Farm   D   E
365   Buckland House   Nottington

Broad Coppice 64   **Buckland Ripers**   CHURCH   NOTTINGTON   FRANKLIN'S LANE   66   River

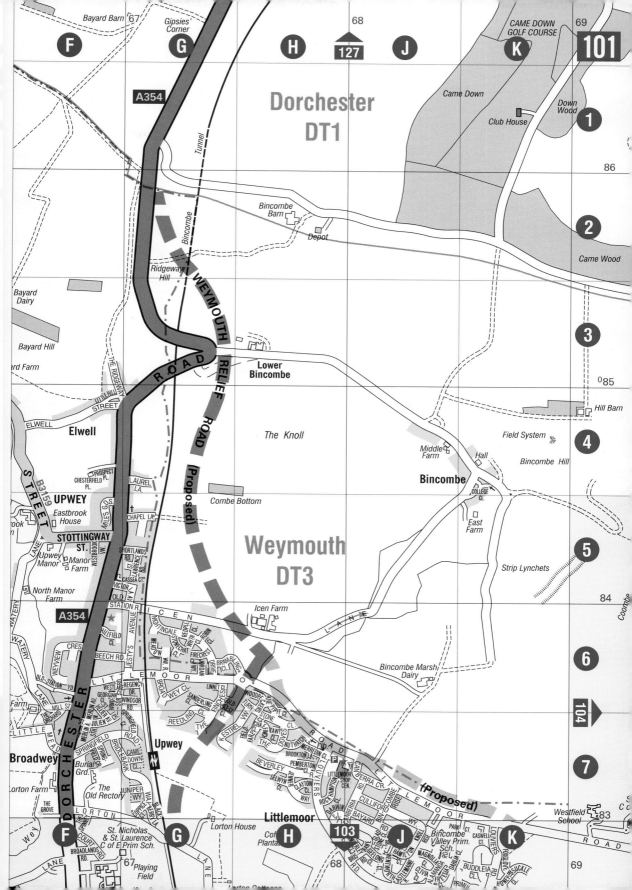

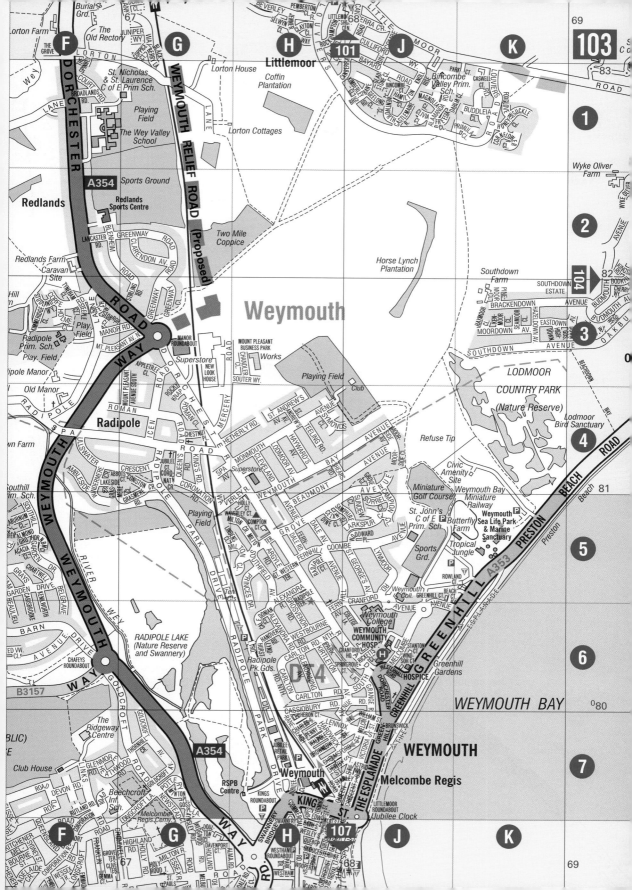

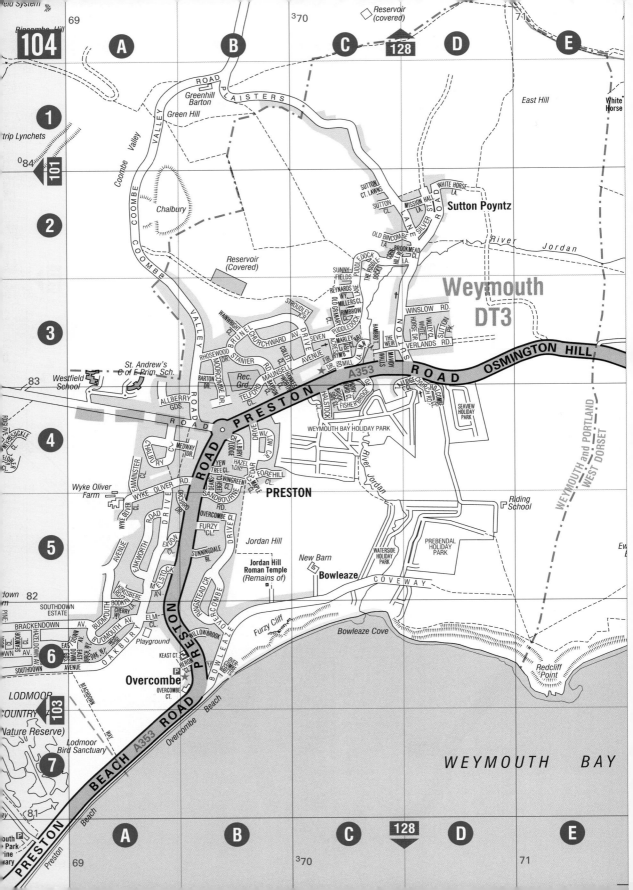

72 73 74

F **G** **H** **J** **K**

POXWELL
DROVE

1

White Horse
Hill

**Dorchester
DT2**

Poxwell

⁰84

2

Poxwell
Manor

Coombe
Bottom

Pixon Barn

Hall's
Farm

LANE

CHURCH

Strip
Lynchets

Grove Lodge

A353

3

Netherton
Farm

White Horse
Farm

CHURCH

ROMAN   ROAD

Grove
Farmhouse

Upton

128 83

West
Farm

VILLAGE ST.

Osmington
House

GROVE
HILL

A353

Osmington

Fir
Coppice

WAY

CHAPEL LA.

Manor House
(remains of)

THATCH
COTTS.

†

MILLS

4

PLOUGH
COTTS.

PLOUGH CL.

MAIN   ROAD

Hall

Play.
Fld.

East Farm

East Farm
Dairy

Osmington
Hill

Hitts
Farm

HILL
W.

LANE

GLEBE CL.

ROAD

Osmington
Mills

5

OSMINGTON BAY
HOLIDAY CENTRE

Camping
Site

UPTON FORT RD.

82

eleaze
Barn

P

SHORTLAKE

Osmington Bay
Centre

OSMINGTON
MILLS
HOLIDAY CLUB

Sewage
Works

Black Head

6

Upton Fort

7

81

F **G** **H** **J** **K**

72 73 74

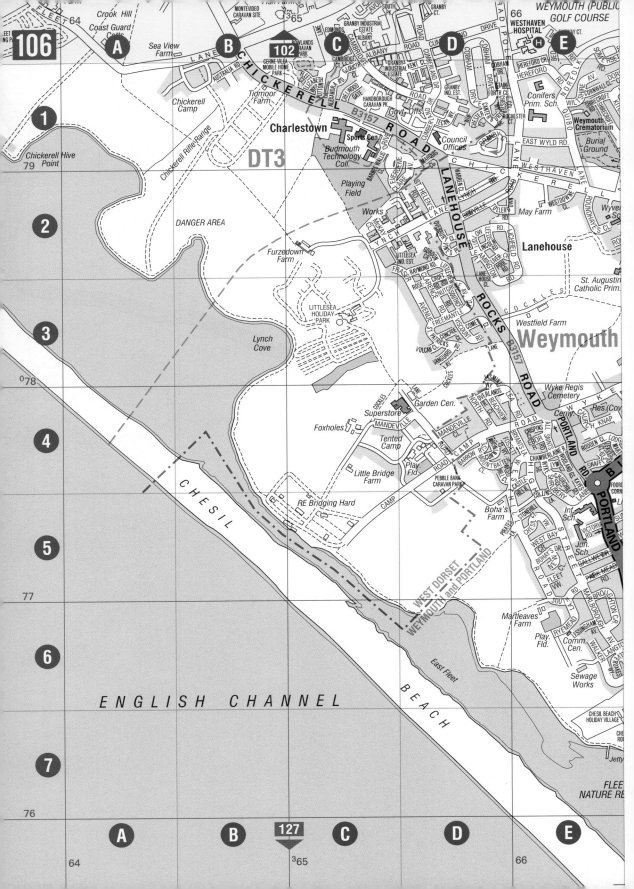

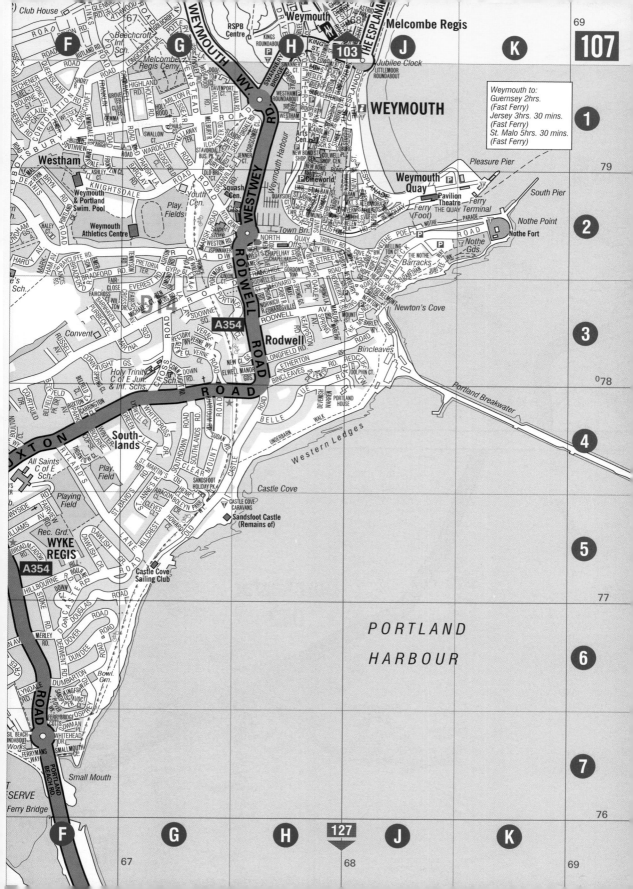

Weymouth to:
Guernsey 2hrs.
(Fast Ferry)
Jersey 3hrs. 30 mins.
(Fast Ferry)
St. Malo 5hrs. 30 mins.
(Fast Ferry)

WEYMOUTH

Melcombe Regis

Weymouth

Westham

PORTLAND

HARBOUR

WYKE REGIS

Rodwell

Southlands

Portland Breakwater

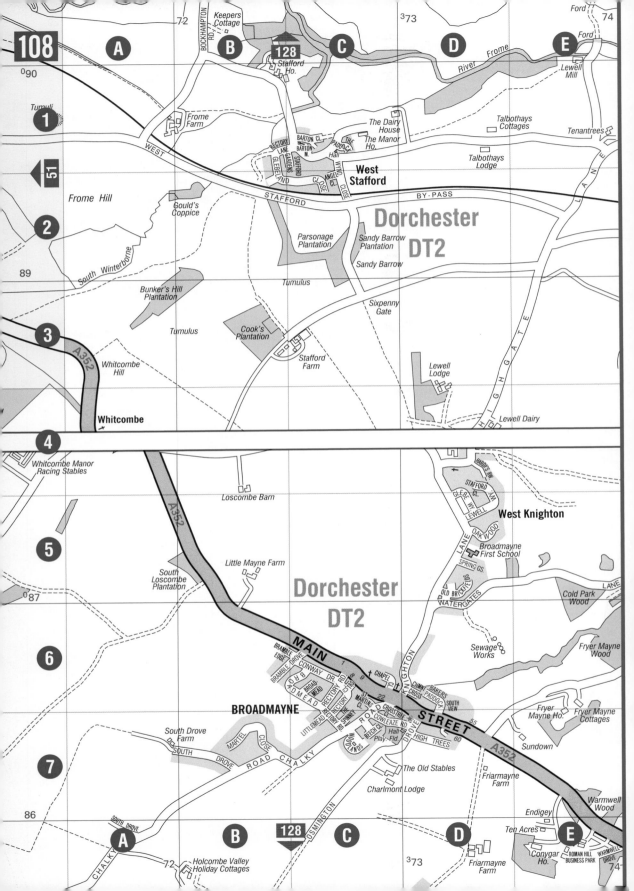

108

⁰90

A B **128** C D E Ford 74 Ford

Ford

Keepers Cottage

BOCKHAMPTON RD.

Stafford Ho.

Lewell Mill

River Frome

1 Tumuli

Frome Farm

The Dairy House

Talbothays Cottages

Tenantrees

The Manor Ho.

RECTORY LANE

BARTON CL.

BARTON M.

THE PADDOCK

STAFFORD GARDENS GLEBELAND

Hall

Talbothays Lodge

51

WEST STAFFORD RD.

ANGEL CL.

WIND CLOSE

CLOSE

West Stafford

2 Frome Hill

Gould's Coppice

STAFFORD

BY-PASS

Dorchester DT2

Parsonage Plantation

Sandy Barrow Plantation

89 South Winterborne

Sandy Barrow

Tumulus

Bunker's Hill Plantation

Sixpenny Gate

HIGHGATE

3 A352

Tumulus

Cook's Plantation

Stafford Farm

Lewell Lodge

Whitcombe Hill

Lewell Dairy

Whitcombe

4

Whitcombe Manor Racing Stables

HARDY'S INN

STAFFORD CL.

A352

Loscombe Barn

GLEBE WAY

LEWELL

OAK WOOD

LANE

West Knighton

5

South Loscombe Plantation

Little Mayne Farm

Broadmayne First School

SPRING GS.

SOUTH

Cold Park Wood

LANE

⁰87

OLD BRICKW'CS

WATERGATES

Fryer Mayne Wood

6

MAIN

BRAMBLE EDGE

BRAMBLE DROVE

CONWAY DR.

B. RD.

BROADMEAD

RD. MEAD

Chapel

KNIGHTON

Sewage Works

CHIMT BAKERS CROSS PADDOCK

SOUTH VIEW

Fryer Mayne Ho.

Fryer Mayne Cottages

BROADMAYNE

RECTORY RD.

RECTORY RD.

LITTLEMEAD RD.

ST. MARTINS CL.

22

CROSTREE

STREET

55

60

Sundown

7

South Drove Farm

MARTEL CLOSE

SOUTH DROVE

ROAD

CHALKY

COWLEAZE RD.

Hall Play. Fld.

SQUARE

WOOD'S

BEECH CL.

DROVE

HIGH TREES

A352

The Old Stables

Friarmayne Farm

Warmwell Wood

86

SOUTH DROVE

Charlmont Lodge

Endigey

A 72 Holcombe Valley Holiday Cottages B **128** OSMINGTON C ³73 D Friarmayne Farm E Ten Acres Conygar Ho. ROMAN HILL BUSINESS PARK WARMWELL DROVE 74

CHALKY

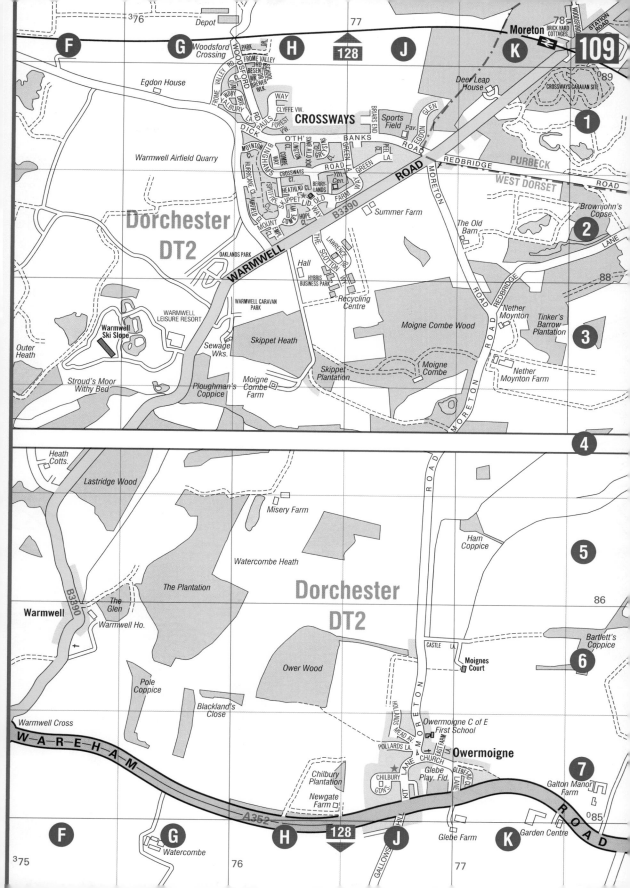

376   77   78   089

Depot

Brick Yard Cottages

STATION ROAD

WOODSFORD

Egdon House

Deer Leap House

Crossways Caravan Site

1

FROME VALLEY RD

SCHOOL

BESCENT

WR DR

BREWER WLK.

PARK DR

FROME VALLEY LA.

WOODSFORD RD

GIN LA.

NDBY

YALBURY

DICK O'TH' BANKS RD

ST PAULS RD.

CLYFFE VW.

WAY

BRIARS END

BANKS

GREEN

O'TH'

SKILLS

GRN.

BINGHAMS

COMBE WAY

MOYNTON CL.

HURRICANE CL.

SPITFIRE CL.

ANFIELD

MOUNT PLT.

COW DRV.

HOPE CL.

EMPT

CROSSWAYS

Sports Field

Pav.

EGDON

GLEN

PURBECK

REDBRIDGE

WEST DORSET

ROAD

1

Warmwell Airfield Quarry

DICK O'TH' BANKS RD

CROSSWAYS CT.

HEATHLND CL.

BERRY-LANDS

SKIPPET

OLD FARM

Ytn. Cen.

GREEN WAY

PEEL LA.

CL.

The Old Barn

Brownjohn's Copse

LANE

2

88

Dorchester DT2

B3390

Summer Farm

ROAD

MORETON

ROAD

REDBRIDGE

OAKLANDS PARK

WARMWELL

THE SCOTTON

LAWRENCE RD

VW.

Hall

HYBRIS BUSINESS PARK

Recycling Centre

Moigne Combe Wood

Nether Moynton

Tinker's Barrow Plantation

3

Outer Heath

Warmwell Ski Slope

WARMWELL LEISURE RESORT

WARMWELL CARAVAN PARK

Sewage Wks.

Skippet Heath

Skippet Plantation

Moigne Combe

Nether Moynton Farm

ROAD

MORETON

Stroud's Moor Withy Bed

Ploughman's Coppice

Moigne Combe Farm

4

Heath Cotts.

Lastridge Wood

Misery Farm

Watercombe Heath

Dorchester DT2

Ham Coppice

ROAD

5

86

B3390

The Plantation

The Glen

Warmwell Ho.

Warmwell

Ower Wood

CASTLE LA.

Moignes Court

Bartlett's Coppice

6

Pole Coppice

Blackland's Close

HOLLANDS MEAD AV.

MORETON LANE

Owermoigne C of E First School

EAST FARM

CASTLE

Owermoigne

7

Warmwell Cross

W A R E H A M

A352

CHURCH LANE

CHILBURY GDNS.

Chilbury Plantation

Newgate Farm

POLLARDS LA.

KIT HILL

Glebe Play. Fld.

GLEBE

CLOSE

GLEBE CROFT

Galton Manor Farm

085

GALLOWS HILL

CHURCH LANE

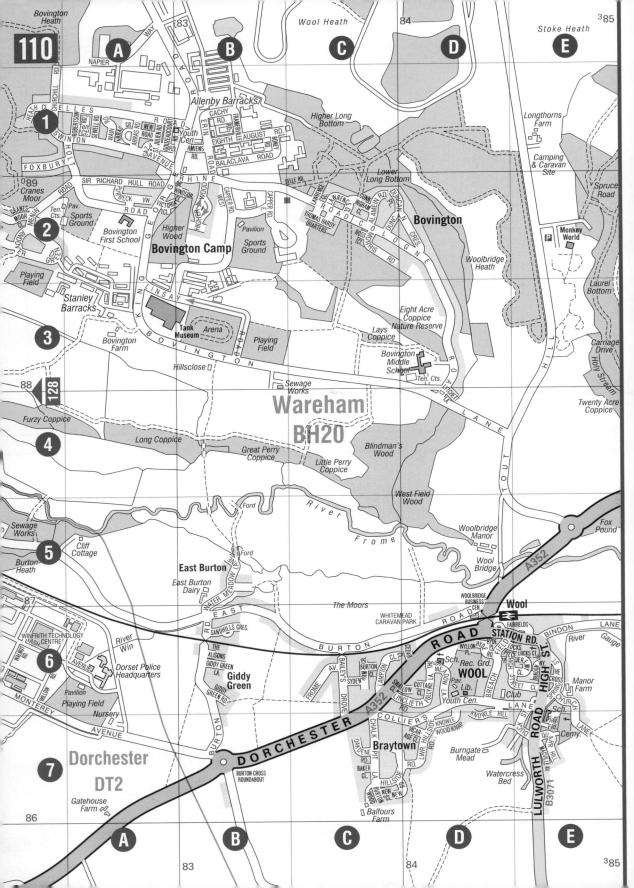

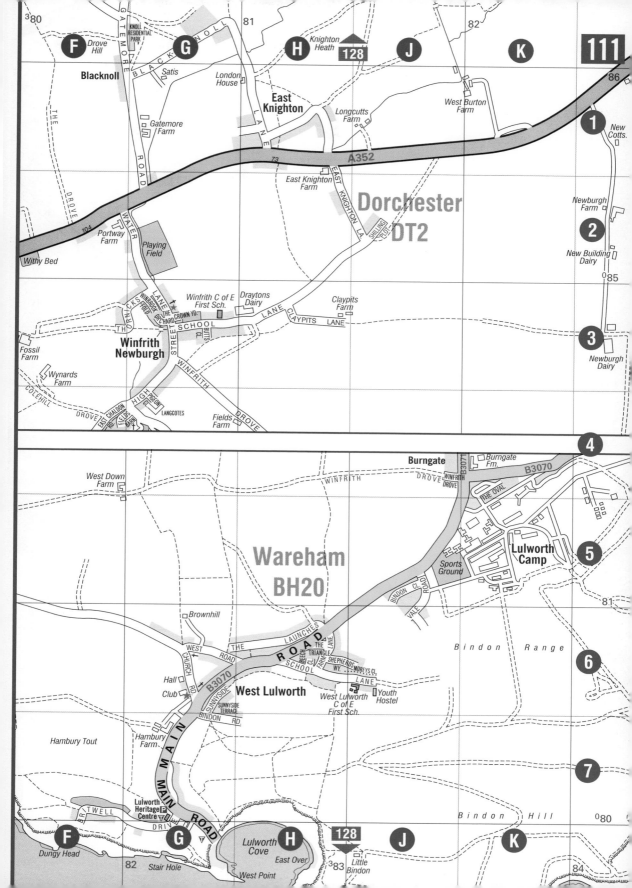

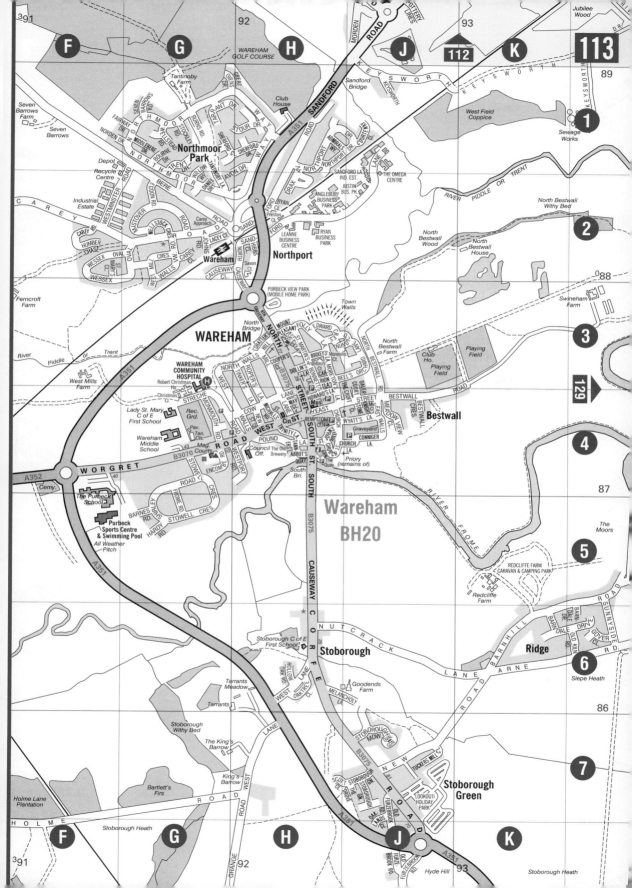

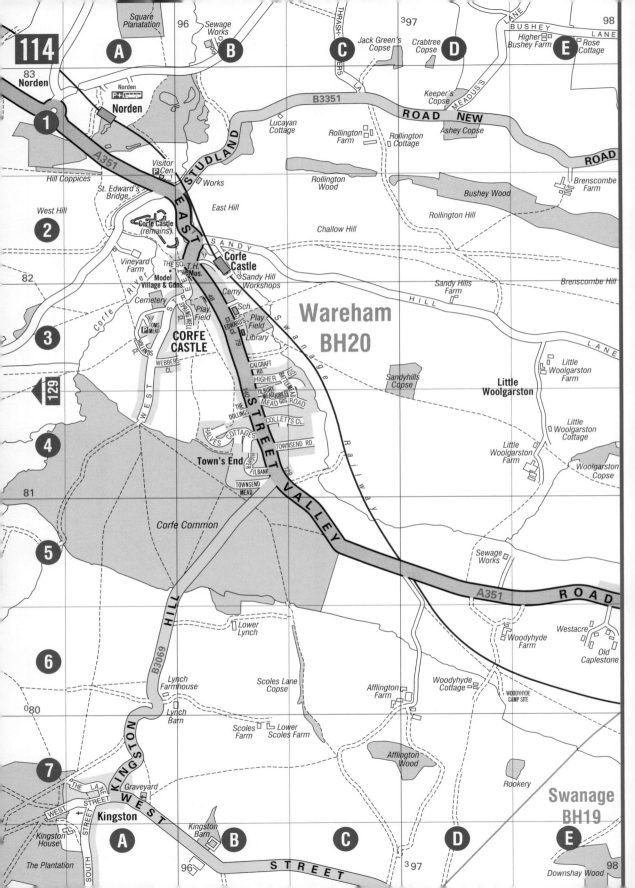

114

83 Norden

Square Planatation

96

Sewage Works

397

Jack Green's Copse

Crabtree Copse

BUSHEY LANE

98

Higher Bushey Farm

Rose Cottage

Norden

P+ Norden

Visitor Cen.

B3351

ROAD NEW

ROAD

Keeper's Copse

MEAD'S S

Hill Coppices

St. Edward's Bridge

Works

East Hill

STUDLAND EAST

Lucayan Cottage

Rollington Farm

Rollington Cottage

Ashey Copse

Brenscombe Farm

West Hill

Corfe Castle (remains)

Rollington Wood

Rollington Hill

Bushey Wood

82

Vineyard Farm

SANDY

Corfe Castle

Sandy Hill Workshops

Challow Hill

Sandy Hills Farm

Brenscombe Hill

THE SQ. T.H. Mus.

Model Village & Gdns

Cemetery

P TOMS MEAD

Corfe River

SPRING WELL

Play Field

Sch.

ST. EDWARD'S CL.

Play Field

Library

Sandy Hills Copse

Wareham BH20

Little Woolgarston Farm

Little Woolgarston

129

CORFE CASTLE

WEBBERS CL.

HOLLANDS

WEST

Cemy.

CALCRAFT RD.

HIGHER

LILBURY MEAD

JUBILEE MEAD GDS. ROAD

THE DOLLINGS

COLLETTS CL.

Sandyhills Copse

Little Woolgarston Cottage

Little Woolgarston Farm

Woolgarston Copse

HALVES COTTAGES

TOWNSEND RD.

SWANAGE Railway

Town's End

HIGHER FILBANK

TOWNSEND MEAD

81

Corfe Common

STREET VALLEY

Sewage Works

A351 ROAD

Westacre

Lower Lynch

Woodyhyde Farm

Old Caplestone

HILL

B3069

Lynch Farmhouse

Scoles Lane Copse

Afflington Farm

Woodyhyde Cottage

WOODYHYDE CAMP SITE

080

Lynch Barn

Scoles Farm

Lower Scoles Farm

Afflington Wood

Rookery

KINGSTON

THE LANE

Graveyard

STREET

WEST STREET

Swanage BH19

SOUTH STREET

Kingston

Kingston Barn

Downshay Wood

Kingston House

The Plantation

96

STREET

397

98

Grid references: A1 B1 C1 D1 E1, A2 B2 C2 D2 E2, A3 B3 C3 D3 E3, A4 B4 C4 D4 E4, A5 B5 C5 D5 E5, A6 B6 C6 D6 E6, A7 B7 C7 D7 E7

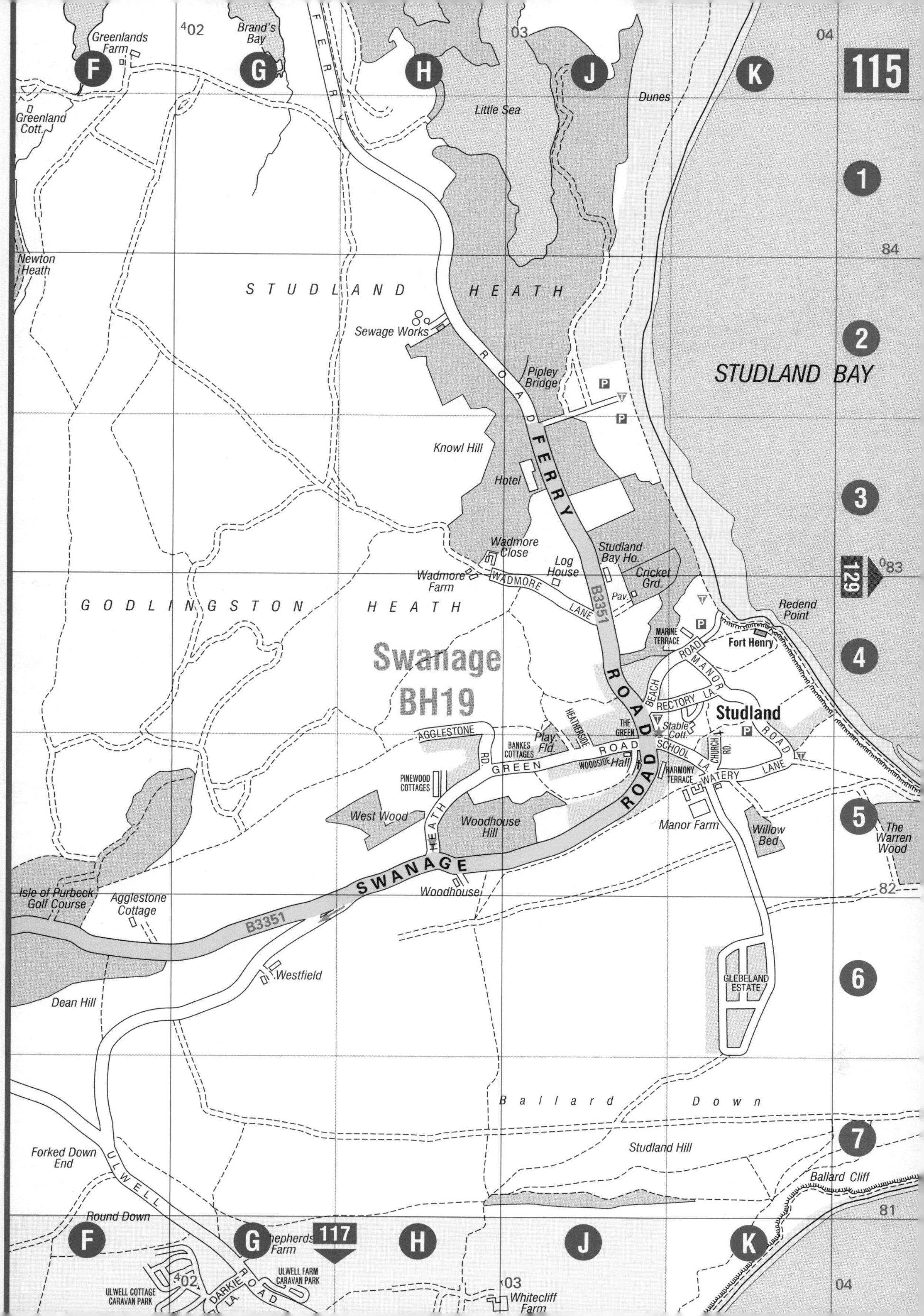

F G H J K

402 03 04

Greenlands Farm

Brand's Bay

Little Sea

Dunes

84

Greenland Cott.

Newton Heath

S T U D L A N D   H E A T H

Sewage Works

STUDLAND BAY

Pipley Bridge

Knowl Hill

FERRY ROAD

Hotel

P

Wadmore Close

Log House

Studland Bay Ho.

Cricket Grd.

Pav.

B3351

WADMORE LANE

Wadmore Farm

083

G O D L I N G S T O N   H E A T H

Redend Point

MARINE TERRACE

Fort Henry

BEACH ROAD

MANOR ROAD

RECTORY LANE

Swanage
BH19

AGGLESTONE

HEATHERSIDE

Play Fld.

THE GREEN

Stable Cott.

Studland

Bankes Cottages

PINEWOOD COTTAGES

GREEN ROAD

WOODSIDE Hall

SCHOOL

CHURCH RD.

HARMONY TERRACE

WATERY LANE

West Wood

Woodhouse Hill

ROAD

Manor Farm

Willow Bed

The Warren Wood

Isle of Purbeck Golf Course

Agglestone Cottage

SWANAGE

Woodhouse

B3351

Westfield

82

GLEBELAND ESTATE

Dean Hill

B a l l a r d   D o w n

Forked Down End

ULWELL ROAD

Studland Hill

Ballard Cliff

Round Down

81

F G H J K

Shepherds Farm

ULWELL COTTAGE CARAVAN PARK

DARKIE LA.

ULWELL FARM CARAVAN PARK

402 03 04

Whitecliff Farm

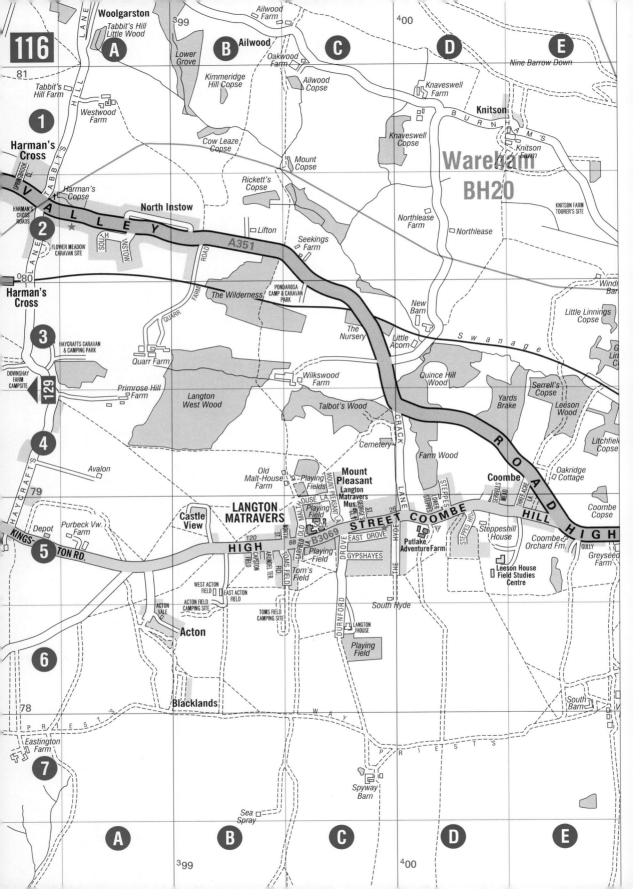

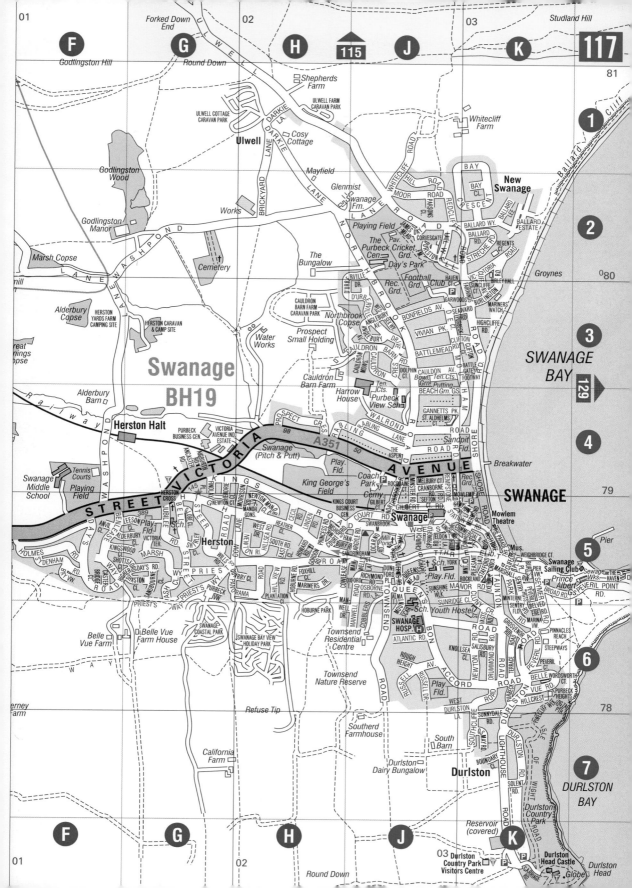

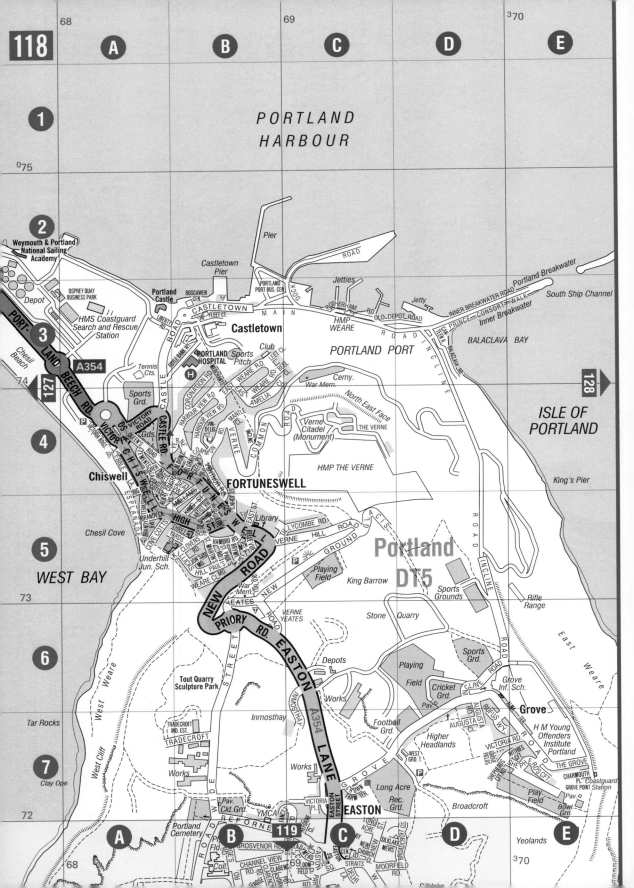

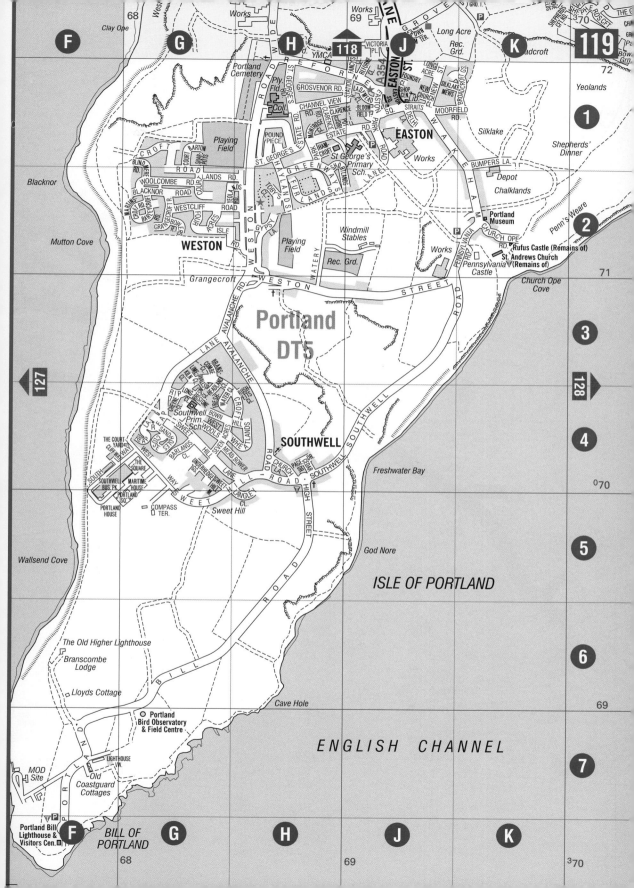

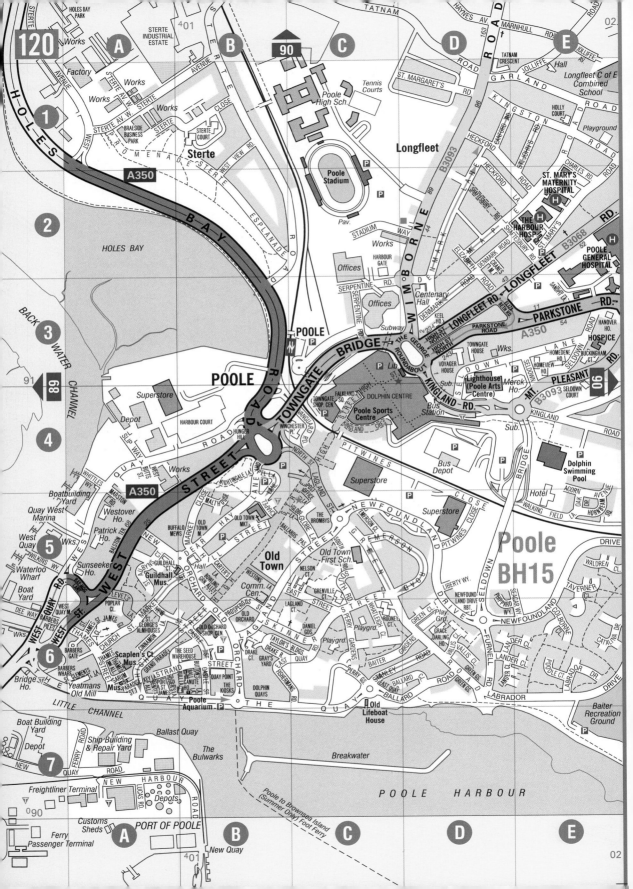

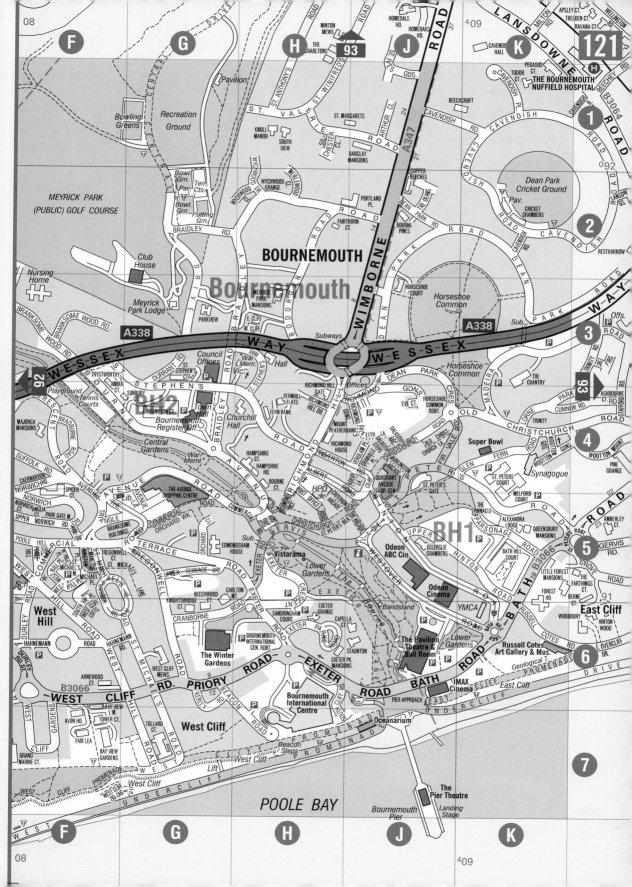

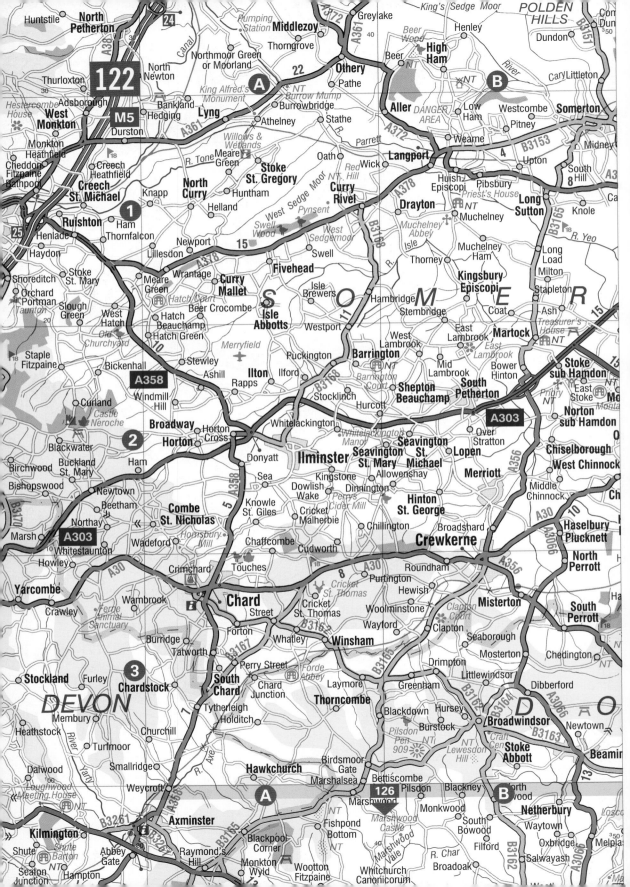

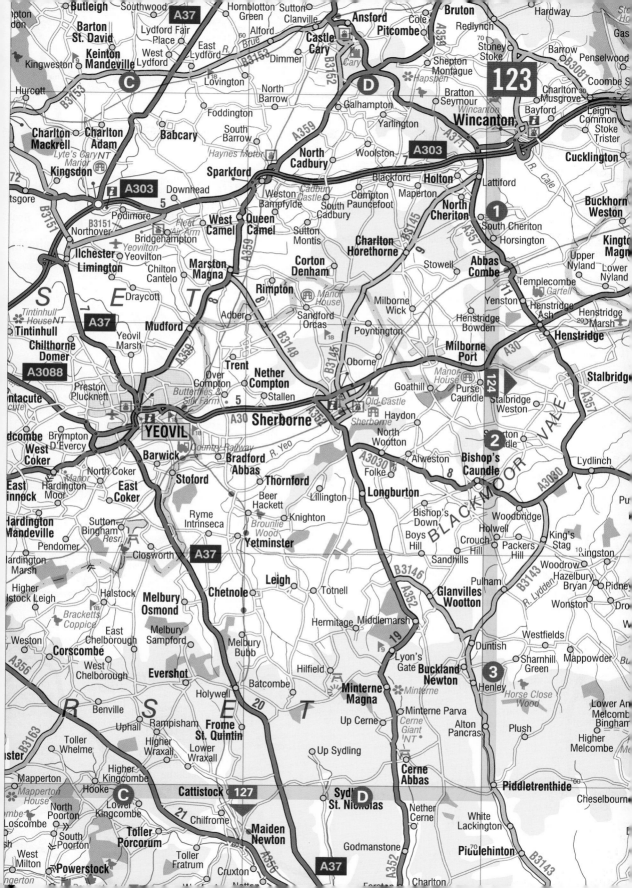

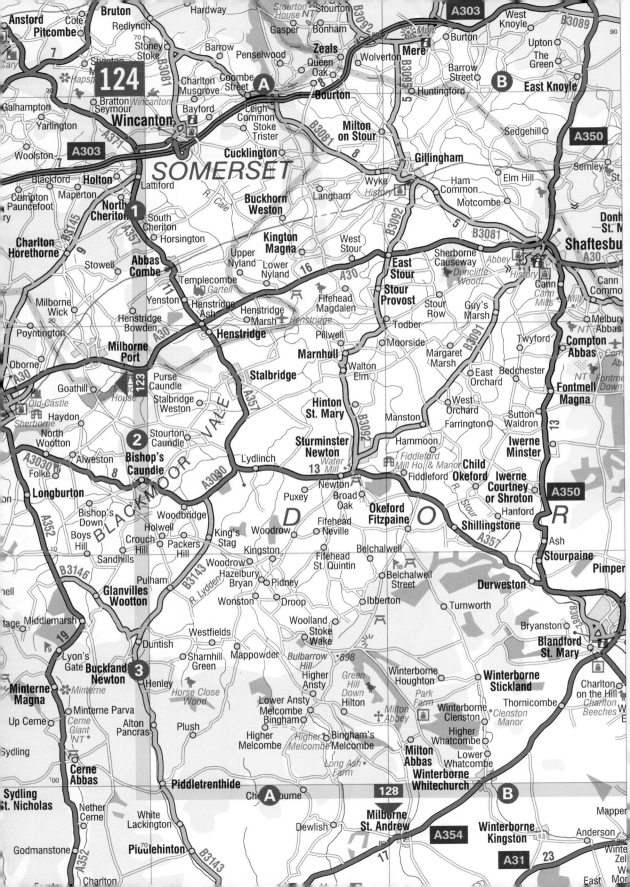

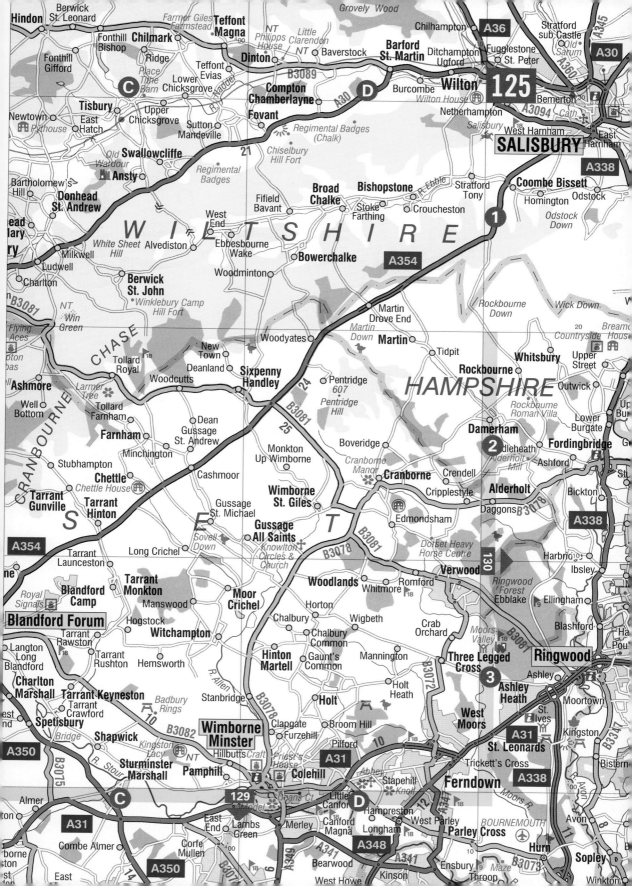

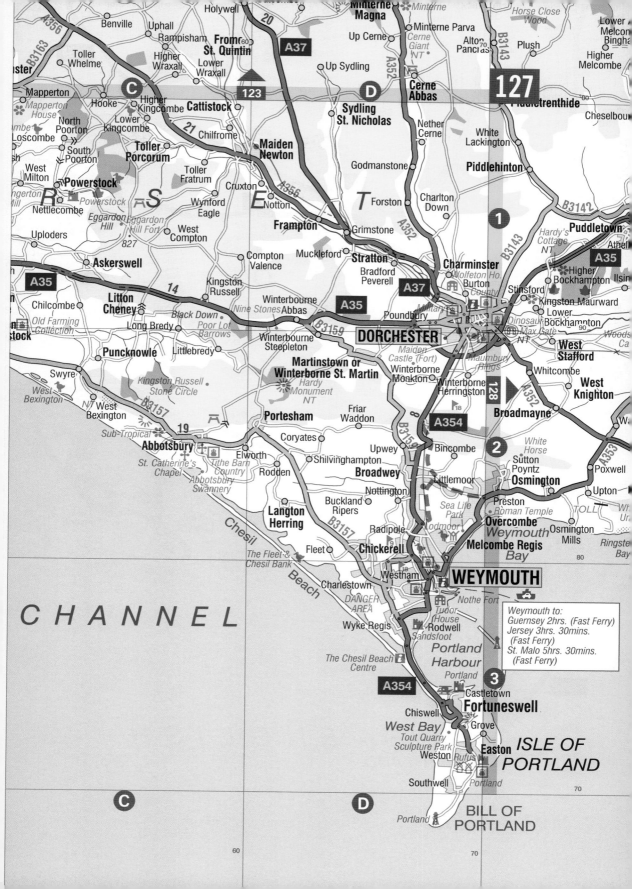

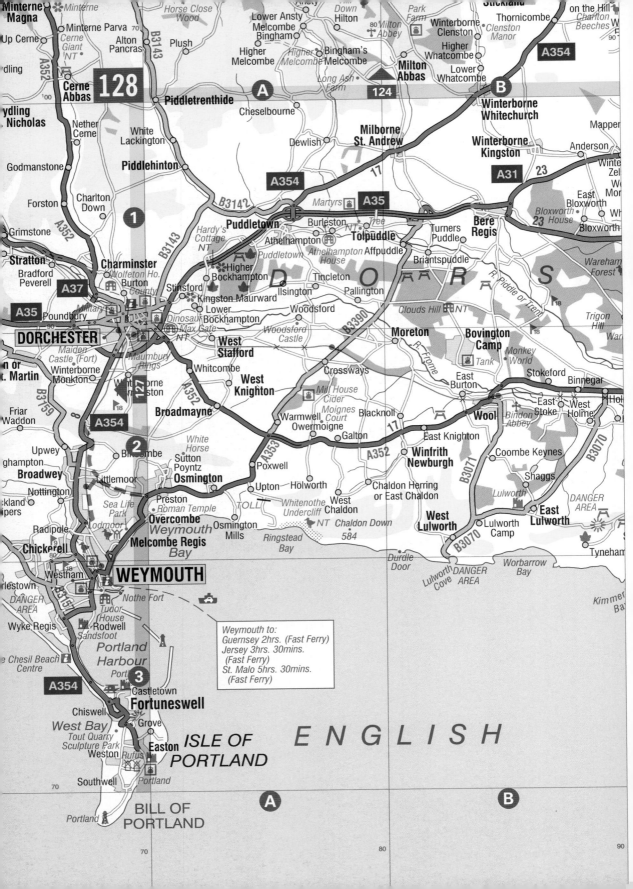

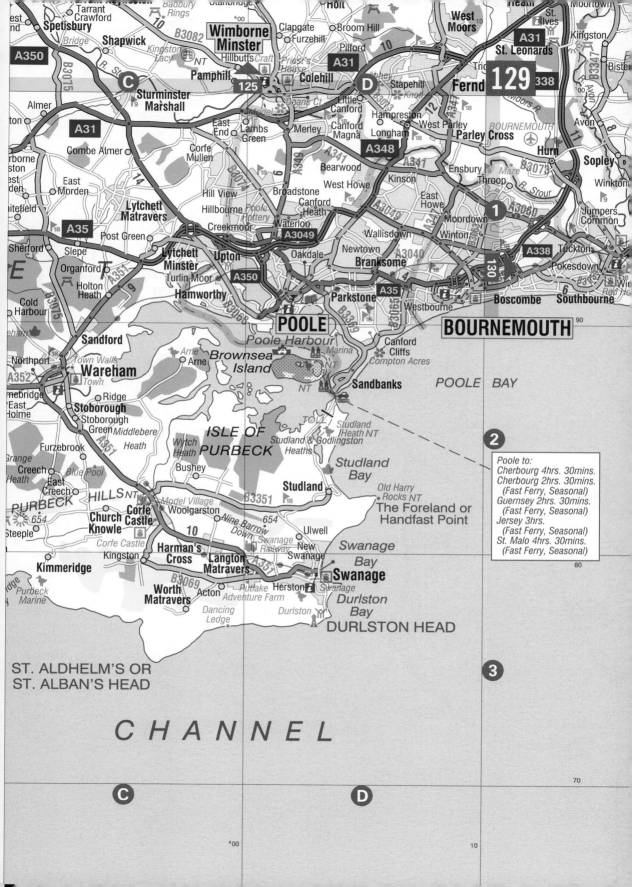

CHANNEL

POOLE

Poole Harbour

BOURNEMOUTH

POOLE BAY

ISLE OF PURBECK

PURBECK HILLS

Wareham

ST. ALDHELM'S OR
ST. ALBAN'S HEAD

DURLSTON HEAD

Durlston Bay

Swanage Bay

Swanage

Studland Bay

Poole to:
Cherbourg 4hrs. 30mins.
Cherbourg 2hrs. 30mins.
(Fast Ferry, Seasonal)
Guernsey 2hrs. 30mins.
(Fast Ferry, Seasonal)
Jersey 3hrs.
(Fast Ferry, Seasonal)
St. Malo 4hrs. 30mins.
(Fast Ferry, Seasonal)

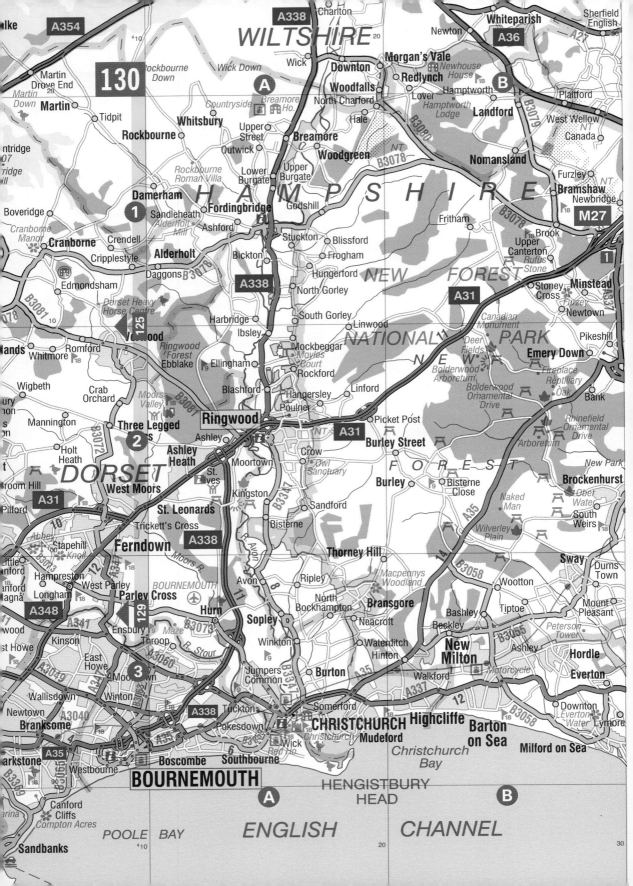

INDEX

Including Streets, Places & Areas, Industrial Estates,
Flats & Walkways, Stations and Places of Interest.

HOW TO USE THIS INDEX

1. Each street name is followed by its Postcode District and then by its Locality abbreviation(s) and then by its map reference; e.g. **Abbey Rd.** BH22: W Moo . . . .4G **67** is in the BH22 Postcode District and the West Moors Locality and is to be found in square 4G on page **67**. The page number is shown in bold type.

2. A strict alphabetical order is followed in which Av., Rd., St., etc. (though abbreviated) are read in full and as part of the street name; e.g. **Abbott St.** appears after **Abbotts Mdw.** but before **Abbotts Way.**

3. Streets and a selection of flats and walkways too small to be shown on street map pages **4-121**, appear in the index with the thoroughfare to which it is connected shown in brackets; e.g. **Acland Ct.** DT1: Dor . . . . 4F **51** (off Linden Av.)

4. Addresses that are in more than one part are referred to as not continuous.

5. Places and areas are shown in the index in **BLUE TYPE** and the map reference is to the actual map square in which the town centre or area is located and not to the place name shown on the map. Map references for entries that appear on street map pages **4-121** are shown first, with references to road map pages **122-130** shown in brackets; e.g. **CRANBORNE** 2H **21** (2D **125**)

6. An example of a selected place of interest is Beaminster Mus. 3D **24**

7. An example of a station is **Bournemouth Station (Rail)** . . . . 3H **93**. Included are Rail **(Rail)** and Park & Ride **(Park & Ride)**

8. Map references for entries that appear on large scale pages **120-121** are shown first, with small scale map references shown in brackets; e.g. **Adelaide La.** BH1: Bourn 4J **121** (4F **93**)

GENERAL ABBREVIATIONS

All. : Alley	**Cres.** : Crescent	**Info.** : Information	**Res.** : Residential
App. : Approach	**Cft.** : Croft	**Junc.** : Junction	**Ri.** : Rise
Arc. : Arcade	**Dr.** : Drive	**La.** : Lane	**Rd.** : Road
Av. : Avenue	**E.** : East	**Lit.** : Little	**Rdbt.** : Roundabout
Bk. : Back	**Ent.** : Enterprise	**Lwr.** : Lower	**Shop.** : Shopping
Bri. : Bridge	**Est.** : Estate	**Mnr.** : Manor	**Sth.** : South
Bldgs. : Buildings	**Fld.** : Field	**Mans.** : Mansions	**Sq.** : Square
Bungs. : Bungalows	**Flds.** : Fields	**Mkt.** : Market	**Sta.** : Station
Bus. : Business	**Gdn.** : Garden	**Mdw.** : Meadow	**St.** : Street
Cvn. : Caravan	**Gdns.** : Gardens	**Mdws.** : Meadows	**Ter.** : Terrace
C'way. : Causeway	**Gth.** : Garth	**M.** : Mews	**Trad.** : Trading
Cen. : Centre	**Ga.** : Gate	**Mt.** : Mount	**Up.** : Upper
Chu. : Church	**Gt.** : Great	**Mus.** : Museum	**Va.** : Vale
Cl. : Close	**Grn.** : Green	**Nth.** : North	**Vw.** : View
Comn. : Common	**Gro.** : Grove	**Pde.** : Parade	**Vs.** : Villas
Cnr. : Corner	**Hgts.** : Heights	**Pk.** : Park	**Vis.** : Visitors
Cott. : Cottage	**Ho.** : House	**Pas.** : Passage	**Wlk.** : Walk
Cotts. : Cottages	**Ho's.** : Houses	**Pl.** : Place	**W.** : West
Ct. : Court	**Ind.** : Industrial	**Prom.** : Promenade	**Yd.** : Yard

LOCALITY ABBREVIATIONS

Abb : Abbotsbury	**Cau M** : Caundle Marsh	**F Clif** : Friars Cliff	**M New** : Maiden Newton
Ald : Alderholt	**Cer A** : Cerne Abbas	**F Wad** : Friar Waddon	**Mann** : Mannington
A Pan : Alton Pancras	**Chalb** : Chalbury	**F Vau** : Frome Vauchurch	**Mans** : Manswood
A'ton : Ashington	**Chalm** : Chalmington	**F Whit** : Frome Whitfield	**Marn** : Marnhull
Ash : Ashley	**Char D** : Charlton Down	**G Com** : Gaunt's Common	**Mart** : Martinstown
Ash H : Ashley Heath	**Char M** : Charlton Marshall	**Gill** : Gillingham	**Matc** : Matchams
Ask : Askerswell	**C'ster** : Charminster	**Green** : Greenham	**M Abb** : Melbury Abbas
Ath : Athelhampton	**C'outh** : Charmouth	**Grim** : Grimstone	**M Osm** : Melbury Osmond
Avon : Avon	**Chet** : Chetnole	**Hal** : Halstock	**M Sam** : Melbury Sampford
Bag : Bagber	**Chick** : Chickerell	**Hamp** : Hampreston	**Melp** : Melplash
Bar : Barton on Sea	**Chid** : Chideock	**Hamw** : Hamworthy	**Merl** : Merley
B Hil : Beacon Hill	**Chilb** : Chilbridge	**Harb** : Harbridge	**M And** : Milborne St Andrew
Bea : Beaminster	**Chilc** : Chilcombe	**H Bot** : Harcombe Bottom	**Mil A** : Milton Abbas
Bee : Beer Hackett	**Chil O** : Child Okeford	**H Cro** : Harman's Cross	**Mil S** : Milton on Stour
Ber : Bere Regis	**Chilf** : Chilfrome	**Hay** : Hayes	**M Cric** : Moor Crichel
Bin : Bincombe	**Chris** : Christchurch	**H Bry** : Hazelbury Bryan	**Morc** : Morcombelake
Bis C : Bishops Caundle	**Clap** : Clapton	**Hen** : Henley	**More** : Moreton
Bist : Bisterne	**Clif M** : Clifton Maybank	**H'ffe** : Highcliffe	**Most** : Mosterton
B Cam : Blandford Camp	**Coke F** : Coker's Frome	**H'own** : Hightown	**Mot** : Motcombe
B For : Blandford Forum	**Coleh** : Colehill	**Hill** : Hillbutts	**Mude** : Mudeford
Blan : Blandford St Mary	**Coles** : Colesbrook	**Hin** : Hinton	**Nea** : Neacroft
Blas : Blashford	**C Abb** : Compton Abbas	**H Mart** : Hinton Martell	**Neth** : Netherbury
Bock : Bockhampton	**Corf C** : Corfe Castle	**H Mary** : Hinton St Mary	**N Com** : Nether Compton
Both : Bothenhampton	**Corf M** : Corfe Mullen	**Holt** : Holt	**N Mil** : New Milton
Bourn : Bournemouth	**Cors** : Corscombe	**Hol H** : Holton Heath	**New** : Newton
B Int : Bournemouth International Airport	**Cow** : Cowgrove	**Holw** : Holwell	**N Chid** : North Chideock
Bour : Bourton	**Cran** : Cranborne	**Holy** : Holywell	**Nott** : Nottington
Bov : Bovington	**Cros** : Crossways	**Hort** : Horton	**O Fitz** : Okeford Fitzpaine
Brad A : Bradford Abbas	**Crow** : Crow	**Hurn** : Hurn	**Organ** : Organford
Brad P : Bradford Peverell	**Dor** : Dorchester	**Hurs** : Hursey	**Osm** : Osmington
Bradp : Bradpole	**Dort** : Dottery	**I Cou** : Iwerne Courtney	**Osm M** : Osmington Mills
Bran : Bransgore	**Drim** : Drimpton	**I Min** : Iwerne Minster	**Over** : Overcombe
Brian : Briantspuddle	**Droo** : Droop	**K Stag** : King's Stag	**O Com** : Over Compton
Brid : Bridport	**Dur** : Durweston	**K'ton** : Kingston	**Ower** : Owermoigne
Broad : Broadmayne	**E Knig** : East Knighton	**K Maur** : Kingston Maurward	**Pamp** : Pamphill
Bro O : Broad Oak	**E Par** : East Parley	**K Mag** : Kington Magna	**Pens** : Penselwood
B'tone : Broadstone	**E Sto** : East Stour	**Knig** : Knighton	**P'ton** : Piddlehinton
B'wey : Broadwey	**East** : Easton	**Knit** : Knitson	**P'hide** : Piddletrenthide
B'sor : Broadwinsor	**Ecc** : Eccliffe	**Lan M** : Langton Matravers	**P'erne** : Pimperne
Bro H : Broom Hill	**E'ham** : Edmondsham	**Leig** : Leigh	**Pool** : Poole
Bryan : Bryanston	**Ever** : Evershot	**L Can** : Little Canford	**Port** : Portesham
Buck N : Buckland Newton	**Fern** : Ferndown	**Lit** : Littlemoor	**Poul** : Poulner
Buck R : Buckland Ripers	**Fid** : Fiddleford	**Lod** : Loders	**Poun** : Poundsbury
Burs : Burstock	**F Mag** : Fifehead Magdalen	**L'ton** : Longburton	**Pox** : Poxwell
Burt : Burton	**F Nev** : Fifehead Neville	**L'ham** : Longham	**Pres** : Preston
Burt B : Burton Bradstock	**Fle** : Fleet	**Low E** : Lower Eype	**Pud** : Puddletown
Can M : Canford Magna	**Folk** : Folke	**L Cam** : Lulworth Camp	**Pun** : Puncknowle
Can : Cann	**Fon M** : Fontmell Magna	**L Reg** : Lyme Regis	**Pym** : Pymore
Cast : Castletown	**Ford** : Fordingbridge	**L Mat** : Lytchett Matravers	**Rad** : Radipole
Catt : Cattistock	**Fort** : Fortuneswell	**L Min** : Lytchett Minster	**Red** : Redlands
	Fram : Frampton	**Mad** : Madjeston	**Rid** : Ridge

A-Z Dorset Atlas 131

Aaron Cl.—Anncott Cl.

Ring : **Ringwood**
Ripl : **Ripley**
Rock : **Rockford**
Ryal : **Ryall**
R Int : **Ryme Intrinseca**
S Ive : **St Ives**
S Leo : **St Leonards**
Sandb : **Sandbanks**
Sandf : **Sandford**
S Hou : **School House**
Sea : **Seatown**
Sed : **Sedgehill**
Shaf : **Shaftesbury**
Shap : **Shapwick**
Sher : **Sherborne**
Shil : **Shillingstone**
Ship G : **Shipton Gorge**
Silt : **Silton**
Six H : **Sixpenny Handley**
Sop : **Sopley**
S'hill : **Southill**
S Per : **South Perrott**
S'well : **Southwell**
S'bury : **Spetisbury**
Stalb : **Stalbridge**
Stall : **Stallen**
Stap : **Staplehill**
Stin : **Stinsford**
Stob : **Stoborough**
Stoc : **Stockwood**
S Wak : **Stoke Wake**
Stour : **Stourpaine**
S Pro : **Stour Provost**
S Cau : **Stourton Caundle**
Strat : **Stratton**
Stud : **Studland**
S Mar : **Sturminster Marshall**
S New : **Sturminster Newton**
Sutt : **Sutton**
S Poy : **Sutton Poyntz**
S Wal : **Sutton Waldron**
Swan : **Swanage**
Swy : **Swyre**
Syd N : **Sydling St Nicholas**
Sym : **Symondsbury**
T Raw : **Tarrant Rawston**
T'ombe : **Thorncombe**
T'ford : **Thornford**
T Leg : **Three Legged Cross**
Tod : **Todber**
Toll : **Tollerford**
T Por : **Toller Porcorum**
Tolp : **Tolpuddle**
Twy : **Twyford**
Uplo : **Uploders**
Uply : **Uplyme**
Upp : **Uppington**
Upt : **Upton**
Upw : **Upwey**
Ver : **Verwood**
Wald : **Walditch**
Walk : **Walkford**
Ware : **Ware**
W'ham : **Wareham**
Warm : **Warmwell**
Water : **Waterditch**
Watt : **Watton**
W Bay : **West Bay**
W Bex : **West Bexington**
W Bou : **West Bourton**
W Knig : **West Knighton**
W Lul : **West Lulworth**
W Moo : **West Moors**
W Par : **West Parley**
W Staf : **West Stafford**
W Stou : **West Stour**
West : **Weston**
Wey : **Weymouth**
What : **Whatcombe**
Whit C : **Whitchurch Canonicorum**
Wim M : **Wimborne Minster**
W New : **Winfrith Newburgh**
Wink : **Winkton**
Wins : **Winsham**
W Hou : **Winterborne Houghton**
W Kin : **Winterborne Kingston**
W Mus : **Winterborne Muston**
W Stic : **Winterborne Stickland**
W Whi : **Winterborne Whitechurch**
W Her : **Winterbourne Herringston**
W Mon : **Winterbourne Monkton**
Wit : **Witchampton**
Won : **Wonston**
Woodl : **Woodlands**
Woods : **Woodsford**
Wool : **Wool**
Woolg : **Woolgarston**
Wools : **Woolsbridge**
W Mat : **Worth Matravers**
Wrack : **Wrackleford**
W Reg : **Wyke Regis**
Yet : **Yetminster**
Zea : **Zeals**

A

Aaron Cl. BH17: Pool .7D **80**
ABBAS COMBE .1A **124**
Abbey Cl. DT9: Sher .5C **12**
SP7: Shaf .4B **8**
Abbey Ct. DT2: Cer A .2C **42**
SP7: Shaf .4B **8**
Abbey Gdns. BH21: Stap .7H **65**
ABBEY GATE .1A **126**
Abbey Rd. BH22: W Moo .4G **67**
DT9: Sher .4C **12**
Abbey St. DT2: Cer A .2C **42**
Abbey Vw. DT11: S'bury .6D **32**
Abbey Wlk. SP7: Shaf .4B **8**
ABBOTSBURY .5D **46** (2C **127**)
Abbotsbury Hill DT3: Abb .4A **46**
Abbotsbury Rd. BH18: B'tone .1G **79**
DT4: Wey .2F **107**
Abbotsbury Sub-Tropical Gdns. .5A **46**
Abbotsbury Swannery .7C **46**
Abbots Cl. BH23: H'ffe .7K **87**
Abbots Ct. BH16: L Mat .6H **53**
DT3: Rad .4F **103**
Abbot's Quay BH20: W'ham .4H **113**
Abbots Wlk. DT2: Cer A .2C **42**
Abbots Way DT9: Sher .5A **12**
Abbott Cl. BH9: Bourn .6G **83**
Abbott Rd. BH9: Bourn .6G **83**
Abbotts Mdw. BH16: L Mat .6H **53**
Abbott St. BH21: Hill, Pamp .6D **62**
Abbotts Way BH22: W Moo .4G **67**
SP8: Gill .3H **5**
Aberdare Rd. BH10: Bourn .3E **82**
Abingdon Dr. BH23: H'ffe .6K **97**
Abingdon Rd. BH17: Pool .6B **80**
Abinger Rd. BH7: Bourn .1C **94**
Abney Rd. BH10: Bourn .3D **82**
Acacia Av. BH31: Ver .6J **55**
Acacia Cl. DT4: S'hill .5F **103**
Acacia Dr. DT2: Char D .2H **49**
Acer Av. DT6: Bradp .2F **39**
Ackerman Rd. DT1: Dor .4H **51**
Acland Ct. *DT1: Dor .4F 51*
(off Linden Av.)
Acland Rd. BH9: Bourn .6H **83**
DT1: Dor .3F **51**
Aconbury Av. DT1: Poun .4B **50**
Acorn Av. BH15: Pool .5E **120** (5B **90**)
Acorn Bus. Pk. BH12: Pool .6F **81**
Acorn Cl. BH23: Chris .6H **85**
BH24: S Leo .1A **68**
Acorns, The BH21: Hay .1E **72**
Acorn Way BH31: Ver .4G **55**
Acreman Cl. DT2: Cer A .2B **42**
Acreman Ct. DT9: Sher .4B **12**
Acreman Pl. DT9: Sher .5C **12**
Acreman St. DT2: Cer A .2B **42**
DT9: Sher .4B **12**
Acres Rd. BH11: Bourn .4B **82**
ACTON .6B **116** (3C **129**)
Acton Fld. Camping Site
BH19: Lan M .5B **116**
Acton Rd. BH10: Bourn .5B **82**
Acton Vale BH19: Lan M .6A **116**
Adamsfield Gdns. BH10: Bourn .4C **82**
ADAM'S GREEN .3K **25**
Adams La. SP5: Six H .2C **20**
Adastral Rd. BH17: Pool .5C **80**
Adastral Sq. BH17: Pool .6D **80**
ADBER .1D **123**
Addington Pl. BH23: Chris .1B **96**
Addiscombe Rd. BH23: Chris .7J **85**
Addison Cl. SP8: Gill .6J **5**
Addison Sq. BH24: Ring .4K **61**
Addison Ter. SP8: Gill .6J **5**
Adelaide Cl. BH23: Chris .6H **85**
Adelaide Cres. DT4: Wey .1F **107**
Adelaide La.
BH1: Bourn .4J **121** (4F **93**)
Adeline Rd. BH5: Bourn .3A **94**
Admirals Cl. DT9: Sher .3D **12**
Admirals Wlk. BH2: Bourn .5D **92**
Admirals Way BH20: W'ham .1H **113**
Admiralty Rd. BH6: Bourn .4H **95**
ADSBOROUGH .1A **122**
AFC Bournemouth .1A **94**
AFFPUDDLE .7C **52** (1B **128**)
Aggis Farm Rd. BH31: Ver .4E **54**
Agglestone Rd. BH19: Stud .4H **115**
Agra Pl. DT1: Dor .4F **51**
Aigburth Rd. BH19: Swan .4G **117**
AILWOOD .1B **116**
Aireton's Cl. BH18: B'tone .3A **80**
Airfield Cl. DT2: Cros .2H **109**
Airfield Ind. Est. BH23: Chris .7E **86**
Airfield Rd. BH23: Chris .7D **86**
Airfield Way BH23: Chris .7D **86**
Airspeed Rd. BH23: Chris .7F **87**
Alamanda Rd. DT3: Lit .1J **103**
Alamein Rd. BH20: Bov .2C **110**
Alan Ct. BH23: H'ffe .7J **97**
Albany BH1: Bourn .4J **93**
Albany Cl. DT9: Sher .2D **12**
Albany Ct. DT1: Dor .4E **50**
DT4: Wey .7C **102**
Albany Dr. BH21: T Leg .3E **58**
Albany Gdns. BH15: Hamw .5H **89**
Albany Pk. BH17: Pool .6K **79**
Albany Pl. DT6: Brid .3E **38**
Albany Rd. DT4: Wey .7C **102**
Albemarle Rd. BH3: Bourn .7F **83**
Albert Pl. *DT11: B For .4C 30*
(off Albert St.)
Albert Rd. BH1: Bourn .4H **121** (4F **93**)
BH12: Pool .2H **91**
BH21: Corf M .1E **78**
BH22: Fern .7C **66**
(not continuous)
DT1: Dor .4E **50**
Albert Row DT9: Sher .4D **12**
Albert St. DT4: Wey .1H **107**
DT11: B For .4C **30**
Albert Ter. DT5: Fort .1A **118**
Albert Vs. DT5: Fort .5A **118**
Albion Cl. BH12: Pool .7F **81**
Albion Cres. DT5: Fort .4B **118**
Albion Rd. BH23: Chris .5H **85**
Albion Way BH31: Ver .4D **54**
Alby Rd. BH12: Pool .2K **91**
ALCESTER .4A **8**
Alcester Rd. BH12: Pool .1H **91**
Aldabrand Cl. DT3: Chick .6B **102**
Alderbury Cl. BH19: Swan .5F **117**
Alder Cl. BH20: Sandf .5C **112**
BH23: Burt .5B **86**
DT10: S New .4D **16**
Alder Cres. BH12: Pool .7K **81**
Alder Dr. SP6: Ald .7H **21**
Alder Hgts. BH12: Pool .1A **92**
Alder Hills BH12: Pool .7A **82**
Alder Hills Ind. Pk. BH12: Pool .7K **81**
Alder Hills Nature Reserve .7A **82**
ALDERHOLT .7J **21** (1A **130**)
Alderholt Mill .1A **130**
Alderley Rd. BH10: Bourn .2D **82**
ALDERNEY .4F **81**
Alderney Av. BH12: Pool .5G **81**
Alderney Rdbt. BH12: Pool .4H **81**
Alder Pk. BH12: Pool .7A **82**
Alder Rd. BH12: Pool .2J **91**
DT10: S New .4D **16**
Aldis Gdns. BH15: Hamw .5G **89**
Aldridge Rd. BH10: Bourn .2C **82**
BH22: Fern .2E **74**
Aldridge Way BH22: Fern .2F **75**
Alexander Cl. BH23: Chris .1C **96**
Alexandra Ct. DT6: Brid .5C **38**
DT11: B For .4C 30
(off Oakfield St.)
Alexandra Gdns. DT4: Wey .2J **107**
Alexandra Lodge
BH1: Bourn .5K **121** (4G **93**)
Alexandra Rd. BH6: Bourn .2E **94**
BH14: Pool .3G **91**
DT1: Dor .4E **50**
DT4: Wey .1C **106**
(Charlestown)
DT4: Wey .5H **103**
(Radipole)
DT6: Brid .4C **38**
Alexandra St. DT11: B For .4C **30**
Alexandra Ter. *DT1: Dor .3F 51*
(off Somerleigh Rd.)
Alexandria Ct. BH22: W Par .2D **74**
ALFORD .1D **123**
Alford Rd. BH3: Bourn .7D **82**
Alfred Pl. DT1: Dor .4G **51**
Alfred Rd. DT1: Dor .4F **51**
Alfred St. DT11: B For .4C **30**
Alice in Wonderland Family Pk. .6A **76**
Alice Rd. DT1: Dor .4D **50**
Alington Av. DT1: Dor .4H **51**
Alington Cl. BH14: Pool .1G **99**
Alington Rd. BH3: Bourn .1G **93**
BH14: Pool .1G **99**
DT1: Dor .4G **51**
Alington St. DT1: Dor .3F **51**
Alington Ter. DT1: Dor .3F **51**
Alipore Cl. BH14: Pool .4H **91**
Alisons, The BH20: Wool .6B **110**
Allberry Gdns. DT3: Pres .4A **104**
Allenby Cl. BH17: Pool .4K **79**
Allenby Rd. BH17: Pool .5K **79**
Allen Cl. DT11: Chil O .3G **19**
Allen Ct. BH21: Wim M .7A **64**
Allen Rd. BH21: Wim M .1A **72**
Allens La. BH16: Hamw .2F **89**
Allens Rd. BH16: Upt .1E **88**
Allenview Rd. BH21: Wim M .6A **64**
ALLER .1B **122**
All Fools La. BH21: Pamp .7E **62**
ALLINGTON .3C **38**
Allington Gdns. DT6: Brid .2B **38**
Allington Hill La. DT6: Brid .2B **38**
Allington Mead DT6: Brid .2C **38**
Allington Pk. DT6: Brid .3B **38**
ALLOWENSHAY .2A **122**
All Saints Rd. DT1: Dor .3G **51**
DT4: W Reg .4E **106**
Alma Rd. BH9: Bourn .7F **83**
DT4: Wey .1H **107**
Alma Ter. BH19: Swan .5J **117**
DT5: East .7E **118**
ALMER .1C **129**
Almer Rd. BH15: Hamw .4G **89**
Almond Gro. BH12: Pool .7H **81**
DT4: S'hill .5F **103**
Alpha Cen., The BH17: Pool .7J **79**
Alpine Rd. BH24: Matc .3E **68**
Alton La. DT2: Cer A .2C **42**
Alton Mead La. DT9: Leig .4C **14**
ALTON PANCRAS .3A **124**
Alton Rd. BH10: Bourn .5B **82**
BH14: Pool .4F **91**
Alton Rd. E. BH14: Pool .5H **91**
Alum Chine Rd. BH4: Bourn .4B **92**
Alumdale Rd. BH4: Bourn .5B **92**
Alumhurst Rd. BH4: Bourn .4B **92**
ALVEDISTON .1C **125**
Alverton Rd. BH15: Pool .4C **90**
ALWESTON .2D **123**
Alyth Rd. BH3: Bourn .1C **92**
Ambassador Cl. BH23: Mude .1E **96**
Ambassador Ind. Est.
BH23: Chris .1E **96**
Amberley Cl. BH23: H'ffe .6J **87**
Amberley Ct.
BH1: Bourn .5K **121** (4G **93**)
Amber Rd. BH21: Corf M .2E **78**
Amberwood BH22: Fern .6E **66**
BH25: N Mil .7K **97**
Amberwood Dr. BH23: Walk .4K **87**
Amberwood Gdns. BH23: Walk .4H **97**
Amberwood Lodge BH22: Fern .7D **66**
Ambleside BH23: Chris .3F **85**
DT3: Rad .4F **103**
Ambleside Cl. BH18: B'tone .4A **80**
Ambrose Cl. DT9: Brad A .6G **11**
Ambury La. BH23: Chris .6C **86**
Amelia Cl. DT5: Fort .4B **118**
Amesbury Rd. BH6: Bourn .1E **94**
Amethyst Rd. BH23: Chris .7D **86**
AMEYSFORD .3B **66**
Ameysford Rd. BH22: Fern .3B **66**
(not continuous)
Ameys La. BH22: Fern .5F **67**
Amiens Rd. BH20: Bov .1B **110**
Amira Ct. BH2: Bourn .4F **121** (4E **92**)
Ampfield Rd. BH8: Bourn .3K **83**
Amsterdam Sq. BH23: Chris .1A **96**
Ancaster Rd. BH19: Swan .4G **117**
Anchor Cl. BH11: Bourn .1K **81**
BH23: Mude .2E **96**
Anchor Rd. BH11: Bourn .1K **81**
Ancrum Lodge BH13: Pool .4B **92**
Andbourne Ct. BH6: Bourn .4H **95**
ANDERSON .1B **128**
Andover Cl. BH23: Chris .7F **87**
Andover Grn. BH20: Bov .2A **110**
Andrew Cl. DT11: B For .3D **30**
Andrews Cl. BH11: Bourn .3A **82**
Androse Gdns. BH24: Ring .5H **61**
Angel Cl. DT2: W Staf .2C **108**
Angel Ct. *SP7: Shaf .3B 8*
(off Angel La.)
Angeline Cl. BH23: H'ffe .6K **87**
Angel La. BH22: Fern .2B **74**
SP7: Shaf .3B **8**
Angers La. DT10: Fid .3A **18**
Anglebury Av. BH19: Swan .3J **117**
Anglebury Bus. Pk.
BH20: W'ham .2H **113**
Anglebury Ct. BH20: W'ham .3H **113**
Anglesey Cotts.
DT10: Stalb .2H **15**
Anglia Ct. BH2: Bourn .5F **121**
Angus Cl. DT11: B For .3D **30**
Anjou Cl. BH11: Bourn .1H **81**
Anna La. BH23: Avon .1H **77**
Anncott Cl. BH16: L Mat .6H **53**

Anne Cl.—Barnack Wlk.

Anne Cl. BH23: Chris 5J 85
DT11: B For 4D 30
Annerley Rd. BH1: Bourn 3J 93
Annet Cl. BH15: Hamw 5G 89
Anning Rd. DT7: L Reg 4C 34
Annings La. DT6: Burt B 6H 37
ANSFORD 1D 123
Anson Cl. BH23: Mude 1D 96
Anstey Cl. BH11: Bourn 7A 74
Anstey Rd. BH11: Bourn 1A 82
ANSTY 1C 125
Ansty La. DT11: M And 6A 44
Antell's Way SP6: Ald 6J 21
Antelope Wlk. DT1: Dor 3F 51
Anthony's Av. BH14: Pool 7F 91
Anvil Cl. BH19: Swan 5F 117
Anvil Cres. BH18: B'tone 1G 79
Anvil Rd. DT11: P'erne 3G 31
Aplands Cl. DT11: Chil O 1F 19
Apollo Cl. BH12: Pool 7H 81
DT1: Dor 5E 50
Apple Acre DT11: Chil O 2G 19
Applebee Way DT7: L Reg 4D 34
Apple Cl. BH12: Pool 3A 92
Applefield Rd. DT8: Drim 2B 22
Apple Gro. BH23: Chris 4G 85
Appletree Cl. BH6: Bourn 2E 94
DT3: Rad 3G 103
Apple Tree Gro. BH22: Fern 6E 66
Apple Tree Rd. SP6: Ald 7H 21
Apple Trees La. DT6: Chid 5B 36
Approach Rd. BH14: Pool 4F 91
April Cl. BH11: Bourn 2A 82
April Ct. BH11: Bourn 2A 82
Apsley Cres. BH17: Pool 5K 79
Apsley Ct BH8: Bourn 1K 121
Aragon Cl. DT4: Wey 5G 107
Aragon Way BH9: Bourn 2H 83
Arbutus Cl. DT1: Dor 4F 51
Arcade, The BH1: Bourn 5J 121 (4F 93)
Arcade Ter. *BH19: Swan 5K 117*
(off High St.)
Arcadia Av. BH8: Bourn 7H 83
Arcadia Rd. BH23: Chris 5H 85
Archdale Cl. BH10: Bourn 4D 82
Archway Ho. DT11: B For 5C 30
Archway Rd. BH14: Pool 3J 91
Arden Rd. BH9: Bourn 3F 83
Ardmore Rd. BH14: Pool 3F 91
Arena Bus. Pk. BH17: Pool 6K 79
Argyle Rd. BH19: Swan 5J 117
BH23: Mude 2C 96
DT4: Wey 5H 103
Argyll Rd. BH5: Bourn 3A 94
BH12: Pool 1H 91
Ariel Cl. BH6: Bourn 3K 95
Ariel Dr. BH6: Bourn 3K 95
Ark Dr. BH22: Fern 2F 75
Arlecks La. DT11: P'erne 2F 31
Arley Rd. BH14: Pool 5E 90
Arlington DT4: S'hill 6E 102
Armada Way DT1: Dor 5H 51
Armoury Yd. SP7: Shaf 3B 8
Armstrong Rd. DT6: Brid 2C 38
ARNE 2C 129
Arne Av. BH12: Pool 7J 81
Arne Bird Sanctuary 2C 129
Arne Cres. BH12: Pool 7J 81
Arne Rd. BH20: Rid 6K 113
Arne Vw. Cl. BH16: Upt 7D 78
Arnewood Ct.
BH2: Bourn 6F 121 (5E 92)
Arnewood Rd. BH6: Bourn 3E 94
Arnhem Grn. DT1: Dor 3D 50
Arnold Cl. BH22: W Moo 1E 66
Arnold Rd. BH22: W Moo 1E 66
Arran Way BH23: Walk 5J 97
Arras Cres. BH20: Bov 1A 110
Arras Rd. BH20: Bov 1A 110
Arrowfield DT6: Brid 4C 38
(not continuous)
Arrowsmith Ct. *BH18: B'tone 2J 79*
(off Station App.)
Arrowsmith La. BH21: Merl 6C 72
Arrowsmith Rd. BH21: Merl 1B 80
Arthur Cl. BH2: Bourn 1J 121 (2F 93)
Arthur La. BH23: Chris 7J 85
Arthur Rd. BH23: Chris 7J 85
Artist Row DT5: Fort 5B 118
Arun Cl. SP8: Gill 3H 5
Arundell DT6: Chid 5B 36
Arundel Ter. BH19: Lan M 5B 116
Arundel Way BH23: H'ffe 7K 87
Ascham Rd. BH8: Bourn 2H 93
Ascot Rd. BH18: B'tone 2J 79
ASH
Blanford Forum 1H 29 (2B 124)
Martock 1B 122
Ash Av. BH16: Sandf 3C 112
Ashbourne Ct. *BH1: Bourn 4K 121*
(off Lorne Pk. Rd.)
Ashbourne Rd. BH5: Bourn 2D 94
Ashbrook Wlk. BH16: L Min 1A 88
Ashburton Gdns. BH10: Bourn 5D 82
Ashbury Cotts. BH21: H Mart 2A 56
(not continuous)
Ash Cl. BH16: Upt 6D 78
BH19: Swan 5G 117
BH20: Sandf 6B 112
SP6: Ald 7J 21
SP7: Shaf 2D 8
Ashdene Cl. BH21: Wim M 7B 64
Ashdown BH2: Bourn 5D 92
Ashdown Cl. BH17: Pool 5C 80
Ashdown Leisure Cen. 5C 80
ASHFORD 1A 130
Ashford Rd. BH6: Bourn 7F 85
Ash Gro. BH24: Ring 4K 61
Ash Hill DT2: Strat 4D 48
ASHILL 2A 122
ASHINGTON 4J 71
Ashington La. BH21: A'ton 3J 71
Ashington St. DT1: Poun 4C 50
Ashleigh Av. DT2: M New 6H 41
Ashleigh Ri. BH10: Bourn 4D 82
ASHLEY
New Milton 3B 130
Ringwood 6F 61 (2A 130)
Ashley Cl. BH1: Bourn 1A 94
Ashley Ct. BH22: W Moo 4G 67
DT4: Wey 2F 107
Ashley Dr. Nth. BH24: Ash H 5B 60
(not continuous)
Ashley Dr. Sth. BH24: Ash H 6B 60
Ashley Dr. W. BH24: Ash H 6B 60
ASHLEY HEATH 6A 60 (2A 130)
Ashley Heath Ind. Est.
BH21: Wools 4H 59
Ashley Pk. BH24: Ash H 5C 60
Ashley Rd. BH1: Bourn 1A 94
BH14: Pool 2F 91
DT1: Dor 5F 51
DT10: Marn 4J 9
Ashley Wood Rd. DT11: B Cam 7H 31
Ashling Cl. BH8: Bourn 6J 83
Ashling Cres. BH8: Bourn 6H 83
Ashmeads Cl. BH21: Coleh 6E 64
Ashmeads Way BH21: Coleh 6E 64
Ashmede BH4: Bourn 5C 92
ASHMORE 2C 125
Ashmore BH21: Wim M 1B 72
Ashmore Av. BH15: Hamw 6H 89
Ashmore Cl. DT11: B For 3C 30
Ashmore Cres. BH15: Hamw 6H 89
Ashmore Gro. BH23: Chris 5J 87
Ashridge Av. BH10: Bourn 1D 82
Ashridge Gdns. BH10: Bourn 1D 82
Ashridge Pde. BH10: Bourn 1D 82
Ash Rd. DT2: Char D 2H 49
Ashstead Gdns. BH8: Bourn 3J 83
Ashton Ct. BH13: Pool 5A 92
Ashton Rd. BH9: Bourn 4F 83
DT4: Wey 2G 107
Ash Tree Cl. DT2: Pud 2C 52
Ash Tree Ct. DT2: Mart 2J 47
Ashtree Mdws. BH23: Chris 1B 96
Ashurst Rd. BH8: Bourn 3K 83
BH22: W Moo 1E 66
Ash Way DT3: Over 6A 104
Ashwood Dr. BH18: B'tone 2A 80
Asker Gdns. DT6: Brid 4D 38
Asker Mead DT6: Both 4E 38
ASKERSWELL 1C 127
Asker Ter. DT6: Brid 4D 38
Askwith Cl. DT9: Sher 6A 12
Aspen, The BH19: Swan 4J 117
Aspen Dr. BH31: Ver 4H 55
Aspen Gdns. BH12: Pool 6K 81
Aspen Rd. BH12: Pool 7K 81
DT2: Char D 1J 49
Aspen Way BH12: Pool 7K 81
Asquith Cl. BH23: Chris 2B 96
Astbury Av. BH12: Pool 6K 81
Aston Mead BH23: Chris 2G 85
Astrid Way DT4: Wey 7J 103
ATHELHAMPTON 2E 52 (1A 128)
Athelhampton House 1A 128
Athelhampton Rd. DT2: Ath, Pud 2D 52
ATHELNEY 1A 122
Athelstan Rd. BH6: Bourn 2G 95
DT1: Dor 4G 51
Athelstan Way DT11: Mil A 1C 44
Atlantic Rd. BH19: Swan 6J 117
Attwood Cl. SP6: Ald 7H 21
Auburn Mans. BH12: Pool 3B 92
Auckland Rd. BH23: Chris 7G 87
Augusta Cl. DT5: East 7D 118
Augustan Av. DT11: Shil 6F 19
Augustan Cl. DT1: Dor 6E 50
Augusta Pl. *DT4: Wey 2J 107*
(off New St.)
Augusta Rd. DT5: East 7D 118
Austen Av. BH10: Bourn 7D 74
Auster Cl. BH23: Mude 7F 87
Austin Av. BH14: Pool 6F 91
Austin Cl. BH1: Bourn 2K 93
Australia Rd. DT3: Chick 1B 106
Autumn Cl. BH22: Fern 5B 66
Autumn Rd. BH11: Bourn 3H 81
Avalanche Rd. DT5: S'well 3G 119
Avalon BH14: Pool 7G 91
Avebury Av. BH10: Bourn 7E 74
Avebury Ct. DT11: B For 3C 30
Avenue, The BH9: Bourn 4F 83
BH13: Pool 7A 92
BH22: W Moo 1D 66
BH24: S Leo 4H 67
DT9: Sher 3D 12
Avenue Cl. DT7: L Reg 5C 34
Avenue Ct. BH13: Pool 4A 92
Avenue La. BH2: Bourn 5G 121 (4E 92)
Avenue Rd. BH2: Bourn 5F 121 (4E 92)
BH21: Wim M 1B 72
BH23: Chris 7H 85
BH23: Walk 5K 97
DT4: Wey 6J 103
DT7: L Reg 5C 34
Avenue Shop. Cen., The
BH2: Bourn 5G 121 (4E 92)
Avenue Stadium 6E 50
Aviation Pk. BH23: B Int 4B 76
Aviation Pk. W. BH23: B Int 4K 75
Avocet Cl. DT3: Chick 6B 102
DT4: W Reg 6F 107
AVON 3H 77 (3A 130)
Avon Av. BH24: Ash 1F 69
Avon Bldgs. BH23: Chris 7K 85
AVON CASTLE 7F 61
Avon Castle Dr. BH24: Ash 7F 61
Avon C'way. BH23: Hurn 6D 76
Avoncliffe Rd. BH6: Bourn 4G 95
Avon Cl. BH8: Bourn 1K 93
DT4: Wey 7C 102
Avon Ct. BH12: Pool 3A 92
DT4: Wey 7C 102
Avondale Gdns. SP8: Gill 3H 5
Avon Dr. BH20: W'ham 2G 113
Avon Heath Country Pk. (North Pk.) 7C 60
Avon Heath Country Pk. (South Pk.) 3C 68
Avon Heath Country Pk. Vis. Cen. 2C 68
Avon Ho. BH2: Bourn 7F 121 (5E 92)
Avon M. BH8: Bourn 1J 93
Avon Pk. BH24: Ash 5F 61
Avon Rd. BH8: Bourn 1J 93
BH22: W Moo 3E 66
Avon Rd. E. BH23: Chris 6J 85
Avon Rd. W. BH23: Chris 6H 85
Avon Run Cl. BH23: F Clif 2F 97
Avon Run Rd. BH23: F Clif 2F 97
Avon Trad. Pk. BH23: Chris 7J 85
Avon Vw. Pde. BH23: Burt 3A 86
Avon Vw. Rd. BH23: Burt 3A 86
Avon Wharf BH23: Chris 1A 96
Avorns, The BH24: S Leo 4H 67
Award Rd. BH21: Stap 7K 65
Axe Mill Ind. Est. DT8: Drim 1A 22
Axe Rd. DT8: Drim 1A 22
TA18: Clap 1A 22
Axe Valley Cl. DT8: Most 2J 23
Axford Cl. BH8: Bourn 3A 84
AXMINSTER 1A 126
Axminster Rd. DT6: C'outh 6G 35
AXMOUTH 1A 126
Aylesbury Rd. BH1: Bourn 3K 93
Aynsley Ct. DT4: Wey 7G 103
Azalea Cl. BH24: S Ive 6C 60
Aztec Cen. BH17: Pool 6B 80
Azura Cl. BH21: Wools 5H 59

B

BABCARY 1C 123
Babeny Wlk. DT1: Poun 4B 50
Babylon Hill DT9: Brad A, Sher 3F 11
Back Drove DT9: Leig 6D 14
Back La. BA22: Hal 1H 25
BH20: Ber 1G 53
BH21: S Mar 5H 33
DT2: Cer A 2B 42
DT2: Ever 5B 26
DT2: F Vau 6G 41
DT2: Swy 3B 46
DT2: Syd N 6C 42
DT8: B'sor 6H 23
DT9: Brad A 7G 11
DT9: Chet 6A 14
DT9: Sher 4C 12
DT10: K'ton 3D 28
DT11: O Fitz 6B 18
Back La. SP5: Six H 2C 20
SP8: K Mag 7B 4
SP8: Mil S 1F 5
Bk. Rivers La. DT6: Brid 4D 38
Back St. DT3: Abb 5D 46
DT3: Port 6G 47
SP8: E Sto 1J 7
Backwater DT2: Pud 1C 52
Badbury Cl. BH18: B'tone 3A 80
Badbury Dr. DT11: B For 3C 30
Badbury Rings 2A 62
Badbury Vw. BH21: Wim M 7B 64
Badbury Vw. Rd. BH21: Corf M 5F 71
Bader Rd. BH17: Pool 6C 80
Badgers Cl. BH24: Ash H 6B 60
SP8: Bour 2C 4
Badger Sett DT11: Blan 6B 30
Badgers Wlk. BH10: Bourn 2D 82
BH22: Fern 5E 66
Badgers Way DT10: S New 4C 16
Badger Way BH31: Ver 5F 55
Bagman's La. BH21: Hort, Woodl 6A 20
(not continuous)
Bagwood Rd. DT11: W Kin 7F 45
Bailey Cres. BH15: Pool 7A 80
Bailey Dr. BH23: Chris 7H 85
Bailey's Drove BH20: Wool 6C 110
Bailie Gate Ind. Est. BH21: S Mar 7J 33
Baiter Gdns. BH15: Pool 6C 120 (6A 90)
Bakehouse Cnr. DT3: Chick 5A 102
Bakehouse La. DT9: Brad A 6G 11
Baker Cl. BH20: Wool 7C 110
Baker Rd. BH11: Bourn 1K 81
Bakers Farm Rd. BH31: Ver 3E 54
Bakers La. BH21: Holt 2D 56
Bakers Paddock DT2: Broad 6D 108
Bakers Vw. BH21: Corf M 7F 71
Balaclava Pl. DT6: Brid 4C 38
Balaclava Rd. BH20: Bov 1B 110
DT5: Cast 3D 118
Balcombe Rd. BH13: Pool 4A 92
Baldwin Cl. BH23: Chris 1B 96
Balena Cl. BH17: Pool 6J 79
Balfour Cl. BH23: Chris 6H 87
Balfour Rd. BH9: Bourn 5F 83
Ballam Cl. BH16: Upt 7E 78
Ballard Cl. BH15: Pool 6C 120 (6B 90)
BH16: L Mat 5H 53
Ballard Est. BH19: Swan 2K 117
Ballard Lee BH19: Swan 2K 117
Ballard Rd. BH15: Pool 6C 120 (6A 90)
BH19: Swan 2K 117
Ballards Pas.
BH15: Pool 5B 120 (5A 90)
Ballard Way BH19: Swan 2K 117
Ball La. BH15: Pool 6B 120 (6A 90)
Ball's La. BH21: S Mar 5H 33
Balmer Rd. DT11: B For 2D 30
Balmoral Av. BH8: Bourn 5A 84
Balmoral Cres. DT1: Dor 5H 51
Balmoral Ho. BH2: Bourn 4D 92
Balmoral Rd. BH14: Pool 4G 91
Balston Rd. BH14: Pool 1E 90
Balston Ter. BH15: Pool 5A 120 (5K 89)
Banbury Rd. BH17: Pool 7A 80
BANK 2B 130
Bank Chambers *BH14: Pool 3J 91*
(off Penn Hill Av.)
Bank Cl. BH23: Chris 1K 95
Bankes Cotts. BH19: Stud 5J 115
BANKLAND 1A 122
Bankside DT2: Cors 5H 25
Bankside Rd. BH9: Bourn 3G 83
Banks Rd. BH13: Sandb 5F 99
Banstead Rd. BH18: B'tone 1J 79
Banton Shard DT6: Bradp 1F 39
Barberry Way BH31: Ver 5J 55
Barbers Ga.
BH15: Pool 6A 120 (6K 89)
Barber's La. DT7: Uply 4A 34
Barbers Piles
BH15: Pool 6A 120 (6K 89)
Barbers Wharf BH15: Pool 6A 120
Barclay Mans.
BH2: Bourn 1J 121 (2F 93)
Barclay Rd. DT4: Wey 2G 107
BARFORD ST MARTIN 1D 125
Bargates BH23: Chris 7J 85
Baring Rd. BH6: Bourn 3J 95
Barlake Ct. *DT1: Poun 4C 50*
(off Wardbrook St.)
Barlands Cl. BH23: Burt 4A 86
DT5: S'well 4G 119
Bar La. DT6: Lod 2J 39
Barley Cl. DT2: M Osm 2B 26
Barleycroft Rd. DT5: West 2G 119
Barleyfields SP8: Gill 2G 5
Barley Way DT4: Wey 3J 107
Barnaby Mead SP8: Gill 4H 5
Barnaby Mill SP8: Gill 4H 5
Barnack Wlk. DT11: B For 5B 30

Bindells, The—Branksome Wood Gdns.

Bindells, The DT3: Chick ... 6B **102**
Bindon Cl. BH12: Pool ... 7J **81**
BH20: W Lul ... 5J **111**
Bindon La. BH20: Wool ... 6E **110**
Bindon Rd. BH20: W Lul ... 7G **111**
Bindon Way BH20: Wool ... 6E **110**
Bingham Av. BH14: Pool ... 1G **99**
Bingham Cl. BH23: Chris ... 7C **86**
BH31: Ver ... 6H **55**
Bingham Dr. BH31: Ver ... 6G **55**
Bingham Rd. BH9: Bourn ... 6G **83**
BH23: Chris ... 7C **86**
BH31: Ver ... 6G **55**
BINGHAM'S MELCOMBE ... **3A 124**
Binghams Rd. DT2: Cros ... 1H **109**
BINNEGAR ... **2B 128**
Binnie Rd. BH12: Pool ... 2J **91**
Birch Av. BH16: Sandf ... 3C **112**
BH22: W Par ... 4F **75**
BH23: Burt ... 3A **86**
DT11: Blan ... 7B **30**
Birch Cl. BH14: Pool ... 4J **91**
BH21: Corf M ... 7F **71**
BH24: S Leo ... 1K **67**
Birch Copse BH17: Pool ... 5J **79**
Birchdale Rd. BH21: Wim M ... 7B **64**
Birch Dr. BH8: Bourn ... 4C **84**
Birch Gro. BH22: W Moo ... 2D **66**
Birch La. DT9: Yet ... 7G **13**
Birch Rd. BH24: S Ive ... 7D **60**
Birch Wlk. BH22: Fern ... 2F **75**
Birch Way DT2: Char D ... 2H **49**
DT3: Over ... 6A **104**
BIRCHWOOD ... **2A 122**
Birchwood Cl. BH23: Chris ... 6J **87**
Birchwood Dr. SP6: Ald ... 7J **21**
Birchwood M. BH14: Pool ... 4H **91**
Birchwood Rd. BH14: Pool ... 4H **91**
BH16: Upt ... 1D **88**
Birds Hill Gdns. BH15: Pool ... 4C **90**
Birds Hill Rd. BH15: Pool ... 3C **90**
BIRDSMOOR GATE ... **3A 122**
Birkdale Ct. BH18: B'tone ... 1J **79**
Birkdale Rd. BH18: B'tone ... 1J **79**
Birley Hall BH19: Swan ... 2K **117**
Bishop Cl. BH12: Pool ... 7C **82**
Bishop Ct. BH24: Ring ... 4J **61**
BISHOPDOWN ... **1D 125**
Bishop Rd. BH9: Bourn ... 6G **83**
BISHOP'S CAUNDLE ... **5G 15 (2D 123)**
Bishops Cl. BH7: Bourn ... 7B **84**
DT3: Abb ... 5D **46**
BISHOP'S DOWN ... **2D 123**
Bishops La. DT9: Brad A ... 6G **11**
Bishop's Rd. DT3: Abb ... 5E **46**
Bishops Row BH19: Swan ... 5H **117**
BISHOPSTONE ... **1D 125**
BISHOPSWOOD ... **2A 122**
BISTERNE ... **5H 69 (2A 130)**
BISTERNE CLOSE ... **2B 130**
Bitchams Mead BH20: Ber ... 2G **53**
Bitterne Way BH31: Ver ... 5G **55**
BITTLES GREEN ... **5D 6**
Blackberry La. BH23: Chris ... 1D **96**
DT3: B'wey ... 7G **101**
DT9: Sher ... 3B **12**
Blackbird Cl. BH17: Pool ... 6G **79**
Blackbirds DT9: T'ford ... 2K **13**
Blackburn Rd. BH12: Pool ... 1F **91**
BLACKDOWN ... **3A 122**
Blackfield La. BH22: W Moo ... 1E **66**
Blackfield Rd. BH8: Bourn ... 3K **83**
BLACKFORD ... **1D 123**
Black Hill BH31: Ver ... 4G **55**
Blackhill Rd. BH16: Hol H ... 3E **112**
Blackhill Rd. W. BH16: Hol H ... 4E **112**
BLACKLANDS ... **6B 116**
Black La. DT11: B Cam, B For ... 5D **30**
Black Lawn SP8: Gill ... 2H **5**
Black Moor Rd. BH31: Ver ... 5J **55**
Blackmore Rd. DT10: Stalb ... 2H **15**
SP7: Shaf ... 2D **8**
BLACKNEY ... **1B 126**
BLACKNOLL ... **1F 111 (2B 128)**
Blacknoll La.
DT2: E Knig, W New ... 1G **111**
Blacknor Rd. DT5: West ... 2G **119**
BLACKPOOL CORNER ... **1A 126**
Blacksmith Cl. BH21: Corf M ... 1F **79**
Blacksmith's La. DT9: T'ford ... 2K **13**
Blackthorn Way BH31: Ver ... 5H **55**
BLACKWATER
Chard ... **2A 122**
Christchurch ... **2F 85**
Blackwater Cl. SP6: Ald ... 7G **21**
Blackwater Dr. BH21: Merl ... 6B **72**
Blackwater Gro. SP6: Ald ... 7G **21**
Bladen Valley DT2: Brian ... 7E **52**
Bladen Vw. DT11: M And ... 6B **44**
Blagdon Cl. DT2: Mart ... 3J **47**
Blagdon Rd. DT1: Dor ... 4C **50**
Blair Av. BH14: Pool ... 3G **91**
Blake Dene Rd. BH14: Pool ... 6F **91**
Blake Hill Av. BH14: Pool ... 6H **91**
Blake Hill Cres. BH14: Pool ... 6G **91**
BLANDFORD CAMP ... **5J 31 (3C 125)**
Blandford Camp Track ... 4K **31**
Blandford Cl. BH15: Hamw ... 6H **89**
BLANDFORD FORUM ... **5C 30 (3B 124)**
Blandford Forum Mus. ... 5C **30**
Blandford Hgts. Ind. Est.
DT11: B For ... 2C **30**
Blandford Hill DT11: M And ... 6B **44**
DT11: W Whi ... 2H **45**
Blandford Leisure Cen. ... 4B **30**
Blandford Rd. BH15: Hamw ... 3F **89**
BH16: Hamw, Upt ... 7E **78**
BH21: Corf M ... 4D **70**
BH21: Hill, Pamp ... 5F **63**
BH21: S Mar ... 6G **33**
DT2: Pud ... 2C **52**
DT11: I Min ... 2J **17**
DT11: Shap ... 2A **62**
DT11: Shil ... 5F **19**
Blandford Rd. Nth.
BH16: B Hil, Upt ... 3A **78**
BLANDFORD ST MARY ... **6C 30 (3B 124)**
Blaney Way BH21: Corf M ... 7E **70**
BLASHFORD ... **1J 61 (2A 130)**
Bleak St. BA9: Pens ... 1A **4**
Bleet La. SP8: Ecc ... 7F **5**
Bleke St. SP7: Shaf ... 3B **8**
Blenheim BH13: Pool ... 4B **92**
Blenheim Ct. BH23: Chris ... 6J **85**
Blenheim Dr. BH23: Mude ... 1F **97**
Blenheim Rd. DT3: Red ... 2F **103**
Blind La. BH21: Wim M ... 6K **63**
DT2: Holy ... 5E **26**
DT3: Abb ... 4D **46**
DT9: Bis C ... 6J **15**
DT9: L'ton ... 4B **14**
TA20: T'ombe ... 5C **22**
Blind La. Cl. DT6: Bradp ... 1F **39**
Blindmere Rd. DT5: West ... 1G **119**
Blind St. BH20: Ber ... 2H **53**
BLISSFORD ... **1A 130**
Blockhouse La. *DT4: Wey* ... *1J 107*
(off New St.)
Bloomfield Av. BH9: Bourn ... 4F **83**
Bloomfield Pl. BH9: Bourn ... 4F **83**
Bloomfield Ter. DT5: East ... 1J **119**
BLOXWORTH ... **1B 128**
Bloxworth Rd. BH12: Pool ... 6K **81**
Bluebell Cl. BH23: Chris ... 6F **87**
Bluebell La. BH17: Pool ... 5H **79**
Blue Pool ... 2C **129**
Blue Waters Dr. DT7: L Reg ... 5A **34**
Bluff, The BH10: Bourn ... 2F **83**
Blyth Cl. BH23: Chris ... 2F **85**
Blythe Rd. BH21: Corf M ... 7F **71**
Bob Hann Cl. BH12: Pool ... 2H **91**
Bockhampton La. DT2: W Staf ... 1B **108**
Bockhampton Rd. BH23: Bock ... 1B **86**
Bodkin La. DT3: Over ... 6A **104**
Bodley Rd. BH13: Pool ... 1J **99**
Bodorgan Rd.
BH2: Bourn ... 3H **121** (3F **93**)
Bodowen Cl. BH23: Burt ... 4B **86**
Bodowen Rd. BH23: Burt ... 4B **86**
Bognor Rd. BH18: B'tone ... 2H **79**
Bohay's Dr. DT4: W Reg ... 5E **106**
Boldre Cl. BH12: Pool ... 7H **81**
BH25: N Mil ... 6K **97**
Boleyn Cres. BH9: Bourn ... 2J **83**
DT4: Wey ... 5G **107**
Bolter's Drove DT9: Leig ... 7E **14**
Bolton Cl. BH6: Bourn ... 4G **95**
Bolton Cres. BH22: Fern ... 6G **67**
Bolton Pl. DT6: Brid ... 4D **38**
Bolton Rd. BH6: Bourn ... 4G **95**
Bon Accord Rd. BH19: Swan ... 6J **117**
Bond Av. BH22: W Moo ... 7D **58**
Bond Rd. BH15: Pool ... 2D **90**
Bond St. DT4: Wey ... 1H **107**
(not continuous)
Boney Rd. BH20: Bov ... 1B **110**
Bonfields Av. BH19: Swan ... 3J **117**
BONHAM ... **1A 124**
Bonham Rd. BH9: Bourn ... 7F **83**
Bonhole La. DT6: Ship G ... 6K **39**
Bonington Cl. BH23: Chris ... 6C **86**
Bonnett's La. BH20: W'ham ... 3H **113**
Bonscombe La. DT6: Ship G ... 5J **39**
Bonslea Mead DT10: S New ... 5C **16**
BOOKHAM ... **7K 27**
Bookham La. DT2: A Pan, Buck N ... 7K **27**
Boot La. DT9: T'ford ... 2J **13**
Border Dr. BH16: Upt ... 2E **88**
Border Rd. BH16: Upt ... 2E **88**
Boreham Rd. BH6: Bourn ... 2F **95**
Borley Rd. BH17: Pool ... 6J **79**
BOROUGH, THE ... **7H 15**
Borthwick Rd. BH1: Bourn ... 2A **94**
Boscawen Cen. DT5: Cast ... 3J **118**
BOSCOMBE ... **3B 94 (3A 130)**
Boscombe Cliff Rd. BH5: Bourn ... 4A **94**
Boscombe Cres. BH1: Bourn ... 3A **94**
Boscombe Gro. Rd. BH1: Bourn ... 2K **93**
(not continuous)
Boscombe Overcliff Dr.
BH5: Bourn ... 4B **94**
Boscombe Prom. BH5: Bourn ... 4A **94**
Boscombe Spa Grange
BH5: Bourn ... 3A **94**
Boscombe Spa Rd. BH5: Bourn ... 3K **93**
Bosley Cl. BH23: Chris ... 4G **85**
Bosley Way BH23: Chris ... 4G **85**
Boswell's Cl. BH20: Ber ... 2H **53**
Bosworth M. BH9: Bourn ... 2H **83**
Bothen Dr. DT6: Both ... 4E **38**
BOTHENHAMPTON ... **6D 38 (1B 126)**
Bothenhampton Nature Reserve ... 7E **38**
Bottom Rd. DT11: Stour ... 1H **29**
Boulnois Av. BH14: Pool ... 4J **91**
Boulton Cl. DT4: W Reg ... 4F **107**
Boundary Cl. BH19: Swan ... 7K **117**
Boundary Dr. BH21: Coleh ... 6B **64**
Boundary La.
BH24: Matc, S Leo ... 3J **67**
Boundary Rd. BH9: Bourn ... 6D **82**
BH10: Bourn ... 6D **82**
Boundary Rdbt. BH12: Pool ... 6D **82**
Boundary Vw. DT11: B For ... 4C **30**
Bound La. DT9: Leig ... 7B **14**
Bounty's La. BH12: Pool ... 2J **91**
Bourne Av. BH2: Bourn ... 3F **121** (4E **92**)
Bourne Cl. BH2: Bourn ... 4D **92**
Bourne Ct. BH2: Bourn ... 4H **121** (4F **93**)
BH21: Wim M ... 7B **64**
Bourne Dr. BH20: W'ham ... 1G **113**
Bourne Drove DT2: P'ton ... 7K **43**
BOURNEMOUTH ... **5H 121 (1D 129)**
BOURNEMOUTH AIRPORT
... **5B 76 (3A 130)**
Bournemouth Aviation Mus. ... 5C **76**
Bournemouth Central Bus. Pk.
BH1: Bourn ... 2J **93**
Bournemouth Crematorium
BH8: Bourn ... 5J **83**
Bournemouth FC ... 5E **82**
Bournemouth Ho. BH1: Bourn ... 4H **93**
Bournemouth Indoor Bowls Cen. ... 2B **94**
Bournemouth International Cen.
... 6H **121** (5F **93**)
Bournemouth Intl. Cen. Rdbt.
BH2: Bourn ... 6H **121**
Bournemouth Memorial Homes
BH8: Bourn ... 5B **84**
Bournemouth Rd. BH14: Pool ... 3F **91**
DT11: Blan, Char M, S'bury ... 6B **30**
Bournemouth Sports Club ... 4J **75**
Bournemouth Station (Rail) ... 3H **93**
Bournemouth Sta. Rdbt.
BH8: Bourn ... 3H **93**
Bournemouth W. Rdbt.
BH2: Bourn ... 3D **92**
Bourne Pk. DT2: P'ton ... 6K **43**
Bourne Pines BH1: Bourn ... 2J **121**
Bourne River Ct. BH4: Bourn ... 3D **92**
BOURNE VALLEY ... **2A 92**
Bourne Valley Bus. Pk.
BH12: Pool ... 2A **92**
Bourne Valley Nature Reserve ... 1A **92**
... 5J **81**
Bourne Valley Rd. BH12: Pool ... 3A **92**
Bourne Way SP8: Gill ... 3H **5**
Bournewood Dr. BH4: Bourn ... 3C **92**
BOURTON ... **3B 4 (1A 124)**
Bourton Gdns. BH7: Bourn ... 6D **84**
BOVERIDGE ... **2D 125**
Boveridge Gdns. BH9: Bourn ... 2H **83**
BOVINGTON ... **2C 110**
BOVINGTON CAMP ... **2A 110 (2B 128)**
Bovington Cl. BH17: Pool ... 5D **80**
Bovington La. BH20: Bov ... 3A **110**
Bow, The DT1: Dor ... 3F **51**
BOWDEN ... **6D 4**
Bowden Rd. BH12: Pool ... 4G **81**
Bowdowns DT6: Neth ... 7A **24**
Bower DT11: Chil O ... 1F **19**
BOWERCHALKE ... **1D 125**
Bower Ct. DT9: Yet ... 7H **13**
BOWER HINTON ... **2B 122**
Bower Rd. BH8: Bourn ... 6K **83**
Bowers Rd. DT5: West ... 2G **119**
Bowes La. DT8: Most ... 1J **23**
Bowey DT11: O Fitz ... 5A **18**
Bowgrove Rd. DT8: Bea ... 1D **24**
Bowhayes DT6: Both ... 5E **38**
BOWLEAZE ... **5C 104**
Bowleaze Coveway
DT3: Over ... 6B **104**
Bowling All. Wlk. DT1: Dor ... 4F **51**
Bowling Grn. All. BH15: Pool ... 5B **120**
Bowling Grn. Chalets
DT7: L Reg ... 6C **34**
Bowlpex
Alderney ... 6E **80**
Branksome ... 3K **91**
Bown Hill DT5: S'well ... 4G **119**
BOWRIDGE HILL ... **1J 5**
Box Cl. BH17: Pool ... 7K **79**
Boyd Rd. BH12: Pool ... 1K **91**
Boyle Cl. DT10: Stalb ... 2H **15**
Boyne Mead SP7: Shaf ... 4C **8**
BOYS HILL ... **2D 123**
Boyte Rd. DT11: P'erne ... 2G **31**
Bozley Hill SP7: Can ... 7D **8**
Brabazon Dr. BH23: Chris ... 7F **87**
Brabazon Rd. BH21: Merl ... 4D **72**
Brabourne Av. BH22: Fern ... 1C **74**
Bracken Cl. BH24: Ash H ... 7K **59**
Brackendale Ct. BH21: T Leg ... 3E **58**
Brackendale Rd. BH8: Bourn ... 6J **83**
Brackendown Av. DT3: Over ... 3K **103**
Bracken Glen BH15: Pool ... 2C **90**
Brackenhill BH13: Pool ... 6A **92**
Brackenhill Rd. BH21: Coleh ... 5E **64**
Bracken Rd. BH6: Bourn ... 3E **94**
BH22: Fern ... 5B **66**
Brackens Way BH13: Pool ... 7K **91**
Bracken Way BH23: Walk ... 5J **97**
Brackley Cl. BH23: B Int ... 5C **76**
Bradburne Rd.
BH2: Bourn ... 4F **121** (4E **92**)
BRADFORD ABBAS ... **7G 11 (2C 123)**
Bradford Abbas Sports & Recreation Club
... 6F **11**
Bradford La. DT9: L'ton ... 4A **14**
BRADFORD PEVERELL ... **6D 48 (1D 127)**
Bradford Rd. BH9: Bourn ... 2J **83**
DT4: Wey ... 2F **107**
DT9: Sher ... 5A **12**
BRADPOLE ... **1G 39 (1B 126)**
Bradpole Rd. BH8: Bourn ... 4A **84**
Bradstock Cl. BH12: Pool ... 6K **81**
Bradstock Working Horse Farm ... 7K **37**
Braemar Av. BH6: Bourn ... 3J **95**
Braemar Cl. BH6: Bourn ... 3J **95**
Braemar Dr. BH23: H'ffe ... 5J **87**
Braemar Rd. DT1: Dor ... 5H **51**
Braeside Bus. Pk.
BH15: Pool ... 1A **120** (3K **89**)
Braeside Rd. BH22: W Moo ... 1E **66**
BH24: S Leo ... 7A **60**
Braidley Rd.
BH2: Bourn ... 4G **121** (4E **92**)
Brailswood Rd. BH15: Pool ... 3B **90**
Braishfield Gdns. BH8: Bourn ... 4K **83**
Brakes Hill DT2: M Osm ... 2C **26**
Bramble Cl. SP6: Ald ... 7J **21**
Bramble Dr. DT6: Brid ... 1J **37**
Bramble Drove DT2: Broad ... 6B **108**
Bramble Edge DT2: Broad ... 6B **108**
Bramble La. BH23: H'ffe ... 5J **97**
Brambling Cl. DT3: B'wey ... 6G **101**
Bramdon Cl. DT3: Port ... 6G **47**
Bramdon La. DT3: Port ... 6G **47**
Bramley Ct. BH22: Fern ... 6C **66**
Bramley Hill DT6: Brid ... 2E **38**
Bramley Rd. BH10: Bourn ... 1C **82**
BH22: Fern ... 6C **66**
Brampton Ct.
BH2: Bourn ... 4G **121** (4E **92**)
Brampton Rd. BH15: Pool ... 1B **90**
BRAMSHAW ... **1B 130**
Bramshaw BH25: N Mil ... 7K **97**
Bramshaw Gdns. BH8: Bourn ... 3K **83**
Bramshaw Way BH25: N Mil ... 6K **97**
Branders Cl. BH6: Bourn ... 3J **95**
Branders La. BH6: Bourn ... 2J **95**
Brandon Ct. *BH12: Pool* ... *3B 92*
(off Poole Rd.)
Brandy La. DT5: Fort ... 5A **118**
Brandy Row DT5: Fort ... 5A **118**
Branksea Av. BH15: Hamw ... 6F **89**
Branksea Castle ... 4D **98**
Branksea Cl. BH15: Hamw ... 6G **89**
BRANKSOME ... **2J 91 (1D 129)**
Branksome Bldgs. BH2: Bourn ... 5F **121**
Branksome Bus. Pk. BH12: Pool ... 7A **82**
Branksome Chine Pleasure Gdns.
... 7A **92**
Branksome Ct. BH13: Pool ... 7K **91**
Branksome Dene Chine ... 6B **92**
Branksome Dene Rd. BH4: Bourn ... 5B **92**
Branksome Dorset Provincial
Masonic Mus. ... 2A **94**
Branksome Hill Rd. BH4: Bourn ... 1B **92**
BRANKSOME PARK ... **5A 92**
Branksome Station (Rail) ... 3K **91**
Branksome Towers BH13: Pool ... 7B **92**
Branksome Wood Gdns.
BH2: Bourn ... 3D **92**

Branksome Wood Rd.—Bute Dr.

Branksome Wood Rd.
BH2: Bourn 3D 92
BH4: Bourn 2B 92
BH12: Pool 2B 92
Branscombe Cl. DT5: S'well 3G 119
Bransford BA22: Hal 2J 25
BRANSGORE 3A 130
Brantwood DT8: Bea 2C 24
Branwell Cl. BH23: Chris 5J 85
Brassey Cl. BH9: Bourn 5G 83
Brassey Rd. BH9: Bourn 5F 83
Brassey Ter. BH9: Bourn 5F 83
BRATTON SEYMOUR 1D 123
BRAYTOWN 7C 110
Breach Cl. SP8: Bour 2C 4
Breach Fld. BH20: Wool 6D 110
Breach La. SP7: Shaf 4A 8
SP8: K Mag 6B 4
BREAMORE 1A 130
Brecon Cl. BH10: Bourn 7E 74
Bredy Cl. BH17: Pool 5B 80
Bredy Farm Old Farming Collection 1C 127
Bredy Rd. DT6: Burt B 7J 37 & 1A 46
Bremble Cl. BH12: Pool 4G 81
Breston Cl. DT5: S'well 4G 119
Brewer's Quay 2J 107 (off Hope Sq.)
Brewer Wlk. DT2: Cros 1H 109
Brewery La. SP8: Gill 4F 5
Brian Cl. BH20: Sandf 6B 112
BRIANTSPUDDLE 7E 52 (1B 128)
Briar Cl. BH15: Pool 2C 90
BH23: Chris 1D 96
DT4: S'hill 6E 102
SP8: Gill 4G 5
Briars End DT2: Cros 1J 109
Briarswood Rd. BH16: Upt 7E 78
Briar Way BH21: Hay 7F 65
Brickenswood BH25: N Mil 7K 97
Brickfield Ind. Est. SP8: Gill 6H 5
Brickfields Bus. Pk. SP8: Gill 6H 5
Brick Kiln La. DT9: Sher 2D 12
Brick Yd. Cotts. DT2: More 1K 109
Brickyard La. BH19: Swan 2H 117
BH21: Corf M 5C 70
BH22: Fern 6A 66
BH31: Ver 3D 54
SP8: Bour 3C 4
SP8: Gill 6H 5
Bridewell La. SP7: Mot 1B 6
Bridge App. BH15: Hamw 6K 89
Bridge Cl. SP8: Gill 5J 5
Bridge Ct. DT1: Dor 3G 51
BRIDGEHAMPTON 1C 123
Bridge Inn La. DT3: Pres 3C 104
Bridge Pl. BH10: Bourn 6D 74
DT9: N Com 1J 11
Bridge Rd. DT6: C'outh 6J 35
Bridges, The BH24: Ring 4G 61
Bridges Cl. BH22: W Moo 1F 67
Bridge St. BH21: S Mar 6H 33
BH23: Chris 1A 96
DT6: Neth 7B 24
DT7: L Reg 5D 34
DT10: S New 6B 16
SP8: Bour 2C 4
Bridge Vw. DT11: Blan 6B 30
Bridgewater Rd. BH12: Pool 1H 91
Bridlebank Way DT3: B'wey 7F 101
Bridle Cl. BH16: Upt 7F 79
Bridle Cres. BH7: Bourn 6E 84
Bridle Way BH21: Coleh 6F 65
Bridleways BH31: Ver 4E 54
BRIDPORT 4D 38 (1B 126)
Bridport Arts Cen. 4D 38
Bridport Leisure Cen. 5C 38
Bridport Mus. 4D 38
Bridport Rd. BH12: Pool 6K 81
BH31: Ver 4F 55
DT1: Dor, Poun 4A 50
DT2: Dor 4A 50
DT8: Bea 3D 24
DT8: B'sor 7H 23
DT8: Drim 2B 22
Brierley Av. BH22: W Par 4E 74
Brierley Cl. BH10: Bourn 1E 82
Brierley Hay DT9: Yet 7H 13
Brierley Rd. BH10: Bourn 2D 82
Brighthay La. DT6: N Chid 3B 36
Brightlands Av. BH6: Bourn 3H 95
Bright Rd. BH15: Pool 1C 90
Brinscombe La. SP7: Shaf 5C 8
Brinsley Cl. DT10: S New 5B 16
Brinsley Ct. DT10: S New 5B 16
Brinsons Cl. BH23: Burt 3A 86
Brionne Way SP7: Shaf 3D 8
Brisbane Rd. BH23: Chris 5G 85
DT3: Lit 1J 103
Brister End DT9: Yet 7H 13
Bristol Rd. DT9: Sher 3C 12
Briston Cl. DT1: Poun 4B 50
Brit, The DT8: Bea 3D 24
Britannia Ct. BH12: Pool 7F 81
Britannia Rd. BH14: Pool 4E 90
Britannia Way BH23: Mude 7F 87
DT1: Dor 5D 50
Brit Vw. Rd. DT6: W Bay 1G 37
Britwell Dr. BH20: W Lul 7F 111
Brixey Cl. BH12: Pool 7G 81
Brixey Rd. BH12: Pool 7G 81
Brixey's La. BH20: W'ham 3H 113
Broadacres SP8: Gill 3H 5
Broad Av. BH8: Bourn 5K 83
BROAD CHALKE 1D 125
Broad Cl. DT11: W Kin 6H 45
SP8: K Mag 6B 4
Broadcroft Gdns. DT5: East 1K 119
Broadhurst Av. BH10: Bourn 2E 82
Broadlands Av. BH6: Bourn 3H 95
Broadlands Cl. BH8: Bourn 3K 83
BH23: Walk 4J 97
Broadlands Rd. DT3: B'wey 1F 103
Broad La. DT6: Low E, Watt 5A 38
BROADMAYNE 6C 108 (2A 128)
Broadmayne Rd. BH12: Pool 7K 81
Broadmead DT2: Broad 6C 108
DT6: Chid 5C 36
Broadmead Av. DT6: Brid 3C 38
Broadmead Cl. DT8: Most 2J 23
Broadmead La. SP8: K Mag 7A 4
Broadmeadow Rd. DT4: W Reg 5F 107
Broad Mead Rd. BH21: T Leg 2F 59
Broadmoor Rd. BH21: Corf M 7D 70
BROADOAK 1B 126
BROAD OAK 7C 16 (2A 124)
Broad Oak Av. DT8: Most 3J 23
Broad Rd. BH19: Swan 5K 117
Broad Robin SP8: Gill 5G 5
Broads, The BH21: Wim M 6H 63
BROADSHARD 2B 122
Broadshard Ct. BH24: Ring 2J 61
Broadshard La. BH24: Ring 2J 61
BROADSTONE 2J 79 (1D 129)
Broadstone Leisure Cen. 1J 79
Broadstone Way BH15: Pool 1K 89
BH17: Pool 5H 79
BH18: B'tone 4H 79
Broad St. DT7: L Reg 5D 34
Broadwater Av. BH14: Pool 5F 91
BROADWAY 2A 122
Broadway BH6: Bourn 3H 95
Broadway, The BH10: Bourn 1D 82
BH18: B'tone 2J 79
Broadway Gables BH14: Pool 3H 91
Broadway Gdns. BH10: Bourn 7D 74
BH21: Wim M 1A 72
Broadway La. BH8: Bourn 3J 83
Broadway M. BH14: Pool 4D 90 (off Park Rd.)
BROADWEY 7F 101 (2D 127)
Broadwey Cl. DT3: B'wey 6G 101
BROADWINDSOR 6H 23 (3B 122)
Broadwindsor Craft and Design Cen. 7H 23
Broadwindsor Rd. DT8: Bea 2B 24
Broadwindsor Rd. Ind. Est.
DT8: Bea 2A 24
BROCKENHURST 2B 130
Brockenhurst Rd. BH9: Bourn 4H 83
Brockley Rd. BH10: Bourn 2E 82
Brocks Pine BH24: S Leo 1B 68
Brock Way BH31: Ver 3E 54
Brockwood BH24: S Leo 2K 67
Brodham Way DT11: Shil 7E 18
BROG STREET 3F 71
Brog St. BH21: Corf M 4E 70
Broke La. DT9: Folk 1C 14
Broken Cross DT2: C'ster 6J 49
Brombys, The BH15: Pool 5C 120
Bronte Av. BH23: Chris 5J 85
BROOK 1B 130
Brook Cl. BH10: Bourn 2C 82
DT2: C'ster 5H 49
Brookdale Cl. BH18: B'tone 2J 79
Brookdale Farm BH18: B'tone 2J 79
Brook Dr. BH31: Ver 6H 55
Brookhouse St. DT1: Poun 4C 50
Brooklands DT11: M And 6B 44
Brooklands Farm Conservation Cen. 1F 49
Brook La. BH21: Corf M 7E 70
BH21: Woodl 6E 20
Brookmead Cl. DT3: S Poy 2D 104
Brook Pk. Ind. Est.
BH21: Wim M 2C 72
Brook Rd. BH10: Bourn 2C 82
BH12: Pool 2G 91
BH21: Wim M 1C 72
Brooks Cl. BH24: Ring 5K 61
Brookside SP8: Gill 3H 5
Brookside Cl. DT3: Pres 4C 104
Brookside Pk. Homes
BH21: Corf M 2D 78
Brookside Rd. BH21: Wim M 1D 72
Brookside Way BH23: H'ffe 5J 87
Brook St. DT6: Ship G 6K 39
Brookton La. DT3: Lit 7H 101
Brook Vw. BH22: W Moo 1D 66
Brook Way BH23: F Clif 7G 87
Broomfield Ct. BH22: Fern 6E 66
Broomfiled Dr. SP6: Ald 7J 21
BROOM HILL 2F 65 (3D 125)
Broom La. BH6: Bourn 3D 94 (off Pine Av.)
Broom Rd. BH12: Pool 5F 81
Broom Rd. Bus. Pk. BH12: Pool 5G 81
Broughton Av. BH10: Bourn 2E 82
Broughton Cl. BH10: Bourn 3E 82
Broughton Cres. DT4: W Reg 5E 106
Brownen Rd. BH9: Bourn 6H 83
Browning Av. BH5: Bourn 3B 94
Browning Rd. BH12: Pool 1H 91
Brownlow St. DT4: Wey 7H 103
Brown's Cres. DT3: Chick 6C 102
Brownsea Av. BH21: Corf M 7F 71
Brownsea Ct. BH14: Pool 7F 91
BROWNSEA ISLAND 3B 98
Brownsea island Nature Reserve 3D 98
Brownsea Rd. BH13: Sandb 5F 99
Brownsea Vw. Av. BH14: Pool 6F 91
Brownsea Vw. Cl. BH14: Pool 6G 91
Brown's La. SP8: E Sto 1K 7
Brown St. DT9: Bis C 6H 15
Brudenell Av. BH13: Sandb 1H 99
Brudenell Rd. BH13: Sandb 1H 99
Brunel Cl. BH31: Ver 6J 55
Brunel Ct. DT1: Dor 4F 51
Brunel Dr. DT3: Pres 3B 104
Brune Way BH22: W Par 2D 74
Brunstead Pl. BH12: Pool 3B 92
Brunstead Rd. BH12: Pool 3A 92
Brunswick Ter. DT4: Wey 7J 103
Brushy Bush La. SP5: Six H 4A 20
BRUTON 1D 123
Brutus Cl. DT1: Dor 6D 50
BRYANSTON 5A 30 (3B 124)
Bryanston Cl. DT11: Blan 6B 30
Bryanstone Rd. BH3: Bourn 7E 82
Bryanston St. DT11: B For 5B 30
Bryant Rd. BH12: Pool 6A 82
Bryants La. DT4: W Reg 1E 106
Brydian Ct. DT6: Brid 3D 38 (off Barrack St.)
Brymer Rd. DT2: Pud 2C 52
Brymers Av. DT5: Fort 5B 118
BRYMPTON D'EVERCY 2C 123
Bryn Rd. BH20: Sandf 6B 112
DT4: Wey 2F 107
Bryony Cl. BH18: B'tone 4G 79
Bryony Gdns. BH6: Bourn 1E 94
SP8: Gill 4F 5
Bub La. BH23: Chris 1C 96
Buccaneers Cl. BH23: Chris 1B 96
Buccleuch Rd. BH13: Pool 6A 92
Bucehayes Cl. BH23: H'ffe 6H 97
Buchanan Av. BH7: Bourn 1A 94
Buckbury M. DT1: Dor 5G 51
BUCKHORN WESTON 1A 124
Buckingham Ct.
BH15: Pool 3E 120 (4B 90)
Buckingham Mans. BH1: Bourn 4G 93
Buckingham Rd. BH12: Pool 7H 81
SP8: Gill 5H 5
Buckingham Way DT1: Dor 5H 51
Buckland Gro. BH23: Chris 4J 87
BUCKLAND NEWTON 6G 27 (3D 123)
BUCKLAND RIPERS 1C 102 (2D 127)
Buckland Rd. BH12: Pool 2G 91
BUCKLAND ST MARY 2A 122
Buckland Ter. BH12: Pool 2G 91
Bucklers Mead DT9: Yet 7G 13
Bucklers Way BH8: Bourn 3K 83
Buckthorn Cl. BH17: Pool 5H 79
Buddens Mdw. BH21: Corf M 2E 78
Buddleia Cl. DT3: Lit 1K 103
Budmouth Av. DT3: Over 6A 104
Budmouth Community Sports Cen. 1C 106
Budmouth Dr. SP8: Gill 2G 5
Buffalo M. BH15: Pool 5A 120 (5K 89)
Buffets Rd. DT10: S New 4C 16
Buffetts Cl. DT10: S New 4C 16
Bugden's Copse Nature Reserve 4F 55
Bugdens La. BH31: Ver 4F 55
Bull Bri. Mead BA22: Hal 2J 25
Bull Cl. DT2: Strat 4C 48
Buller's Way DT3: Abb 6A 46
Bullfinch Cl. BH17: Pool 5H 79
Bull Ground La. DT10: S New 5D 16
Bull Inn Cvn. Pk., The DT2: Swy 3B 46
Bull La. BH15: Pool 6B 120 (6A 90)
Bull La. DT2: M New 6H 41
DT2: Swy 3B 46
Bumpers La. DT5: East 1K 119
Bungalows, The SP8: Gill 3G 5
Bunting Rd. BH22: Fern 4B 66
Burbidge Cl. BH16: L Mat 7G 53
Burbitt La. DT6: Ship G 6H 39
Burbridge Cl. BH17: Pool 6C 80
BURCOMBE 1D 125
Burcombe Rd. BH10: Bourn 1C 82
Burdens DT10: K'ton 2D 28
Burdock Cl. BH23: Chris 5F 87
Bure Cl. BH23: F Clif 1F 97
Bure Ct. BH23: Mude 1F 97
Bure Haven Dr. BH23: Mude 1E 96
Bure Homage Gdns. BH23: Mude 1F 97
Bure Homage La. BH23: Mude 1E 96
Bure La. BH23: Mude 2F 97
Bure Pk. BH23: F Clif 1F 97
Bure Rd. BH23: F Clif 1F 97
Burford Cl. BH23: Chris 5F 85
Burford Ct. BH1: Bourn 4H 93
Burges Cl. DT10: Marn 2G 9
Burgess Cl. BH11: Bourn 2K 81
Burgess Fld. BH21: Woodl 4A 54
Burleigh Rd. BH6: Bourn 1F 95
BURLESTON 1A 128
BURLEY 2B 130
Burley Cl. BH25: N Mil 6K 97
BH31: Ver 5E 54
Burley Rd. BH12: Pool 1G 91
BH23: Wink 1A 86
BURLEY STREET 2B 130
Burling Ter. BH12: Pool 3A 92
Burlington Arc.
BH1: Bourn 4J 121 (4F 93)
Burlington Rd. BH19: Swan 3K 117
Burnaby Ct. BH4: Bourn 6B 92
Burnaby Rd. BH4: Bourn 6C 92
Burnbake Rd. BH31: Ver 5F 55
Burnbrae Rd. BH22: W Par 4D 74
Burn Cl. BH31: Ver 6H 55
Burnett Av. BH23: Chris 6G 85
Burnett Rd. BH23: Chris 7H 85
BURNGATE 4J 111
Burngate Rd. BH15: Hamw 5G 89
Burnham Dr. BH8: Bourn 7J 83
Burnham Rd. BH23: Burt 4A 86
Burnham's La. BH20: Knit 1D 116
Burnside BH23: Chris 6H 87
DT2: Mart 3H 47
Burns Rd. BH6: Bourn 7F 85
BH20: W'ham 1G 113
Burn Vw. DT2: C'ster 7K 49
Burraton Sq. DT1: Poun 4C 50
Burraton Yd. DT1: Poun 4C 50 (off Burraton Sq.)
BURRIDGE 3A 122
BURROWBRIDGE 1A 122
Burrows La. BH31: Ver 1F 55
Burr Stone Mead BH19: Swan 5J 117 (off High St.)
BURSTOCK 3B 122
Burstock La. DT8: Drim 3A 22
Burtley Rd. BH6: Bourn 4G 95
BURTON
Christchuch 3A 130
Dorchester 1E 50 (1D 127)
Warminster 1B 124
BURTON BRADSTOCK 6H 37 (2B 126)
Burton Cl. BH20: Wool 6C 110
BH23: Burt 5A 86
BH24: Ash H 6K 59
SP7: Shaf 3D 8
Burtoncroft BH23: Burt 3A 86
Burton Cross Rdbt. BH20: Wool 7B 110
Burton Hall BH23: Burt 3B 86
Burton Hall Pl. BH23: Burt 3B 86
Burtonhayes DT10: Marn 3H 9
Burton Rd. BH13: Pool 4A 92
BH20: Wool 7B 110
BH23: Chris 7C 86
DT1: Dor 2E 50
DT3: Abb 6A 46
DT6: Both, Burt B 6D 38
Burton St. DT10: Marn 3G 9
Burton Wood BH20: Wool 7C 110
Burt's Hill BH21: Coleh, Wim M 6A 64
Burt's La. BH21: Mann 5A 58
Burt's Pl. BH19: Swan 5K 117
Bury Rd. BH13: Pool 6J 91
Bushell Rd. BH15: Pool 7A 80
Bushes Rd. DT11: Stour 3H 29
BUSHEY 2C 129
Bushey La. BH20: Corf C 1E 114
Bushey Rd. BH8: Bourn 5J 83
Bushmead Dr. BH24: Ash H 6A 60
Bush Pk. DT11: W Kin 6H 45
Bush Rd. DT2: Dor 6B 50
Butchers Cl. DT2: K Maur 2K 51
Bute Dr. BH23: H'ffe 6J 97

Chapel Ga.—Cineworld

Chapel Ga. BH23: E Par 5J 75
Chapelhay Hgts. DT4: Wey 2H 107
Chapelhay Steps *DT4: Wey 2H 107*
(off North Quay)
Chapelhay St. DT4: Wey 2H 107
Chapel Hill SP8: K Mag 7C 4
Chapel La. BA9: Pens 1A 4
BH15: Pool 4B 120 (5A 90)
BH19: Swan 5J 117
BH21: Corf M 1E 78
BH21: Wim M 7K 63
BH21: Woodl 6E 20
BH23: E Par 4J 75
DT2: M New 6H 41
DT3: Abb 5D 46
DT3: Osm 3H 105
DT3: Upw 5G 101
DT9: Yet 7H 13
DT11: P'erne 4F 31
Chapel Mdw. DT9: Yet 7H 13
Chapel Ri. BH24: Ash 2F 69
Chapel Rd. BH14: Pool 3E 90
Chapel Row BH21: Wit 3H 33
Chapel St. DT6: Ship G 6K 39
DT11: M And 6B 44
Chapel Vw. DT2: Pud 3C 52
Charberry Ri. DT6: C'outh 7G 35
Charborough Cl. BH16: L Mat 5G 53
Charborough Rd. BH18: B'tone 3K 79
Charborough Way BH21: S Mar 6H 33
CHARD 3A 122
CHARD JUNCTION 3A 122
Chard Rd. DT8: Drim 3B 22
Chardsmead Ct. *DT6: Brid 3D 38*
(off North St.)
Chards Mead Rd. DT6: Brid 3C 38
CHARDSTOCK 3A 122
Chard St. TA20: T'ombe 6C 22
Charing Cl. BH24: Ring 5J 61
CHARING CROSS 7H 21
Charles Gdns. BH10: Bourn 4C 82
Charles Garrett Cl. SP7: Shaf 3C 8
Charles Keightley Ct.
BH21: Wim M 2B 72
Charles Rd. BH15: Pool 1E 120 (3B 90)
BH23: Chris 6D 86
DT6: Burt B 6H 37
Charles St. DT1: Dor 3F 51
DT4: Wey 7H 103
DT11: B For 4C 30
CHARLESTOWN 1C 106 (3D 127)
Charlmont Cross DT2: Broad 6D 108
Charlotte Cl. BH12: Pool 6C 82
BH23: Mude 1E 96
DT2: C'ster 7J 49
CHARLTON
Salisbury 1A 130
Shaftesbury 1C 125
CHARLTON ADAM 1C 123
Charlton Beeches DT11: Char M 2A 32
Charlton Cl. BH9: Bourn 2J 83
CHARLTON DOWN 2H 49 (1D 127)
CHARLTON HORETHORNE 1D 123
Charlton Ho. Ct. DT11: Char M 2A 32
CHARLTON MACKRELL 1C 123
Charlton Mnr. DT11: Char M 3B 32
CHARLTON MARSHALL 3B 32 (3C 125)
Charlton Mead DT11: Char M 3A 32
CHARLTON MUSGROVE 1A 124
CHARLTON ON THE HILL
.... 2A 32 (3B 124)
Charltons, The
BH2: Bourn 1H 121 (2F 93)
CHARMINSTER
Bournemouth 4H 83
Dorchester 6J 49 (1D 127)
Charminster Av. BH9: Bourn 5H 83
Charminster Cl. BH8: Bourn 4H 83
Charminster La. DT2: Pud 2A 52
Charminster Pl. BH8: Bourn 4H 83
Charminster Rd. BH8: Bourn 1G 93
CHARMOUTH 6H 35 (1A 126)
Charmouth Cl. DT7: L Reg 4D 34
Charmouth Gro. BH14: Pool 3E 90
Charmouth Heritage Coast Cen. 7H 35
Charmouth Ho. *DT7: L Reg 5B 34*
(off Portland Ct.)
Charmouth Pl. DT5: East 7E 118
Charmouth Rd. DT7: L Reg 3D 34
Charnwood Av. BH9: Bourn 3H 83
Charnwood Cl. BH22: W Moo 2E 66
Charnwood Ho. BH6: Bourn 4H 95
Charris Camping & Cvn. Pk.
BH21: Corf M 3F 71
Chartcombe BH13: Pool 7J 91
Charter Rd. BH11: Bourn 7H 73
Chartwell BH13: Pool 4B 92
DT4: S'hill 5F 103
Chase, The BH24: Ash 6F 61
BH31: Ver 4H 55
Chaseborough Sq. DT1: Poun 4C 50
Chaseside BH7: Bourn 6C 84
Chatsworth Rd. BH8: Bourn 1H 93
BH14: Pool 2F 91
Chaucer Cl. BH21: Wim M 6A 64
Chaucer Rd. BH13: Pool 7K 91
Cheam Rd. BH18: B'tone 2H 79
Cheap St. DT9: Sher 4C 12
Cheddington Rd. BH9: Bourn 2G 83
CHEDDON FITZPAINE 1A 122
CHEDINGTON 3B 122
Chedington Cl. BH17: Pool 4C 80
Chedington La. DT8: Most 1J 23
Chelmsford Rd. BH16: Upt 7D 78
Chelmsford St. DT4: Wey 7H 103
Cheltenham Rd. BH12: Pool 2G 91
Chelwood Ga. DT4: Wey 1C 106
Chene Rd. BH21: Wim M 1B 72
Cherford Rd. BH11: Bourn 4B 82
Cherita Ct. BH15: Pool 1D 90
Cheriton Av. BH7: Bourn 6E 84
Cheriton Way BH21: Wim M 6A 64
Cherrett Cl. BH11: Bourn 2K 81
Cherries Dr. BH9: Bourn 4E 82
Cherrybrook La. DT1: Poun 4A 50
Cherry Cl. BH14: Pool 2F 91
BH20: Sandf 6C 112
Cherryfields SP8: Gill 2H 5
Cherry Gro. BH22: Fern 6C 66
Cherry Hill Gdns. BH16: Upt 1D 88
Cherry Hill Gro. BH16: Upt 1D 88
Cherry Tree DT6: Brid 2B 38
Cherry Tree Cl. BH24: S Leo 1K 67
Cherry Tree Ct. DT11: P'erne 3G 31
Cherry Tree La. DT6: Brid 1B 38
Cherry Tree Wlk. BH4: Bourn 5D 92
Cherry Way DT3: Over 6A 104
Chescombe DT2: Cer A 2C 42
Chescombe Cl. DT2: Cer A 2C 42
Chescombe Ct. DT11: W Whi 2H 45
Chescombe La. DT11: W Whi 2F 45
CHESELBOURNE 1A 128
Cheshire Dr. BH8: Bourn 5C 84
Chesil Beach 2D 127
Chesil Beach Cen. 3D 127
Chesil Beach Holiday Village
DT4: W Reg 7E 106
Chesil Beach Rdbt. DT4: W Reg 7E 106
Chesilbourne Gro. BH8: Bourn 3K 83
Chesildene Av. BH8: Bourn 3K 83
(not continuous)
Chesildene Dr. BH8: Bourn 3J 83
Chesil Gdns. BH12: Pool 6G 81
Chesil Ho. DT6: W Bay 2H 37
Chesil Pl. *DT1: Dor 4F 51*
(off Somerleigh Rd.)
Chesil Vw. DT4: W Reg 5E 106
Chessel Av. BH5: Bourn 2B 94
Chester Cl. DT1: Dor 5H 51
Chesterfield Cl. BH13: Pool 7K 91
Chesterfield Ct. BH1: Bourn 4J 93
Chesterfield Pl. DT3: Upw 4F 101
DT4: Wey 1J 107
(off The Esplanade)
Chester Rd. BH13: Pool 5A 92
Chestnut Av. BH6: Bourn 3E 94
BH16: Sandf 3C 112
BH23: Chris 6F 85
Chestnut Cl. BH20: Sandf 6C 112
Chestnut Gro. BH21: Stap 6J 65
DT11: B For 4B 30
Chestnut Pl. DT3: Rad 4G 103
Chestnut Rd. DT2: Char D 2H 49
DT6: Both 6D 38
Chestnut Way BH23: Burt 3A 86
DT1: Dor 3C 50
SP8: Gill 5F 5
CHETNOLE 6A 14 (3D 123)
Chetnole Cl. BH17: Pool 5E 80
Chetnole Rd. DT9: Leig 6B 14
Chetnole Station (Rail) 7A 14
Chettell Way DT11: Blan 6B 30
CHETTLE 2C 125
Chettle House 2C 125
Chetwode Way BH17: Pool 4K 79
Cheviot Ct. Flats BH23: Chris 6C 86
Cheviots, The BH14: Pool 4G 91
Cheviot Way BH31: Ver 5F 55
Chewton Comn. Rd. BH23: H'ffe 5H 97
Chewton Farm Est. BH23: H'ffe 6K 97
Chewton Farm Rd. BH23: Walk 5K 97
Chewton Lodge BH23: H'ffe 6J 97
Chewton M. BH23: Walk 5H 97
Chewton Way BH23: Walk 5J 97
Cheyne Cl. DT5: S'well 4G 119
Cheyne Gdns. BH4: Bourn 5C 92
Chichester Wlk. BH21: Merl 4C 72
Chichester Way BH23: Mude 2E 96
CHICKERELL 5B 102 (2D 127)
Chickerell Cl. BH9: Bourn 2H 83
Chickerell Hill DT3: Chick 5A 102
Chickerell Rd. DT3: Chick 6A 102
Chickerell Rd. DT4: Wey 2E 106
CHIDEOCK 5B 36 (1B 126)
Chideock Cl. BH12: Pool 1J 91
Chideock Ct. BH12: Pool 1J 91
DT7: L Reg 5B 34
(off Clappentail La.)
Chideock Hill DT6: Chid 4A 36
Chigwell Rd. BH8: Bourn 5H 83
CHILBRIDGE 5G 63
Chilbury Gdns. DT2: Ower 7J 109
CHILCOMBE 1C 127
Chilcombe La. DT2: Pun 1C 46
DT6: Chilc 7E 40
Chilcombe Rd. BH6: Bourn 2D 94
CHILD OKEFORD 2G 19 (2B 124)
CHILFROME 4F 41 (1C 127)
Chilfrome Cl. BH17: Pool 5A 80
Chilfrome La. DT2: Chilf, Toll 4F 41
CHILHAMPTON 1D 125
CHILLINGTON 2A 122
CHILMARK 1C 125
Chiltern Cl. BH4: Bourn 2B 92
Chiltern Dr. BH31: Ver 4F 55
CHILTHORNE DOMER 2C 123
CHILTON CANTELO 1C 123
Chine Cres. BH2: Bourn 5D 92
Chine Cres. Rd. BH2: Bourn 5D 92
Chine Hill La. DT2: Pud 1A 52
Chine Wlk. BH22: W Par 3E 74
Chinnocks DT10: S New 5C 16
Chippel La. DT10: Marn 5H 9
CHISELBOROUGH 2B 122
Chisels La. BH23: Nea 1F 87
Chislehurst Flats BH4: Bourn 4C 92
CHISWELL 4A 118 (3D 127)
Chiswell DT5: Fort 4A 118
Chiswell Rd. BH17: Pool 5B 80
Chivrick Cl. DT10: S New 3D 16
Chloe Gdns. BH12: Pool 7H 81
Chorley Cl. BH15: Pool 1A 90
Chris Cres. BH16: Upt 7E 78
CHRISTCHURCH 7K 85 (3A 130)
Christchurch By-Pass BH23: Chris 7K 85
Christ Chu. Ct. DT1: Dor 3E 50
Christchurch Priory 1A 96
Christchurch Rd. BH1: Bourn 4H 93
BH7: Bourn 2B 94
BH22: L'ham, W Par 3B 74
BH23: Hurn 7D 76
BH24: K'ton, Ring 4H 61
BH25: N Mil 6K 97
Christchurch Ski Cen. 2D 76
Christchurch Station (Rail) 7J 85
Christmas Cl. BH20: W'ham 4G 113
Christopher Cres. BH15: Pool 1A 90
Christophers BH21: Merl 4B 72
Christy's Gdns. SP7: Shaf 3C 8
Christy's La. SP7: Shaf 3C 8
Chrysanthemum Flats
DT9: Sher 4D 12
(off Knotts Paddock)
Chrysanthemum Row *DT9: Sher 4D 12*
(off Tinneys La.)
Chubbs M. BH12: Pool 2G 91
Church Acre DT1: Dor 3G 51
Church Cl. BH19: Swan 5J 117
DT1: Dor 3F 51
(off Church St.)
DT2: Brad P 6D 48
DT6: Bradp 1F 39
DT9: Bee 5J 13
DT9: Chet 6A 14
DT9: L'ton 2B 14
DT10: Tod 7K 7
SP7: Fon M 4B 10
SP8: Bour 3B 4
Church Farm DT2: Cors 6J 25
Church Farm Cvn. & Camping Pk.
SP5: Six H 2C 20
Churchfield BH31: Ver 4E 54
Churchfield Ct. BH15: Pool 4C 90
Churchfield Cres. BH15: Pool 3C 90
Churchfield Rd. BH15: Pool 4C 90
Churchfoot La. DT10: Won 5C 28
Church Grn. BH20: W'ham 4H 113
DT9: Bis C 5H 15
Church Hill BH19: Swan 5J 117
BH21: Woodl 6D 20
BH31: Ver 4E 54
DT2: P'ton 7K 43
DT10: Stalb 1G 15
DT11: I Min 2J 17
DT11: M And 7B 44
SP7: Shaf 3A 8
SP8: K Mag 6C 4
SP8: W Stou 1F 7
Church Hill Vw. DT2: Syd N 7C 42
CHURCHILL 3A 122
Churchill Cl. BH21: S Mar 6H 33
DT4: W Reg 4E 106
SP6: Ald 7G 21
Churchill Ct. BH1: Bourn 3A 94
DT11: W Stic 4J 29
Churchill Cres. BH12: Pool 1G 91
Churchill Gdns. BH12: Pool 2G 91
Churchill Rd. BH1: Bourn 2K 93
BH12: Pool 2G 91
BH20: Bov 1A 110
BH21: Wim M 2B 72
DT11: B For 4C 30
Church Knap DT4: W Reg 4E 106
CHURCH KNOWLE 2C 129
Church La. BH20: Ber 2H 53
BH20: W'ham 4H 113
BH20: Wool 6E 110
BH22: W Par 7F 75
BH23: Chris 1K 95
DT2: C'ster 6H 49
DT2: Ower 7J 109
DT2: P'hide 1G 43
DT2: Stin 2K 51
DT2: Syd N 7C 42
DT3: Buck R 1B 102
DT3: Osm 3G 105
DT3: Port 6G 47
DT5: S'well 4H 119
DT9: Leig 4C 14
DT9: Sher 5C 12
DT10: S New 6C 16
DT10: Tod 7K 7
DT11: B For 5C 30
DT11: Blan 7D 30
DT11: Char M 3A 32
DT11: S Wal 7B 10
SP7: Shaf 4B 8
SP8: S Pro 5H 7
Church Mead DT2: T Por 2C 40
SP8: Bour 3B 4
(off W. Bourton Rd.)
Church M. BH14: Pool 3F 91
Churchmoor Rd. BH21: Coleh 7E 64
Church Ope Rd. DT5: East 2K 119
Church Orchard *DT11: S Wal 7B 10*
(off Church La.)
Church Pas. *DT4: Wey 2H 107*
(off St Edmund St.)
Church Path DT8: B'sor 6H 23
DT11: I Min 3J 17
Church Rd. BH6: Bourn 4H 95
BH14: Pool 3E 90
BH19: Stud 5K 115
BH20: W Lul 6G 111
BH21: T Leg 2E 58
BH22: Fern 6C 66
DT2: M New 6H 41
DT3: Pres 3D 104
DT9: Brad A 7G 11
DT9: T'ford 2J 13
DT11: Dur 3G 29
DT11: I Min 3J 17
DT11: P'erne 2F 31
DT11: Shil 5E 18
SP8: Silt 4D 4
Church St. BA22: Hal 2H 25
BH15: Pool 6A 120 (6K 89)
BH20: W'ham 4H 113
BH21: Cran 2G 21
BH21: S Mar 5J 33
BH21: Wim M 7K 63
BH23: Chris 1K 95
DT1: Dor 3F 51
DT2: Pun 2C 46
DT3: Abb 5D 46
DT3: Upw 3D 100
DT6: Brid 4D 38
DT6: Burt B 6H 37
DT7: L Reg 5D 34
DT7: Uply 3A 34
DT8: Bea 3C 24
DT9: Yet 7G 13
DT10: S New 5C 16
DT11: W Kin 6H 45
SP7: Fon M 4C 10
SP8: K Mag 6B 4
SP8: W Stou 2F 7
Church Track SP8: Bour 3B 4
Church Vw. DT2: Strat 4B 48
SP8: Bour 3B 4
SP8: Gill 5G 5
Church Wlk. DT10: S New 6C 16
DT10: Stalb 2G 15
SP7: Mot 5D 6
SP7: Shaf 4B 8
(off Lyons Wlk.)
SP8: Gill 4H 5
(off Le Neubourg Way)
Churchward Av. DT3: Pres 3B 104
Churchwell Cl. DT9: Brad A 7G 11
Churchwell La. DT9: Brad A 7G 11
Churchwell St. DT9: Brad A 7G 11
Cineworld
Weymouth 2H 107

Darracott Rd.—Duncan Pl.

Darracott Rd. BH5: Bourn 3C 94
Darrian Ct. BH16: Upt 7D 78
Dartmeet Ct. DT1: Poun 3A 50
Darwin Av. BH23: Chris 5G 85
Darwin Cl. DT3: Lit 7H 101
Darwin Ct. BH12: Pool 3A 92
Dashwood Cl. DT10: S New 4D 16
Davenant Cl. SP8: Gill 5G 5
Davenport Cl. BH16: Upt 7E 78
Davenport Ct. DT4: Wey 1G 107
David Lloyd Leisure
Bournemouth 3K 93
Ringwood 6J 61
David's La. BH24: Ash 6E 60
David Way BH15: Hamw 5F 89
Davies Ct. BH12: Pool 2J 91
Davis Gdns. DT11: B For 2D 30
Davis Rd. BH12: Pool 2J 91
Dawkins Bus. Cen.
BH15: Hamw 4F 89
Dawkins Rd. BH15: Hamw 3F 89
Dawlish Cres. DT4: W Reg 5F 107
Dawn Chorus BH14: Pool 4F 91
Dawn Cl. BH10: Bourn 4C 82
Daws Av. BH11: Bourn 5A 82
Daylesford Cl. BH14: Pool 5E 90
Day's Ct. BH21: Wim M 1B 72
(not continuous)
Day's Rd. BH19: Swan 5F 117
Deacon Gdns. BH11: Bourn 1A 82
Deacon Rd. BH11: Bourn 1A 82
DEAN 2C 125
Dean Cl. BH15: Hamw 4G 89
Dean Court 1A 94
Deane Av. SP8: Gill 5F 5
DEANLAND 1B 20 (2C 125)
Dean La. SP5: Six H 1B 20
Dean La. Drove SP5: Six H 1A 20
Dean Pk. Cres.
BH1: Bourn 3J 121 (3F 93)
Dean Pk. Rd.
BH1: Bourn 3J 121 (3F 93)
Deans, The BH1: Bourn . . .2J 121 (3F 93)
Deans Court Gdns. 1K 71
Dean's Ct. La. BH21: Wim M 1A 72
Deanscroft Rd. BH10: Bourn 2E 82
Deans Drove BH16: L Mat 7G 53
DEANS GROVE 5B 64
Deans Gro. BH21: Wim M 5B 64
Deansleigh Cl. DT3: Over 4B 104
Deansleigh Pk. SP7: Shaf 3D 8
Deansleigh Rd. BH7: Bourn 5D 84
Deans Rd. BH5: Bourn 2D 94
Dean Swift Cres. BH14: Pool 7G 91
Dear Hay La.
BH15: Pool 5B 120 (5A 90)
De Briane Cl. DT10: Won 5B 28
Decies Rd. BH14: Pool 2F 91
De Courtenai Cl. BH11: Bourn 1H 81
Deepdene La. BH11: Bourn 1J 81
Deepford La. DT9: Chet 6A 14
Deep La. DT9: Chet 5A 14
Deep Sea Adventure 2J 107
(off Custom House Quay)
Dee Way BH15: Pool 6A 120 (6K 89)
De Haviland Cl. BH21: Merl 3D 72
De Havilland Way BH23: Mude 2D 96
Delamere Gdns. BH10: Bourn 3E 82
Delapre Gdns. DT6: Brid 3E 38
Delegh Gro. DT6: Brid 3B 38
Delft M. BH23: Chris 1B 96
Delhi Cl. BH14: Pool 4H 91
Delhi La. DT5: East 1J 119
Delhi Rd. BH9: Bourn 4E 82
Delilah Rd. BH15: Hamw 5F 89
De Lisle Rd. BH3: Bourn 7F 83
Delkeith Ct. BH22: Fern 1D 74
Dell, The BH25: N Mil 6K 97
Dell Cl. BH18: B'tone 3G 79
Delph Rd. BH21: Merl 5B 72
Delta Cl. BH23: Chris 7E 86
De Mauley Rd. BH13: Pool 7J 91
De Montfort Rd. BH21: Merl 4B 72
De Moulham Rd. BH19: Swan 3J 117
Denby Rd. BH15: Pool 3B 90
Dene Cl. DT9: L'ton 1B 14
Deneve Av. BH17: Pool 5A 80
Dene Wlk. BH22: W Par 4E 74
Denewood Copse BH22: W Moo 1D 66
Denewood Rd. BH4: Bourn 4B 92
BH22: W Moo 7D 58
Denhall Cl. DT10: S New 4C 16
Denham Cl. BH17: Pool 3C 80
Denham Dr. BH23: H'ffe 5K 87
Denison Rd. BH17: Pool 5A 80
Denmark La.
BH15: Pool 3D 120 (4B 90)
Denmark Rd. BH9: Bourn 5F 83
BH15: Pool 3D 120 (4B 90)
(not continuous)
Denmead Rd. BH6: Bourn 7F 85
Dennets La. BH15: Pool 6A 120
(off High St.)
Dennis Rd. BH21: Corf M 1F 79
DT4: Wey 2F 107
Dennistoun Av. BH23: Chris 7D 86
Denziloe DT6: Neth 7B 24
Derby Rd. BH1: Bourn 3J 93
Derby St. DT4: Wey 7H 103
De Redvers Rd. BH14: Pool 5G 91
Dereham Way BH12: Pool 1K 91
Derritt La. BH23: Sop 7K 77
Derwent Cl. BH9: Bourn 4G 83
BH22: Fern 6G 67
Derwent Rd. DT4: W Reg 6F 107
Derwentwater Rd. BH21: Merl 3B 72
Devenish Cl. DT4: Wey 3H 107
Devenish Gdns. DT4: Wey 3G 107
(off Rodwell Rd.)
Devenish Warren DT4: Wey 4H 107
Deverel Cl. BH23: Chris 6J 85
Deverel Rd. DT2: Char D 2H 49
Devonedge La. DT6: C'outh 6J 35
Devon Rd. BH15: Pool 2C 90
BH23: Chris 6G 85
DT4: Wey 7F 103
Deweys La. BH24: Ring 4H 61
Dewey's Way SP8: Gill 4H 5
Dewlands Common Nature Reserve
. . . . .4D 54
Dewlands Orchard DT9: Leig 6D 14
Dewlands Pk. (Mobile Home Pk.)
BH31: Ver 4D 54
Dewlands Rd. BH31: Ver 5D 54
Dewlands Way BH31: Ver 4E 54
DEWLISH 1A 128
Dewlish Cl. BH17: Pool 4E 80
Dewlish Rd. DT11: M And 6A 44
Dewsall Pl. DT1: Poun 4B 50
Diana Cl. BH22: Fern 6D 66
DT1: Dor 6E 50
Diana Ct. BH23: H'ffe 7H 97
Diana Way BH21: Corf M 6G 71
DIBBERFORD 3B 122
Dibden Cl. BH8: Bourn 3K 83
Dickens Rd. BH6: Bourn 7G 85
Dick O'th Banks Cl. DT2: Cros 1H 109
Dick O'th Banks Rd. DT2: Cros 1H 109
Didcot Rd. BH17: Pool 7B 80
Digby Cres. DT9: T'ford 3J 13
Digby Ho. BH2: Bourn 4D 92
(off Suffolk Rd.)
Digby Rd. DT9: Sher 5C 12
Diggory Cres. DT1: Dor 5G 51
Dillons Gdns. BH16: L Mat 7G 53
Diments Ct. DT6: Brid 2C 38
Diments Gdns. DT6: Brid 2C 38
DIMMER .1D 123
Dingle Rd. BH5: Bourn 3D 94
Dingley Rd. BH15: Pool 1B 90
Dinham Wlk. DT1: Poun 4B 50
Dinhay DT10: Marn 2G 9
DINNINGTON 2B 122
Dinosaurland 5D 34
(off Coombe St.)
Dinosaur Mus., The 3F 51
DINTON .1D 125
Diprose Rd. BH21: Corf M 6G 71
Dirty La. DT2: Ever 5B 26
Discovery Ct. BH12: Pool 4J 81
Disraeli Rd. BH23: Chris 1B 96
DITCHAMPTON 1D 125
Dock Rd. DT5: Cast 3C 118
Doctor Roberts Cl. DT6: Brid 5D 38
Dodhams Farm Cl. DT6: Bradp 1F 39
Dodhams La. DT6: Bradp 1E 38
DOE'S HATCH 4D 54
Doe's La. BH31: Ver 4D 54
Dogdean BH21: Wim M 5A 64
Dogwood Rd. BH18: B'tone 4G 79
Dolbery Rd. Nth. BH12: Pool 4H 81
Dolbery Rd. Sth. BH12: Pool 5G 81
Dollings, The BH20: Corf C 4B 114
Dollin's La. BH20: W'ham 3H 113
Dolmans Hill BH16: L Mat 6F 53
Dolphin Av. BH10: Bourn 1E 82
Dolphin Cen.
BH15: Pool 4C 120 (5A 90)
Dolphin Cl. DT7: L Reg 5D 34
Dolphin Ct. BH13: Pool 5B 92
BH19: Swan 3J 117
DT4: Wey 3J 107
Dolphin Indoor Bowls Club 6K 79
Dolphin La. SP8: Gill 2G 5
Dolphin Quays
BH15: Pool 6B 120 (6A 90)
Dolphin Swimming Pool
. . . . .4E 120 (5B 90)
Dominion Cen. BH11: Bourn 3J 81
Dominion Rd. BH11: Bourn 3J 81
Doncaster Rd. DT4: W Reg 6F 107
DONHEAD ST ANDREW 1C 125
DONHEAD ST MARY 1C 125
Donkey La. DT6: Brid 2C 38
DT6: Burt B 6H 37
Donnelly Rd. BH6: Bourn 2H 95
Donnington Dr. BH23: Chris 7F 87
Donoughmore Rd. BH1: Bourn 3K 93
DONYATT 2A 122
DORCHESTER 3F 51 (1D 127)
Dorchester Arts Cen. 3E 50
(off School La.)
Dorchester By-Pass DT1: Dor 5H 51
DT2: Dor 4A 50
Dorchester Gdns. BH15: Pool 2C 90
Dorchester Health Club 3F 51
Dorchester Hill DT11: Blan 7B 30
DT11: M And 6B 44
DT11: W Whi 3G 45
Dorchester Rd. BH15: Pool 1B 90
BH16: L Min, Upt 1A 88
BH20: Wool 7B 110
BH21: S Mar 3A 70
DT2: Cer A 3B 42
DT2: Grim, Strat 2A 48
DT2: M New 6H 41
DT2: Syd N 7C 42
DT2: Tolp 5A 52
(not continuous)
DT3: B'wey, Rad, Red 7F 101
DT4: Wey 6J 103
DT6: Ask, Uplo, Wald 3G 39
Dorchester South Station (Rail) . . .4F 51
Dorchester Tennis & Squash Club
. . . . .6E 50
(off Sawmills La.)
Dorchester Town FC 6E 50
Dorchester West Station (Rail) 4E 50
Dornie Rd. BH13: Pool 1J 99
Dorset Av. BH22: Fern 1C 74
Dorset Cl. DT4: Wey 1E 106
Dorset County Mus. 3F 51
Dorset Cricket Cen., The 7D 76
Dorset Heavy Horse Cen. 2D 125
Dorset Ho. BH13: Pool 5A 92
Dorset Lake Av. BH14: Pool 7F 91
Dorset Lake Mnr. BH14: Pool 5E 90
Dorset Rd. BH4: Bourn 2C 92
BH23: Chris 6D 86
Dorset St. DT4: Wey 2H 107
DT11: B For 4C 30
Dorset Way BH17: Pool 7A 80
DOTTERY 1B 126
Dottery Rd. DT6: Brid, Dort 1B 38
Double Comn. DT6: C'outh 7H 35
Douglas Av. BH23: Chris 1H 95
Douglas Cl. BH16: Upt 6E 78
Douglas Ct. BH23: Chris 1H 95
Douglas Gdns. BH12: Pool 2J 91
Douglas M. BH6: Bourn 2E 94
BH16: Upt 6D 78
Douglas Rd. BH6: Bourn 3G 95
BH12: Pool 2J 91
DT4: W Reg 6F 107
Doulton Cl. DT4: Wey 1G 107
Doulton Gdns. BH14: Pool 5F 91
Doussie Cl. BH16: Upt 6C 78
Dover Cl. BH13: Pool 4A 92
Dover Rd. BH13: Pool 4A 92
DT4: W Reg 6F 107
Dover St. DT10: Tod 7K 7
Doves, The DT3: B'wey 7H 101
Doveshill Cres. BH10: Bourn 3D 82
Doveshill Gdns. BH10: Bourn 3D 82
Doveshill Mobile Home Pk.
BH10: Bourn 3D 82
Dowden Ct. BH23: Chris 1H 95
DOWLANDS 1A 126
Dowlands Cl. BH10: Bourn 2D 82
Dowlands Rd. BH10: Bourn 2D 82
DOWLISH WAKE 2A 122
Dowman Pl. DT4: W Reg 7F 107
Down Cl. DT4: W Reg 5F 107
Downe Hall DT6: Brid 3D 38
Down End DT2: C'ster 6J 49
Down End Ct. DT6: Both 4E 38
Downes St. DT6: Brid 4D 38
Downey Cl. BH11: Bourn 4K 81
Downfield DT11: W Stic 4J 29
DOWNHEAD 1C 123
Downlands SP7: Shaf 3D 8
Downlands Pl. BH17: Pool 6C 80
Down Lodge Cl. SP6: Ald 6J 21
Down Rd. DT4: Wey 3G 107
DT8: Most 1J 23
DT11: P'erne 3G 31
Downshay Farm Campsite
BH19: H Cro 3A 116
Downside Cl. DT6: C'outh 7H 35
DT11: B For 4D 30
Downside La. DT1: Poun 4B 50
Downs La. DT9: Yet 7H 13
Downsview Dr. SP8: Gill 3H 5
DOWNTON
Lymington 3B 130
Salisbury 1A 130
Downton Cl. BH8: Bourn 3J 83
Down Wood Rd. DT11: B Cam 7H 31
Doyne Rd. BH14: Pool 3J 91
Dragon La. BH24: Bist, Sandf 4H 69
Dragons Hill DT7: L Reg 3D 34
Dragoon Way BH23: Chris 7H 85
Drake Av. DT3: Chick 6B 102
Drake Cl. BH23: Mude 1D 96
Drake Ct. BH15: Pool 6B 120 (6A 90)
Drake Rd. BH15: Pool 6B 120 (6A 90)
Drakes Rd. BH22: Fern 2F 75
Drakes Way DT7: L Reg 5D 34
(off Broad St.)
Draper Rd. BH11: Bourn 2A 82
BH23: Chris 7C 86
Drax Av. BH20: W'ham 2H 113
DRAYCOTT 1C 123
Draycott Rd. BH10: Bourn 4D 82
DRAYTON 1B 122
Dreadnought Trad. Est. DT6: Brid . . .4C 38
Dreswick Cl. BH23: Chris 2F 85
Drew Cl. BH12: Pool 7C 82
DT6: Bradp 1F 39
Drew Grange BH15: Hamw 3G 89
Drewitt Ind. Est. BH11: Bourn 4H 81
Drew's La. DT10: Stalb 1G 15
Drift Rd. DT2: Fram, M New 5J 41
Driftwood Pk. BH23: Chris 5G 85
DRIMPTON 2B 22 (3B 122)
Drimpton Rd. DT8: B'sor 4C 22
Drive, The BH12: Pool 2H 91
BH13: Sandb 1H 99
DT11: Bryan 3A 30
DRIVE END 1C 126
Drives, The DT2: Pun 3D 46
Drone, The BH21: Wit 3H 33
Drones La. SP7: C Abb, Twy 1A 10
DROOP 5D 28 (3A 124)
Drove, The BH20: Stob 7J 113
DT2: W New 1F 111
DT9: T'ford 2K 13
Drovers DT10: S New 5C 16
Droxford Rd. BH6: Bourn 1D 94
Druce La. DT2: Pud 1A 52
(not continuous)
Druids Cl. BH22: W Par 3D 74
Druid's Wlk. DT1: Dor 6E 50
Druitt Rd. BH23: Chris 6D 86
Drum La. DT10: Won 5B 28
Drummond Rd. BH1: Bourn 3K 93
BH19: Swan 6K 117
Drury La. DT6: Neth 7B 24
Drury Rd. BH4: Bourn 5B 92
Dryden Cl. BH24: Ash H 6A 60
Duchy Cl. DT1: Dor 5H 51
Ducking Stool La. BH23: Chris 1K 95
Duck Island La. BH24: Ring 5H 61
Duck La. BH11: Bourn 1K 81
(Dalewood Av.)
BH11: Bourn 2K 81
(Poole La.)
DT10: Stalb 1H 15
Duck St. BH20: Wool 7E 110
DT2: Catt 2G 41
DT2: Cer A 1B 42
DT6: Both 6E 38
DT6: Chid 5B 36
DT6: Sym 3A 38
DT11: Chil O 3H 19
DT11: W Kin 7H 45
Dudley Gdns. BH10: Bourn 1D 82
Dudley Rd. BH10: Bourn 1D 82
Dudmoor Farm Rd. BH23: Chris 2H 85
Dudmoor La. BH23: Chris 2H 85
BH23: Hurn 6F 77
DUDSBURY 4D 74
Dudsbury Av. BH22: Fern 1D 74
Dudsbury Cres. BH22: Fern 1D 74
Dudsbury Fort 5D 74
Dudsbury Gdns. BH22: W Par 5E 74
Dudsbury Rd. BH22: W Par 4D 74
Dudsway Ct. BH22: Fern 1D 74
Dugdell Cl. BH22: Fern 6F 67
Duke's Av. DT1: Dor 4G 51
Dukes Cl. BH6: Bourn 1F 95
DT2: Mart 3H 47
Dukes Ct. BH31: Ver 3F 55
(off Jenner Cl.)
Dukes Dr. BH11: Bourn 1J 81
Dukesfield BH23: Chris 4F 85
Dullar La. BH21: S Mar 7G 33
Dulsie Rd. BH3: Bourn 1C 92
Dumbarton Rd. DT4: W Reg 6F 107
Dunbar Cres. BH23: Chris 4K 87
Dunbar Rd. BH3: Bourn 1E 92
Dunbury La. DT11: W Stic 7F 29
Duncan Cres. BH20: Bov 2C 110
Duncan Pl. BH20: Bov 2C 110

A-Z Dorset Atlas 141

Dunch La.—Excelsior Rd.

Dunch La. DT9: Chet 6A **14**
Duncliffe Cl. DT10: Stalb 2H **15**
Duncliffe Vw. SP8: E Sto 1K **7**
Duncliff Rd. BH6: Bourn 3J **95**
Duncombe Dr. BH24: Harb 1D **60**
Dundas Rd. BH17: Pool 6C **80**
Dundee Rd. DT4: W Reg 6F **107**
DUNDON **1B 122**
Dune Crest BH13: Sandb 5G **99**
Dunedin Cl. BH22: Fern 2B **74**
Dunedin Dr. BH22: Fern 2B **74**
Dunedin Gdns. BH22: Fern 2B **74**
Dunedin Gro. BH23: Chris 7G **87**
Dunford Pl. BH19: Swan 5J **117**
Dunford Rd. BH12: Pool 2H **91**
Dunkeld Rd. BH3: Bourn 1D **92**
Dunlin Cl. BH23: Mude 2F **97**
Dunnabridge Sq. DT1: Poun 3A **50**
Dunnock Cl. BH22: Fern 4B **66**
Dunn's La. DT11: I Min 2J **17**
SP8: Silt 3E **4**
Dunstans La. BH15: Pool 1E **90**
Dunstan St. DT9: Sher 3D **12**
DUNTISH . . . .**4H 27 (3D 123)**
Dunyeats Rd. BH18: B'tone 2K **79**
Dunyeats Rdbt. BH17: Pool 1B **80**
D'Urberville Cl. DT1: Dor 6E **50**
Durberville Dr. BH19: Swan 3H **117**
Durdells Av. BH11: Bourn 7A **74**
Durdells Gdns. BH11: Bourn 1A **82**
Durdle Door 2B **128**
Durley Chine BH2: Bourn 5D **92**
Durley Chine Ct. BH2: Bourn 5D **92**
Durley Chine Rd. BH2: Bourn 4D **92**
Durley Chine Rd. Sth. BH2: Bourn. . . .5D **92**
Durley Gdns. BH2: Bourn 5D **92**
Durley Rd. BH2: Bourn 6F **121** (5E **92**)
Durley Rd. Sth.
BH2: Bourn 6F **121** (5D **92**)
DURLSTON **7K 117**
Durlston Country Pk. 7K **117**
Durlston Country Pk. Vis. Cen. . . .7K **117**
Durlston Cres. BH23: Chris 2F **85**
Durlston Farm BH19: Swan 2J **117**
Durlston Head Castle 7K **117**
Durlston Point *BH19: Swan 6K 117*
(off Park Rd.)
Durlston Rd. BH14: Pool 5G **91**
BH19: Swan 7K **117**
Durnford Drove BH19: Lan M 6C **116**
Durngate St. DT1: Dor 3F **51**
Durnover Ct. DT1: Dor 3G **51**
DURNS TOWN **3B 130**
Durrant DT10: S New 6B **16**
Durrant Cl. DT9: Sher 5C **12**
Durrant Rd. BH2: Bourn . . .3G **121** (3E **92**)
BH14: Pool 4G **91**
Durrington Pl. BH7: Bourn 1D **94**
Durrington Rd. BH7: Bourn 1D **94**
DURSTON **1A 122**
DURWESTON . . . .**3G 29 (3B 124)**
Durweston Cl. BH9: Bourn 3H **83**
Dyke Head DT9: L'ton 4A **14**
Dymewood Rd. BH21: T Leg 4E **58**

E

Eadon Cl. DT3: Over 5A **104**
Eagle Ho. Gdns. DT11: B For 4B **30**
Eaglehurst *BH12: Pool 3A 92*
(off Poole Rd.)
Eagle Rd. BH12: Pool 3A **92**
Earl Cl. DT1: Dor 4G **51**
Earle Rd. BH4: Bourn 6C **92**
Earles Rd. BH21: T Leg 3E **58**
Earlham Dr. BH14: Pool 3G **91**
Earls Cl. DT9: Sher 3E **12**
Earlsdon Way BH23: H'ffe 6K **87**
Earlswood Dr. SP6: Ald 7H **21**
E. Acton Fld. BH19: Lan M 5B **116**
East Av. BH3: Bourn 1C **92**
BH25: N Mil 7K **97**
East Av. Roundabout BH3: Bourn . . .1E **92**
EAST BLOXWORTH **1B 128**
East Borough BH21: Wim M 6K **63**
(not continuous)
EAST BROOK **1A 72**
Eastbrook Row BH21: Wim M 1A **72**
EAST BURTON . . . .**5B 110 (2B 128)**
E. Burton Rd. BH20: Wool 6B **110**
EAST CHALDON **2A 128**
E. Chaldon Rd. DT2: W New 4F **111**
EAST CHELBOROUGH **3C 123**
EAST CHINNOCK **2B 122**
EAST CLIFF . . . .**5K 121 (4G 93)**
East Cliff BH2: Bourn 3H **121** (3F **93**)
DT6: W Bay 2H **37**
DT7: L Reg 5D **34**
E. Cliff Prom.
BH1: Bourn 6J **121** (5G **93**)
E. Cliff Way BH23: F Clif 7G **87**
EAST COKER **2C 123**
EAST COMPTON **1E 10**
Eastcott Cl. BH7: Bourn 6C **84**
EAST CREECH **2C 129**
East Dorset Indoor Bowls Club 1A **96**
East Dorset Sailing Club 1G **99**
Eastdown Av. DT3: Over 3K **103**
Eastdown Gdns. DT3: Over 6A **104**
East Dr. BH24: S Leo 4H **67**
East Drove BH19: Lan M 5C **116**
EAST END . . . .**4G 71 (1C 129)**
Easter Rd. BH9: Bourn 4G **83**
E. Farm La. DT2: Ower 7J **109**
Eastfield DT9: T'ford 2K **13**
Eastfield Ct. BH24: Ring 4K **61**
Eastfield La. BH24: Ring 4K **61**
EAST HARNHAM **1D 125**
EAST HATCH **1C 125**
Easthay La. TA20: S Hou 7A **22**
East Hill DT2: C'ster 6H **49**
DT2: Ever 5C **26**
EAST HOLME **2B 128**
EAST HOLTON **4A 88**
EAST HOWE . . . .**2C 82 (1D 129)**
E. Howe La. BH10: Bourn 3C **82**
EAST KNIGHTON . . . . . .**1H 111 (2B 128)**
East Knighton La. DT2: E Knig 2H **111**
EAST KNOYLE **1B 124**
Eastlake Av. BH12: Pool 1F **91**
EAST LAMBROOK **2B 122**
Eastlands DT9: Yet 7H **13**
Eastleaze Rd. DT11: B For 2C **30**
EAST LULWORTH **2B 128**
EAST LYDFORD **1C 123**
E. Mill La. DT9: Sher 4D **12**
EAST MORDEN **1C 129**
EASTON . . . .**1J 119 (3D 127)**
Easton La. DT5: East 6C **118**
Easton Pl. SP8: Bour 1E **4**
Easton Shop. Cen. DT5: East 1J **119**
Easton Sq. DT5: East 1J **119**
Easton St. DT5: East 1J **119**
EAST ORCHARD **2B 124**
E. Overcliff Dr.
BH1: Bourn 6K **121** (5G **93**)
EAST PARLEY **5J 75**
EAST PARLEY COMMON **2H 75**
East Quay BH15: Pool 6C **120** (6A **90**)
E. Quay Rd. BH15: Pool . . .6B **120** (6A **90**)
East Rd. DT6: Brid 4E **38**
East Rd. Bus. Pk. DT6: Both 4E **38**
EAST STOKE
Stoke sub Hamdon **2B 122**
Wareham **2B 128**
EAST STOUR . . . .**2J 7 (1B 124)**
East St. BH15: Pool 5C **120** (5A **90**)
BH20: Corf C 2B **114**
BH20: W'ham 4H **113**
BH21: Wim M 1A **72**
DT2: Syd N 7C **42**
DT3: Chick 5A **102**
DT4: Wey 2J **107**
DT5: Fort 5B **118**
DT6: Brid 4D **38**
DT8: Bea 3D **24**
DT11: B For 5C **30**
DT11: W Kin 6H **45**
SP8: Bour 3C **4**
East St. La. *DT11: B For 5C 30*
(off The Close)
East Vw. Rd. BH24: Ring 4K **61**
East Walls BH20: W'ham 4J **113**
East Way BH8: Bourn 5H **83**
BH21: Corf M 1F **79**
E. Weare Rd. DT5: Fort 4B **118**
Eastwell La. DT10: Marn 6J **9**
Eastwood Av. BH22: Fern 6E **66**
Eastworth Rd. BH31: Ver 3E **54**
E. Wyld Rd. DT4: Wey 1E **106**
Eaton Rd. BH13: Pool 5A **92**
EBBESBOURNE WAKE **1C 125**
EBBLAKE . . . .**5K 55 (2A 130)**
Ebblake Cl. BH31: Ver 7J **55**
Ebblake Ent. Pk. BH31: Ver 5J **55**
Ebblake Ind. Est. BH31: Ver 6K **55**
Ebenezer La. BH24: Ring 4H **61**
Ebor Cl. BH22: W Par 3E **74**
Ebor Rd. BH12: Pool 1H **91**
DT4: W Reg 4E **106**
Eccles Rd. BH15: Hamw 5J **89**
ECCLIFFE **7F 5**
Eddison Av. DT1: Dor 4H **51**
Eddy Grn. Rd. BH16: L Mat 7F **53**
Eden Gro. BH21: Wim M 2B **72**
Edgarton Rd. BH17: Pool 3B **80**
Edgcumbe Mnr. *DT1: Dor 3F 51*
(off Somerleigh Rd.)
Edgehill Rd. BH9: Bourn 6E **82**
DT6: Brid 5B **38**
Edgemoor Rd. BH22: W Moo 3G **67**
Edifred Rd. BH9: Bourn 2G **83**
Edith Ct. SP8: Gill 5G **5**
EDMONDSHAM **2D 125**
Edmondsham Ho.
BH2: Bourn 5G **121** (4E **92**)
Edmondsham Rd. BH31: Ver 2E **54**
Edmonds Pl. DT4: Wey 7C **102**
Edward Cres. BH20: W'ham 3H **113**
Edward May Ct. BH11: Bourn 2A **82**
Edward Rd. BH11: Bourn 3B **82**
(not continuous)
BH14: Pool 2G **91**
BH23: Chris 6D **86**
DT1: Dor 4E **50**
Edwards Ct. DT1: Dor 3G **51**
Edward St. DT4: Wey 7H **103**
DT11: B For 4C **30**
Edwardsville DT4: Wey 3H **107**
Edwina Cl. BH24: Poul 2K **61**
Edwina Dr. BH17: Pool 4K **79**
Egdon Cl. BH20: Ber 2H **53**
BH22: Fern 2B **74**
Egdon Ct. BH16: Upt 7D **78**
Egdon Dr. BH21: Merl 5C **72**
Egdon Glen DT2: Cros 1J **109**
Egdon Rd. BH20: W'ham 2G **113**
DT1: Dor 6G **51**
Egerton Gdns. BH8: Bourn 1K **93**
Egerton Rd. BH8: Bourn 1K **93**
Eggardon Cl. DT8: Bea 2B **24**
Eggardon Hill Fort 1C **127**
Egmont Cl. BH24: Ash 2E **68**
Egmont Dr. BH24: Ash 2F **69**
Egmont Gdns. BH24: Ash 2F **69**
Egmont Rd. BH16: Hamw 3D **88**
Eight Acre Coppice Nature Reserve
. . . . .3D **110**
Eighth August Rd. BH20: Bov 1B **110**
Elbury Vw. SP7: Fon M 4B **10**
Elderberry La. BH23: Mude 1D **96**
Elder Rd. BH20: Ber 2G **53**
Eldon Pl. BH4: Bourn 4B **92**
Eldon Rd. BH9: Bourn 5E **82**
Eldons Drove BH16: L Mat 6G **53**
Eldon Ter. BH19: Swan 5J **117**
Eldridge Cl. DT1: Dor 6E **50**
Eleanor Dr. BH11: Bourn 1H **81**
Eleanor Gdns. BH23: Chris 6G **85**
Elfin Dr. BH22: Fern 5C **66**
Elgar Rd. BH10: Bourn 2D **82**
Elgin Ct. BH13: Pool 5B **92**
Elgin Rd. BH3: Bourn 7D **82**
BH4: Bourn 1D **92**
BH14: Pool 6F **91**
Elijah Cl. BH15: Hamw 5G **89**
Elise Cl. BH7: Bourn 6D **84**
Elizabethan Way DT4: Wey 2J **107**
Elizabeth Av. BH23: Chris 6H **85**
DT6: Brid 5C **38**
Elizabeth Cl. DT7: L Reg 4D **34**
Elizabeth Ct. BH1: Bourn 4G **93**
BH22: Fern 7D 66
(off Victoria Rd.)
Elizabeth Gdns. BH23: Chris 7H **87**
Elizabeth Pl. DT1: Dor 4C **50**
Elizabeth Rd. BH15: Pool. . .2D **120** (4B **90**)
(not continuous)
BH16: Upt 7E 78
(off Douglas Cl.)
BH21: Wim M 6A **64**
DT11: B For 4D **30**
Elizabeth Way DT3: Chick 1C **106**
Ellerslie Chambers
BH1: Bourn 5J **121** (4F **93**)
Ellerslie Cl. DT2: C'ster 6J **49**
Ellesdon DT6: C'outh 6J **35**
Ellesfield Dr. BH22: W Par 2D **74**
Elles Rd. BH20: Bov 1A **110**
ELLINGHAM **2A 130**
Ellingham Rd. BH25: N Mil 6K **97**
Elliott Rd. BH11: Bourn 3J **81**
Elm Av. BH16: Sandf 3C **112**
BH23: Chris 5G **85**
Elm Cl. DT3: Over 6A **104**
DT10: S New 5D **16**
SP7: Mot 3C **6**
Elmes Rd. BH9: Bourn 4E **82**
Elm Gdns. BH4: Bourn 2C **92**
Elmgate Dr. BH7: Bourn 7C **84**
ELM HILL . . . .**2C 6 (1B 124)**
Elmhurst Rd. BH11: Bourn 1A **82**
BH22: W Moo 3F **67**
Elmhurst Way BH22: W Moo 3F **67**
Elm La. DT2: Char D 1H **49**
Elmore Dr. BH24: Ash H 5A **60**
Elms Av. BH14: Pool 6E **90**
Elms Cl. BH14: Pool 6E **90**
Elmsdown Ct. BH24: Ring 4H **61**
Elmstead Rd. BH13: Pool 7K **91**
Elmsway BH6: Bourn 3G **95**
Elm Tree Wlk. BH22: W Par 5E **74**
Elmwood Way BH23: H'ffe 7K **87**
Elphinstone Rd. BH23: H'ffe 6J **97**
Eltham Cl. BH7: Bourn 6D **84**
Elvastone St. DT1: Poun 4B **50**
Elveroakes Way DT4: W Reg 6E **106**
ELWELL **4F 101**
Elwell DT6: Both 5E **38**
Elwell Mnr. Gdns. DT4: Wey 3G **107**
Elwell St. DT3: Upw 4F **101**
Elwood Cl. BH20: Sandf 6A **112**
ELWORTH . . . .**7F 47 (2C 127)**
Elwyn Rd. BH1: Bourn 2J **93**
Elysium Ct. BH22: Fern 2E **74**
Elziver Cl. DT3: Chick 6B **102**
Embankment Way BH24: Ring 5K **61**
Emberley Cl. BH22: Fern 5G **67**
Emerald Cl. BH24: Ash H 5A **60**
Emerson Cl. BH15: Pool . . .5C **120** (5A **90**)
Emerson Rd.
BH15: Pool 5C **120** (5A **90**)
DT4: Wey 2F **107**
EMERY DOWN **2B 130**
Emily Cl. BH23: Chris 5J **85**
Emily Ct. BH12: Pool 2J **91**
Emlet DT9: Brad A 6G **11**
Emley La. BH21: H Mart 3A **56**
Emmadale Cl. DT4: Wey 1F **107**
Emmadale Rd. DT4: Wey 1F **107**
Emminster Cl. DT3: Over 4A **104**
Empool Cl. DT2: Cros 2H **109**
Emsbury Rd. DT10: S New 3D **16**
Encombe Cl. BH12: Pool 6K **81**
Encombe Rd. BH20: W'ham 4G **113**
Endeavour Pk. BH17: Pool 5B **80**
BH24: Ring 5K **61**
Endfield Cl. BH23: Chris 5H **85**
Endfield Rd. BH9: Bourn 4G **83**
BH23: Chris 5G **85**
Enefco Ho. *BH15: Pool 6A 120*
(off The Quay)
Enfield Av. BH15: Pool 1C **90**
Enfield Cres. BH15: Pool 1C **90**
Enfield Rd. BH15: Pool 1C **90**
Englands Way BH11: Bourn 2H **81**
Enkworth Rd. DT3: Over 5A **104**
ENMORE GREEN **3A 8**
ENSBURY . . . .**1D 82 (1D 129)**
Ensbury Av. BH10: Bourn 5D **82**
Ensbury Cl. BH10: Bourn 5D **82**
Ensbury Ct. BH10: Bourn 4E **82**
ENSBURY PARK **4C 82**
Ensbury Pk. Rd. BH9: Bourn 4E **82**
Enterprise Pk. DT2: P'ton 7K **43**
Enterprise Way BH23: B Int 4J **75**
Erica Dr. BH21: Corf M 7F **71**
Ericksen Rd. BH11: Bourn 3C **82**
Erinbank Mans. BH1: Bourn 4J **93**
Erin Rd. BH20: Bov 1B **110**
Erpingham Rd. BH12: Pool 3A **92**
Esmonde Way BH17: Pool 6D **80**
Esplanade BH13: Pool 1K **99**
DT5: Fort 5A **118**
DT6: W Bay 2G **37**
Esplanade, The DT4: Wey 1J **107**
(not continuous)
Esporta Health & Fitness Club
Poole .6K **79**
Essex Av. BH23: Chris 5H **85**
Essex Rd. DT4: Wey 1G **107**
Ethelbert Rd. BH21: Wim M 1B **72**
Ethelston's Cl. DT7: Uply 3A **34**
Eton Gdns. BH4: Bourn 3C **92**
Ettrick Rd. BH13: Pool 6A **92**
Eucalyptus Av. BH24: Matc 2C **68**
Euston Gro. BH24: Ring 5J **61**
Evans Cl. BH11: Bourn 5K **81**
BH24: Ash H 5A **60**
Evelyn M. BH9: Bourn 5F **83**
Evelyn Rd. BH9: Bourn 5F **83**
Evening Glade BH22: Fern 1E **74**
Eventide Homes BH8: Bourn 4A **84**
Everdene Cl. BH22: Fern 3C **74**
Everdene Dr. DT3: Chick 2C **106**
Everdene Ho. BH7: Bourn 5D **84**
Everdene Rd. DT1: Dor 5G **51**
Everest Rd. BH23: Chris 6C **86**
DT4: Wey 3G **107**
Everetts La. DT11: Shil 6F **19**
Everglades Cl. BH22: Fern 5D **66**
Evergreen Cl. BH21: T Leg 3E **58**
Evergreens BH24: Ash H 6A **60**
Evering Av. BH12: Pool 5G **81**
Evering Gdns. BH12: Pool 5G **81**
EVERSHOT . . . .**5B 26 (3C 123)**
Evershot Rd. BH8: Bourn 4A **84**
Evershot Wlk. DT1: Poun 4C **50**
EVERTON **3B 130**
Evesham Cl. BH7: Bourn 6D **84**
Evesham Ct. BH13: Pool 5A **92**
Exbury Dr. BH11: Bourn 1K **81**
Excelsior Rd. BH14: Pool 4G **91**

Exeter Ct.—Foxglove Cl.

Exeter Ct. BH23: H'ffe 7J 97
Exeter Cres.
BH2: Bourn 5H 121 (5F 93)
Exeter Grange BH2: Bourn 6H 121
Exeter La. BH2: Bourn 5H 121 (4F 93)
Exeter Pk. Mans. BH2: Bourn 6H 121
Exeter Pk. Rd.
BH2: Bourn 6H 121 (5F 93)
Exeter Rd. BH2: Bourn 5H 121 (4F 93)
BH19: Swan 5K 117
Exton Rd. BH6: Bourn 7E 84
Eynon M. BH24: Ring 5H 61
Eype Down Rd. DT6: Brid 5E 36

F

Factory Hill SP8: Bour 2C 4
Factory La. DT2: Buck N 5G 27
Factory Rd. BH16: Upt 7E 78
Fairclose DT4: Wey 3F 107
Faircross Av. DT4: Wey 3G 107
Faircross Ct. DT4: Wey 3F 107
Fairey Cl. SP8: Gill 3H 5
Fairey Cres. SP8: Gill 3H 5
Fairfax DT6: Chid 5B 36
Fairfield BH23: Chris 7K 85
DT3: Chick 6B 102
DT8: Bea 2C 24
DT9: Sher 3C 12
Fairfield Bungs. DT11: B For 4C 30
Fairfield Cl. BH21: Coleh 7D 64
BH23: Chris 7K 85
DT11: O Fitz 5A 18
Fairfield Hgts. DT9: Sher 3C 12
Fairfield Pk. DT7: L Reg 4D 34
Fairfield Rd. BH21: Wim M 1B 72
DT1: Dor 4F 51
DT11: B For 4C 30
DT11: I Cou 6G 17
Fairfields BH20: Wool 6E 110
Fairhaven Ct. BH5: Bourn 3A 94
Fairies Dr. BH22: Fern 2F 75
Fair La. SP7: Shaf 4D 8
Fair Lea BH2: Bourn 7F 121 (5E 92)
Fairlie BH24: Poul 2K 61
Fairlie Pk. BH24: Poul 2K 61
Fairmead DT11: W Stic 4J 29
FAIRMILE 6J 85
Fairmile Ho. BH23: Chris 6H 85
Fair Mile La. DT11: Bryan 7A 30
Fairmile Rd. BH23: Chris 4G 85
Fairmont Ter. DT9: Sher 4D 12
Fairoak Way DT8: Most 3J 23
Fairthorn Ct.
BH2: Bourn 2H 121 (3F 93)
Fairview Cres. BH18: B'tone 1J 79
Fairview Dr. BH18: B'tone 1J 79
Fairview Pk. BH14: Pool 4G 91
Fairview Rd. BH18: B'tone 1J 79
DT4: W Reg 5F 107
Fairway Ct. DT4: Wey 7E 102
Fairway Dr. BH20: W'ham 1F 113
BH23: Chris 1H 95
Fairway Est. BH11: Bourn 2H 81
Fairway Rd. BH14: Pool 7G 91
Fairways BH22: Fern 6F 67
Fairwinds BH13: Sandb 5F 99
BH19: Swan 3K 117
Fairwood Rd. BH31: Ver 5J 55
Fairy Bri. Wlk. SP8: Gill 3H 5
Falcon Dr. BH23: Mude 2E 96
Falconer Dr. BH15: Hamw 3G 89
Falkland Sq.
BH15: Pool 4C 120 (5A 90)
Fancy Rd. BH12: Pool 6F 81
Fancy's Cl. DT5: East 7B 118
Fancy's Row BH16: Hol H 2C 112
Fannybrook's La. DT9: Brad A 6H 11
Fantley La. BA12: Zea 1E 4
SP8: Bour, Silt 2E 4
Farcroft Rd. BH12: Pool 2F 91
Farfrae Cres. DT1: Dor 5G 51
Farm Cl. BH24: Ring 3J 61
DT4: S'hill 6E 102
Farm Ct. BH21: Hay 1E 72
Farmdene Cl. BH23: Chris 6H 87
Farmer Palmer's Farm Pk. 1C 112
Farmers Wlk. BH21: Wim M 6K 63
Farm La. BH20: W Lul 6H 111
BH23: Mude 2E 96
Farm Rd. BH22: W Moo 2D 66
DT9: Brad A 6F 11
FARNHAM 2C 125
Farnham Rd. BH12: Pool 7A 82
Farriers Cl. BH21: Coleh 6F 65
Farringdon Cl. DT1: Dor 6E 50
FARRINGTON 2B 124
Farrington BH4: Bourn 5C 92
Farthings, The BH23: H'ffe 6H 97
Farthings Ct. BH1: Bourn 4J 93
Farthings Ct., The
BH1: Bourn 5K 121 (4G 93)
Farwell Cl. BH23: Burt 3A 86
Farwell Rd. BH12: Pool 4G 81
Faversham DT4: S'hill 5E 102
Fawley Grn. BH8: Bourn 3K 83
Fayrewood Ct. BH31: Ver 3F 55
Fellowsmead DT10: Marn 4H 9
Felton Ct. BH14: Pool 2D 90
Felton Cres. BH23: H'ffe 6K 87
Felton Rd. BH14: Pool 2D 90
Fendalls Wlk. DT6: Brid 4C 38
Fenn Bank BH2: Bourn 4H 121 (4F 93)
Fenton Rd. BH6: Bourn 1E 94
Fenway Cl. DT1: Dor 4J 51
Fenwick Ct. BH8: Bourn 2H 93
Fern Bank BH2: Bourn 4F 93
BH21: T Leg 4E 58
Fern Barrow BH12: Pool 6B 82
Fern Brook La. SP8: Gill 5K 5
Fern Cl. BH23: Burt 4A 86
SP6: Ald 7J 21
Ferncroft Gdns. BH10: Bourn 1D 82
Ferncroft Rd. BH10: Bourn 1D 82
Ferndale Rd. DT4: Wey 5H 103
FERNDOWN 7D 66 (3D 125)
Ferndown Cen. BH22: Fern 7D 66
Ferndown Ind. Est. BH21: Stap 5A 66
Ferndown Leisure Cen. 6B 66
Ferndown Rd. DT7: L Reg 5D 34
Fernheath Cl. BH11: Bourn 4A 82
Fernheath Rd. BH11: Bourn 3A 82
Fernhill Av. DT4: Wey 5H 103
Fernhill Cl. BH17: Pool 4E 80
Fernhill Flats
BH2: Bourn 4H 121 (4F 93)
Fernhill Hgts. DT6: C'outh 6F 35
Fernlea BH23: Chris 1B 96
Fernlea Av. BH22: Fern 1D 74
Fernlea Cl. BH22: Fern 1D 74
BH24: Ash H 7A 60
Fernlea Gdns. BH22: Fern 1D 74
Fernside Av. BH14: Pool 3D 90
Fernside Pk. Ind. Est.
BH21: Stap 5A 66
Fernside Rd. BH9: Bourn 6D 82
BH15: Pool 2B 90
BH22: W Moo 3E 66
Fern Sq. *DT3: Chick 5B 102*
(off Wheat Farland)
Fernway Cl. BH21: Hay 1F 73
Fernwood Cl. BH24: S Ive 6D 60
Ferris Av. BH8: Bourn 4J 83
Ferris Cl. BH8: Bourn 4K 83
Ferris Pl. BH8: Bourn 4K 83
Ferrybridge Cotts. DT4: W Reg 7F 107
Ferrymans Way DT4: W Reg 7F 107
Ferry Rd. BH6: Bourn 4H 95
BH15: Hamw 7A 120 (6K 89)
BH19: Stud 7E 98 & 1G 115
Ferry Way BH13: Sandb 5F 99
Feversham Av. BH8: Bourn 5A 84
FIDDLEFORD 1A 18 (2B 124)
Fiddleford Manor 2B 124
Fiddleford Mill House 2B 124
Fld. Barn Dr. DT4: S'hill 6E 102
Field Cl. DT10: S New 4D 16
Fieldfare Cl. DT3: B'wey 7H 101
Fieldings, The SP8: E Sto 1J 7
Field La. BA9: Pens 1A 4
SP8: K Mag 7C 4
SP8: Mil S 2F 5
Field Pl. BH25: N Mil 6K 97
BH31: Ver 3E 54
Fields Barn DT2: W New 4F 111
Field's Cl. DT11: W Whi 2H 45
Fields Oak DT11: B For 5C 30
Field Vw. Rd. DT11: B For 4C 30
Field Way BH21: Corf M 5G 71
BH23: Chris 5H 87
Fieldway BH24: Ring 3K 61
FIFEHEAD MAGDALEN 4F 7 (1A 124)
FIFEHEAD NEVILLE 2A 124
FIFEHEAD ST QUINTIN 2A 124
FIFIELD BAVANT 1D 125
Filbridge Ri. DT10: S New 4D 16
FILFORD 1B 126
Filleul Rd. BH20: Sandf 5A 112
Fillymead DT10: Marn 5H 9
Finches, The DT3: B'wey 7G 101
Finchfield Av. BH11: Bourn 7K 73
Findlay Pl. BH19: Swan 4G 117
Finger Cnr. DT10: Marn 4H 9
Finger La. DT9: Sher 5C 12
Fippenny Hollow DT11: O Fitz 6B 18
Fir Av. BH16: Sandf 3C 112
Firbank Rd. BH9: Bourn 6H 83
Firch La. DT6: Wald 3H 39
Fir Cl. BH22: W Moo 1E 66
Fir Dr. DT3: Pres 3C 104
Firecrest Cl. DT3: B'wey 6G 101
Firmain Rd. BH12: Pool 5H 81
Firs, The BH1: Bourn 3K 121 (3G 93)
Firs Glen Rd. BH9: Bourn 6D 82
BH22: W Moo 2E 66
BH31: Ver 5F 55
Firshill BH23: Chris 5J 87
Firside Rd. BH21: Corf M 2E 78
Firs La. BH14: Pool 7F 91
First Cliff Wlk. DT6: W Bay 1G 37
Firsway BH16: Upt 7E 78
Fir Tree Cl. BH24: S Leo 2K 67
DT1: Dor 3C 50
Fir Tree Hill SP6: Ald 6J 21
Fir Tree La. BH23: Chris 5H 87
Fir Va. Rd. BH1: Bourn 4J 121 (4F 93)
Fisherbridge Rd. DT3: Pres 4C 104
Fishermans Av. BH6: Bourn 3D 94
Fishermans Bank BH23: Mude 2C 96
Fishermans Cl. DT3: Chick 5B 102
Fishermans Rd.
BH15: Pool 6B 120 (6A 90)
Fishermans Wlk. BH6: Bourn 3D 94
Fishers Barn DT2: Mart 2J 47
Fisher's Cl. DT11: B For 5C 30
FISHPOND BOTTOM 1A 126
Fish St. BH23: Ripl 3K 77
Fishweir Flds. DT6: Bradp 1F 39
Fishweir La. DT6: Bradp 1F 39
Fishweir Ter. *DT6: Bradp 1F 39*
(off Fishweir La.)
Fitness First
Bournemouth 1A 94
Poole 1K 89
Fitzharris Av. BH9: Bourn 7G 83
Fitzmaurice Rd. BH23: Chris 6G 85
Fitzpain Cl. BH22: W Par 3D 74
Fitzpain Rd. BH22: W Par 3D 74
Fitzwilliam Cl. BH11: Bourn 1J 81
Fitzworth Av. BH16: Hamw 3E 88
Five Acres DT6: C'outh 7H 35
Five Ct. Row DT6: Brid 5C 38
FIVEHEAD 1A 122
Flag Farm BH13: Sandb 1H 99
Flaghead Chine Rd. BH13: Pool 2J 99
Flaghead Rd. BH13: Pool 1J 99
Flambard Av. BH23: Chris 5H 85
Flambard Rd. BH14: Pool 5G 91
Flanders Cl. DT10: Marn 4J 9
Flaxfield Rd. DT8: Bea 3E 24
Flaxhayes DT6: Brid 2C 38
Flax La. DT9: N Com 1J 11
Flazen Cl. BH11: Bourn 3H 81
FLEET 2D 127
Fleet Ct. DT3: Chick 1C 106
DT5: Cast 3B 118
Fleet La.
DT3: Chick, Fle 7A 102 & 6A 102
Fleet Nature Reserve 7E 106
Fleetsbridge Bus. Cen.
BH17: Pool 7K 79
Fleetsbridge Retail Pk.
BH15: Pool 1K 89
Fleets Cnr. BH17: Pool 7A 80
Fleets Est. BH15: Pool 1K 89
Fleets La. BH15: Pool 7K 79
Fleetspont Bus. Cen. BH15: Pool 2K 89
Fleet St. DT8: Bea 3D 24
Fleet Vw. DT4: W Reg 5E 106
Fletcher Cl. BH10: Bourn 3D 82
Fletcher Rd. BH10: Bourn 3D 82
Flintcombe Sq. DT1: Poun 4C 50
Flood La. DT6: Brid 6D 38
Floral Farm BH21: Merl 3D 72
Floramour Pl. SP8: Gill 4H 5
Florence Ct. BH5: Bourn 3K 93
Florence Rd. BH5: Bourn 3A 94
BH14: Pool 3G 91
DT1: Dor 5D 50
Florin Mall *BH1: Bourn 3A 94*
(off Royal Arc.)
Flower Ct. BH21: Wim M 2B 72
Flower Mdw. Cvn. Site
BH19: H Cro 2A 116
Flowers Drove BH16: L Mat 5H 53
FODDINGTON 1C 123
FOLKE 1D 14 (2D 123)
Folke La. DT9: Folk 1D 14
Folly, The DT2: Cer A 2B 42
Folly Farm La. BH24: Ash 5E 60
Folly La. BH20: W'ham 3H 113
BH20: Wool 6D 110
DT9: N Com 1J 11
DT11: Blan 7B 30
SP8: K Mag 5D 4
Folly Mill Gdns. DT6: Brid 4D 38
Folly Mill La. DT6: Brid 4D 38
Folly Sq. *DT6: Brid 4D 38*
(off Folly Mill La.)
FONTHILL BISHOP 1C 125
FONTHILL GIFFORD 1C 125
Fontmell Down Nature Reserve 3E 10
FONTMELL MAGNA 4C 10 (2B 124)
Fontmell Rd. BH18: B'tone 4A 80
Foord's Cnr. DT4: W Reg 4E 106
Footners La. BH23: Burt 4A 86
FOOT'S HILL 7E 8
Foot's Hill SP7: Can 7D 8
Ford Cl. BH22: Fern 5F 67
Ford Ct. DT9: Chet 5A 14
Ford Down La. DT2: Hen 7H 27
Forde Abbey 3A 122
FORDINGBRIDGE 1A 130
Fordingbridge Rd. SP6: Ald, Ford 5J 21
Fordington DT1: Dor 3G 51
Fordington Cross DT1: Dor 4H 51
Fordington Dairy *DT1: Dor 4G 51*
(off Athelstan Rd.)
Fordington Farm DT1: Dor 4H 51
Fordington Gdns. DT1: Dor 4G 51
Fordington Grn. DT1: Dor 4G 51
Fordington Hill Ho. *DT1: Dor 3G 51*
(off High St.)
Ford La. BH22: Fern 5G 67
DT2: Cors 7J 25
Forehill Cl. DT3: Pres 4B 104
Foreland Cl. BH23: Chris 2F 85
Foreland Rd. BH16: Hamw 3D 88
Forelle Cen., The BH31: Ver 6J 55
Forest Cl. BH23: Chris 5H 87
BH31: Ver 6K 55
Forest Edge Cl. BH24: Ash H 6K 59
Forest Edge Dr. BH24: Ash H 6K 59
Forest Edge Rd. BH20: Sandf 7A 112
Forest Ho. BH1: Bourn 5K 121 (5G 93)
Forest La. BH31: Ver 3E 54
Forest Links Rd. BH21: Stap 3B 66
BH22: Fern 3B 66
Fore St. DT2: Ever 6B 26
TA20: T'ombe 6C 22
Forest Ri. BH23: Chris 4H 87
Forest Rd. BH13: Pool 6A 92
BH22: W Moo 1F 67
Forestside, The BH31: Ver 5K 55
Forestside Gdns. BH24: Poul 2K 61
Forest Vw. DT2: Cros 1H 109
Forest Vw. Cl. BH9: Bourn 4G 83
Forest Vw. Dr. BH21: Stap 6A 66
Forest Vw. Rd. BH9: Bourn 3G 83
Forest Way BH21: Stap 7A 66
BH23: Chris 4H 87
Forge End SP8: E Sto 1J 7
Forge La. BH31: Ver 5D 54
SP8: Bour 1D 4
Forsters La. DT6: Bradp 1G 39
FORSTON 1F 49 (1D 127)
Forsyth Gdns. BH10: Bourn 5C 82
Fort Cumberland Cl.
BH15: Hamw 5F 89
Fortescue Rd. BH3: Bourn 1G 93
BH12: Pool 7H 81
Fort Henry 4K 115
FORTON 3A 122
Forton Cl. BH10: Bourn 2E 82
Fortress Grn. DT1: Dor 6D 50
FORTUNESWELL 5B 118 (3D 127)
Fortuneswell DT5: Fort 4B 118
Forty Foot Way DT6: W Bay 1H 37
Forum Cen., The DT1: Dor 3F 51
Forum Grn. DT1: Dor 6C 50
Forum Vw. DT11: Bryan 5A 30
Fosse Grn. DT1: Dor 6D 50
Fossett Way DT4: W Reg 4D 106
Foss Orchard DT6: Chid 5B 36
Fosters DT9: Sher 4D 12
Fosters Hill DT9: Holw 2F 27
Fosters Mdws. DT11: W Whi 2H 45
Fosters Spring BH16: L Mat 7H 53
Foundry Cl. DT5: East 1J 119
DT6: Brid 3A 38
Foundry Ct. DT1: Dor 3G 51
Foundry Knapp DT6: Brid 3A 38
Foundry La. DT6: Brid 4C 38
Fountain Ct. BH13: Pool 5B 92
SP7: Shaf 3A 8
Fountain Mead SP7: Shaf 2C 8
Fountain Rdbt. BH23: Chris 1K 95
Fountain Way BH23: Chris 1K 95
Fouracre Cl. DT6: Brid 2D 38
Four Acres DT5: West 2G 119
Fourgates Rd. DT1: Dor 4D 50
Fourth Cliff Wlk. DT6: W Bay 1G 37
Four Wells Rd. BH21: Coleh 5E 64
FOVANT 1D 125
Foxbury BH20: Bov 1A 110
Foxbury Rd. BH24: Matc 6A 68
BH24: S Leo 3B 68
(not continuous)
Fox Cl. DT6: Bradp 1G 39
Foxcroft Dr. BH21: Hay 7F 65
Foxes Cl. BH31: Ver 5F 55
Foxglove Cl. BH23: Chris 6G 87
SP8: Gill 4G 5

Foxglove Way—Gordon Rd.

Foxglove Way DT3: Lit 1K 103
DT6: Brid 7D 38
Foxhill Cl. BH19: Swan 5H 117
Foxhills BH31: Ver 4H 55
Foxhills Cres. BH16: L Mat 6H 53
Foxhills Dr. BH16: L Mat 6H 53
Foxhills La. BH16: L Mat 7H 53
Foxhills Rd. BH16: L Mat 6H 53
FOX HOLES 7E 80
Foxholes Rd. BH6: Bourn 3H 95
BH15: Pool 1D 90
Fox La. BH21: L Can 7G 65
(not continuous)
Fox's Cl. DT9: Holw 2F 27
Foxwold Ho. BH6: Bourn 3H 95
Foxwood Av. BH23: Mude 2D 96
Foyle Bank Way DT5: Cast 3B 118
Foyle Hill SP7: Shaf 5A 8
Framerville Rd. BH20: Bov 1B 110
FRAMPTON 1D 127
Frampton Cotts. DT3: Nott 7E 100
Frampton Pl. BH24: Ring 4H 61
Frampton Rd. BH9: Bourn 6G 83
DT11: P'erne 2G 31
Francesca Ct. BH23: Chris 7C 86
Francesca Grange BH23: Chris 7C 86
Francesca Lodge BH23: Chris 7C 86
Frances Ct. BH23: H'ffe 7J 97
Frances Rd. BH1: Bourn 3H 93
Franchise St. DT4: Wey 2H 107
Francis Av. BH11: Bourn 3H 81
Francis Rd. BH12: Pool 2J 91
DT4: Wey 2F 107
Francis Wlk. DT9: Sher 3D 12
Frankland Cres. BH14: Pool 4J 91
Franklin Cl. DT4: Wey 1F 107
Franklin Rd. BH9: Bourn 3G 83
DT4: Wey 1F 107
Franklyn Cl. BH16: Upt 7D 78
Frankston Rd. BH6: Bourn 3E 94
Franks Way BH12: Pool 7F 81
Franwill Ind. Est. DT11: P'erne 2F 31
Fraser Av. DT4: Wey 2D 106
Fraser Rd. BH12: Pool 5K 81
Freame Way SP8: Gill 5F 5
Freda Rd. BH23: Chris 1H 95
Frederica Rd. BH9: Bourn 6E 82
Frederick Pl. *DT4: Wey 1H 107*
(off Gt. George St.)
Freemans Cl. BH21: Coleh 7F 65
Freemans La. BH21: Coleh 7F 65
Freemantle Rd. DT4: Wey 3D 106
Freesia Cl. DT3: Lit 1J 103
French Mill La. SP7: Shaf 4C 8
French Mill Ri. SP7: Shaf 5C 8
French Rd. BH17: Pool 5K 79
French's Farm Rd. BH16: Upt 7C 78
Frensham Cl. BH10: Bourn 3E 82
Freshwater Beach Holiday Pk.
DT6: Burt B 6F 37
Freshwater Cl. DT5: S'well 4G 119
Freshwater Dr. BH15: Hamw 4F 89
Freshwater Rd. BH23: F Clif 1G 97
FRIARS CLIFF 1G 97
Friars Cl. DT1: Dor 5H 51
Friars Ct. BH16: L Mat 6H 53
Friars Moor DT10: S New 5D 16
Friars Moor Ct. DT10: S New 5D 16
Friars Rd. BH23: F Clif 1F 97
FRIAR WADDON 2A 100 (2D 127)
Friar Waddon Rd.
DT3: F Wad, Upw 2A 100
Friary Ct. *DT1: Dor 3F 51*
(off North Sq.)
Friary Hill DT1: Dor 3F 51
Friary La. DT1: Dor 3F 51
Friday's Heron BH21: Cran 2H 21
FRITHAM 1B 130
Fritham Gdns. BH8: Bourn 3K 83
Frizzel's Hill DT10: K'ton 3C 28
Frobisher Av. BH12: Pool 5K 81
Frobisher Cl. BH23: Mude 1D 96
FROGHAM 1A 130
Frog La. DT11: I Cou 6G 17
SP7: Mot 4D 6
Frogmore La. DT2: T Por 2C 40
Frog Rd. SP8: Gill 6K 5
Frome Av. BH20: Wool 6C 110
Frome La.
DT2: F Vau, M New 6H 41
Frome Rd. BH20: W'ham 5G 113
FROME ST QUINTIN 3C 123
Frome Ter. DT1: Dor 3F 51
Frome Valley Rd. DT2: Cros 1G 109
FROME VAUCHURCH 7H 41
Frome Vw. DT2: Brad P 6E 48
DT2: M New 6J 41
FROME WHITFIELD 1F 51
Frome Whitfield Cotts.
DT2: F Whit 1E 50
Front La. BH21: S Mar 5H 33
Front St. DT3: Port 6G 47
SP8: E Sto 2K 7
Froom's La. BH20: Ber 3J 53
Frost Rd. BH11: Bourn 2K 81
Froud Way BH21: Corf M 2E 78
Froxfield Rd. DT11: B For 3C 30
Fryer Cl. BH11: Bourn 1B 82
Fryer M. BH22: W Moo 3E 66
Fryers Copse BH21: Coleh 6G 65
Fryers Rd. BH21: T Leg 3E 58
Frys Cl. BH16: L Mat 5G 53
DT3: Port 6G 47
Fudge Hill DT2: Cors 6H 25
FUGGLESTONE ST PETER 1D 125
Fulbrooks Cl. DT6: Brid 3C 38
Fulbrooks La. DT6: Brid 3C 38
Fullers DT8: B'sor 7H 23
Fulmar Rd. BH23: Mude 2E 96
Fulwood Av. BH11: Bourn 1J 81
Furbers Paddock DT2: Strat 4C 48
Furlands DT5: East 2H 119
FURLEY 3A 122
Furlong, The BH24: Ring 4H 61
Furlong M. BH24: Ring 4H 61
Furlongs, The DT9: Sher 3C 12
Furlong Shop. Cen., The
BH24: Ring 4H 61
Furnell Rd. BH15: Pool 6D 120 (6B 90)
Furze Bank La. BH10: Bourn 4C 82
Furze Brach La. BH21: E'ham 1A 54
FURZEBROOK 2C 129
Furzebrook Cl. BH17: Pool 3C 80
Furzebrook Rd. BH20: Stob 7J 113
FURZEHILL 3B 64 (3D 125)
Furzehill BH21: Holt, Wim M 4A 64
Furze Hill Dr. BH14: Pool 6G 91
Furzelands Rd. BH21: T Leg 3E 58
Furze La. DT8: Bea 4D 24
Furzey Rd. BH16: Upt 1D 88
FURZLEY 1B 130
Furzy Cl. DT3: Over 5B 104

G

Gables, The DT1: Dor 3E 50
Gabriel Grn. DT1: Dor 5G 51
Gainsborough Ct. BH5: Bourn 2D 94
Gainsborough Dr. DT9: Sher 5A 12
Gainsborough Hill DT9: Sher 5D 12
Gainsborough Rd. BH7: Bourn 7B 84
BH24: Ash H 6A 60
Gainsford Theatre 6A 78
Gale Cres. DT6: Brid 5C 38
GALHAMPTON 1D 123
Gallop Way BH12: Pool 7C 82
Galloway Rd. BH15: Hamw 3F 89
Gallows Dr. BH22: W Par 4D 74
Gallows Hill DT2: Ower 7J 109
Gallwey Rd. DT4: W Reg 5E 106
GALTON 2A 128
Galton Av. BH23: Chris 1H 95
Gannetts Pk. BH19: Swan 4J 117
Garden Cl. DT6: Brid 3D 38
Garden Ct. BH1: Bourn 1K 93
Garden Ct. Cotts. BH22: W Moo 1D 66
Garden Ho. BH1: Bourn 4G 93
Garden La. BH24: S Leo 1A 68
Gardens, The DT9: Sher 5B 12
DT11: I Cou 5G 17
Gardens Ct. BH15: Pool 4C 90
Gardens Cres. BH14: Pool 7F 91
Gardenside DT6: C'outh 7H 35
Gardens Rd. BH14: Pool 7F 91
Garden Wlk. BH22: Fern 5E 66
Gardner Rd. BH23: Chris 6G 85
BH24: Ring 5K 61
Garfield Av. BH1: Bourn 2K 93
DT1: Dor 5D 50
Garfield La. BH19: Lan M 5C 116
Garibaldi Row *DT4: Wey 2G 107*
(off Weston Rd.)
Garland Cres. DT1: Dor 5G 51
Garland Rd. BH15: Pool 1D 120 (3B 90)
Garlands Ct. *DT1: Dor 3F 51*
(off Princes St.)
Garnet Ct. *DT4: Wey 1H 107*
(off Park St.)
Garsdale Cl. BH11: Bourn 7A 74
Garston Hill DT3: Chick 5A 102
Garston Wood Bird Sanctuary 2D 125
Gartells DT10: K'ton 2C 28
Garth Cl. BH24: S Leo 7K 59
Garth Rd. BH9: Bourn 5G 83
Garwoods BH19: Swan 3J 117
Gascoigne's La. SP7: Shaf 5B 8
Gascoyne La. DT2: Brad P, Wrack 7E 48
Gas Ho. Hill DT9: Sher 5D 12
GASPER 1A 124
Gassons La. DT6: Whit C 1F 35
Gatcombe Cl. DT1: Dor 5H 51
Gatemore Rd. DT2: W New 1F 111
Gateway, The BH13: Pool 3K 91
GAUNT'S COMMON 4C 56 (3D 125)
Gaydon Ri. BH11: Bourn 2J 81
Gaza Rd. BH20: Bov 1A 110
Geelong Cl. DT3: Lit 1J 103
Gemma Ct. DT4: Wey 1F 107
General Wolfe Cl. DT11: I Cou 6G 17
Geneva Av. BH6: Bourn 2F 95
Gent Cl. DT11: B For 3D 30
George M., The BH24: Ring 4H 61
George Rd. BH21: Corf M 6F 71
George Roundabout, The
BH15: Pool 3D 120 (4B 90)
Georges Cl. DT6: C'outh 6J 35
George's Ct. BH1: Bourn 2A 94
Georges M. BH21: Corf M 6F 71
George's Sq. *DT7: L Reg 5D 34*
(off Monmouth St.)
George St. DT6: W Bay 1H 37
DT9: Sher 4C 12
Georgian Cl. BH24: Ring 3J 61
DT3: B'wey 6F 101
Georgian Way BH10: Bourn 2F 83
Georgina Cl. BH12: Pool 6C 82
Georgina Talbot Ho. BH12: Pool 6B 82
Gerald Rd. BH3: Bourn 1G 93
Germaine Cl. BH23: H'ffe 6K 87
Gerrards Grn. DT8: Bea 3E 24
Gervis Cres. BH14: Pool 3E 90
Gervis Pl. BH1: Bourn 5H 121 (4F 93)
Gervis Rd. BH1: Bourn 5K 121 (4G 93)
Gibbs Grn. BH16: L Mat 7H 53
Gibbs La. DT6: Morc 3H 35
Gibson Rd. BH17: Pool 7C 80
GIDDY GREEN 6B 110
Giddy Grn. La. BH20: Wool 6B 110
Giddy Grn. Rd. BH20: Wool 6B 110
Giddylake BH21: Wim M 6A 64
Gifle Vw. DT9: T'ford 1J 13
Gilbert Cl. SP6: Ald 6K 21
Gilbert Ct. BH19: Swan 5J 117
Gilbert Rd. BH8: Bourn 1K 93
BH19: Swan 5J 117
Giles Cl. DT2: Brad P 6E 48
Giles Cross DT2: Brad P 7F 49
Giles's La. DT9: Bis C 6G 15
Gillam Rd. BH10: Bourn 1D 82
Gillett Rd. BH12: Pool 7C 82
GILLINGHAM 5H 5 (1B 124)
Gillingham Cl. BH9: Bourn 3J 83
Gillingham Leisure Cen. 5J 5
Gillingham Mus. 5H 5
Gillingham Station (Rail) 5H 5
Gipsy La. DT6: Brid 1E 38
Girt La. DT2: Ever 5A 26
Glacis DT5: Fort 5C 118
Gladdis Rd. BH11: Bourn 2K 81
Glade, The BH23: Chris 5G 85
BH24: Ash H 6A 60
Gladelands Cl. BH18: B'tone 2G 79
Gladelands Mobile Home Pk.
BH22: Fern 5F 67
Gladelands Way BH18: B'tone 2G 79
Gladiator Grn. DT1: Dor 6D 50
Gladstone Cl. BH23: Chris 1B 96
DT3: Lit 1J 103
DT6: Brid 3E 38
Gladstone Rd. BH7: Bourn 2B 94
BH12: Pool 2G 91
Gladstone Rd. E. BH7: Bourn 2B 94
Gladstone Rd. W. BH1: Bourn 2A 94
Glamis Av. BH10: Bourn 1E 82
GLANVILLES WOOTTON 3D 123
Gleadowe Av. BH23: Chris 1H 95
Glebe, The DT11: Dur 4G 29
DT11: I Cou 6H 17
DT11: I Min 3J 17
Glebe Cl. DT2: M New 6H 41
DT3: Abb 5E 46
DT3: Osm 4G 105
DT4: Wey 3G 107
DT6: Both 5D 38
DT9: T'ford 2J 13
Glebe Ct. DT8: Bea 3C 24
DT11: I Min 3J 17
Glebefields DT2: Brad P 5D 48
Glebeford Cl. DT2: Ower 7K 109
Glebe Gdns. SP7: Mot 4C 6
Glebeland Cl. DT2: W Staf 1B 108
Glebeland Est. BH19: Stud 6K 115
Glebelands DT7: Uply 3A 34
Glebe Rd. BH16: L Mat 7G 53
Glebe Way DT2: W Knig 5D 108
Glen, The BH12: Pool 1H 91
BH13: Pool 7J 91
DT7: Uply 3A 34
Glenair Av. BH14: Pool 4E 90
Glenair Cres. BH14: Pool 4E 90
Glenair Rd. BH14: Pool 4E 90
Glen Av. DT4: Wey 2G 107
Glenavon Rd. BH23: H'ffe 5K 87
Glencoe Rd. BH7: Bourn 7B 84
BH12: Pool 2H 91
Glendale Av. BH22: Fern 6D 66
Glendale Cl. BH21: Wim M 7A 64
BH23: Chris 3F 85
Glendale Ct. BH23: Chris 3F 85
Glendale Rd. BH6: Bourn 3J 95
Glendinning Av. DT4: Wey 6H 103
Glendon Av. BH10: Bourn 7C 74
Glen Dr. BH25: N Mil 6K 97
Gleneagles BH23: Chris 1H 95
Gleneagles Av. BH14: Pool 5H 91
Gleneagles Cl. BH22: Fern 6F 67
Glenferness Av. BH3: Bourn 3C 92
BH4: Bourn 3C 92
Glen Fern Rd.
BH1: Bourn 4K 121 (4G 93)
Glengariff Rd. BH14: Pool 5G 91
Glengarry Way BH23: F Clif 1G 97
Glenives Cl. BH24: S Ive 7B 60
Glenmeadows Dr. BH10: Bourn 1B 82
Glenmoor Cl. BH10: Bourn 5D 82
Glenmoor Rd. BH9: Bourn 6D 82
BH22: W Par 2C 74
Glenmore Bus. Cen. BH16: Hol H. 3E 112
Glenmore Rd. DT4: Wey 7F 103
Glenmount Dr. BH14: Pool 2F 91
Glennie Way DT3: Chick 7B 102
Glen Rd. BH5: Bourn 3A 94
BH14: Pool 2F 91
Glenroyd Gdns. BH6: Bourn 3G 95
Glenside BH25: N Mil 7J 97
Glenville Cl. BH23: Walk 4J 97
Glenville Gdns. BH10: Bourn 4C 82
Glenville Rd. BH10: Bourn 4C 82
BH23: Walk 4H 97
Glenwood Cl. BH22: W Moo 2E 66
Glenwood La. BH22: W Moo 2E 66
Glenwood Rd. BH22: W Moo 2E 66
BH31: Ver 5F 55
Glenwood Way BH22: W Moo 2E 66
Glissons BH22: L'ham 3A 74
Globe Cl. BH19: Swan 5G 117
Globe La. BH15: Pool 5C 120 (5A 90)
(not continuous)
DT6: Brid 4D 38
Gloucester Cl. DT4: Wey 1C 106
Gloucester M. DT4: Wey 1H 107
Gloucester Rd. BH7: Bourn 1B 94
BH12: Pool 2J 91
DT1: Dor 4D 50
Gloucester Row *DT4: Wey 1H 107*
(off Gloucester M.)
Gloucester St. DT4: Wey 1H 107
Glue Hill DT10: New 7A 16
Glyde Ct. *DT1: Dor 3F 51*
(off Glyde Path Rd.)
Glyde Path Rd. DT1: Dor 3F 51
Glynville Cl. BH21: Coleh 5E 64
Glynville Ct. BH21: Coleh 5E 64
Glynville Rd. BH21: Coleh 5E 64
GOATHILL 2D 123
Goathorn Cl. BH16: Hamw 3F 89
Godmanston Cl. BH17: Pool 5E 80
GODMANSTONE 1D 127
GOD'S BLESSING GREEN 1E 64
God's Blessing La. BH21: Holt 1C 64
GODSHILL 1A 130
Godshill Cl. BH8: Bourn 3K 83
GODWINSCROFT 1G 87
Goldcrest Cl. DT3: B'wey 6G 101
Goldcroft Av. DT4: Wey 7G 103
Goldcroft Rd. DT4: Wey 6F 103
Golden Acre Holiday Bungs.
DT6: Low E 6A 38
Golden Cap Holiday Pk.
DT6: Sea 6B 36
Golden Gates BH13: Sandb 5F 99
Goldenleas Dr. BH11: Bourn 3H 81
Goldfinch Rd. BH17: Pool 6G 79
GOLD HILL 1G 19
Gold Hill DT11: Chil O 1F 19
SP7: Shaf 4B 8
Gold St. DT10: Stalb 2G 15
Golf Links Rd. BH18: B'tone 1K 79
BH22: Fern 3E 74
Goliath Rd. BH15: Hamw 5F 89
Good Rd. BH12: Pool 7G 81
Gooseberry La. BH24: Ring 4H 61
Goose Gallery 1F 5
Goose Hill DT3: Port 6F 47
Gordon Cl. BH4: Bourn 3D 92
Gordon Cres. DT4: Wey 2D 106
Gordon Mt. BH23: H'ffe 5J 97
Gordon Mt. Flats BH23: H'ffe 6H 97
Gordon Rd. BH1: Bourn 3K 93
BH12: Pool 2A 92
BH19: Swan 5H 117
BH21: Wim M 1C 72
BH23: H'ffe 6H 97

Gordon Rd. Sth.—Hampshire Ct.

Gordon Rd. Sth. BH12: Pool 2A **92**
Gordon Row DT4: Wey 2H **107**
Gordon Way BH23: Burt 5A **86**
Gore Cross Bus. Pk. DT6: Bradp 1E **38**
Gore Cross Way DT6: Bradp 1F **39**
Gore Flds. La. BH16: Hol H 1B **112**
Gore Hill BH20: Sandf 6A **112**
Gore La. DT6: Bradp 1F **39**
DT7: Uply 5A **34**
DT9: N Com, Stall 2J **11**
Gore Rd. BH25: N Mil 4K **97**
Gore Ter. DT6: Bradp 1G **39**
Gorey Rd. BH12: Pool 5H **81**
Gorleston Rd. BH12: Pool 2K **91**
Gorley Rd. BH24: Poul 3K **61**
Gorsecliff Ct. BH5: Bourn 3K **93**
Gorsecliff Rd. BH10: Bourn 5D **82**
Gorse Cl. BH24: S Leo 7K **59**
Gorse Hill Cl. BH15: Pool 2C **90**
Gorse Hill Cres. BH15: Pool 2C **90**
Gorse Hill Rd. BH15: Pool 2C **90**
Gorse Knoll Dr. BH31: Ver 3E **54**
Gorseland Ct. BH22: W Par 2D **74**
Gorselands Cvn. Pk. DT2: W Bex . . .4B **46**
Gorse La. BH16: Upt 7E **78**
Gorse Rd. BH21: Corf M 1E **78**
Gort Rd. BH11: Bourn 3B **82**
BH17: Pool 5J **79**
Gosling Cl. BH17: Pool 6D **80**
Goss Pl. DT4: Wey 7G **103**
Gotts Cnr. DT10: S New 5C **16**
Gough Cres. BH17: Pool 5K **79**
Goughs Cl. DT10: S New 5B **16**
Gould's Hill DT3: Upw 3E **100**
Goulds Hill Cl. DT3: Upw 3E **100**
Gouzeaucourt Rd. BH20: Bov 1A **110**
Gover Cl. BH20: Rid 6K **113**
Governors La. DT4: Wey 2J **107**
Gower Rd. SP7: Shaf 4D **8**
Grace Darling Ho. BH15: Pool 6D **120**
Gracie Ct. BH10: Bourn 1D **82**
Gracie M. BH10: Bourn 1D **82**
Grafton Av. DT4: S'hill 5E **102**
Grafton Cl. BH3: Bourn 7G **83**
BH23: Chris 1B **96**
Grafton Rd. BH3: Bourn 1G **93**
Grammar School La.
BH21: Wim M 1K **71**
Granby Cl. DT4: Wey 1D **106**
Granby Ct. DT4: Wey 7D **102**
Granby Ind. Est. DT4: Wey 7C **102**
(not continuous)
Granby Rd. BH9: Bourn 2G **83**
Granby Way DT4: Wey 6E **102**
Grand Av. BH6: Bourn 3E **94**
Grand Marine Ct.
BH2: Bourn 7F **121** (5D **92**)
Grand Pde. BH10: Bourn 7C **74**
BH15: Pool 6A **120**
GRANGE .2B **64**
Grange BH21: Wim M 2A **64**
Grange Ct. BH1: Bourn 4H **93**
Grangecroft Rd. DT5: West 2G **119**
GRANGE ESTATE 4B **68**
Grange Gdns. BH12: Pool 7J **81**
Grange La. DT8: Burs, Hurs 6F **23**
Grange Pk. DT9: T'ford 1J **13**
Grange Rd. BH6: Bourn 4F **95**
BH18: B'tone 2J **79**
BH20: Stob 7H **113**
BH23: Chris 7F **87**
BH24: S Leo 2K **67**
DT4: Wey 6J **103**
Grange Rd. Bus Cen.
BH23: Chris 7E **86**
Grangewood Hall BH21: Wim M 7B **64**
Grantham Rd. BH1: Bourn 2A **94**
Grantley Rd. BH5: Bourn 3B **94**
Grants Av. BH1: Bourn 1K **93**
Grants Cl. BH1: Bourn 1K **93**
Grants Hill DT9: Brad A 7H **11**
Granville Gdns. SP7: Shaf 3C **8**
Granville Pl. BH1: Bourn 4J **121**
Granville Rd. BH5: Bourn 2C **94**
BH12: Pool 2F **91**
DT4: Wey 2G **107**
Granville Way DT9: Sher 2D **12**
Grasmere Cl. BH23: Chris 3F **85**
DT3: Rad 4F **103**
Grasmere Rd. BH5: Bourn 3C **94**
BH13: Sandb 5F **99**
DT3: Rad 5G **103**
Gravel Hill BH17: Pool 4A **80**
BH21: Merl 1B **80**
Gravel La. BH24: Ring 4H **61**
(not continuous)
DT11: Char M 1A **32**
Gravel Pits DT9: Sher 5C **12**
Gray Cl. BH17: Pool 6D **80**
Graycot Cl. BH10: Bourn 1C **82**
Grays DT4: S'hill 5F **103**
Grays Cl. SP7: Mot 4C **6**
Grayson Ct. BH22: Fern 1E **74**
Gray's Yd. BH15: Pool 6B **120**
Gt. Cranford St. DT1: Poun 3A **50**
Gt. Down La. DT10: Marn, Tod 2K **9**
Gt. George St. DT4: Wey 1H **107**
Gt. Ground SP7: Shaf 2D **8**
Great Ho. Wlk. SP8: Gill 3H **5**
Great La. SP7: Shaf 4C **8**
Gt. Ovens Dr. BH20: W'ham 1G **113**
Gt. Western Ct. DT1: Dor 4E **50**
Gt. Western Ind. Est. DT1: Dor 4E **50**
Gt. Western Rd. DT1: Dor 4F **51**
Gt. Western Ter. DT4: Wey 5H **103**
Greaves Cl. BH10: Bourn 3C **82**
Grebe Cl. BH17: Pool 6G **79**
BH23: Mude 1E **96**
DT3: Chick 6B **102**
Green, The BH4: Bourn 2C **92**
BH19: Stud 4J **115**
DT2: Pud 2C **52**
DT2: Strat 4B **48**
DT8: Bea 3D **24**
DT9: Sher 4C **12**
DT10: K'ton 2D **28**
Greenacre DT2: C'ster 6J **49**
Green Acre Cvn. Site BH23: Chris . .7D **86**
Greenacre Cl. BH16: Upt 1E **88**
Greenacres BH13: Pool 4A **92**
DT2: Pud 1B **52**
Green Acres Cl. BH24: Ash 6F **61**
Greenacres Cl. BH10: Bourn 7E **74**
Greenbanks SP8: Gill 5G **5**
Green Bottom BH21: Coleh 5E **64**
Green Cl. BH15: Pool 6D **120** (6B **90**)
BH20: Ber 3H **53**
DT6: Bradp 2F **39**
DT10: S New 4D **16**
DT11: Char M 3B **32**
SP5: Six H 2C **20**
Greenclose La. BH21: Wim M 7B **64**
Green Dr. SP6: Ald 6K **21**
Greenfield Rd. BH15: Pool 1C **90**
DT11: Char M 3B **32**
Greenfields BH12: Pool 6K **81**
Greenfinch Cl. BH17: Pool 5H **79**
Greenford La. DT2: Toll 7G **41**
Greenford Vw. DT2: Toll 6G **41**
Green Gdns.
BH15: Pool 6D **120** (6B **90**)
(not continuous)
GREENHAM 3A **22** (3B **122**)
Greenham La. DT8: Drim 3A **22**
TA18: Green 3A **22**
Greenham Yd. TA18: Green 3A **22**
Greenhayes BH18: B'tone 4A **80**
DT6: C'outh 7G **35**
DT11: O Fitz 6B **18**
Greenhayes Ri. BH21: Wim M 7A **64**
Greenhill DT4: Wey 7J **103**
DT9: Sher 4C **12**
DT11: B For 3C **30**
Greenhill Cl. BH21: Coleh 6B **64**
Greenhill Ct. DT4: Wey 5J **103**
Greenhill La. BH21: Coleh 6B **64**
Greenhill Rd. BH21: Coleh 6B **64**
Greenhill Ter. DT5: Fort 4B **118**
Greenings Ct. DT1: Dor 3F **51**
Green La. BH10: Bourn 2C **82**
BH21: S Mar 5F **33**
BH22: L'ham 4A **74**
BH24: Crow 1K **69**
BH24: Ring 4J **61**
DT2: Cros 1H **109**
DT3: Chick 6C **102**
DT4: Wey 4G **107**
DT6: Both 5E **38**
DT6: Wald 3G **39**
DT8: Hurs 6F **23**
DT9: Folk 1C **14**
DT9: T'ford 3K **13**
SP8: K Mag 6B **4**
Green Loaning BH23: Mude 2D **96**
Green Pk. BH1: Bourn 4K **93**
Green Pit Knapp DT6: C'outh 4J **35**
Green Pleck SP8: E Sto 2H **7**
Green Rd. BH9: Bourn 6G **83**
BH15: Pool 5C **120** (5A **90**)
Greens Cross Dr. DT8: Bea 3B **24**
Greensleeves Av. BH18: B'tone 7K **71**
Greensome Dr. BH22: Fern 6F **67**
GREEN, THE 1B **124**
Greenway DT7: L Reg 5B **34**
DT11: Chil O 2G **19**
Greenway Cl. DT3: Red 3G **103**
Greenway Cres. BH16: Upt 7C **78**
Greenway La. DT10: H Mary 1B **16**
DT11: Chil O 2F **19**
Greenway Rd. DT3: Red 2G **103**
Greenways BH23: H'ffe 6K **87**
DT5: East 2H **119**
Greenways Av. BH8: Bourn 3J **83**
Greenways Ct. BH22: Fern 2E **74**
Greenwood Av. BH14: Pool 6G **91**
BH22: Fern 6D **66**
Greenwood Copse BH24: S Ive 7B **60**
Greenwood Ho. DT2: Char D 2H **49**
Greenwood Rd. BH9: Bourn 5E **82**
Greenwood Way BH24: S Ive 7C **60**
Grenfell Rd. BH9: Bourn 3F **83**
Grenville Ct. BH4: Bourn 3D **92**
BH15: Pool 5C **120** (5A **90**)
Grenville Rd. BH21: Wim M 1B **72**
Gresham Ct. DT6: Brid 3C **38**
Gresham Rd. BH9: Bourn 5G **83**
Greville Ct. DT2: Char D 2J **49**
Greycot Cl. BH21: T Leg 3E **58**
Greyhound Yd. DT2: Syd N 6C **42**
GREYLAKE 1A **122**
Grey School Pas. DT1: Dor 3F **51**
Greystoke Av. BH11: Bourn 1K **81**
Greystones Cl. DT2: Cros 1H **109**
Greywell BH23: Hurn 6D **76**
GRIBB 5B **22**
Gribb Vw. TA20: T'ombe 6B **22**
Griffin Ct. BH21: Wim M 2B **72**
Griffiths Gdns. BH10: Bourn 1B **82**
Grimsey La. SP8: Silt . . . . . . .4B **4** & 4D **A**
GRIMSTONE 3A **48** (1D **127**)
Grosvenor Cl. BH24: Ash H 6K **59**
Grosvenor Ct. BH1: Bourn 3K **93**
Grosvenor Cres. DT1: Dor 5F **51**
Grosvenor Gdns. BH1: Bourn 3A **94**
Grosvenor Rd. BH4: Bourn 4C **92**
BH19: Swan 6K **117**
DT1: Dor 5F **51**
DT4: Wey 6H **103**
DT5: East 1H **119**
DT10: Stalb 2H **15**
SP7: Shaf 2C **8**
GROVE 7E **118** (3A **128**)
Grove, The BH9: Bourn 3F **83**
BH22: Fern 1C **74**
BH23: Chris 5G **85**
BH31: Ver 5G **55**
DT1: Dor 2E **50**
DT3: B'wey 7F **101**
DT5: East 7E **118**
DT9: Sher 5C **12**
DT11: M And 7B **44**
Grove Av. DT4: Wey 5H **103**
Grove Ct. DT1: Dor 2E **50**
Grove Farm Mdw. Cvn. Pk.
BH23: Chris 4F **85**
Grove Flds. DT5: East 7D **118**
Grove Hill DT3: Osm 3H **105**
Grove La. DT3: Abb 6D **46**
DT6: Wald 4H **39**
DT10: Stalb 2G **15**
Grove La. Cl. DT10: Stalb 2G **15**
Groveley Bus. Cen. BH23: Chris 1C **96**
Groveley Rd. BH4: Bourn 5B **92**
BH23: Chris 1C **96**
Grovely Av. BH5: Bourn 3B **94**
Grove Orchard DT6: Burt B 6H **37**
Grove Point DT5: East 7E **118**
Grove Rd. BH1: Bourn 5K **121** (4G **93**)
BH12: Pool 1F **91**
BH21: Wim M 1B **72**
DT5: East 7C **118**
DT6: Burt B 6H **37**
Grove Rd. E. BH23: Chris 6J **85**
Grove Rd. W. BH23: Chris 6H **85**
Grove Ter. DT4: Wey 1F **107**
Grove Trad. Est. DT1: Dor 2E **50**
Grower Gdns. BH11: Bourn 2A **82**
Grugs La. BH21: Cran 2G **21**
Gryphon Leisure Cen. 1C **12**
Guernsey Rd. BH12: Pool 5H **81**
Guernsey St. DT5: Fort 5B **118**
Guest Av. BH12: Pool 1K **91**
Guest Cl. BH12: Pool 1A **92**
Guest Rd. BH16: Upt 7D **78**
Guildhall Ct.
BH15: Pool 5A **120** (5K **89**)
Guildhall Mus. 5A **120** (5K **89**)
Guildhill Rd. BH6: Bourn 3G **95**
Gulliver Cl. BH14: Pool 7G **91**
Gulliver Ct. BH21: Wim M 7A **64**
Gullivers Orchard DT6: Ship G 6K **39**
Gully BH19: Swan 5E **116**
Gundry La. DT6: Brid 4C **38**
Gundrymoor Trad. Est.
BH21: W Moo 5E **58**
Gundry Rd. DT6: Both 3F **39**
Gunn La. DT11: Shil 6F **19**
Gunville Cres. BH9: Bourn 3H **83**
Gunville Down Rd. DT11: B Cam . . .3K **31**
Gunville Rd. DT11: B Cam 3K **31**
Gurjun Cl. BH16: Upt 6C **78**
Gurney Rd. BH21: Corf M 7G **71**
GUSSAGE ALL SAINTS 2D **125**
Gussage Rd. BH12: Pool 6J **81**
GUSSAGE ST ANDREW 2C **125**
GUSSAGE ST MICHAEL 2C **125**
Guy's Cl. BH24: Ring 4K **61**
GUY'S MARSH 1B **124**
Gwenlyn Rd. BH16: Upt 1E **88**
Gwynne Rd. BH12: Pool 2J **91**
Gyllas Way SP8: Gill 2H **5**
Gypshayes BH19: Lan M 5C **116**
Gypsy La. BH24: Ring 3K **61**
DT4: Wey 2G **107**
DT5: West 2H **119**

H

Haarlem M. BH23: Chris 7B **86**
Hackney DT2: Cors 7F **25**
Hadden Rd. BH8: Bourn 6K **83**
Haddons Dr. BH21: T Leg 4D **58**
Haddons Farm Cvn. & Camping Site
BH21: T Leg 4D **58**
Hadley Way BH18: B'tone 3G **79**
Hadow Rd. BH10: Bourn 3C **82**
Hadrian Cl. BH22: W Par 3D **74**
Hadrian Way BH21: Corf M 5G **71**
Hahnemann Rd.
BH2: Bourn 6F **121** (5E **92**)
Haig Av. BH13: Pool 6J **91**
Haimes La. SP7: Shaf 3B **8**
Hainault Dr. BH31: Ver 4G **55**
Hains La. DT10: Marn 2G **9**
Haking Rd. BH23: Chris 7B **86**
HALE 1A **130**
Halebrose Ct. BH6: Bourn 4G **95**
Halewood Way BH23: Chris 6H **85**
Haley Ct. DT4: Wey 2F **107**
Halfacre La. DT8: Bea 3B **24**
Half Acres DT9: Sher 5B **12**
Half Moon St. DT9: Sher 5C **12**
Halifax Way BH23: Chris 7F **87**
Hall & Woodhouse Brewery 6C **30**
Hallett Ct. DT7: L Reg 4C **34**
Hall Rd. BH11: Bourn 3K **81**
HALSTOCK 2H **25** (3C **123**)
Halstock Cl. DT3: Pres 4C **104**
Halstock Cres. BH17: Pool 4B **80**
Halter Path BH15: Hamw 4G **89**
(not continuous)
Halter Ri. BH21: Coleh 6G **65**
Halves Cotts. BH20: Corf C 4B **114**
HAM
Chard .2A **122**
Gillingham 5K **5**
Taunton 1A **122**
Hambledon Cl. DT10: Tod 7J **7**
DT11: B For 4D **30**
Hambledon Gdns. BH6: Bourn 1E **94**
DT11: B For 4D **30**
Hambledon Hill Nature Reserve 3J **19**
Hambledon Rd. BH6: Bourn 1E **94**
BH7: Bourn 7D **84**
Hambledon Row *DT11: Shil* *6F 19*
(off Blandford Rd.)
Hambledon Vw. DT10: S New 4D **16**
Hamble Rd. BH15: Pool 7D **80**
Hamblin Way BH8: Bourn 4A **84**
HAMBRIDGE 1A **122**
Hambro Rd. DT5: Fort 5B **118**
Hambro Ter. DT3: Pres 3C **104**
HAM COMMON 6J **5** (1B **124**)
Ham Common Nature Reserve 5D **88**
Ham Ct. SP8: Gill 6K **5**
Hamcroft DT5: East 1H **119**
Hamilton Cl. BH1: Bourn 2K **93**
BH15: Hamw 5G **89**
BH23: Mude 3D **96**
DT3: Lit 1J **103**
Hamilton Ct. BH8: Bourn 2H **93**
Hamilton Cres. BH15: Hamw 5G **89**
Hamilton Rd. BH1: Bourn 2K **93**
BH15: Hamw 5G **89**
BH21: Corf M 1G **79**
Ham La. BH21: Hamp, L Can 1H **73**
BH21: Hay 1F **73**
BH22: L'ham 1H **73**
DT10: Marn 2F **9**
DT10: S New 6C **16**
SP8: Gill 5K **5**
HAMLET 5A **14**
Ham Mdw. DT10: Marn 2F **9**
Hammett Cl. DT2: Tolp 6B **52**
Hammond Av. DT4: S'hill 5E **102**
Hammonds Mead DT6: C'outh 7H **35**
HAMMOON 2B **124**
Hampden La. BH6: Bourn 2D **94**
HAMPRESTON 3K **73** (1D **129**)
Hampreston Rd. BH22: L'ham 3A **74**
Hampshire Cl. BH23: Chris 4H **85**
Hampshire Ct.
BH2: Bourn 4H **121** (4E **92**)

Hampshire Hatches La.—Hibberd Ct.

Hampshire Hatches La.
BH24: Ring 1H 69
Hampshire Ho. BH2: Bourn 4H 121
Hampshire Rd. DT4: Wey 7D 102
HAMPTON 1A 126
Hampton DT3: Port 5G 47
Hampton Ct. BH2: Bourn 3D 92
Hampton Dr. BH24: Poul 2K 61
Hamptons, The DT9: Sher 5A 12
HAMPTWORTH 1B 130
Hams DT8: Bea 3C 24
HAMWORTHY 4G 89 (1C 129)
Hamworthy Lodge BH15: Hamw 5H 89
Hamworthy Sports Club 5F 73
Hamworthy Station (Rail) 3F 89
Hanbury Rd. BH19: Swan 5H 117
Handborough Cvn. Pk.
DT4: Wey 1C 106
HANDLEY COMMON 1A 20
Handley Ct. BH24: Ring 4H 61
Handley Pk. SP5: Six H 2C 20
Hands La. DT3: Abb 5D 46
HANFORD 5K 19 (2B 124)
HANGERSLEY 2A 130
Hanham Rd. BH21: Corf M 1F 79
BH21: Wim M 7A 64
Hankinson Rd. BH9: Bourn 6G 83
Hanlon Cl. BH11: Bourn 2A 82
Hannah's La. DT3: Abb 5C 46
Hannam's Cl. BH16: L Mat 6H 53
Hannington Pl. BH7: Bourn 2C 94
Hannington Rd. BH7: Bourn 2C 94
Hanover Cl. DT10: S New 4C 16
Hanover Ct. *DT6: Both* *4E 38*
(off Lwr. Walditch La.)
DT8: Bea 3C 24
DT11: B For 4B 30
Hanover Grn. BH17: Pool 6D 80
Hanover Ho. BH15: Pool 3E 120 (4B 90)
Hanover La. SP8: Gill 5F 5
Hanover Rd. DT4: Wey 6H 103
HAPPY BOTTOM 4H 71
Happy Island Way DT6: Brid 3F 39
Harbeck Rd. BH8: Bourn 3J 83
Harbour Cl. BH13: Sandb 2C 120
Harbour Ct. BH15: Pool 4B 120 (5A 90)
Harbour Cres. BH23: Chris 2C 96
Harbour Ga. BH15: Pool 2C 120 (4A 90)
Harbour Hill DT3: Chick 3D 102
Harbour Hill Cres. BH15: Pool 2C 90
Harbour Hill Rd. BH15: Pool 3C 90
Harbour Life Mus. 1H 37
Harbour Prospect BH14: Pool 7G 91
Harbour Rd. BH6: Bourn 4J 95
DT9: Sher 3D 12
Harbour Vw. Cl. BH14: Pool 2E 90
Harbour Vw. Ct. BH23: Chris 2K 95
Harbour Vw. Rd. BH14: Pool 2E 90
DT5: Fort 4B 118
Harbour Watch BH14: Pool 1G 99
Harbour Way DT9: Sher 3D 12
HARBRIDGE 1A 130
HARCOMBE BOTTOM 1A 126
Harcombe Cl. BH17: Pool 3C 80
Harcombe Rd. DT7: H Bot 1B 34
Harcourt Rd. BH5: Bourn 2C 94
Harding's Ho. La. DT9: Sher 2A 12
Harding's La. SP8: Gill 5J 5
HARDINGTON MANDEVILLE 2C 123
HARDINGTON MARSH 3C 123
HARDINGTON MOOR 2C 123
HARDWAY 1A 124
Hardwick St. DT4: Wey 7H 103
Hardy Av. *DT1: Dor* *3G 51*
(off Kings Rd.)
DT1: Dor 3G 51
(River Cres.)
DT4: Wey 2F 107
Hardy Cl. BH22: W Moo 3F 67
DT2: Mart 3J 47
DT8: Bea 3E 24
DT10: Marn 3J 9
Hardy Cres. BH21: Wim M 2B 72
DT10: Stalb 2H 15
Hardye Arc. *DT1: Dor* *3F 51*
(off South St.)
DT1: Dor 4F 51
(Charles St.)
Hardy Monument 2D 127
Hardy Rd. BH14: Pool 3H 91
BH20: W'ham 5G 113
BH22: W Moo 3F 67
DT6: Brid 3E 38
Hardy's Cottage 1A 128
Hardy's Cottage Garden 1A 128
Hardy's Row DT2: W Knig 4D 108
Hares Grn. BH7: Bourn 6C 84
Hare's La. DT2: Swy 2B 46
Harewood Av. BH7: Bourn 7B 84
Harewood Cres. BH7: Bourn 7B 84
Harewood Gdns. BH7: Bourn 7B 84
Harewood Pl. BH7: Bourn 1D 94
DT11: B For 5B 30
Harewood Rd. DT1: Poun 4B 50
Harford Rd. BH12: Pool 6G 81
Harkwood Dr. BH15: Hamw 3G 89
Harland Rd. BH6: Bourn 3J 95
Harleston Vs. BH21: Wim M 1B 72
HARMAN'S CROSS 1A 116 (2C 129)
Harman's Cross Roads
BH20: H Cro 2A 116
Harman's Cross Station
Swanage Railway 2A 116
Harmony Ter. BH19: Stud 5K 115
Harness Cl. BH21: Coleh 6F 65
Harpitts La. SP8: K Mag 6D 4
Harpway La. BH23: Sop 1A 86
Harraby Grn. BH18: B'tone 3J 79
Harrier Dr. BH21: Merl 3B 72
Harriers Cl. BH23: Chris 6H 87
Harrison Av. BH1: Bourn 1K 93
Harrison Cl. BH23: Burt 3A 86
Harrison Way BH22: W Moo 1E 66
Harry Barrows Cl. BH24: Ring 5J 61
Harting Rd. BH6: Bourn 7F 85
Hartlebury Ter. *DT4: Wey* *2H 107*
(off Franchise St.)
Hartmoor Gdns. BH10: Bourn 5D 82
Hartnell Ct. BH21: Corf M 1F 79
Hartsbourne Dr. BH7: Bourn 6D 84
Hart's Farm Camping & Cvn. Site
BH21: Hort 1K 57
Hart's La. BH21: Bro H, Holt 7D 56
DT9: Stall 1K 11
Hartwell Rd. BH17: Pool 7B 80
Harvey Rd. BH5: Bourn 2C 94
BH21: Merl 5C 72
(not continuous)
Harveys Cl. DT2: M New 6J 41
Harveys Ter. *DT1: Dor* *3G 51*
(off Holloway Rd.)
Harwell Rd. BH17: Pool 7B 80
Hascombe Ct. *DT1: Dor* *4F 51*
(off Somerleigh Rd.)
HASELBURY PLUCKNETT 2B 122
Haskells Rd. BH12: Pool 7F 81
Haslemere Av. BH23: H'ffe 6K 87
Haslemere Pl. BH23: H'ffe 5H 97
Hasler Rd. BH17: Pool 4A 80
Haslop Rd. BH21: Coleh 5E 64
Hastings Rd. BH8: Bourn 4B 84
BH17: Pool 4K 79
HATCH BEAUCHAMP 1A 122
HATCH GREEN 2A 122
Hatch Pond Rd. BH17: Pool 6A 80
Hatfield Gdns. BH7: Bourn 6D 84
Hathaway Rd. BH6: Bourn 3F 95
Hatherden Av. BH14: Pool 2D 90
Havelins DT11: Stour 1G 29
Havelock Rd. BH12: Pool 2A 92
Havelock Way BH23: Chris 4H 87
Haven, The BH19: Swan 5K 117
Haven Ct. BH13: Sandb 5F 99
BH19: Swan 2J 117
Haven Rd. BH13: Sandb 2H 99
BH21: Corf M 7E 70
Haverstock Rd. BH9: Bourn 4H 83
Haviland Ct. BH7: Bourn 2B 94
Haviland M. BH7: Bourn 2B 94
Haviland Rd. BH1: Bourn 3B 94
BH7: Bourn 2B 94
BH21: Stap 5A 66
Haviland Rd. E. BH7: Bourn 2B 94
Hawden Rd. BH11: Bourn 5A 82
HAWKCHURCH 3A 122
Hawkchurch Gdns. BH17: Pool 4C 80
Hawk Cl. BH21: Coleh 5E 64
Hawkcombe La. SP7: C Abb, Twy 2A 10
Hawker Cl. BH21: Merl 4D 72
Hawkers Cl. DT11: B For 3D 30
Hawkesdene SP7: Shaf 5C 8
Hawkesdene La. SP7: Shaf 4C 8
Hawkesworth Cl. DT3: Pres 3B 104
Hawkins Rd. BH12: Pool 5K 81
Hawkwood Rd. BH5: Bourn 3A 94
Haworth Cl. BH23: Chris 5J 85
Hawthorn Av. SP8: Gill 4G 5
Hawthorn Cl. DT1: Dor 3E 50
DT4: S'hill 5E 102
SP7: Shaf 2D 8
Hawthorn Dr. BH17: Pool 5H 79
Hawthorn Flats DT1: Dor 3D 50
Hawthorn Rd. BH9: Bourn 6F 83
BH23: Bock 1C 86
DT1: Dor 3D 50
DT2: Char D 2H 49
Hawthorns, The BH23: Chris 1D 96
DT10: Stalb 3J 15
Haycock Way BH21: S Mar 6H 33
Haycombe DT11: Dur 4G 29
Haycrafts Cvn. & Camping Pk.
BH19: H Cro 3A 116
Haycrafts La. BH19: H Cro 5A 116
HAYDON
Sherborne 2D 123
Taunton 1A 122
Haydon Rd. BH13: Pool 6B 92
Haye Cl. DT7: L Reg 4B 34
Haye La. DT7: L Reg 3B 34
HAYES 1F 73
Hayes, The DT8: B'sor 6H 23
Hayes Av. BH7: Bourn 1A 94
Hayes Cl. BH21: Hay 1E 72
Hayes Ct. DT7: L Reg 5C 34
Hayesend Drove DT2: Cer A 2A 42
Hayes La. BH21: Coleh, Hay 1F 73
Hayes Mead SP7: Mot 4D 6
Hayeswood Rd. BH21: Coleh 6E 64
Haylands DT5: East 2H 119
Haylands Cl. DT1: Poun 4B 50
Haymoor Cl. DT3: Over 3K 103
Haymoor Rd. BH15: Pool 7D 80
Haynes Av. BH15: Pool 1D 120 (3B 90)
Hayters Way SP6: Ald 6J 21
Hayward Cres. BH31: Ver 5E 54
Hayward La. DT11: Chil O 3E 18
Hayward's Av. DT3: Rad 4H 103
Haywards Farm Cl. BH31: Ver 5E 54
Haywards La. BH21: Corf M 5E 70
DT11: Chil O 3G 19
Hayward Way BH31: Ver 5D 54
HAZELBURY BRYAN 4B 28 (3A 124)
Hazel Cl. BH23: Chris 5G 87
SP6: Ald 7J 21
Hazeldene BH18: B'tone 2J 79
Hazeldown Av. DT3: Over 3K 103
Hazel Dr. BH22: Fern 4C 66
DT3: Pres 4B 104
Hazel La. DT2: Pun 1C 46
Hazell Av. BH10: Bourn 4B 82
Hazelton Cl. BH7: Bourn 6C 84
Hazelwood Dr. BH31: Ver 6H 55
Hazlebury Rd. BH17: Pool 7J 79
Hazlemere Dr. BH24: S Leo 1A 68
Headland Cl. DT5: S'well 4G 119
Headlands Adventure Cen. 2J 61
Headlands Bus. Pk. BH24: Blas 1J 61
Headland Warren DT1: Poun 3B 50
Head La. SP8: E Sto 1J 7
Headlinglea BH13: Pool 4B 92
Heads Farm Cl. BH10: Bourn 1E 82
Heads La. BH10: Bourn 1E 82
Headswell Av. BH10: Bourn 2E 82
Headswell Cres. BH10: Bourn 2E 82
Headswell Gdns. BH10: Bourn 1E 82
Heanor Cl. BH10: Bourn 4C 82
Heath Av. BH15: Pool 1B 90
Heath Cl. BH20: Bov 1A 110
BH21: Coleh 5F 65
Heathcote Cl. DT1: Dor 4G 51
Heathcote Ho. BH5: Bourn 4A 94
Heathcote Rd. BH5: Bourn 3B 94
Heatherbank Rd. BH4: Bourn 4C 92
Heatherbrae La. BH16: Upt 1D 88
Heather Cl. BH8: Bourn 2K 83
BH19: Swan 5H 117
BH21: Corf M 7G 71
BH23: Walk 5H 97
BH24: S Leo 1A 68
Heatherdell BH16: Upt 1D 88
Heatherdown Rd. BH22: W Moo 3G 67
Heatherdown Way BH22: W Moo 3G 67
Heather Dr. BH22: Fern 5D 66
Heather Flds. SP8: Gill 2H 5
Heather Grange BH24: Ash H 6A 60
Heatherlands Ri. BH12: Pool 2H 91
Heatherlea Rd. BH6: Bourn 3F 95
Heather Rd. BH10: Bourn 3D 82
Heatherside BH19: Stud 4J 115
Heather Vw. Rd. BH12: Pool 7K 81
Heather Way BH22: Fern 5D 66
Heath Farm Cl. BH22: Fern 2C 74
Heath Farm Rd. BH22: Fern 2C 74
Heath Farm Way BH22: Fern 2C 74
Heathfield Av. BH12: Pool 6A 82
Heathfield Rd. BH22: W Moo 3F 67
Heathfields Way SP7: Shaf 2C 8
Heathfield Way BH22: W Moo 3F 67
Heath Grn. Rd. BH19: Stud 5H 115
Heathland Cl. DT2: Cros 2H 109
Heathlands Av. BH22: W Par 3D 74
Heathlands Cl. BH23: Burt 3A 86
BH31: Ver 4G 55
Heath Rd. BH23: Walk 5J 97
BH24: S Leo 7K 59
Heath Rd. E. BH23: Hurn 1B 76
Heath Rd. W. BH24: Matc 6A 68
HEATHSTOCK 3A 122
Heathwood Rd. BH9: Bourn 6E 82
DT4: Wey 7F 103
Heaton Rd. BH10: Bourn 4B 82
Heavland La. SP8: E Sto 1H 7
Heavytree Rd. BH14: Pool 3F 91
Heckford La.
BH15: Pool 2D 120 (4B 90)
Heckford Rd.
BH15: Pool 1D 120 (3B 90)
BH21: Corf M 1E 78
Hectors Way DT11: Blan 7B 30
Heddington Dr. DT11: B For 3B 30
HEDGING 1A 122
Heights App. BH16: Upt 7E 78
Heights Rd. BH16: Upt 6E 78
Helen La. DT4: Wey 2J 107
Helic Ho. BH21: Wim M 7A 64
HELLAND 1A 122
Hell La. DT6: Chid, N Chid 2B 36
Helston Cl. DT3: Port 5G 47
Helyar Rd. BH8: Bourn 4B 84
Hembury Rd. DT6: Ask 6E 40
Hemlet's Cl. DT6: Bradp 1F 39
HEMSWORTH 3C 125
Henbest Cl. BH21: Hay 7G 65
HENBURY 3A 70
Henbury Cl. BH17: Pool 4E 80
BH21: Corf M 7F 71
Henbury Ho. Gdns. BH21: S Mar 4A 70
Henbury Ri. BH21: Corf M 7F 71
Henbury Vw. Rd. BH21: Corf M 7E 70
Henchard Cl. BH22: Fern 3C 74
Henchard Ct. DT1: Dor 3E 50
Henchard Ho. DT1: Dor 3D 50
Hendford Gdns. BH10: Bourn 4D 82
Hendford Rd. BH10: Bourn 4D 82
Hendrie Cl. BH19: Swan 4G 117
Hengistbury Head Nature Reserve
5D 96
Hengistbury Rd. BH6: Bourn 3H 95
Hengist Pk. BH6: Bourn 3K 95
Hengist Rd. BH1: Bourn 3K 93
HENLADE 1A 122
HENLEY
Dorchester 7H 27 (3D 123)
Langport 1B 122
Henley Council Ho's. DT2: Hen 7H 27
Henley Gdns. BH7: Bourn 7C 84
Hennings Pk. Rd. BH15: Pool 2B 90
Henry Cl. DT4: Wey 4G 107
Henry's Way DT7: L Reg 4D 34
HENSTRIDGE 2A 124
HENSTRIDGE ASH 1A 124
HENSTRIDGE BOWDEN 1D 123
HENSTRIDGE MARSH 1A 124
Henville Rd. BH8: Bourn 2J 93
Hepburn Ct. *BH23: Chris* *1H 95*
(off Kings Av.)
Herbert Av. BH12: Pool 6G 81
Herbert Ct. BH12: Pool 6H 81
Herberton Rd. BH6: Bourn 2E 94
Herbert Pl. DT4: Wey 2H 107
Herbert Rd. BH4: Bourn 5B 92
Herbury La. DT9: Chet 4A 14
Hercules Rd. BH15: Hamw 4F 89
Hereford Ct. BH23: Chris 1H 95
Hereford Cres. DT4: Wey 1E 106
Hereford Rd. DT4: Wey 1E 106
HERMITAGE 3D 123
Hermitage Cl. BH21: T Leg 3E 58
Hermitage Ct. DT1: Poun 4B 50
Hermitage Rd. BH14: Pool 1E 90
Herm Rd. BH12: Pool 5H 81
Heron Cl. DT3: Chick 6B 102
DT3: Over 6B 104
Heron Ct. DT4: Wey 7H 103
DT6: W Bay 2H 37
Heron Ct. Rd. BH3: Bourn 7G 83
BH9: Bourn 7G 83
Heron Dr. BH21: Coleh 5E 64
Herons Mead BH8: Bourn 1K 83
Herringston Rd. DT1: Dor 7E 50
DT2: Dor, W Her 7E 50
Herrison Ho. DT2: Char D 2H 49
Herrison Rd. DT2: Char D 3H 49
HERSTON 5G 117 (3D 129)
Herston Cvn. & Camp Site
BH19: Swan 3G 117
Herston Cross BH19: Swan 4G 117
Herstone Cl. BH17: Pool 5D 80
Herston Halt Station
Swanage Railway 4G 117
Herston Yards Farm Camping Site
BH19: Swan 3F 117
Hesketh Cl. BH24: S Ive 6C 60
Hessary Pl. DT1: Poun 4B 50
Hessary St. DT1: Poun 4B 50
Hestan Cl. BH23: Chris 2F 85
Heston Way BH22: W Moo 1D 66
Hetherly Rd. DT3: Rad 4G 103
HEWISH 3B 122
Hewitt Rd. BH15: Hamw 3G 89
Hexworthy Ct. DT1: Poun 3A 50
Heysham Rd. BH18: B'tone 3J 79
Heytesbury Rd. BH6: Bourn 1F 95
Hibberd Ct. BH10: Bourn 5D 82

Hibberds Fld.—Honeysuckle Cl.

Hibberds Fld. BH21: Cran . . . 2H 21
Hibberd Way BH10: Bourn . . . 5D 82
Hibbs Cl. BH16: Upt . . . 7E 78
BH20: W'ham . . . 2H 113
Hibernia Cl. DT6: Brid . . . 2C 38
Hickes Cl. BH11: Bourn . . . 2K 81
Hickory Cl. BH16: Upt . . . 6C 78
Highacres DT6: Lod . . . 1K 39
Highbridge Rd. BH14: Pool . . . 4G 91
HIGHCLIFFE . . . 6H 97 (3B 130)
Highcliffe Castle . . . 7J 87
Highcliffe Cnr. BH23: H'ffe . . . 6J 97
Highcliffe Rd. BH19: Swan . . . 3K 117
BH23: Chris . . . 6E 86
Highcliff Rd. DT7: L Reg . . . 5B 34
High Cl. BH21: S Mar . . . 5J 33
Highdown DT3: Over . . . 3K 103
Highdown Av. DT1: Poun . . . 4C 50
High East St. DT1: Dor . . . 3F 51
HIGHER ANSTY . . . 3A 124
Higher Blandford Rd.
BH18: B'tone . . . 7H 71
BH21: Corf M . . . 6G 71
SP7: Can, Shaf . . . 5D 8
HIGHER BOCKHAMPTON . . . 1A 128
Higher Cheap St. DT9: Sher . . . 4C 12
Higher Day's Rd. BH19: Swan . . . 5F 117
Higher Drove DT2: Chilf . . . 3F 41
Higher End DT3: Chick . . . 6A 102
Higher Eype Rd. DT6: Low E . . . 5A 38
Higher Filbank BH20: Corf C . . . 4B 114
HIGHER FROME VAUCHURCH . . . 5G 41
Higher Gdns. BH20: Corf C . . . 3B 114
Higher Grn. DT8: Bea . . . 2E 24
HIGHER HALSTOCK LEIGH . . . 3C 123
HIGHER KINGCOMBE . . . 1C 127
Higher La. DT5: Fort . . . 4A 118
HIGHER MELCOMBE . . . 3A 124
Higher Merley La. BH21: Corf M . . . 5G 71
HIGHER ROW . . . 6H 57
Higher Sea La. DT6: C'outh . . . 7H 35
Higher Shaftesbury Rd.
DT11: B For . . . 1C 30
Higher St. DT6: Bradp . . . 1G 39
DT11: I Min . . . 2J 17
DT11: O Fitz . . . 6B 18
Higher Westbury DT9: Brad A . . . 7G 11
HIGHER WHATCOMBE . . . 3B 124
Higher Wood BH20: Bov . . . 2B 110
HIGHER WRAXALL . . . 3C 123
Highfield Av. BH24: Ring . . . 3J 61
Highfield Cl. BH21: Corf M . . . 1G 79
DT2: C'ster . . . 5H 49
Highfield Dr. BH24: Ring . . . 2J 61
Highfield Gdns. DT6: Neth . . . 7B 24
Highfield Rd. BH9: Bourn . . . 4E 82
BH21: Corf M . . . 2G 79
BH22: W Moo . . . 7D 58
BH24: Ring . . . 3J 61
Highfields DT11: B For . . . 4D 30
Highford La. DT2: M Osm . . . 3A 26
Highgate La. DT2: W Knig . . . 4D 108
High Glebe DT11: I Min . . . 3J 17
Highgrove SP8: Gill . . . 2H 5
Highgrove Cl. DT1: Dor . . . 5G 51
HIGH HAM . . . 1B 122
High Howe Cl. BH11: Bourn . . . 2J 81
High Howe Gdns. BH11: Bourn . . . 2J 81
High Howe La. BH11: Bourn . . . 2J 81
Highland Av. BH23: H'ffe . . . 5J 97
Highland Rd. BH14: Pool . . . 2F 91
BH21: Coleh, Wim M . . . 6B 64
DT4: Wey . . . 1G 107
HIGHLANDS . . . 6A 38
Highlands Cres. BH10: Bourn . . . 2C 82
Highlands End Farm Holiday Pk.
DT6: Low E . . . 7A 38
Highland Vw. Cl. BH21: Wim M . . . 7B 64
High Mead BH22: L'ham . . . 3A 74
High Mead La. BH22: L'ham . . . 4A 74
Highmoor Cl. BH14: Pool . . . 4F 91
BH21: Corf M . . . 1F 79
Highmoor Rd. BH11: Bourn . . . 5A 82
BH14: Pool . . . 4G 91
BH21: Corf M . . . 1F 79
Highmore Rd. DT9: Sher . . . 3B 12
High Oaks Gdns. BH11: Bourn . . . 2J 81
High Pk. Rd. BH18: B'tone . . . 2G 79
High Pines BH23: Chris . . . 7H 87
High Point BH14: Pool . . . 3G 91
High St. BH15: Pool . . . 6A 120 (6K 89)
(not continuous)
BH16: L Mat . . . 5F 53
BH19: Lan M . . . 5B 116
BH19: Swan . . . 5E 116
BH20: Wool . . . 6E 110
BH21: Cran . . . 2G 21
BH21: S Mar . . . 6H 33
BH21: Wim M . . . 7K 63
BH23: Chris . . . 1K 95
BH24: Ash H . . . 5A 60
High St. BH24: Ring . . . 4H 61
DT1: Dor . . . 3G 51
DT2: Cors . . . 5G 25
DT2: P'ton, P'hide . . . 6J 43
DT2: Pud . . . 2C 52
DT2: Syd N . . . 7C 42
DT2: T Por . . . 3B 40
DT2: W New . . . 4G 111
DT4: W Reg . . . 4E 106
DT5: Fort . . . 5B 118
DT5: S'well . . . 5H 119
DT6: Burt B . . . 7H 37
DT8: B'sor . . . 6H 23
DT9: Yet . . . 7G 13
DT10: Stalb . . . 1G 15
DT11: Chil O . . . 2G 19
DT11: S'bury . . . 5C 32
SP5: Six H . . . 2C 20
SP7: Shaf . . . 3B 8
SP8: Bour . . . 2D 4
SP8: Gill . . . 4H 5
TA20: T'ombe . . . 7B 22
High St. Cl. BH20: Wool . . . 6D 110
High St. Nth.
BH15: Pool . . . 3D 120 (4B 90)
Hightown Gdns. BH24: Ring . . . 5K 61
Hightown Ind. Est.
BH24: Ring . . . 5K 61
Hightown Rd. BH24: Ring . . . 5J 61
High Trees BH13: Pool . . . 7A 92
DT2: Broad . . . 7D 108
Hightrees Av. BH8: Bourn . . . 5A 84
High Trees Wlk. BH22: Fern . . . 5D 66
Highview Cl. BH23: Chris . . . 3G 85
Highview Gdns. BH12: Pool . . . 7G 81
High Way BH18: B'tone . . . 3H 79
High W. St. DT1: Dor . . . 3E 50
DT4: Wey . . . 2H 107
Highwood Cl. SP6: Ald . . . 6F 21
Highwood Rd. BH14: Pool . . . 3J 91
Hilary Rd. BH17: Pool . . . 5A 80
Hilcot Way DT11: B For . . . 3C 30
Hilda Rd. BH12: Pool . . . 1J 91
Hiley Rd. BH15: Pool . . . 1A 90
HILFIELD . . . 3D 123
Hillary Rd. BH23: Chris . . . 6C 86
HILLBOURNE . . . 4H 79 (1D 129)
Hillbourne Cl. DT4: W Reg . . . 5F 107
Hillbourne Rd. BH17: Pool . . . 4J 79
DT4: W Reg . . . 5F 107
Hillbrook Ct. DT9: Sher . . . 4B 12
Hill Brow DT9: Sher . . . 6A 12
Hillbrow Rd. BH6: Bourn . . . 1D 94
Hillbury Pk. SP6: Ald . . . 7J 21
Hillbury Rd. SP6: Ald . . . 6J 21
HILLBUTTS . . . 6H 63 (3C 125)
Hill Cl. DT6: W Bay . . . 1G 37
Hillcrest BH19: Swan . . . 6K 117
Hillcrest Av. BH22: Fern . . . 4C 66
Hillcrest Cl. BH9: Bourn . . . 3G 83
DT10: New . . . 7A 16
Hillcrest Rd. BH9: Bourn . . . 3G 83
BH12: Pool . . . 2E 90
BH21: Corf M . . . 1E 78
DT4: Wey . . . 5G 107
Hillfield Cl. DT3: Upw . . . 6F 101
Hillfort Cl. DT1: Dor . . . 6D 50
Hillfort M. *DT1: Dor . . . 6D 50*
(off Hillfort Cl.)
Hill Ho. Cl. DT9: Sher . . . 3D 12
Hillingdon DT6: Brid . . . 2E 38
Hilling La. DT2: Buck N, Hen . . . 6G 27
Hill La. BH23: Water . . . 4C 86
DT4: Wey . . . 2J 107
Hillman Rd. BH14: Pool . . . 2H 91
Hill Mdw. BH31: Ver . . . 6G 55
Hill Ri. DT6: W Bay . . . 1G 37
Hill Ri. Rd. DT7: L Reg . . . 5C 34
Hill Rd. BH19: Swan . . . 2J 117
BH24: Matc . . . 6C 68
DT7: L Reg . . . 5C 34
DT11: B For . . . 2D 30
Hillsea Rd. BH19: Swan . . . 5H 117
Hillside Dr. BH23: Chris . . . 2F 85
Hillside Gdns. BH21: Corf M . . . 2E 78
Hillside M. BH21: Corf M . . . 2E 78
Hillside Rd. BH12: Pool . . . 5K 81
BH20: Wool . . . 7C 110
BH21: Corf M . . . 2E 78
BH21: Woodl . . . 4A 54
BH31: Ver . . . 3F 55
DT11: B Cam . . . 4J 31
Hillside Ter. DT1: Dor . . . 4G 51
Hillside Wlk.
BH21: Woodl . . . 4A 54
Hill St. BH15: Pool . . . 5B 120 (5A 90)
Hill Ter. BH21: Merl . . . 3E 72
Hilltop Cl. BH22: Fern . . . 5B 66
Hilltop Rd. BH21: Corf M . . . 1G 79
BH22: Fern . . . 5B 66
HILL VIEW . . . 1F 79 (1C 129)
Hill Vw. DT2: C'ster . . . 6G 49
DT2: M New . . . 7J 41
DT3: Osm . . . 4G 105
DT6: Bradp . . . 1F 39
DT9: Bis C . . . 6G 15
DT10: K'ton . . . 3D 28
Hillview Est. DT6: Brid . . . 2C 38
Hill Vw. Rd. BH19: Swan . . . 5H 117
BH22: Fern . . . 5C 66
Hillview Rd. BH10: Bourn . . . 2D 82
Hill Way BH24: Ash H . . . 6B 60
Hillyard Ct. *BH20: W'ham . . . 4H 113*
(off Mill La.)
Hilmar Dr. SP8: Gill . . . 4G 5
Hiltom Rd. BH24: Ring . . . 4K 61
HILTON . . . 3A 124
Hilton Cl. BH15: Pool . . . 1E 90
Hinchcliffe Cl. BH15: Hamw . . . 5H 89
Hinchcliffe Rd. BH15: Hamw . . . 5H 89
HINDON . . . 1C 125
Hine Cl. SP8: Gill . . . 6K 5
HINE TOWN . . . 5F 19
Hine Town La. DT11: Shil . . . 5F 19
Hingsdon La. DT6: Neth . . . 7A 24
Hintock St. DT1: Poun . . . 4C 50
HINTON . . . 3K 87 (3B 130)
Hinton Admiral M. BH23: Hin . . . 4J 87
Hinton Admiral Station (Rail) . . . 4J 87
Hinton Cl. DT11: B For . . . 3C 30
Hinton La. DT2: Syd N . . . 7C 42
DT10: H Mary . . . 7K 9 & 1D 16
HINTON MARTELL . . . 2A 56 (3D 125)
Hinton Rd. BH1: Bourn . . . 5J 121 (4F 93)
HINTON ST GEORGE . . . 2B 122
HINTON ST MARY . . . 1C 16 (2A 124)
Hinton Vw. DT10: S New . . . 4C 16
Hinton Wood
BH1: Bourn . . . 6K 121 (5G 93)
Hinton Wood Av. BH23: Chris . . . 4J 87
Hinton Wood La. BH23: Hin . . . 4J 87
Hive Cl. DT6: Burt B . . . 7J 37
Hive Gdns. BH13: Sandb . . . 2H 99
Hobbs Pk. BH24: S Leo . . . 7B 60
Hobbs Rd. BH12: Pool . . . 6G 81
Hobgoblin DT11: I Min . . . 3J 17
Hoburne Cvn. Pk. BH23: Chris . . . 6G 87
Hoburne Gdns. BH23: Chris . . . 5G 87
Hoburne La. BH23: Chris . . . 5G 87
Hoburne Pk. BH19: Swan . . . 6H 117
Hoburne Rd. BH19: Swan . . . 5H 117
Hoburne Rdbt. BH23: Chris . . . 6F 87
Hodder's La. DT7: H Bot . . . 1B 34
Hod Dr. DT11: Stour . . . 1F 29
Hodges Cl. BH17: Pool . . . 7C 80
Hod Vw. DT11: Stour . . . 1H 29
Hodway La. DT11: Shil . . . 7J 19
Hogarth Way BH8: Bourn . . . 4C 84
Hogshill Mead DT8: Bea . . . 3C 24
Hogshill St. DT8: Bea . . . 3C 24
HOGSTOCK . . . 3C 125
Hogue Av. BH10: Bourn . . . 1D 82
Holbaek Cl. DT1: Dor . . . 6G 51
Holbury Cl. BH8: Bourn . . . 3A 84
Holcombe Cl. DT3: Pres . . . 4D 104
Holcombe Rd. BH16: Upt . . . 1D 88
HOLDENHURST . . . 3D 84
Holdenhurst Av. BH7: Bourn . . . 1E 94
Holdenhurst Rd. BH8: Bourn . . . 4H 93
(Landsdowne Cres.)
BH8: Bourn . . . 3B 84
(Throop Rd.)
HOLDITCH . . . 3A 122
Hole Ho. La. DT10: New . . . 7B 16
Holes Bay Nth. Rdbt. BH17: Pool . . . 1J 89
Holes Bay Pk.
BH15: Pool . . . 1A 120 (3K 89)
Holes Bay Rd.
BH15: Pool . . . 1A 120 (1K 89)
Holes Bay Rdbt. BH15: Pool . . . 1K 89
HOLFLEET . . . 1B 86
Holland Rd. DT4: Wey . . . 1G 107
Hollands Cl. BH20: Corf C . . . 3A 114
Hollands Ho. DT1: Dor . . . 3E 50
Hollands Mead Av.
DT2: Ower . . . 6J 109
Holland Way BH18: B'tone . . . 1H 79
DT11: B For . . . 3C 30
Holland Way Ind. Est.
DT11: B For . . . 2C 30
Hollenden BH12: Pool . . . 3A 92
Hollis Cl. BA22: Hal . . . 2J 25
HOLLIS HILL . . . 6H 23
Hollis Way BA22: Hal . . . 2J 25
Hollow, The DT11: Chil O . . . 1G 19
SP5: Six H . . . 2C 20
Holloway Av. BH11: Bourn . . . 1K 81
Holloway La. DT11: Shil . . . 6G 19
Holloway Rd. DT1: Dor . . . 3G 51
Hollow Hill DT2: Stin . . . 2K 51
Hollow Oak Rd. BH20: Stob . . . 6H 113
Hollow Way DT6: Both . . . 6D 38
Holly Cl. BH16: Upt . . . 7C 78
BH20: Sandf . . . 5B 112
BH22: W Moo . . . 2D 66
BH24: S Leo . . . 7K 59
DT1: Dor . . . 3C 50
Holly Ct. BH2: Bourn . . . 4D 92
BH15: Pool . . . 1E 120 (3B 90)
BH22: W Moo . . . 2D 66
DT3: Rad . . . 5H 103
Holly Gdns. BH23: Burt . . . 5B 86
Holly Grn. Ri. BH11: Bourn . . . 2J 81
Holly Gro. BH31: Ver . . . 5D 54
Holly Hedge La. BH17: Pool . . . 6A 80
Holly La. BH21: Cow . . . 7F 63
BH23: Walk . . . 4K 97
DT8: Drim . . . 2C 22
Holly Lodge BH13: Pool . . . 3A 92
Hollymoor Cl. DT8: Bea . . . 3E 24
Hollymoor Comn. La. DT8: Bea . . . 3E 24
Hollymoor Gdns. DT8: Bea . . . 3E 24
Hollymoor La. DT8: Bea . . . 3E 24
Holly Rd. DT4: Wey . . . 1G 107
Holmead Wlk. DT1: Poun . . . 4C 50
HOLMEBRIDGE . . . 2B 128
Holme Cl. DT3: Red . . . 3F 103
Holme Rd. BH20: Stob . . . 7F 113
BH23: H'ffe . . . 6J 97
Holmes Place
Corfe Mullen . . . 6F 71
Holmes Rd. BH19: Swan . . . 5F 117
Holmfield Av. BH7: Bourn . . . 7E 84
Holmhurst Av. BH23: H'ffe . . . 5J 87
Holmlea DT11: B For . . . 3D 30
Holm Oak Cl. BH31: Ver . . . 3E 54
HOLMWOOD . . . 3B 74
Holnest Rd. BH17: Pool . . . 5B 80
HOLT . . . 7D 56 (3D 125)
Holt Forest Nature Reserve . . . 4F 57
HOLT HEATH . . . 5K 57 (3D 125)
Holt Ho. BH1: Bourn . . . 2K 93
Holt La. BH21: Holt . . . 1C 64
DT2: M Osm . . . 1B 26
DT9: Bis C . . . 4G 15
HOLTON . . . 1D 123
HOLTON HEATH . . . 3C 112 (1C 129)
Holton Heath Nature Reserve . . . 3E 112
Holton Heath Pk. BH16: Hol H . . . 2D 112
Holton Heath Station (Rail) . . . 5E 112
Holton Heath Trading Pk.
BH16: Hol H . . . 4E 112
Holton Rd. BH16: Hol H . . . 4E 112
Holt Rd. BH12: Pool . . . 1K 91
BH20: Bov . . . 1A 110
BH21: Holt . . . 6E 56
BH21: Mann, T Leg . . . 5A 58
HOLT WOOD . . . 2E 56
HOLWAY . . . 5D 22
Holway La. DT2: Ever . . . 6A 26
HOLWELL . . . 2F 27 (2A 124)
Holwell Drove DT9: Holw . . . 2F 27
Holwell Rd. DT10: K Stag . . . 2J 27
HOLWORTH . . . 2A 128
Holworth Cl. BH11: Bourn . . . 3J 81
Holyrood Cl. BH17: Pool . . . 6J 79
Holyrood Ter. DT4: Wey . . . 1G 107
HOLYWELL . . . 3C 123
Holywell Cl. BH17: Pool . . . 3B 80
Homedale Ho.
BH2: Bourn . . . 1J 121 (2F 93)
Homedene Ho.
BH15: Pool . . . 3E 120 (4B 90)
Home Farm DT11: I Min . . . 2J 17
Home Farm Cvn. & Camp Site
DT2: Pun . . . 2D 46
Home Farm Cl. DT6: Uplo . . . 5A 40
Home Farm Rd. BH31: Ver . . . 4E 54
Home Farm Way BH31: Ver . . . 4E 54
DT6: Ship G . . . 7K 39
Home Farris Ho. SP7: Shaf . . . 3B 8
Homefield DT11: Chil O . . . 2G 19
DT11: M And . . . 7C 44
SP7: Shaf . . . 2C 8
Homelake Ho. BH14: Pool . . . 4F 91
Homelands Est. BH23: Chris . . . 1H 95
Homelands Ho. BH22: Fern . . . 7D 66
Homeleigh Ho. BH8: Bourn . . . 2G 93
Homemead DT10: K'ton . . . 2C 28
Homeoaks Ho.
BH2: Bourn . . . 1J 121 (2F 93)
Home Rd. BH11: Bourn . . . 7B 74
Homeside Rd. BH9: Bourn . . . 4G 83
Homeview Ho.
BH15: Pool . . . 3E 120 (4B 90)
HOMINGTON . . . 1D 125
Honeybourne Cres. BH6: Bourn . . . 3J 95
Honeybrook Farm Pk. . . . 2K 63
Honeybun Mdw. DT10: H Bry . . . 3B 28
Honeycombe Ri. DT9: Sher . . . 6A 12
Honeyfields SP8: Gill . . . 2H 5
Honeymead La. DT10: S New . . . 4C 16
Honeysuckle Cl. DT3: Lit . . . 1K 103

Honeysuckle Gdns.—Kernella Ct.

Honeysuckle Gdns. DT11: Shil 6F 19
Honeysuckle La. BH17: Pool 5H 79
Honeysuckle Way BH23: Chris 6F 87
Hood Cl. BH10: Bourn 5B 82
Hood Cres. BH10: Bourn 5B 82
HOOKE 3C 123
Hooke Cl. BH17: Pool 4E 80
Hook Farm Camping and Cvn. Pk.
DT7: Uply 4A 34
Hoopers La. DT2: Pun 2D 46
Hop Cl. BH16: Upt 7B 78
Hope Bottom DT8: Bea 6C 24
Hope Cl. DT2: Cros 2H 109
Hopegood Cl. DT11: Char M 3B 32
Hope Sq. DT4: Wey 2J 107
Hope St. DT4: Wey 2J 107
Hope St. Sth. DT4: Wey 2J 107
Hope Ter. DT2: Mart 3J 47
Hopkins Cl. BH8: Bourn 4C 84
Hopmans Cl. BH16: L Mat 5F 53
Hopsfield DT11: M And 6B 44
Horace Rd. BH5: Bourn 3A 94
HORDLE 3B 130
Hornbeam Cl. DT4: S'hill 5F 103
Hornbeam Rd. DT2: Char D 1H 49
Hornbeam Sq.
BH15: Pool 5E 120 (5B 90)
Hornbeam Way BH21: Coleh 7C 64
HORNBLOTTON GREEN 1C 123
Horn Hill Vw. DT8: Bea 2B 24
Horning Rd. BH12: Pool 2K 91
Horsa Cl. BH6: Bourn 3G 95
Horsa Ct. BH6: Bourn 3G 95
Horsa Rd. BH6: Bourn 3G 95
Horsecastles DT9: Sher 5B 12
Horsecastles La. DT9: Sher 4A 12
(not continuous)
Horsefields SP8: Gill 2H 5
Horseponds SP7: Shaf 3A 8
Horsepool La. DT9: T'ford 3J 13
Horseshoe, The BH13: Sandb 4G 99
Horseshoe Cl. BH21: Coleh 6F 65
Horseshoe Comn. Rdbt.
BH1: Bourn 4J 121
Horseshoe Ct.
BH1: Bourn 3J 121 (3F 93)
Horseshoe Rd. TA20: T'ombe 4A 22
Horsey Knap DT2: Ever 6A 26
Horsford St. DT4: Wey 3J 107
Horsham Av. BH10: Bourn 7C 74
HORSINGTON 1A 124
HORTON
Ilminster 2A 122
Wimborne 1D 56 (3D 125)
Horton Cl. BH9: Bourn 3J 83
HORTON CROSS 2A 122
HORTON HEATH 2A 58
HORTON HOLLOW 1D 56
Horton Rd. BH21: T Leg 2B 58
BH21: Woodl 7B 20
BH24: Ash, Ash H 5J 59
Horton Way BH31: Ver 5D 54
Horyford Cl. DT3: Pres 4C 104
Hosey Rd. DT10: S New 3D 16
Hosier's La. BH15: Pool . . 6A 120 (6K 89)
Hosker Rd. BH5: Bourn 2D 94
Hospital La. DT6: Brid 2B 38
DT9: Sher 4C 12
Houlton Rd. BH15: Pool 3C 90
HOUND HILL 5H 63
Houndsell Way DT6: Brid 3B 38
Hound St. DT9: Sher 4C 12
Hounds Way BH21: Hay 7F 65
Hounslow Cl. BH15: Hamw 5H 89
Howard Cl. BH23: Mude 1D 96
DT4: Wey 5G 107
DT6: Both 3F 39
Howard Rd. BH8: Bourn 7J 83
BH19: Swan 5H 117
BH31: Ver 4F 55
(not continuous)
DT6: Both 4F 39
Howard's La. BH20: W'ham 4H 113
Howarth Cl. DT6: Burt B 6H 37
Howe Cl. BH23: Mude 2D 96
Howe La. BH31: Ver 5E 54
Howell Ho. BH21: Coleh 5D 64
Howeth Cl. BH10: Bourn 3D 82
Howeth Rd. BH10: Bourn 4C 82
HOWLEY 3A 122
Howton Cl. BH10: Bourn 1C 82
Howton Rd. BH10: Bourn 1C 82
Hoxley Rd. BH10: Bourn 2D 82
Hoyal Rd. BH15: Hamw 4F 89
Hudson Cl. BH12: Pool 4G 81
Hughs Bus. Cen. BH23: Chris 7E 86
HUISH 7C 42
HUISH EPISCOPI 1B 122
Hull Cres. BH11: Bourn 2H 81
Hull Rd. BH11: Bourn 2H 81
Hull Way BH11: Bourn 2J 81
Humber Chase BH20: W'ham 2F 113
Humber Rd. BH22: Fern 6G 67
Humphrey's Bri. BH23: Chris 7G 87
HUNGERFORD 1A 130
Hungerford Rd. BH8: Bourn 3K 83
Hunger Hill BH15: Pool 4B 120
Hunter Cl. BH21: Coleh 6G 65
BH23: Chris 7E 86
Hunters Cl. BH31: Ver 5J 55
Hunters Lodge *DT1: Dor 4G 51*
(off Linden Av.)
Hunters Mead SP7: Mot 3C 6
Huntfield Rd. BH9: Bourn 3H 83
HUNTHAM 1A 122
Huntick Est. BH16: L Mat 6H 53
Huntick Farm Cvn. Site
BH16: L Mat 7K 53
Huntick Rd. BH16: L Mat, L Min . . . 6H 53
Huntingdon Dr. BH21: Merl 4C 72
Huntingdon Gdns. BH23: Chris 4J 85
HUNTINGFORD 1B 124
Huntley Down DT11: M And 5B 44
Huntly Rd. BH3: Bourn 1D 92
Hunt Rd. BH15: Pool 3C 90
BH23: Chris 6C 86
DT11: B For 3D 30
Hunt's Hill DT10: Tod 7K 7
Hunts Mead DT9: Sher 6A 12
HUNTSTILE 1A 122
Huntvale Rd. BH9: Bourn 3H 83
HURCOTT
Ilminster 2A 122
Somerton 1C 123
Hurdles, The BH23: Chris 6G 85
HURN 6D 76 (3A 130)
Hurn Bridge Sports Club 6D 76
Hurn Cl. BH24: Ash 5F 61
Hurn Ct. BH23: Hurn 2C 84
Hurn Ct. La. BH23: Hurn 7B 76
Hurn La. BH24: Ash 5F 61
Hurn Rd. BH23: Chris 2F 85
BH24: Ash, Matc 3E 68
Hurn Way BH23: Chris 5F 85
Hurricane Cl. DT2: Cros 1H 109
HURSEY 6G 23 (3B 122)
Hursley Cl. BH7: Bourn 6E 84
Hurst DT8: Bea 1C 24
Hurstbourne Av. BH23: Chris 5J 87
Hurst Cl. BH23: Walk 4K 97
BH25: N Mil 6K 97
Hurstdene Rd. BH8: Bourn 4J 83
Hurst Hill BH14: Pool 7G 91
Hurst Rd. BH24: Ring 2J 61
Hussar Cl. BH23: Chris 7H 85
Hussey's DT10: Marn 5G 9
Hutchins Cl. DT1: Dor 6D 50
Hyacinth Cl. BH17: Pool 5H 79
Hybris Bus. Pk. DT2: Cros 2H 109
HYDE 4F 39
Hyde, The BH19: Lan M 5C 116
Hyde Gdns. DT11: P'erne 3G 31
Hyde Pl. BH20: Wool 6D 110
Hyde Rd. BH10: Bourn 1C 82
BH20: Wool 6D 110
SP8: Gill 3G 5
Hylands Farm DT2: Buck N 6G 27
Hynesbury Rd. BH23: F Clif 1G 97
Hythe, The DT3: Chick 6B 102
Hythe Rd. BH15: Pool 7E 80

I

IBBERTON 3A 124
Ibbertson Cl. BH8: Bourn 4B 84
Ibbertson Rd. BH8: Bourn 5B 84
Ibbertson Way BH8: Bourn 4B 84
Ibbett Rd. BH10: Bourn 4C 82
IBSLEY 2A 130
Ibsley Cl. BH8: Bourn 1J 93
Icen La. DT3: Upw 6G 101
DT6: Ship G . . . . 7K 39 & 7D 40
Icen Rd. DT3: Rad 4G 103
Icen Way DT1: Dor 3F 51
Iddesleigh Rd. BH3: Bourn 1F 93
IFORD 7E 84
Iford Bri. Home Pk. BH6: Bourn . . . 7F 85
Iford Cl. BH6: Bourn 1G 95
Iford Gdns. BH7: Bourn 7E 84
Iford La. BH6: Bourn 7F 85
Iford Rdbt. BH7: Bourn 7E 84
Iford Sports Complex 6F 85
ILCHESTER 1C 123
Ilchester Rd. DT4: Wey 1G 107
ILFORD 2A 122
ILMINSTER 2A 122
Ilminster Rd. BH19: Swan 4J 117
ILSINGTON 1A 128
ILTON 2A 122
Imax Cinema
Bournemouth 6J 121 (5F 93)
Imber Dr. BH23: H'ffe 6K 87
Imber Rd. SP7: Shaf 3D 8
Imbre Ct. BH13: Pool 1J 99
Incledon Ct. *BH19: Swan 4J 117*
(off Cranborne Rd.)
Incline Rd. DT5: Cast, East 3D 118
Inglesham Way BH15: Hamw 3G 89
Inglewood Av. BH8: Bourn 5B 84
Ingram Wlk. BH21: Wim M 1B 72
Ingworth Rd. BH12: Pool 2A 92
Inmosthay DT5: East 6C 118
Inner Breakwater Rd. DT5: Cast . . . 3D 118
Innes Ct. DT10: S New 5C 16
Insley Cres. BH18: B'tone 1G 79
Institute Rd. BH19: Swan 5K 117
Inveravon BH23: Mude 2D 96
Inverclyde Rd. BH14: Pool 3F 91
Inverleigh Rd. BH6: Bourn 1E 94
Inverness Rd. BH13: Pool 1J 99
Ipswich Rd. BH4: Bourn 3B 92
BH12: Pool 3B 92
Iris Gdns. SP8: Gill 5G 5
Iris Rd. BH9: Bourn 5F 83
Irvine Way BH23: Chris 6C 86
Irving La. BH6: Bourn 2F 95
Irving Rd. BH6: Bourn 3E 94
Isaacs Cl. BH12: Pool 7B 82
Isambard Ct. *DT1: Dor 4E 50*
(off Damer's Rd.)
Island Vw. BH25: N Mil 7K 97
Island Vw. Av. BH23: F Clif 1F 97
Island Vw. Rd. BH25: N Mil 7K 97
ISLE ABBOTTS 1A 122
ISLE BREWERS 1A 122
Isle of Wight Rd. BH19: Swan . . . 7K 117
Isle Rd. DT5: West 2G 119
Ivamy Pl. BH11: Bourn 4K 81
Ivel Cl. DT1: Dor 5G 51
Ivor Rd. BH15: Hamw 6J 89
BH21: Corf M 2F 79
Ivy Cl. BH24: S Leo 7K 59
SP8: Gill 4F 5
IVY CROSS 3C 8
Ivy Ho. BH2: Bourn 4D 92
Ivy La. BH24: Blas, Rock 1J 61
Ivy Rd. BH21: Merl 5B 72
Iwerne Cl. BH9: Bourn 2H 83
IWERNE COURTNEY 6G 17 (2B 124)
IWERNE MINSTER 3J 17 (2B 124)

J

Jacklin Ct. BH18: B'tone 1K 79
Jackson Gdns. BH12: Pool 1G 91
Jackson Rd. BH12: Pool 1G 91
Jacobean Cl. BH23: Walk 5J 97
Jacobs Ladder DT11: Chil O 2G 19
Jacobs Rd. BH15: Hamw 5G 89
Jacqueline Rd. BH12: Pool 7F 81
James Cl. DT1: Dor 5D 50
DT11: B For 4E 30
James Day Mead BH19: Swan 2J 117
Jameson Rd. BH9: Bourn 5E 82
James Rd. BH12: Pool 2A 92
DT1: Dor 5D 50
James St. DT4: Wey 2H 107
Jamie Ct. BH16: Upt 7F 79
Jarvis Cl. DT10: Stalb 3H 15
Jarvis Way DT10: Stalb 2H 15
Jasmine Way DT4: W Reg 3D 106
Jays Ct. BH23: H'ffe 6J 97
Jay Wlk. SP8: Gill 6K 5
Jeanneau Cl. SP7: Shaf 3C 8
Jefferson Av. BH1: Bourn 1K 93
Jellicoe Cl. BH14: Pool 2D 90
Jellicoe Dr. BH23: Mude 1D 96
Jellicoe Theatre 2D 90
Jenner Cl. BH31: Ver 3E 54
Jenner Ct. DT4: Wey 1H 107
Jenner Way DT3: Lit 7H 101
Jennings Rd. BH14: Pool 5G 91
Jennys La. BH16: L Mat 5F 53
Jephcote Rd. BH11: Bourn 2K 81
Jeremy Cl. BH20: Wool 6E 110
Jersey Cl. BH12: Pool 5H 81
Jersey Rd. BH12: Pool 5H 81
Jesmond Av. BH23: H'ffe 6K 87
Jessica Av. BH31: Ver 3D 54
Jessop Cl. SP8: Gill 5G 5
Jessop Ho. BH21: Wim M 7A 64
Jessopp Av. DT6: Brid 3E 38
Jessopp Cl. BH10: Bourn 2F 83
Jessopp Rd. BH21: Coleh 6F 65
Jesty's Av. DT3: Upw 6G 101
Jewell Rd. BH8: Bourn 5B 84
Jimmy Brown Av. BH22: W Moo . . . 6E 58
John Shoobridge Ct. *SP7: Shaf 3B 8*
(off Beleke St.)
Johnson Rd. BH21: Stap 5A 66
Johnsons Courtyard DT9: Sher 5C 12
Johns Rd. BH20: W'ham 2G 113
Johnstone Rd. BH23: Chris 1C 96
Johnston Rd. BH15: Pool 7B 80
John St. DT4: Wey 2H 107
Jolliffe Av. BH15: Pool . . . 1E 120 (3B 90)
Jolliffe Rd. BH15: Pool . . . 1E 120 (3B 90)
Jonson Trad Pk. DT1: Dor 4H 51
Jopps Cnr. BH23: Wink 2A 86
Jordan Hill Roman Temple (remains of)
. . . . 5B 104
Jordan Way DT3: B'wey 6G 101
Joselin Ct. DT9: Sher 3C 12
Joshua Cl. BH15: Hamw 5G 89
Journeys End DT6: Brid 4C 38
Joyce Dickson Cl. BH24: Ring 5K 61
Joys Rd. BH21: T Leg 3E 58
Juan's La. SP8: K Mag 6B 4
Jubilee Cl. BH21: Corf M 6G 71
BH24: Poul 3K 61
DT4: Wey 7H 103
Jubilee Ct. DT1: Dor 3F 51
DT3: Rad 4G 103
Jubilee Cres. BH12: Pool 2H 91
Jubilee Gdns. BH10: Bourn 4D 82
BH20: Corf C 4B 114
Jubilee Path SP7: Shaf 4B 8
Jubilee Retail Pk. DT4: Wey 7H 103
Jubilee Rd. BH12: Pool 2H 91
BH19: Swan 5G 117
BH21: Corf M 6G 71
Jubilee Wlk. DT4: Wey 2J 107
Jubilee Way DT11: B For 3B 30
Julia Cl. BH23: H'ffe 6K 87
Julian's Rd. BH21: Wim M 1J 71
Julyan Av. BH12: Pool 6A 82
Jumpers Av. BH23: Chris 6G 85
JUMPERS COMMON 5G 85 (3A 130)
Jumpers Rd. BH23: Chris 6H 85
Junction Rd. BH9: Bourn 6F 83
BH16: Hamw 3E 88
Juniper Cen., The BH23: Chris 6H 85
Juniper Cl. BH21: T Leg 3E 58
BH22: Fern 4C 66
Juniper Gdns. SP8: Gill 5G 5
Juniper Way DT3: B'wey 7G 101
Jupiter Way BH21: Corf M 5G 71
(not continuous)
Justin Bus. Pk. BH20: W'ham 2H 113
Justin Gdns. BH10: Bourn 2E 82

K

Kangaw Pl. BH15: Hamw 5F 89
Katherine Chance Cl. BH23: Burt . . . 3A 86
Katterns Cl. BH23: Chris 4G 85
Kay Cl. BH23: Chris 1C 96
Kayes Cl. DT4: W Reg 4E 106
Keast Ct. DT3: Over 6A 104
Keats Mdw. BH16: L Mat 7H 53
SP5: Six H 2D 20
Keeble Cl. BH10: Bourn 7D 74
Keeble Cres. BH10: Bourn 7D 74
Keeble Rd. BH10: Bourn 7D 74
Keel Ho. BH15: Pool 3D 120
Keepers La. BH21: Stap 7J 65
Keep Military Mus., The 3E 50
Keighley Av. BH18: B'tone 4H 79
KEINTON MANDEVILLE 1C 123
Keith Rd. BH3: Bourn 1C 92
Kellaway Ct. *DT4: Wey 2J 107*
(off Barrack Rd.)
Kellaway Rd. BH17: Pool 6D 80
Kellaway Ter. DT4: Wey 1G 107
Kelly Cl. BH17: Pool 6D 80
Kemp Rd. BH9: Bourn 6F 83
Kempston Rd. DT4: Wey 3H 107
Kemp Welch Leisure Cen. 6H 81
Kendall La. SP8: Mil S 1F 5
Kenilworth DT4: S'hill 5F 103
Kenilworth Ct. BH13: Pool 7K 91
BH23: Chris 7J 85
Kenmoor Cl. DT3: Over 3K 103
Kennart Rd. BH17: Pool 7K 79
Kennel La. DT2: Catt 2G 41
Kenneth Ct. BH23: H'ffe 7J 97
Kennington Rd. BH17: Pool 6B 80
Kennington Sq. *BH20: W'ham 3H 113*
(off St Martin's La.)
Ken Rd. BH6: Bourn 3G 95
Kensington Dr. BH2: Bourn 3D 92
Kensington Wlk. DT1: Dor 5H 51
Kent Cl. DT4: Wey 1D 106
Kentisworth Rd. DT10: Marn 5G 9
Kent Rd. BH12: Pool 1J 91
Kenwyn Rd. DT6: Brid 3E 38
Kenyon Cl. BH15: Pool 7C 80
Kenyon Rd. BH15: Pool 7C 80
Keppel Cl. BH24: Ring 4K 61
Kerley Rd. BH2: Bourn 6G 121 (5E 92)
Kernella Ct. BH4: Bourn 3B 92

Lotmoor Hill—Marnhull

Lotmoor Hill SP8: E Sto 2H 7
Louise Rd. DT1: Dor 4D 50
Louse La. DT11: S'bury 7E 32
Louviers Rd. DT3: Lit 7H 101
Lovelands DT2: Cors 4G 25
Love La. DT4: Wey 2H 107
DT10: Marn 3H 9
SP7: Shaf 4A 8
Lovells Mead DT10: Marn 3G 9
LOVER 1B 130
Loves La. DT6: Morc 3H 35
LOVINGTON 1C 123
Lwr. Acreman St. DT9: Sher 5C 12
LOWER ANSTY 3A 124
LOWER BINCOMBE 3H 101
Lwr. Blakemere Rd. DT1: Poun 4B 50
Lwr. Blandford Rd. BH18: B'tone . . .3K 79
SP7: Can, Shaf 4C 8
LOWER BLANDFORD ST MARY 7D 30
LOWER BOCKHAMPTON 1A 128
LOWER BRYANSTON 6B 30
LOWER BURGATE 1A 130
Lwr. Burton Cotts. DT2: Burt 1E 50
Lwr. Catherston Rd. DT6: C'outh 5J 35
LOWER CHICKSGROVE 1C 125
Lower Common La. BH21: T Leg . . .4G 59
Lower Common Rd. DT11: Chil O . . .1F 19
Lower Cross DT10: H Mary 1B 16
LOWER EYPE 7A 38 (1B 126)
Lower Farm DT9: O Com 1G 11
LOWER FROME VAUCHURCH 7J 41
Lwr. Golf Links Rd. BH18: B'tone . . .1K 79
LOWER HALSTOCK LEIGH 3F 25
LOWER HAMWORTHY 6J 89
Lwr. Hillside Rd. BH20: Wool 7D 110
LOWER KINGCOMBE 1C 127
LOWER MANNINGTON 4B 58
LOWER NYLAND 1A 124
LOWER PARKSTONE 3D 90
Lwr. Putton La. DT3: Chick 5B 102
Lower Rd. DT2: T Por 2C 40
DT10: Stalb 2H 15
LOWER ROW 5G 57
Lwr. St Alban St. DT4: Wey 2H 107
Lwr. St Edmund St. DT4: Wey 2H 107
Lwr. School La. DT11: Blan 7B 30
Lwr. Sea La. DT6: C'outh 7H 35
Lower Steppes BH19: Lan M 5D 116
LOWER STREET 3J 45
Lower St. BH21: Wit 3H 33
DT11: O Fitz 5A 18
Lower Townsend DT6: Burt B 6H 37
Lwr. Walditch La.
DT6: Both, Wald 4E 38
Lower Way DT3: Chick 5B 102
LOWER WHATCOMBE 1H 45 (3B 124)
LOWER WRAXALL 3C 123
LOW HAM 1B 122
Lowther Gdns. BH8: Bourn 2J 93
Lowther Rd. BH8: Bourn 1G 93
Lox La. SP7: Mot 7A 6
Lubbecke Way DT1: Dor 3H 51
Lucas Rd. BH12: Pool 1G 91
BH15: Hamw 7A 120 (6K 89)
Luccombe Bus. Pk. DT11: Mil A 3E 44
Lucerne Av. BH6: Bourn 2F 95
Lucetta La. DT1: Dor 5G 51
Luckham Cl. BH9: Bourn 4H 83
Luckham Gdns. BH9: Bourn 4J 83
Luckham Pl. BH9: Bourn 4H 83
Luckham Rd. BH9: Bourn 4H 83
Luckham Rd. E. BH9: Bourn 4H 83
Ludbourne Rd. DT9: Sher 5D 12
Ludlow Rd. DT4: Wey 2D 106
LUDWELL 1C 125
Lugger Cl. DT3: Chick 5A 102
Lulworth Av. BH15: Hamw 6G 89
LULWORTH CAMP 5K 111 (2B 128)
Lulworth Castle 2B 128
Lulworth Cl. BH15: Hamw 6G 89
Lulworth Ct. BH15: Hamw 5G 89
BH19: Swan 4J 117
(off Cranborne Rd.)
Lulworth Cove 7H 111
Lulworth Cres. BH15: Hamw 6G 89
Lulworth Heritage Cen. 7G 111
Lulworth Rd. BH20: Wool 7E 110
Lumby Dr. BH24: Poul 3K 61
Lumby Dr. Mobile Home Pk.
BH24: Poul 3K 61
Lurmer St. SP7: Fon M 4C 10
Luscombe Rd. BH14: Pool 5G 91
Lush Path DT9: Sher 4D 12
Luther Rd. BH9: Bourn 6F 83
Luton Down Rd. DT11: B Cam 7J 31
Luton Drove DT11: T Raw 7K 31
Lychett La. BH20: Bov 4D 110
Lych Ga. Ct. BH24: H'own 5K 61
Lydden Va. DT10: H Bry 4B 28
LYDFORD FAIR PLACE 1C 123
Lydford Gdns. BH11: Bourn 4A 82
Lydford Rd. BH11: Bourn 4A 82
Lydfords La. SP8: Gill 4F 5
Lydgate St. DT1: Poun 3B 50
LYDLINCH 2A 124
Lydlinch Cl. BH22: W Par 4D 74
Lydwell Cl. BH11: Bourn 1K 81
DT4: Wey 4G 107
Lyell Rd. BH12: Pool 1G 91
Lym Cl. DT7: L Reg 5D 34
Lyme Cres. BH23: H'ffe 6K 87
LYME REGIS 5D 34 (1A 126)
Lyme Regis Ind. Est.
DT7: L Reg 4B 34
Lyme Regis Marine Aquarium
(& Cobb History) 6D 34
Lyme Regis Mus. 5D 34
Lyme Rd. DT7: Uply 3A 34
Lymes Cl. DT4: W Reg 4E 106
Lymington Rd. BH23: Chris 7G 87
LYMORE 3B 130
Lynch, The SP8: W Stou 1F 7
Lynch Cl. DT11: M And 6A 44
Lynch La. DT4: Wey 2C 106
Lynch Rd. DT4: Wey 2D 106
Lyndale Rd. DT4: W Reg 6F 107
Lyndhurst Rd. BH23: Bock 2D 86
BH23: Chris 6E 86
DT4: Wey 6H 103
Lynes Ct. BH24: Ring 4H 61
Lyne's La. BH24: Ring 4H 61
LYNG .1A 122
Lynmoor Rd. DT4: Wey 5J 103
Lynn Rd. BH17: Pool 6D 80
Lynton Cres. BH23: Chris 3F 85
Lynwood Cl. BH22: Fern 5D 66
Lynwood Dr. BH21: Merl 5C 72
Lyon Rd. BH12: Pool 4J 81
Lyons Ct. *SP7: Shaf 4B 8*
(off Lyons Wlk.)
LYON'S GATE 3D 123
Lyons Wlk. SP7: Shaf 4B 8
Lysander Cl. BH23: Chris 7F 87
Lystra Rd. BH9: Bourn 3G 83
Lytchett Dr. BH18: B'tone 4H 79
LYTCHETT MATRAVERS
. . . . .6H 53 (1C 129)
LYTCHETT MINSTER 1A 88 (1C 129)
Lytchett Minster & Upton By-Pass
BH16: Upt 6C 78
Lytchett Way BH16: Upt 1D 88
Lytham Rd. BH18: B'tone 3J 79
Lytton Cl. DT2: Pun 2D 46
Lytton Rd. BH1: Bourn 2J 93

M

Mabey Av. BH10: Bourn 4D 82
Macandrew Rd. BH13: Pool 1K 99
Macaulay Rd. BH18: B'tone 2J 79
McCreery Rd. DT9: Sher 2C 12
McIntyre Rd. BH23: B Int 5B 76
McKay Cl. DT4: Wey 2C 106
McKinley Rd. BH4: Bourn 5C 92
Maclaren Rd. BH9: Bourn 3F 83
Maclean Rd. BH11: Bourn 3K 81
Macville Av. BH20: Wool 7E 110
McWilliam Cl. BH12: Pool 6C 82
McWilliam Rd. BH9: Bourn 4G 83
Madeira Rd.
BH1: Bourn 3K 121 (4G 93)
BH14: Pool 2H 91
Madeline Cl. BH12: Pool 7F 81
Madeline Cres. BH12: Pool 7F 81
Madison Av. BH1: Bourn 1K 93
MADJESTON 7H 5
Maen Gdns. DT1: Dor 4G 51
Magdalene La. SP7: Shaf 4B 8
Magdalen La. BH23: Chris 1J 95
DT6: Brid 4B 38
Magiston St. DT2: Strat 4B 48
Magna Cl. BH11: Bourn 7K 73
Magna Gdns. BH11: Bourn 7K 73
Magna Rd. BH11: Bourn 5E 72
BH21: Merl 5E 72
Magnolia Cl. BH6: Bourn 2J 95
BH31: Ver 6J 55
DT3: Lit 1J 103
Magnolia Ct. BH4: Bourn 4D 92
Magnolia Dr. DT2: Char D 1H 49
Magnolia Ho. BH10: Bourn 2F 83
Magpie Cl. BH8: Bourn 3J 83
Mag's Barrow BH22: W Par 3E 74
Maiden Castle 7A 50
Maiden Castle Rd. DT1: Dor 6C 50
DT2: Dor 7A 50
MAIDENHAYNE 1A 126
MAIDEN NEWTON 6H 41 (1C 127)
Maiden Newton Station (Rail) 6H 41
Maiden St. DT4: Wey 2H 107
Maidment Cl. BH11: Bourn 2J 81
Main Rd. BH20: W Lul 7G 111
DT2: Tolp 6A 52
DT3: Osm 4G 105
DT5: Cast 3B 118
Main St. DT2: Broad 6C 108
DT6: Both 6E 38
DT6: Chid 5B 36
DT11: I Cou 6G 17
Maitlands, The BH4: Bourn 5D 92
Majorca Mans.
BH2: Bourn 4F 121 (4E 92)
Major's Comn. DT2: Buck N, Hen . . .6H 27
Malan Cl. BH17: Pool 6C 80
Malcomb Cl. BH6: Bourn 4J 95
Mallams DT5: Fort 5B 118
Mallard Cl. BH8: Bourn 5J 83
BH23: Mude 1E 96
Mallard Rd. BH8: Bourn 5K 83
BH21: Coleh 5E 64
Mallory Cl. BH23: Chris 6D 86
Mallow Cl. BH18: B'tone 3G 79
BH23: Chris 6G 87
Malmesbury Ct. BH8: Bourn 1J 93
Malmesbury Pk. Pl. BH8: Bourn 2J 93
Malmesbury Pk. Rd. BH8: Bourn . . .1G 93
Malmesbury Rd. BH24: S Leo 1A 68
Malmsbury Cl. BH23: Chris 2J 95
Maloren Way BH22: W Moo 3G 67
Malta Cl. DT1: Dor 3D 50
Malthouse BH15: Pool 5B 120 (5A 90)
Malthouse Mdw. DT3: Port 6F 47
Maltings, The BH15: Pool 4C 90
DT2: Cer A 2B 42
DT4: Wey 3J 107
DT9: Sher 4D 12
(off Long St.)
DT11: Mil A 2B 44
Malvern Cl. BH9: Bourn 3G 83
Malvern Rd. BH9: Bourn 3G 83
Malvern Ter. DT4: Wey 2F 107
Mampitts La. SP7: Shaf 4D 8
Mampitts Rd. SP7: Shaf 4D 8
Mandalay Cl. BH31: Ver 5E 54
Mandale Cl. BH11: Bourn 2A 82
Mandale Rd. BH11: Bourn 3K 81
Mandeville Cl. DT4: W Reg 4D 106
Mandeville Rd. DT4: W Reg 4C 106
Mangerton La. DT6: Bradp 1G 39
Mangerton Mill 1B 126
Manning Av. BH23: Chris 5G 87
Manningford Rd. DT11: B For 3C 30
Mannings Heath Rd. BH12: Pool 4F 81
Mannings Heath Rdbt. BH17: Pool . . .3F 81
MANNINGTON 3A 58 (3D 125)
Mannington Pl. BH2: Bourn 5F 121
Mannington Way BH22: W Moo 2D 66
Manor Av. BH12: Pool 6G 81
DT7: L Reg 4C 34
Manor Barn DT6: Both 6E 38
Manor Cl. BH22: Fern 7E 66
DT2: Strat 4C 48
DT3: Port 6G 47
DT9: Brad A 6G 11
Manor Ct. BH24: Ring 3H 61
DT9: Sher 4C 12
Mnr. Farm Cvn. & Camping Site
DT6: C'outh 5J 35
Mnr. Farm Cl. DT2: M New 6H 41
DT11: P'erne 3F 31
Mnr. Farm Ct. DT2: Mart 3K 47
Mnr. Farm Ga. SP8: W Stou 2F 7
Mnr. Farm Holiday Cen.
DT6: C'outh 6J 35
Mnr. Farm Rd. BH10: Bourn 7B 74
BH20: Ber 2H 53
Mnr. Farm Wlk. DT3: Port 6G 47
Manor Farmyard BH8: Bourn 3D 84
Manor Flds. DT6: Both 4E 38
Manor Gdns. BH19: Swan 5H 117
BH24: Ring 3H 61
BH31: Ver 4F 55
DT8: Bea 3D 24
Manor Gro. DT2: Mart 3J 47
Manor La. BH31: Ver 5F 55
DT2: Brad P 6D 48
Manor Pk. BH15: Pool 2K 89
Manor Pl. *DT5: Fort 4B 118*
(off Fortuneswell)
Manor Rd. BH1: Bourn 4H 93
BH19: Stud 4K 115
BH19: Swan 5K 117
BH23: Chris 1J 95
BH24: Ring 4J 61
BH31: Ver 4F 55
DT1: Dor 6F 51
DT3: Red 3F 103
DT11: Stour 2H 29
Manor Rdbt. DT3: Rad 3G 103
Manor Va. DT8: Most 2J 23
Manor Way BH31: Ver 3F 55
Mansel Cl. BH12: Pool 7C 82
Mansfield Av. BH14: Pool 3G 91
Mansfield Cl. BH14: Pool 3G 91
BH22: W Par 3D 74
Mansfield Rd. BH9: Bourn 5E 82
BH14: Pool 3G 91
BH24: Ring 4H 61
MANSTON 2B 124
Manston Rd. DT10: S New 4D 16
MANSWOOD 3C 125
Mantle Cl. DT5: Fort 4B 118
Manton Cl. BH15: Hamw 4G 89
Manton Rd. BH15: Hamw 4G 89
(not continuous)
Manwell Dr. BH19: Swan 6H 117
Manwell Rd. BH19: Swan 6J 117
Manwell's La. BH19: Swan 5J 117
MAPERTON 1D 123
Maple Cl. BH20: Sandf 6B 112
BH23: H'ffe 7K 87
DT3: Pres 4B 104
SP7: Shaf 2C 8
Maple Dr. BH22: Fern 4C 66
DT2: Char D 2H 49
(off Cedar Rd.)
Maple Gdns. DT6: Both 5D 38
Maple Lodge BH16: Upt 7E 78
Maple Rd. BH9: Bourn 6F 83
BH15: Pool 2D 120 (4B 90)
Maple Way SP8: Gill 5F 5
MAPPERTON
Beaminster 1C 127
Blandford Forum 1C 129
Mapperton Cl. BH17: Pool 4D 80
Mapperton Gdns. 1C 127
MAPPOWDER 7A 28 (3A 124)
Marabout Cl. BH23: Chris 7B 86
Marabout Ind. Est. DT1: Dor 2E 50
Marchwood Rd. BH10: Bourn 3C 82
Margards La. BH31: Ver 5D 54
MARGARET MARSH 2B 124
Margaret Pl. DT1: Dor 4D 50
Marian Cl. BH21: Corf M 2E 78
Marianne Rd. BH12: Pool 6C 82
BH21: Coleh 5E 64
Marian Rd. BH21: Corf M 2E 78
Marie Cl. BH12: Pool 7H 81
Marie Rd. DT1: Dor 4D 50
Marina, The BH5: Bourn 4A 94
Marina Ct. BH5: Bourn 4A 94
Marina Dr. BH14: Pool 6F 91
Marina Gdns. DT4: Wey 3G 107
Marina Towers BH5: Bourn 4A 94
Marina Vw. BH19: Swan 6K 117
BH23: Chris 2H 95
Marine Pde. DT7: L Reg 6C 34
Marine Rd. BH6: Bourn 4F 95
Mariners Dr. BH19: Swan 5H 117
Mariners Pde. DT1: Dor 3F 51
Mariners Watch BH19: Swan 3K 117
Mariners Way DT3: Chick 5B 102
Marine Ter. BH19: Stud 4J 115
Marine Theatre, The 5D 34
Marion Bradley DT10: S New 4C 16
Maritime Ho. DT5: S'well 4G 119
Market Cl. BH15: Pool 5B 120 (5A 90)
BH20: W'ham 4J 113
Market Cross DT10: S New 5C 16
Market Pl. *BH21: S Mar 5H 33*
(off Front La.)
BH24: Ring 4H 61
DT10: S New 5C 16
DT11: B For 5C 30
Markets La. DT6: Ship G 7K 39
Market St. BH15: Pool 6A 120 (6K 89)
DT3: Abb 5D 46
DT4: Wey 2J 107
Market Way BH21: Wim M 1B 72
Markham Av. BH10: Bourn 7D 74
DT4: Wey 2F 107
Markham Cl. BH10: Bourn 6D 74
Markham Rd. BH9: Bourn 6G 83
Marksmead DT8: Drim 2B 22
Marks Rd. BH9: Bourn 3F 83
Marlborough Av. DT4: W Reg 5E 106
Marlborough Ct. *BH12: Pool 3B 92*
(off Poole Rd.)
BH21: Wim M 7A 64
Marlborough Mans. BH7: Bourn 1D 94
Marlborough Pl. BH21: Wim M 7B 64
Marlborough Rd. BH4: Bourn 4C 92
BH14: Pool 3G 91
Marley Cl. DT3: Pres 3C 104
Marline Rd. BH12: Pool 1H 91
Marl La. DT9: O Com 2G 11
Marlott Rd. BH15: Pool 2A 90
SP8: Gill 2G 5
Marlow Dr. BH23: Chris 3F 85
Marlow Rd. DT4: Wey 3H 107
Marlpit Dr. BH23: Walk 4H 97
Marmion Grn. BH23: Chris 7D 86
MARNHULL 3G 9 (2A 124)

New Quay Rd.—Old Lyme Hill

New Quay Rd.
BH15: Hamw 7A 120 (6K 89)
New Rd. BA12: Zea 1E 4
BH10: Bourn 7E 74
(not continuous)
BH12: Pool 1H 91
BH16: L Min 7A 78
BH20: Bov 1A 110
BH20: Corf C 1D 114
BH20: Stob 7J 113
BH20: Wool 7C 110
BH21: Woodl 4A 54
BH22: Fern, W Par 7D 66
BH24: Ring 7J 61
DT2: Fram, M New 7K 41
DT3: Port 6G 47
DT4: Wey 2H 107
DT5: Fort 6B 118
DT6: Uplo 6A 40
DT9: Sher 6C 12
DT10: Stalb 2H 15
DT11: Bryan 5A 30
SP7: Shaf 3A 8
SP8: Gill 6J 5
Newstead Rd. BH6: Bourn 3F 95
DT4: Wey 7G 103
New St. BH15: Pool 6A 120 (6K 89)
BH20: W'ham 4H 113
BH24: Ring 5J 61
DT1: Dor 4F 51
DT2: Pud 2C 52
DT4: Wey 2J 107
DT5: East 1J 119
DT10: Marn 5H 9
New St. La. DT6: Brid, Low E 4A 38
DT6: Lod 1K 39
NEW SWANAGE 2K 117 (2D 129)
NEWTON
Salisbury 1B 130
Sturminster Newton
. . . . .7B 16 (2A 124)
Newton Cl. DT10: New 7B 16
SP8: Gill 4G 5
Newton Ct. BH19: Swan 5G 117
Newton Ga. DT10: S New 7A 16
Newton Hill DT10: New, S New 7B 16
Newton Mnr. Cl. BH19: Swan 5H 117
Newton Morrell BH14: Pool 4H 91
NEWTON PEVERIL 6F 33
Newton Ri. BH19: Swan 5H 117
Newton Rd. BH13: Pool 7J 91
BH19: Swan 6K 117
BH21: S Mar 6G 33
DT2: M New 6J 41
Newton's Rd. DT4: Wey 3J 107
NEW TOWN
Farnham 2C 125
Gillingham 7B 4
Wimborne 1K 33
NEWTOWN
Beaminster 1C 24 (3B 122)
Chard 2A 122
Lyndhurst 1B 130
Poole 7F 81 (1D 129)
Salisbury 1C 125
Wimborne 6F 71
Newtown DT8: Bea 2C 24
DT11: Char M 1A 32
Newtown Bus. Pk. BH12: Pool 7F 81
Newtown La. BH21: Corf M 6F 71
BH31: Ver 5F 55
Newtown Rd. BH31: Ver 4G 55
(not continuous)
New Zealand Ter. DT6: Brid 4D 38
Nichola Ct. BH12: Pool 7F 81
Nicholas Cl. BH23: Walk 4J 97
Nicholas Gdns. BH10: Bourn 4C 82
Nicholson Cl. BH17: Pool 6C 80
Nicholsons Cotts. DT10: H Mary 1B 16
Nightingale Cl. BH31: Ver 5G 55
Nightingale Ct. *DT4: Wey* *7J 103*
(off Victoria St.)
DT11: B For 5C 30
Nightingale Dr. DT3: B'wey 6G 101
Nightingale La.
BH15: Pool 4B 120 (5A 90)
Nightjar Cl. BH17: Pool 6H 79
Nimrod Way BH21: Stap 5K 65
Nine Stones 1D 127
Noah Henville Cnr. DT11: W Kin . . .6H 45
Noake Rd. DT9: Sher 5A 12
Noble Cl. BH11: Bourn 5K 81
Noel Rd. BH10: Bourn 5B 82
NOMANSLAND 1B 130
Nonesuch Cl. DT1: Dor 5G 51
Noon Gdns. BH31: Ver 4H 55
Noon Hill Dr. BH31: Ver 4H 55
Noon Hill Rd. BH31: Ver 4H 55
Norburton DT6: Burt B 6H 37
Norcliffe Cl. BH11: Bourn 3B 82
NORDEN 1A 114
Norden Dr. BH20: W'ham 1F 113
Norden La. DT2: Catt, M New 5H 41
Norden Station
Swanage Railway 1A 114
Nordon Rd. DT11: B For 3C 30
Nordons DT6: Both 5E 38
Norfolk Av. BH23: Chris 4H 85
Norfolk Ct. DT6: Brid 4D 38
Norfolk Rd. DT4: Wey 1E 106
Norleywood BH23: H'ffe 6K 87
Norman Av. BH12: Pool 1K 91
Norman Cl. DT6: Brid 3F 39
Normandy Dr. BH23: Chris 7B 86
Normandy Way BH15: Hamw 5F 89
DT1: Dor 3D 50
DT6: Brid 4C 38
Norman Gdns. BH12: Pool 1A 92
Normanhurst Av. BH8: Bourn 5K 83
Normanton Cl. BH23: Chris 5H 85
Norris Cl. BH24: Ash H 7A 60
Norrish Rd. BH12: Pool 2G 91
Nth. Allington DT6: Brid 2C 38
North Av. BH10: Bourn 7D 74
DT7: L Reg 4C 34
NORTHAY 2A 122
NORTH BARROW 1D 123
Nth. Bestwall Rd. BH20: W'ham . . .3J 113
NORTH BOCKHAMPTON 3A 130
NORTHBOURNE 2E 82
Northbourne Av. BH10: Bourn 1D 82
Northbourne Gdns. BH10: Bourn . . .1E 82
Northbourne Pl. BH10: Bourn 1D 82
Northbourne Rdbt. BH10: Bourn 7E 74
NORTH BOWOOD 1B 126
Northbrook Rd. BH18: B'tone 4J 79
BH19: Swan 2J 117
NORTH CADBURY 1D 123
Nth. Causeway BH20: W'ham 2H 113
NORTH CHARFORD 1A 130
NORTH CHERITON 1D 123
NORTH CHIDEOCK 3B 36 (1B 126)
North Cl. SP8: Gill 5K 5
NORTH COKER 2C 123
Northcote Rd. BH1: Bourn 3H 93
NORTH CURRY 1A 122
Nth. Dorset Bus. Pk. DT10: S New. . .6A 16
North Dr. BH24: S Leo 4H 67
North E. Ind. Area BH23: B Int 4A 76
NORTH END 1B 6
North End DT9: Leig 5E 14
Northernhay DT1: Dor 2E 50
Northey Rd. BH6: Bourn 1G 95
Northfield Rd. BH24: Poul, Ring 2J 61
North Flds. DT10: S New 3D 16
NORTH GORLEY 1A 130
North Gro. DT9: Chet 7A 14
DT11: B Cam 5J 31
North Hill Cl. DT6: Burt B 6H 37
Nth. Hill Way DT6: Both 6D 38
NORTH INSTOW 2A 116
NORTH KINGSTON 2K 69
North La. DT9: Bis C 4H 15
Northleigh La. BH21: Coleh 6C 64
Nth. Lodge Rd. BH14: Pool 3J 91
Northmead Dr. BH17: Pool 6H 79
Northmere Dr. BH12: Pool 7K 81
Northmere Rd. BH12: Pool 1J 91
North Mills DT6: Brid 3D 38
Nth. Mills Trad. Est. DT6: Brid 2D 38
NORTHMOOR GREEN 1A 122
NORTHMOOR PARK 1G 113
Northmoor Way BH20: W'ham 1G 113
NORTH NEWTON 1A 122
NORTHOVER 1C 123
Northover Cl. DT2: P'hide 3H 43
DT6: Burt B 6J 37
Northover Ct. BH3: Bourn 7D 82
NORTH PERROTT 3B 122
NORTH PETHERTON 1A 122
North Pl. DT11: B For 4C 30
NORTH POORTON 1C 127
NORTHPORT 2H 113 (2C 129)
Northport Dr. BH20: W'ham 1H 113
Nth. Poulner Rd. BH24: Poul 2K 61
North Quay DT4: Wey 2G 107
Nth. Rew La. DT2: Mart 1G 47
North Rd. BH7: Bourn 2A 94
BH14: Pool 3D 90
DT2: M New 5H 41
DT4: W Reg 4D 106
DT6: Chid 4B 36
DT9: Sher 3D 12
North Sq. DT1: Dor 3F 51
DT3: Chick 5A 102
North St. BH15: Pool 4C 120 (5A 90)
BH19: Lan M 5C 116
BH20: Ber 2H 53
BH20: W'ham 3H 113
DT2: C'ster 3H 49
DT6: Brid 3D 38
DT8: Bea 3D 24
North St. DT9: Brad A 6G 11
DT11: W Stic 4J 29
SP7: Fon M 4C 10
(not continuous)
Northumberland Ct. BH24: Ring 4H 61
North Wlk. DT1: Dor 3E 50
North Walls BH20: W'ham 3G 113
North W. Ind. Area BH23: B Int 4K 75
(not continuous)
North Wood BH25: N Mil 7K 97
NORTH WOOTTON 2D 123
Nortoft Rd. BH8: Bourn 1H 93
Norton Cl. BH23: Chris 7B 86
Norton Gdns. BH9: Bourn 5E 82
Norton La. DT6: Neth 6A 24
DT11: Dur 3F 29
Norton Rd. BH9: Bourn 6E 82
NORTON SUB HAMDON 2B 122
Norton Way BH15: Hamw 6J 89
Norway Cl. BH9: Bourn 5F 83
Norwich Av.
BH2: Bourn 4F 121 (4D 92)
Norwich Av. W. BH2: Bourn 4D 92
Norwich Ct. BH2: Bourn 5F 121
Norwich Mans. BH2: Bourn 4D 92
Norwich Rd.
BH2: Bourn 5F 121 (4E 92)
DT4: Wey 3H 107
NORWOOD 5K 25
Norwood Pl. BH5: Bourn 2D 94
Nothe, The DT4: Wey 2J 107
Nothe Fort 2K 107
Nothe Pde. DT4: Wey 2J 107
NOTTINGTON 1D 102 (2D 127)
Nottington Ct. DT3: Nott 1E 102
Nottington La.
DT3: B'wey, Buck R, Nott 1A 102
NOTTON 1D 127
Noyce Gdns. BH8: Bourn 4D 84
Nuffield Ind. Est. BH17: Pool 6B 80
(Abingdon Rd.)
BH17: Pool 6A 80
(Waterloo Rd.)
Nuffield Rd. BH17: Pool 7A 80
Nugent Rd. BH6: Bourn 3H 95
Nundico BH20: W'ham 3H 113
Nursery Gdns. BH21: S Mar 7H 33
DT6: Brid 4E 38
Nursery Rd. BH9: Bourn 3G 83
BH24: Ring 5J 61
DT11: B For 4C 30
Nursling Grn. BH8: Bourn 4K 83
Nutcombe Cl. DT6: C'outh 6H 35
Nutcombe Ter. DT6: C'outh 6H 35
Nutcrack La. BH20: Stob 6H 113
Nutgrove Av. DT4: Wey 3D 106
Nuthatch Cl. BH17: Pool 7H 79
BH22: Fern 4B 66
DT3: B'wey 7H 101
Nutley Cl. BH11: Bourn 2K 81
Nutley Way BH11: Bourn 3K 81
Nutmead Cl. DT11: Chil O 1G 19

O

Oak Av. BH16: Sandf 3C 112
BH23: Chris 6F 85
Oakbury Dr. DT3: Over 6A 104
Oak Cl. BH21: Corf M 1E 78
BH22: W Par 4E 74
Oak Ct. DT11: Shil 5F 19
OAKDALE 1C 90 (1D 129)
Oakdale Rd. BH15: Pool 1C 90
Oakdene Cl. BH21: Wim M 7B 64
Oakdene Holiday Pk.
BH24: S Leo 5J 67
Oakdene Rd. BH20: Wool 7C 110
Oak Dr. BH15: Pool 5E 120 (5B 90)
Oakery Ct. DT1: Poun 3A 50
Oake Woods SP8: Gill 5H 5
Oakfield Ct. DT11: B For 5C 30
Oakfield Rd. BH15: Pool 1A 90
Oakfield St. DT11: B For 4C 30
Oakford Ct. BH8: Bourn 3K 83
Oak Gdns. BH11: Bourn 5B 82
Oak Gdns., The DT2: Pud 2C 52
Oakham Grange BH22: Fern 6E 66
Oakhurst BH13: Pool 4B 92
Oakhurst Cl. BH22: W Moo 2F 67
Oakhurst La. BH22: W Moo 2F 67
Oakhurst Rd. BH22: W Moo 3F 67
Oaklands Cl. BH20: Stob 7J 113
BH31: Ver 4E 54
Oaklands Pk. DT2: Cros 2G 109
Oakland Wlk. BH22: W Par 4F 75
Oak La. BH24: Ring 3K 61
Oakleigh Way BH23: H'ffe 7K 87
OAKLEY 3B 72
Oakley Gdns. BH16: Upt 7C 78
Oakley Hill BH21: Merl 2B 72
Oakley La. BH21: Merl 3B 72
SP5: Six H 1D 20
Oakley Pl. DT4: Wey 3H 107
Oakley Rd. BH21: Merl 3B 72
Oakley Straight BH21: Merl 4C 72
Oakmead Gdns. BH11: Bourn 2J 81
Oakmead Rd. BH17: Pool 6H 79
Oakmead Sports Cen. 2K 81
Oakridge Ct. DT1: Dor 4C 50
Oak Rd. BH8: Bourn 1J 93
BH16: Upt 1E 88
DT2: Char D 1H 49
SP6: Ald 7H 21
Oaks, The BH31: Ver 3E 54
SP8: Gill .5G 5
Oaks Dr. BH24: S Leo 1K 67
Oaks Mead BH31: Ver 4G 55
Oaktree Cl. BH20: Stob 6H 113
Oak Tree Farm Cvn. Pk.
BH24: S Leo 4H 67
Oak Vw. *DT11: B For* *5C 30*
(off Damory Ct. St.)
Oak Way DT3: Over 6A 104
Oakwood BH3: Bourn 7E 82
DT2: Broad 5D 108
Oakwood Cl. BH9: Bourn 4H 83
BH24: Ash H 6B 60
Oakwood Dr. DT11: I Min 3J 17
Oakwood Rd. BH9: Bourn 4G 83
BH23: H'ffe 5J 87
Oasis, The BH13: Pool 3A 92
Oasis M. BH16: Upt 7C 78
Oates Rd. BH9: Bourn 5E 82
OATH 1A 122
Oathill La. TA18: Clap 1A 22
Oban Rd. BH3: Bourn 7E 82
OBORNE 2D 123
Oborne Rd. DT9: Sher 4E 12
Oceanarium 7J 121 (5F 93)
Ocean Hgts. BH5: Bourn 4B 94
Octave Ter. SP8: Gill 4H 5
ODCOMBE 2C 123
Odeon ABC
Bournemouth 5J 121 (4F 93)
Odeon Cinema
Alderney 5F 81
Bourmemouth 5J 121 (4F 93)
ODSTOCK 1D 125
OKEFORD FITZPAINE 6B 18 (2B 124)
Okeford Rd. BH18: B'tone 4A 80
Okeford Row *DT11: Shil* *6G 19*
(off Blandford Rd.)
OK Mobile Home Pk. BH23: Chris . . .6F 87
Old Bakery, The DT8: B'sor 7H 23
Old Bakery Cl. DT11: P'erne 4F 31
Old Barn Cl. BH23: Chris 4F 85
BH24: Ring 4K 61
Old Barn Farm Rd. BH21: Wools . . .6G 59
Old Barn Rd. BH20: Ber 2H 53
BH23: Chris 4F 85
Old Bincombe La. DT3: S Poy 2C 104
Old Boundary Rd. SP7: Shaf 4C 8
Old Bound Rd. BH16: Upt 1E 88
Old Brewery, The BH20: W'ham . . .4H 113
Old Brickfields DT2: Broad 5D 108
Old Bri. Ct. DT4: Wey 2G 107
Old Bri. Rd. BH6: Bourn 6F 85
Old Castle Rd. DT4: Wey 5G 107
Old Chapel Dr. BH16: L Mat 5G 53
Old Christchurch La.
BH1: Bourn 4J 121 (4F 93)
Old Christchurch Rd.
BH1: Bourn 5H 121 (4F 93)
(not continuous)
Old Church M. BH14: Pool 3E 90
Old Church Rd. DT6: Both 6E 38
Old Coastguard Rd. BH13: Sandb . . .4F 99
Old Courthouse, The BH14: Pool . . .2G 91
Old Dairy Cl. BH15: Pool 7B 80
Old Dairy Farm, The DT10: Won . . .5B 28
Old Depot Rd. DT5: Cast 3C 118
Olde Fairfield SP8: Bour 2E 4
Old Farm Ct. DT11: B For 3D 30
Old Farm Gdns. DT11: B For 3C 30
Old Farm Rd. BH15: Pool 1C 90
Old Farm Way DT2: Cros 2H 109
Old Forge, The SP8: Gill 3H 5
Old Forge Cl. BH16: L Min 1A 88
SP6: Ald 6G 21
Old Forge Rd. BH21: Stap 6K 65
Old Furzebrook Rd. BH20: Stob . . .7J 113
Old Granary Cl. DT3: Pres 3C 104
Old Grn., The *DT9: Sher* *4C 12*
(off Greenhill)
Old Ham La. BH21: L Can 7G 65
Old Highways M. BH21: Wim M 1C 72
Old Hill DT5: Fort 5B 118
Old Kiln Rd. BH16: Upt 7F 79
BH20: Rid 6K 113
Old Lifeboat House 6C 120 (6A 90)
Old Lyme Hill DT6: C'outh 7G 35

Old Lyme Rd.—Penelope Ct.

Old Lyme Rd. DT6: C'outh 7G 35
Old Malthouse La.
BH19: Lan M 5C 116
Old Manor, The 2D 52
Old Manor Cl. BH21: Wim M 1C 72
Old Manor Farm BH21: H Mart 2A 56
Old Mkt. Cen. SP8: Gill 5J 5
Old Mkt. Hill DT10: S New 5C 16
Old Mkt. Rd. BH21: Corf M 7A 70
Old Mill Ho. BH24: Ring 5H 61
Old Mill La. DT10: Marn 7F 7
Old Mills DT2: T Por 2B 40
Old Mulberry Cl. BH10: Bourn 5A 82
Old Oak Way DT11: W Whi 2H 45
Old Orchard
BH15: Pool 6B 120 (6A 90)
(not continuous)
Old Orchard Shop. Cen.
BH15: Pool 6B 120 (6A 90)
Old Parish La. DT4: Wey 1F 107
(not continuous)
Old Pines Cl. BH22: Fern 1E 74
Old Pound Cl. BH16: L Mat 6G 53
Old Pound Ct. SP8: Bour 3B 4
Old Priory Rd. BH6: Bourn 3H 95
Old Railway Wlk. DT11: B For 3B 30
Old Rectory Cl. BH21: Corf M 5F 71
DT6: C'outh 6H 35
Old Rd. BH21: Wim M 1K 71
Old Rope Wlk., The BH15: Hamw. . .6H 89
Old St Johns M. BH9: Bourn 3F 83
Old Sandpit La. BH16: B Hil 4C 78
Old Sawmill Cl. BH31: Ver 3D 54
Old School Cl. BH14: Pool 3E 90
BH22: Fern 7C 66
Old School La. DT10: H Mary 1C 16
DT11: I Min 3J 17
Old School Pl. DT9: Sher 5C 12
Old Sherborne Rd. DT2: C'ster 4J 49
Old Shipyard Cen. DT6: W Bay 1H 37
Old Stacks Gdns. BH24: Ring 5K 61
Old Station Rd. DT3: Upw 6F 101
Old Station Yd. DT3: B'wey 6F 101
Old St. BH21: S Mar 6J 33
OLD TOWN 5B 120 (5A 90)
Old Town Mkt.
BH15: Pool 5B 120 (5A 90)
Old Town M. BH15: Pool 5B 120
Old Vicarage Cl. BH10: Bourn 7E 74
DT2: C'ster 6J 49
Old Vicarage Gdns. DT7: L Reg 5C 34
Old Vicarage Rd. DT6: Both 6E 38
Old Wareham Rd. BH12: Pool 7E 80
BH16: B Hil 4C 78
BH21: Corf M 4C 78
Old Watery La. BH16: L Min 1A 88
Olga Rd. DT1: Dor 4E 50
Olivers Mead DT11: Chil O 1G 19
Olivers Rd. BH21: Coleh 6E 64
Olivers Way BH21: Coleh 6E 64
Omega Cen., The BH20: W'ham . . .2J 113
Onslow Gdns. BH21: Wim M 6B 64
Ophir Gdns. BH8: Bourn 2H 93
Ophir Rd. BH8: Bourn 2H 93
Oratory Gdns. BH13: Pool 7K 91
Orchard, The BH11: Bourn 7H 73
DT2: W New 3G 111
DT3: B'wey 7F 101
DT10: Won 5B 28
DT11: B For 3B 30
SP5: Six H 2C 20
Orchard Av. BH14: Pool 5D 90
DT6: Brid 2C 38
Orchard Cl. BH21: Corf M 6F 71
BH22: Fern 7E 66
BH23: Chris 1J 95
BH24: Ring 3J 61
DT2: Syd N 6C 42
DT6: C'outh 7H 35
DT8: Drim 2B 22
DT9: L'ton 1B 14
DT10: New 7A 16
DT11: O Fitz 5A 18
DT11: Stour 2H 29
SP7: Fon M 5B 10
Orchard Ct. BH31: Ver 5G 55
SP8: Gill 4H 5
(off Orchard Rd.)
Orchard Cres. DT6: Brid 2C 38
Orchard Dr. DT3: Over 5B 104
Orchard La. BH21: Corf M 6F 71
DT11: W Kin 6H 45
TA20: T'ombe 6B 22
Orchard Mead BH24: Ring 3J 61
DT8: B'sor 7H 23
Orchard M. SP8: Gill 4F 5
Orchard Mt. BH24: Ring 3J 61
(off Orchard Mead)
ORCHARD PORTMAN 1A 122
Orchard Ri. DT11: M And 6B 44
Orchard Rd. SP8: Gill 4G 5
Orchard St. BH2: Bourn . . .5G 121 (4E 92)
DT1: Dor 3F 51
DT11: B For 4C 30
Orchard Wlk.
BH2: Bourn 5G 121 (4E 92)
Orchard Way DT8: Most 2J 23
Orcheston Rd. BH8: Bourn 1H 93
Orchid Way BH23: Chris 7A 86
Orford Cl. BH23: Chris 2F 85
Orford M. DT2: Pud 1C 52
Orford St. DT2: Pud 2C 52
ORGANFORD 1D 112 (1C 129)
Organford Rd. BH16: Hol H 1C 112
Orion Rd. DT4: Wey 3H 107
Orkney Ct. DT11: B For 4C 30
Ormonde Rd. BH13: Pool 5A 92
Osborne Cl. DT1: Dor 5H 51
Osborne Rd. BH9: Bourn 6E 82
BH14: Pool 4F 91
BH19: Swan 5J 117
BH21: Wim M 1B 72
Osborne Ter. DT5: Fort 4A 118
(off Fortuneswell)
Osbourne Rd. DT6: Brid 3D 38
Osmay Rd. BH19: Swan 7K 117
OSMINGTON 3H 105 (2A 128)
Osmington Bay Cen. 5G 105
Osmington Bay Holiday Cen.
DT3: Osm 5G 105
Osmington Drove DT2: Broad 7C 108
Osmington Hill DT3: Pres 3D 104
OSMINGTON MILLS 5K 105 (2A 128)
Osmington Mills Holiday Club
DT3: Osm M 5K 105
Osprey Cl. BH23: Mude 2E 96
Osprey Quay Bus. Pk. DT5: Cast . . .3A 118
Osprey Rd. DT4: W Reg 7F 107
Oswald Cl. BH9: Bourn 4E 82
Oswald Rd. BH9: Bourn 4E 82
OTHERY 1A 122
Otterbourne BH2: Bourn 3D 92
Otter Cl. BH16: Upt 1D 88
BH31: Ver 5G 55
Otter Rd. BH15: Pool 1D 90
Ottery La. DT9: Sher 5B 12
OUTWICK 1A 130
Oval, The BH20: L Cam 4K 111
Oval Gdn. BH20: Stob 7J 113
Overbury Cl. DT4: Wey 2D 106
Overbury Rd. BH14: Pool 4G 91
Overcliffe Mans. BH1: Bourn 4J 93
OVERCOMBE 6B 104 (2D 127)
Overcombe Cl. BH17: Pool 3C 80
Overcombe Cotts. DT3: Over 6B 104
Overcombe Ct. DT3: Over 6A 104
Overcombe Dr. DT3: Over 6B 104
OVER COMPTON 1G 11 (2C 123)
Overlands Rd. DT4: W Reg 4D 106
Over Links Dr. BH14: Pool 5H 91
OVER STRATTON 2B 122
Overton Cl. DT7: L Reg 3D 34
Overton Wlk. DT11: B For 3C 30
Ovington Av. BH7: Bourn 7E 84
Ovington Gdns. BH7: Bourn 7E 84
OWERMOIGNE 7J 109 (2A 128)
Owls Rd. BH5: Bourn 4K 93
BH31: Ver 4G 55
OXBRIDGE 1B 126
Oxencroft SP7: Shaf 2C 8
Oxford Av. BH6: Bourn 2D 94
Oxford La. BH11: Bourn 7B 74
Oxford Rd. BH8: Bourn 3H 93
Oxford Ter. BH19: Swan 5J 117
Oxhayes DT8: Drim 2B 22
Ozone Ter. DT7: L Reg 6C 34

P

Paceycombe Way DT1: Poun 4B 50
PACKERS HILL 2H 27 (2A 124)
Paddington Cl. BH11: Bourn 2H 81
Paddington Gro. BH11: Bourn 3H 81
Paddock, The BH16: Upt 7D 78
(off Coronation Av.)
BH24: S Leo 4H 67
BH25: N Mil 7K 97
DT2: W Staf 1C 108
Paddock Cl. BH12: Pool 1F 91
BH16: L Mat 5H 53
BH21: Stap 6A 66
BH24: S Ive 7B 60
SP5: Six H 3C 20
SP7: Shaf 5D 8
Paddock Gro. BH31: Ver 5G 55
Paddocks, The BH10: Bourn 2D 82
DT6: Both 6E 38
DT8: Most 1J 23
DT9: T'ford 1J 13
DT10: Stalb 3J 15
DT11: I Min 3J 17
Padfield Cl. BH6: Bourn 1G 95
Pageant Cl. DT9: Sher 5C 12
Pageant Dr. DT9: Sher 5C 12
Pageants Cl. DT6: Bradp 1F 39
Page Dr. DT5: S'well 4H 119
Paget Cl. BH21: Coleh 5E 64
Paget Rd. BH11: Bourn 2A 82
Paisley Rd. BH6: Bourn 2E 94
Palace Ct. DT1: Dor 3F 51
Palace Rd. SP8: Gill 5J 5
Palfrey Rd. BH10: Bourn 2D 82
PALLINGTON 1A 128
Palma Apartments BH25: N Mil 7K 97
Palmer Rd. BH15: Pool 2A 90
Palmers Brewery 5C 38
Palmers La. DT11: Char M 3B 32
Palmers Orchard BH16: L Mat 7G 53
Palmerston Av. BH23: Chris 1B 96
Palmerston Cl. BH16: Upt 7F 79
Palmerston M. BH1: Bourn 2A 94
Palmerston Rd. BH1: Bourn 2A 94
BH14: Pool 3H 91
BH16: Upt 7E 78
PAMPHILL 6G 63 (3C 125)
Panorama Rd. BH13: Sandb 5F 99
BH19: Swan 5G 117
Pans Cnr. BH22: Fern 2F 75
Parade, The BH6: Bourn 4G 95
BH17: Pool 5K 79
BH19: Swan 5K 117
BH21: Corf M 1F 79
DT10: S New 5C 16
SP8: Gill 5H 5
Paradise Rd. BH21: Holt, Hort 5G 57
Paradise St.
BH15: Pool 6A 120 (6K 89)
Pardy's Hill BH21: Corf M 5E 70
Parham Rd. BH10: Bourn 4C 82
Paris Ct. SP8: Gill 5H 5
Parish Rd. BH15: Pool 4C 90
Park, The BH25: N Mil 7K 97
Park & Ride
Dorchester 6E 50
Marshes End 7J 79
Norden 1A 114
Park Av. BH10: Bourn 7C 74
Park Cl. BH23: Burt 3A 86
DT11: Stour 1H 29
Park Ct. BH13: Pool 4B 92
DT3: Lit 1J 103
Park Dr. BH16: Sandf 3C 112
BH31: Ver 3E 54
DT2: Cros 1H 109
Parkelea BH21: S Mar 6H 33
Parker Rd. BH9: Bourn 7F 83
Parkers Cl. BH24: Poul 2K 61
Park Est. Rd. DT5: East 1H 119
Park Farm Cl. DT2: Mart 3K 47
Park Farm Mus. 1D 44
Park Gdns. BH23: Chris 7C 86
PARK GATE 7C 28
Park Ga. M. BH2: Bourn 5F 121
Park Gro. DT10: Stalb 2G 15
Park Hill DT11: Char M 3A 32
Pk. Homer Dr. BH21: Coleh 5D 64
Pk. Homer Rd. BH21: Coleh 5D 64
Pk. Lake Rd. BH15: Pool 5C 90
Parkland Cl. BH31: Ver 6K 55
Park Lands DT11: B For 4B 30
Park La. BH10: Bourn 2F 83
BH21: Wim M 1A 72
BH21: Woodl 7E 20
DT2: Ever 4C 26
DT4: Wey 6H 103
DT11: I Cou 4F 17
DT11: Shap 4A 62
SP6: Ald 6H 21
SP7: Shaf 4B 8
Park Mans. BH8: Bourn 7J 83
Park Mead Rd. DT4: W Reg 5E 106
Park Pl. BH14: Pool 3D 90
Park Rd. BH8: Bourn 3G 93
BH14: Pool 4D 90
BH19: Swan 5K 117
DT5: East 1J 119
DT6: Brid 3C 38
DT10: Stalb 2G 15
DT11: B For 4B 30
Parkside BH23: Chris 5H 87
BH24: Ring 5J 61
Parkside Gdns. BH10: Bourn 4E 82
Parkside Rd. BH14: Pool 3G 91
PARKSTONE 3F 91 (1D 129)
Parkstone Av. BH14: Pool 3G 91
Parkstone Hgts. BH14: Pool 2D 90
(not continuous)
Parkstone Rd.
BH15: Pool 3D 120 (4B 90)
Parkstone Station (Rail) 4F 91
Parkstone Yacht Club 6E 90
Park St. DT4: Wey 1H 107
Park Vw. BH15: Pool 4C 90
Parkview BH2: Bourn 3G 121 (3E 92)
Park Vw. Ct. BH8: Bourn 7J 83
Park Wlk. SP7: Shaf 4B 8
Park Way BH22: W Moo 2D 66
Parkway DT6: C'outh 7J 35
Parkway Dr. BH8: Bourn 6K 83
Parkway Retail Pk. BH8: Bourn 3J 93
Parkwood La. BH5: Bourn 2D 94
(off Hosker Rd.)
Parkwood Rd. BH5: Bourn 2C 94
BH21: Wim M 1A 72
Parley Cl. BH22: W Par 4F 75
PARLEY COMMON 2G 75
PARLEY CROSS 5E 74 (1D 129)
PARLEY GREEN 6H 75
Parley Grn. La. BH23: E Par 6H 75
Parley La. BH23: E Par 5H 75
Parley Rd. BH9: Bourn 4G 83
Parmiter Dr. BH21: Wim M 1C 72
Parmiter Rd. BH21: Wim M 1C 72
Parmiter Way BH21: Wim M 1C 72
Parr Gro. DT11: P'erne 3G 31
Parr Ho. BH14: Pool 3E 90
Parr St. BH14: Pool 3E 90
Parr Way DT4: Wey 5G 107
Parsonage, The SP5: Six H 2D 20
Parsonage Barn La. BH24: Ring 3J 61
Parsonage Rd.
BH1: Bourn 5K 121 (4G 93)
DT6: Brid 2C 38
Parsonage St. SP7: Fon M 5C 10
Parsons Cl. BH19: Swan 2J 117
Parsons Ct. DT1: Dor 3F 51
(off Durngate St.)
Parsons Pool SP7: Shaf 3B 8
Partridge Cl. BH23: Mude 2E 96
Partridge Dr. BH14: Pool 6F 91
Partridge Wlk. BH14: Pool 6G 91
Partway La. DT10: H Bry 4B 28
Pascoe Cl. BH14: Pool 3E 90
Pasture Way DT6: Both 5E 38
Patchins, The BH14: Pool 7G 91
Patchins Rd. BH16: Hamw 3D 88
(not continuous)
PATHE 1A 122
Paul Baker's La. DT11: P'erne 3G 31
(off Church Rd.)
Paul's Mead DT5: Fort 5B 118
Pauls Way DT2: Cros 1H 109
Pauncefote Rd. BH5: Bourn 2C 94
Pauntley Rd. BH23: Chris 1C 96
Pavan Gdns. BH10: Bourn 4C 82
Pavilions, The SP7: Shaf 4C 8
Pavilions, The DT11: B For 3D 30
Pavilion Theatre 2J 107
Pavilion Theatre & Ball Room, The
...............6J 121 (5F 93)
Payne Cl. BH22: W Moo 6E 58
Paynes Cl. DT2: P'ton 7J 43
Peaceful La. DT10: K Stag 1J 27
PEACEMARSH 2F 5
Peacemarsh Farm Cl. SP8: Gill 2G 5
Peacemarsh Ter. SP8: Gill 3H 5
PEAR ASH 1A 4
Pear Ash La. BA9: Pens 1A 4
Pearce Av. BH14: Pool 6E 90
Pearce Gdns. BH14: Pool 6E 90
Pearce Rd. BH16: Upt 1D 88
Pear Cl. BH12: Pool 3B 92
Pearl Gdns. BH10: Bourn 2C 82
Pearl Rd. BH10: Bourn 2C 82
Pearson Av. BH14: Pool 2F 91
Pearson Gdns. BH10: Bourn 7D 74
Peartree Bus. Cen. BH21: Stap 6K 65
Pear Tree Cl. SP6: Ald 6H 21
Pear Tree Farm Cvn. and Camping Pk.
BH16: Hol H 2C 112
Peas Hill DT6: Ship G 6J 39
Peatons La. BH16: L Mat 5F 53
Pebble Bank Cvn. Pk.
DT4: W Reg 4D 106
Pebble La. DT5: Fort 4A 118
Peddlars Wlk. BH24: Ring 4H 61
Peel Cl. BH12: Pool 2G 91
BH31: Ver 3E 54
DT11: B For 3C 30
Peel Ct. BH23: Chris 1H 95
Peelers Ct. DT6: Brid 3D 38
Pegasus Ct. BH1: Bourn . .1K 121 (2G 93)
Pelham BH13: Pool 3A 92
Pelham Cl. BH23: Chris 1B 96
Pemberton Cl. DT3: Lit 7H 101
Pembroke Ct. BH23: H'ffe 7J 97
Pembroke Rd. BH4: Bourn 5B 92
BH12: Pool 7H 81
Penbugle Yd. DT1: Poun 4C 50
Pen Craig BH13: Pool 4B 92
PENDOMER 2C 123
Pendruffle La. DT1: Poun 4C 50
Penelope Ct. BH23: H'ffe 7J 97

Pengelly Av.—Preston La.

Pengelly Av. BH10: Bourn 1E 82
Penhale Wlk. *DT1: Poun 4C 50*
(off Netherton St.)
PENN 1A 126
Pennant Way BH23: Chris 7D 86
Penn Ct. BH22: W Moo 2D 66
Penn Hill Av. BH14: Pool 4H 91
Penn Hill Vw. DT2: Strat 4B 48
Pennine Way BH31: Ver 5F 55
Pennington Cl. BH22: W Moo 3D 66
Pennington Cres.
BH22: W Moo 2D 66
Pennington Rd. BH22: W Moo 3D 66
Pennsylvania Rd. DT5: East 2K 119
Penny Ct. BH24: Poul 3K 61
Penny La. BH1: Bourn 3A 94
Penny Plot DT7: L Reg 4B 34
Penny's Ct. BH22: Fern 7D 66
Penny's La. BH21: Cran 2H 21
Penny's Mead BH21: Cran 2H 21
Penny St. DT4: Wey 7H 103
DT10: S New 5C 16
Penny's Wlk. BH22: Fern 7D 66
Penny Way BH23: F Clif 1G 97
Penrith Cl. BH31: Ver 5E 54
Penrith Rd. BH5: Bourn 3C 94
Penrose Cl. BH16: L Mat 7G 53
Penrose Rd. BH22: Fern 6D 66
PENSELWOOD 1A 4 (1A 124)
PENTRIDGE 2D 125
Peppercorn Cl. BH23: Chris 6C 86
Pepperell Ho. *SP7: Shaf 3B 8*
(off Bleke St.)
Pepper Hill DT11: Shil 6F 19
Percy Gdns. DT11: B For 4C 30
Percy Rd. BH5: Bourn 3A 94
Peregrine Rd. BH23: Mude 1E 96
Pergin Cres. BH17: Pool 7K 79
Pergin Way BH17: Pool 7K 79
Perrin Lock Ct. *BH23: Chris 1H 95*
(off Kings Av.)
Perryfield Gdns. BH7: Bourn 6D 84
Perry Gdns. BH15: Pool . . .6C 120 (6A 90)
(not continuous)
PERRY STREET 3A 122
Persley Rd. BH10: Bourn 2D 82
Perth Cl. BH23: Chris 5G 85
Perth St. DT4: Wey 1F 107
Peter Grant Way BH22: Fern 7C 66
Peters Cl. BH16: Upt 1E 88
Petersfield Pl. BH7: Bourn 7D 84
Petersfield Rd. BH7: Bourn 1C 94
(not continuous)
Petersham La.
BH21: G Com, Holt 6B 56
Petersham Rd. BH17: Pool 6H 79
Peters Rd. BH22: Fern 2F 75
Petit Rd. BH9: Bourn 3G 83
Pettitts Cl. DT9: Brad A 6F 11
Pettycrate La. DT6: Chid 6A 36
Petwyn Cl. BH22: Fern 6G 67
Peverell Av. E. DT1: Poun 3B 50
Peverell Av. W. DT1: Poun 4A 50
Peverell Rd. BH16: Hamw 3D 88
Peveril Cl. BH24: Ash H 5B 60
Peveril Ct. BH19: Swan 6K 117
Peveril Hgts. BH19: Swan 5K 117
Peveril Point Rd. BH19: Swan 5K 117
Peveril Rd. BH19: Swan 6K 117
Pheasant Way SP8: Gill 6K 5
Phelipps Rd. BH21: Corf M 6F 71
Philip Rd. DT11: B For 3D 30
Phillips Rd. DT10: Marn 4J 9
Phippard Way
BH15: Pool 6D 120 (5B 90)
Phoenix Ct. *DT1: Dor 3F 51*
(off High E. St.)
Phyldon Cl. BH12: Pool 2G 91
Phyldon Rd. BH12: Pool 1F 91
PIBSBURY 1B 122
Pickard Rd. BH22: Fern 5F 67
Pickering Cl. BH18: B'tone 4J 79
PICKET POST 2A 130
Pickford Rd. BH9: Bourn 5E 82
PIDDLEHINTON 7K 43 (1A 128)
Piddle La. DT2: Cer A 2C 42
PIDDLETRENTHIDE 2H 43 (3A 124)
PIDNEY 4C 28 (3A 124)
Pier App. BH2: Bourn 6J 121 (5F 93)
Pierston Flds. SP8: Mil S 1F 5
Pier Ter. DT6: W Bay 2H 37
Pier Theatre, The 7J 121 (5F 93)
Pier Vw. BH19: Swan 5K 117
Pigeon Cl. DT2: W New 4G 111
DT11: Blan 6C 30
PIG OAK .1C 64
Pig Shoot La. BH23: Hurn 2B 84
Pigs La. DT2: M Osm 3C 26
PIKESHILL 2B 130
PILFORD 3F 65 (3D 125)
Pilford Heath Rd. BH21: Coleh 4E 64
Pilford La. BH21: Bro H, Coleh 2F 65
BH21: Coleh 4E 64
Pilgrim Pk. Homes BH24: Poul 3K 61
Pilgrims Way BH17: Pool 7J 79
DT4: Wey 2J 107
Pill Mdw. SP8: K Mag 6B 4
PILLWELL 3K 9 (2A 124)
Pilot Hight Rd. BH11: Bourn 2A 82
PILSDON 1B 126
Pilsdon Cl. DT8: Bea 2B 24
Pilsdon Dr. BH17: Pool 4C 80
Pilsdon Pen 277 m (909 ft) 3B 122
Pilwell DT10: Marn 3J 9
Pimpern Cl. BH17: Pool 4C 80
PIMPERNE
Blandford Forum 3G 31 (3C 125)
Dorchester 1B 26
Pimpernel Ct. SP8: Gill 4F 5
Pine Av. BH6: Bourn 3E 94
BH12: Pool 7K 81
Pinebeach Ct. BH13: Pool 7A 92
Pinecliffe Av. BH6: Bourn 3E 94
Pinecliffe Rd. BH25: N Mil 7K 97
Pinecliff Rd. BH13: Pool 7A 92
Pinecliff Wlk. BH19: Swan 7K 117
Pine Cl. BH22: Fern 5C 66
DT2: Cors 6J 25
Pine Cres. BH16: Sandf 3C 112
BH23: H'ffe 7J 87
Pine Dr. BH13: Pool 4K 91
(not continuous)
BH24: S Ive 7B 60
Pine Dr. E. BH13: Pool 5A 92
Pine End BH22: Fern 2F 75
Pine Glen Av. BH22: Fern 4C 66
Pine Grange BH1: Bourn . . .4K 121 (4G 93)
Pineholt Cl. BH24: S Ive 6C 60
Pinehurst Av. BH23: Mude 2D 96
Pinehurst Pk. (Cvn. Site)
BH22: W Moo 4F 67
Pinehurst Rd. BH22: W Moo 3E 66
Pinelands Ct. BH8: Bourn 7J 83
Pine Mnr. Rd. BH24: Ash H 6K 59
Pinemoor Cl. DT3: Over 3K 103
Pine Pk. Mans. BH13: Pool 3A 92
Pine Ridge DT7: L Reg 3D 34
Pine Rd. BH9: Bourn 5F 83
BH21: Corf M 4H 71
SP6: Ald 7H 21
Pines, The BH13: Pool 5A 92
Pines Ct. DT11: B For 5C 30
Pines M. DT8: Bea 3D 24
Pinesprings Dr. BH18: B'tone 3G 79
Pine Springs Nature Reserve 4G 79
Pine Tree Cl. BH21: Coleh 7B 64
Pine Tree Glen BH4: Bourn 4C 92
Pine Tree Wlk. BH17: Pool 6H 79
Pine Va. Cres. BH10: Bourn 3E 82
Pine Vw. DT6: Brid 4B 38
Pine Vw. Cl. BH16: Upt 1E 88
BH31: Ver 3D 54
Pine Vw. Rd. BH31: Ver 3D 54
Pine Wlk. BH22: W Moo 1E 66
BH31: Ver 5H 55
DT7: L Reg 6C 34
SP7: Shaf 4A 8
Pinewood Av. BH10: Bourn 1D 82
Pinewood Cl. BH10: Bourn 1D 82
BH16: Upt 7C 78
BH23: Walk 4H 97
Pinewood Cotts. BH19: Stud 5H 115
Pinewood Ct. BH22: W Moo 2D 66
Pinewood Gdns. BH22: Fern 5D 66
Pinewood Rd. BH13: Pool 6B 92
BH16: Upt 7C 78
BH22: Fern 4C 66
BH23: H'ffe 5K 87
BH24: S Ive 7B 60
Pinford La. DT9: Sher 4E 12
Pinnacle, The BH1: Bourn 5K 121
Pinnacles Reach BH19: Swan 6K 117
Pipers Dr. BH23: Chris 7E 86
Pipit Cl. DT3: B'wey 6H 101
Pippin Cl. BH23: Chris 4G 85
Pirates La. DT4: W Reg 5D 106
Pitcher Cl. *DT11: W Kin 6H 45*
(off North St.)
PITCOMBE 1D 123
Pitcote La. DT1: Poun 4C 50
Pithouse La. BH23: Hurn 4F 77
Pitman's La. DT6: Morc 3G 35
PITNEY .1B 122
Pitt Cl. DT11: Blan 6B 30
Pittmore Rd. BH23: Burt 4A 86
Pitt's Drove BH21: Chilb 2D 62
Pitts Orchard DT10: S New 5C 16
Pitwines Cl. BH15: Pool . . .5D 120 (5A 90)
Pix Mead Gdns. SP7: Shaf 4D 8
Plaisters La. DT3: S Poy 1B 104
PLAITFORD 1B 130
Plantagenet Cres. BH11: Bourn 1H 81
Plantagenet Way SP8: Gill 4F 5
Plantation Cl. BH19: Swan 5H 117
Plantation Ct. BH17: Pool 5A 80
Plantation Dr. BH23: Walk 4H 97
Plantation Rd. BH17: Pool 5A 80
BH23: Hurn 2D 76
Plant Pk. Rd. BH24: Matc 1E 68
Plassey Cl. DT1: Dor 3D 50
Plassey Cres. BH10: Bourn 1C 82
Playfields Dr. BH12: Pool 1J 91
Plaza Cinema
Dorchester 3F 51
Pleasant Vw. SP8: Bour 3B 4
PLECK
Hazelbury Bryan 5A 28
Holwell 2G 27
Marnhull 6G 9
Pleck Hill DT10: Won 5A 28
Plecy Cl. BH22: W Par 2D 74
Plemont Cl. BH12: Pool 5J 81
Plocks, The DT11: B For 5C 30
Plot, The DT9: Holw 2F 27
Plough Cl. DT3: Osm 4G 105
Plough Cotts. DT3: Osm 4G 105
Plough Est. DT11: B For 2C 30
Plover Dr. DT3: Chick 6B 102
Plover Wlk. DT4: W Reg 6F 107
Plowman Cl. DT10: Marn 3J 9
Plumbley Mdws. DT11: W Kin 6H 45
Plumer Rd. BH17: Pool 5J 79
Plum Orchard DT9: N Com 1J 11
Plumptree Gdns. DT6: Both 5E 38
PLUSH .3A 124
PODIMORE 1C 123
Podington Mdws. DT3: Chick 6C 102
Point, The BH5: Bourn 4A 94
POKESDOWN 1B 94 (3A 130)
Pokesdown Station (Rail) 2C 94
Polans DT9: Chet 7A 14
Policemans La. BH16: Upt 7B 78
Pollards La. DT2: Ower 7J 109
Pomona Cl. BH22: Fern 6D 66
Pompey's La. BH22: Fern 1A 74
(not continuous)
Pondarosa Camp & Cvn. Pk.
BH19: H Cro 3B 116
Pond End DT6: Pym 1D 38
Pond Head BH21: Holt 6E 56
Pond Wlk. DT10: Stalb 2G 15
Ponsonby Rd. BH14: Pool 3H 91
Pony Dr. BH16: Upt 7F 79
POOLE 4C 120 (1D 129)
Poole Aquarium 6B 120 (6K 89)
Poole Commerce Cen.
BH12: Pool 2K 91
Poole Crematorium BH21: Merl 1B 80
Poole Hill BH2: Bourn 5F 121 (4D 92)
Poole La. BH11: Bourn 2K 81
Poole La. Rdbt. BH11: Bourn 2J 81
Poole Pottery 5J 79
Poole Rd. BH2: Bourn 4D 92
BH4: Bourn 3B 92
BH12: Pool 3K 91
BH16: L Mat 4K 53
BH16: Upt 7E 78
BH20: Ber 2H 53
BH21: S Mar 7H 33
BH21: Wim M 1A 72
Poole's Ct. DT7: L Reg 5D 34
Poole Sports Cen. 4C 120 (5A 90)
Poole Stadium 2C 120 (4A 90)
Poole Station (Rail) 3C 120 (4A 90)
Pope's Hill DT2: T Por 1C 40
Popes Rd. BH15: Pool 1B 90
Poplar Cl. BH15: Pool 6A 120
BH21: Wim M 7B 64
BH23: H'ffe 6J 97
DT4: S'hill 5E 102
Poplar Cres. BH24: Ring 4K 61
Poplar Dr. DT2: Char D 2H 49
Poplar Hill DT11: Shil 5E 18
Poplar Way BH24: Ring 4K 61
Poppy Cl. BH16: Upt 7B 78
BH23: Chris 6F 87
Poppy Ct. BH6: Bourn 3F 95
Poppyfields SP8: Gill 2H 5
Poppy Way DT6: Brid 1J 37
Portarlington Cl. BH4: Bourn 5D 92
Portarlington Rd. BH4: Bourn 4C 92
Port Bredy *DT6: Brid 3D 38*
(off Barrack St.)
Portchester Ct. BH8: Bourn 2H 93
Portchester Pl. BH8: Bourn 2H 93
Portchester Rd. BH8: Bourn 1G 93
Portelet Cl. BH12: Pool 5H 81
Porter Rd. BH17: Pool 7K 79
Porters La. BH21: Coleh 6G 65
PORTESHAM 6G 47 (2D 127)
Portesham Dairy Farm Campsite
DT3: Port 6G 47
Portesham Gdns. BH9: Bourn 2H 83
Portesham Hill DT3: Port 5G 47
Portesham Way BH17: Pool 3C 80
Portfield Cl. BH23: Chris 6J 85
Portfield Rd. BH23: Chris 7H 85
Portland Beach Rd. DT4: W Reg . . .7F 107
DT5: Fort 3A 118
Portland Bill Lighthouse & Vis. Cen.
. . . . .7F 119
Portland Bill Rd. DT5: S'well 7F 119
Portland Bird Observatory & Field Cen.
. . . . .7G 119
Portland Castle 3A 118
Portland Ct. DT7: L Reg 5B 34
Portland Cres. DT4: Wey 2F 107
Portland Ho. DT4: Wey 4J 107
DT5: S'well 5F 119
Portland Mus. 2K 119
Portland Pl. BH2: Bourn . . .2J 121 (3F 93)
DT6: Brid 3C 38
Portland Port Bus. Cen.
DT5: Cast 3B 118
Portland Rd. BH9: Bourn 5G 83
DT4: W Reg 4E 106
Portland Sq. DT5: S'well 5G 119
Port La. DT6: Ship G 6K 39
Portman Cres. BH5: Bourn 3D 94
Portman Dr. DT11: Chil O 1G 19
Portman M. BH7: Bourn 2B 94
Portman Pl. DT11: B For 4B 30
Portman Rd. BH7: Bourn 2B 94
DT11: P'erne 3G 31
Portman Ter. BH5: Bourn 3D 94
Portmore Cl. BH18: B'tone 7A 72
Portmore Gdns. DT4: Wey 3G 107
Portnell's La. BA12: Zea . . . . .1C 4 & 1E 4
Port St James BH15: Pool 6A 120
Portswood Dr. BH10: Bourn 2G 83
Port Vw. Cvn. Pk. BH23: Hurn 3D 76
Portway DT6: Ask 7E 40
Portwey Cl. DT4: Wey 3G 107
POST GREEN 6A 78 (1C 129)
Post Grn. Rd. BH16: L Min 6A 78
Post Office La. BH15: Pool 4C 120
BH24: S Ive 6C 60
Post Office Rd.
BH1: Bourn 5H 121 (4F 93)
SP8: Mil S 1F 5
Potterne Hill Nature Reserve 6G 55
Potterne Way BH21: T Leg 6G 55
Potterne Wood Cl. BH31: Ver 6J 55
Potters Way BH14: Pool 5G 91
Pottery Junc. BH12: Pool 2J 91
Pottery La. DT4: Wey 7G 103
Pottery Lines BH20: Sandf 7A 112
Pottery Rd. BH14: Pool 5E 90
POULNER 2A 130
POUNDBURY 3C 50 (1D 127)
Poundbury Cres. DT1: Dor 3C 50
Poundbury Ent. Cen. *DT1: Poun 4C 50*
(off Burraton Sq.)
Poundbury Rd. DT1: Dor 3D 50
Poundbury W. Ind. Est. DT1: Dor . . .3D 50
Pound Cl. BH15: Pool 2D 90
BH24: Ring 3J 61
DT2: C'ster 6H 49
DT10: Stalb 2G 15
Pound Hill BH21: Wit 2H 33
DT2: Cors 6K 25
Pound La. BH15: Pool 2C 90
BH20: W'ham 4H 113
BH23: Chris 1K 95
(off High St.)
DT1: Dor 3G 51
DT7: Uply 2A 34
DT9: Bis C 6H 15
DT9: Chet 6A 14
DT11: O Fitz 6B 18
SP7: Shaf 3C 8
SP8: Gill 4F 5
Pound Piece DT2: M New 6H 41
DT5: West 1H 119
Pound Rd. DT7: L Reg 5C 34
DT9: T'ford 2J 13
Pound St. DT7: L Reg 5C 34
Powell Rd. BH14: Pool 4F 91
POWERSTOCK 1C 127
Powys Cl. DT1: Dor 6D 50
Powys Grn. DT9: Sher 4B 12
Powys La. DT9: Sher 4C 12
POXWELL 1K 105 (2A 128)
Poxwell Drove DT2: Pox 1H 105
POYNTINGTON 1D 123
Prebendal Holiday Pk.
DT3: Over 5D 104
Preetz Way DT11: B For 2E 30
PRESTON 3C 104 (2A 128)
Preston Beach Rd. DT3: Over 5K 103
DT4: Wey 5K 103
Preston Cl. BH16: Upt 7E 78
Preston Ct. BH20: W'ham 2H 113
Preston La. BH23: Burt 4B 86

Restharrow—St Aldhelm's Pl.

Restharrow BH1: Bourn . . .2K **121** (3G **93**)
Retreat Rd. BH21: Wim M 1B **72**
REW
Buckland Newton 6J **27**
Martinstown/Winterborne St Martin 1G **47**
Rew Head DT2: Buck N 6J **27**
Rew La. DT2: Buck N 6J **27**
Rex La. DT3: Chick 6B **102**
Rex Wareham Cinema 4H **113**
Reynards Way DT3: S Poy 3C **104**
Rhine Rd. BH20: Bov 2B **110**
Rhode La. DT7: Uply 2A **34**
Rhosewood Dr. DT3: Pres 3B **104**
Ribble Cl. BH18: B'tone 4J **79**
Ribbonwood Hgts. BH14: Pool 3F **91**
Ricardo Cres. BH23: Mude 1E **96**
Rice Gdns. BH16: Hamw 3F **89**
Rice Ter. BH16: Hamw 3F **89**
Richard Cl. BH16: Upt 6D **78**
Richmar Trad. Cen. DT10: S New 4D **16**
Richmond Cl. DT9: Sher 5B **12**
Richmond Ct. BH8: Bourn 7J **83**
Richmond Gdns.
BH1: Bourn 4J **121** (4F **93**)
Richmond Grn. DT9: Sher 4B **12**
Richmond Hill
BH2: Bourn 4H **121** (4F **93**)
Richmond Hill Dr.
BH2: Bourn 4H **121** (4F **93**)
Richmond Hill Ga. BH2: Bourn 4H **121**
Richmond Ho.
BH1: Bourn 4H **121** (4F **93**)
Richmond Pk. Av. BH8: Bourn 7H **83**
Richmond Pk. Cl. BH8: Bourn 1K **93**
Richmond Pk. Cres. BH8: Bourn 7J **83**
Richmond Pk. Rd. BH8: Bourn 7H **83**
Richmond Rd. BH14: Pool 2G **91**
BH19: Swan 5J **117**
BH21: Wim M 1B **72**
DT9: Sher 5B **12**
DT11: B For 3D **30**
Richmond Wood Rd. BH8: Bourn . . .7H **83**
Ricketts Cl. DT4: Wey 6J **103**
Ricketts La. DT10: S New 5C **16**
RIDGE
Salisbury 1C **125**
Wareham 6K **113** (2C **129**)
Ridge Cl. SP8: E Sto 1K **7**
Ridge Drove DT10: H Bry, K Stag . . .1A **28**
Ridgefield Gdns. BH23: Chris 6H **87**
Ridgemount Gdns. BH15: Hamw . . .4G **89**
Ridge Way SP7: Shaf 1C **8**
Ridgeway BH18: B'tone 2K **79**
BH21: Corf M 5F **71**
BH22: W Par 5E **74**
DT6: Bradp 1F **39**
DT9: Sher 5A **12**
Ridgeway, The DT3: Upw 3F **101**
Ridgeway La. DT10: H Mary 1C **16**
DT11: Chil O 1G **19**
Ridgeway Rd. SP8: Gill 3G **5**
Ridley Rd. BH9: Bourn 6F **83**
Ridout Cl. BH10: Bourn 5B **82**
Ridwood DT6: Chid 5B **36**
Riggs Gdns. BH11: Bourn 4K **81**
Rigler Rd. BH15: Hamw 6J **89**
Riley Ct. SP8: Gill 5J **5**
Rimbrow Cl. DT3: S Poy 3C **104**
Rimbury Way BH23: Chris 6J **85**
RIMPTON .1D **123**
Ring, The DT10: Stalb 3H **15**
Ringhill St. DT1: Poun 3B **50**
Rings, The DT11: M And 6C **44**
Ringstead Cres. DT3: Over 6B **104**
Ring St. DT10: Stalb 2H **15**
RINGWOOD 4K **61** (2A **130**)
Ringwood Raceway 6D **68**
Ringwood Recreation Cen. 4J **61**
Ringwood Rd. BH10: Bourn 7K **73**
BH11: Bourn 7K **73**
BH12: Pool 6F **81**
BH14: Pool 3D **90**
BH21: T Leg, Wools 3D **58**
BH22: Fern, L'ham, W Moo 7D **66**
BH23: Avon, Sop 5J **77**
BH23: Bran 1G **87**
BH24: S Ive, S Leo 4G **67**
BH31: Ver 3F **55**
SP6: Ald 7H **21**
Ringwood Rd. Retail Pk.
BH11: Bourn 3J **81**
Ringwood Rd. Service Rd.
BH24: S Leo 1B **68**
Ringwood Trad. Est. BH24: Ring 5J **61**
(not continuous)
Rip Cft. DT5: S'well 4G **119**
RIPLEY 3K **77** (3A **130**)
Ripon Rd. BH9: Bourn 6G **83**
Rise, The DT2: Strat 4B **48**
DT4: S'hill 6E **102**
Ritchie Pl. BH22: W Moo 7D **58**
Ritchie Rd. BH11: Bourn 2B **82**
River Cl. BH21: Wim M 6A **64**
River Ct. BH23: B Int 5C **76**
River Cres. DT1: Dor 3G **51**
Riverdale La. BH23: Chris 1J **95**
River La. DT11: Char M 3B **32**
Riverlea Rd. BH23: Chris 1J **95**
Rivermead Gdns. BH23: Chris 4G **85**
River M. DT11: B For 5B **30**
Rivers Arms Cl. DT10: S New 5C **16**
Riversdale Rd. BH6: Bourn 3J **95**
Rivers Edge DT11: Char M 2A **32**
Riverside BH10: Bourn 2F **83**
BH24: Ring 5H **61**
DT8: Bea 3E **24**
Riverside Av. BH7: Bourn 4D **84**
Riverside Cl. DT2: Cer A 2B **42**
Riverside Ct. BH22: W Moo 1D **66**
DT1: Dor 2F **51**
DT6: Brid 4C **38**
Riverside La. BH6: Bourn 2H **95**
Riverside Pk. BH23: Chris 2J **95**
Riverside Pk. Ind. Est.
BH21: Wim M 2B **72**
Riverside Rd. BH6: Bourn 2H **95**
BH22: W Moo 2C **66**
DT11: B For 5D **30**
Riverslea M. BH23: Chris 1B **96**
Rivers Mead DT10: S New 4D **16**
Rivervale DT6: Brid 2D **38**
River Vw. SP8: Gill 4G **5**
River Way BH23: Chris 5F **85**
Riverway DT6: C'outh 7J **35**
Riviera BH1: Bourn 4H **93**
Riviera Ct. BH2: Bourn 4D **92**
BH13: Pool 1K **99**
RIXON 4D **16**
Rixon Cl. DT10: S New 5D **16**
Rixon Hill DT10: S New 5D **16**
R L Stevenson Av. BH4: Bourn 4B **92**
Robert Christmas Ho.
BH20: W'ham 3G **113**
Roberts Cl. DT6: Burt B 7H **37**
Roberts La. BH17: Pool 7H **79**
Robertson Rd. BH20: Bov 1A **110**
Roberts Pl. DT1: Dor 4D **50**
Roberts Rd. BH7: Bourn 1C **94**
BH17: Pool 5K **79**
Robin Cl. DT3: B'wey 6G **101**
Robin Gdns. BH23: Chris 6J **85**
Robins Gth. DT1: Dor 4G **51**
Robinson Hgts. DT10: Stalb 2H **15**
Robins Way BH23: Mude 2F **97**
Robinswood Dr. BH22: Fern 4D **66**
Robsall Cl. BH12: Pool 7J **81**
Rochester Ct. DT4: Wey 1E **106**
Rochester Rd. BH11: Bourn 2B **82**
ROCKBOURNE 1A **130**
Rockbourne Gdns. BH25: N Mil 6K **97**
ROCKFORD 2A **130**
Rockford Cl. BH6: Bourn 4H **95**
Rockhampton Cl. DT3: Lit 7H **101**
Rockland BH19: Swan 5K **117**
Rockley Cvn. Pk. BH15: Hamw 4D **88**
Rockley M. BH15: Hamw 5G **89**
Rockley Rd. BH15: Hamw 5G **89**
ROCKLEY SANDS 4D **88**
Rocks La. DT2: Ever 5C **26**
Rockway DT6: Ship G 6J **39**
Rocky Knap DT3: Rad 4G **103**
Rocquaine Ct. BH19: Swan 4J **117**
RODDEN 2D **127**
Rodden Cl. DT4: W Reg 4E **106**
Rodden Row DT3: Abb 5D **46**
Rodgett Cres. BH20: Sandf 6A **112**
Rod Hill Cl. DT2: Pud 2C **52**
Rod Hill La. DT2: Pud 4C **52**
Rodney Cl. BH12: Pool 6A **82**
Rodney Ct. BH15: Pool 6C **120** (6A **90**)
Rodney Dr. BH23: Mude 1D **96**
Rodway BH21: Wim M 1A **72**
Rodways Cnr. BH21: Wim M 1A **72**
RODWELL 2H **107** (3D **127**)
Rodwell Av. DT4: Wey 3H **107**
Rodwell Cl. BH10: Bourn 7C **74**
Rodwell Lodge *DT4: Wey 3H 107*
(off Rodwell Rd.)
Rodwell Rd. DT4: Wey 2H **107**
Rodwell St. DT4: Wey 3H **107**
Roeshot Cres. BH23: Chris 5H **87**
Roeshot Hill BH23: Chris 5G **87**
Rogamet Cvn. Pk. BH21: T Leg 2D **58**
Roi-Mar Home Pk. BH8: Bourn 2K **83**
Roke Rd. BH20: Ber 1F **53**
Rolfe Cres. DT3: Chick 5B **102**
Rolls Bri. Bungs. *SP8: Gill 4G 5*
(off Rolls Bri. La.)
Rolls Bri. La. SP8: Gill 4G **5**
Rolls Bri. Way SP8: Gill 4F **5**
Rolls Dr. BH6: Bourn 3K **95**
Rolls Mill Way DT10: S New 7A **16**
Roman Cl. DT3: Rad 4G **103**
Roman Hgts. BH21: Corf M 5G **71**
Roman Hill Bus. Pk. DT2: Broad . . .7E **108**
Roman Rd. BH18: B'tone 2G **79**
(not continuous)
DT1: Dor 5D **50**
DT3: Osm 3H **105**
DT3: Rad 4F **103**
DT7: L Reg 4B **34**
Romans Bus. Cen. SP8: Gill 4H **5**
Roman Way BH21: Cow 7E **62**
DT11: Shil 6F **19**
ROMFORD 3D **54** (3D **125**)
Romney Cl. BH10: Bourn 3E **82**
Romney Rd. BH10: Bourn 2E **82**
Romulus Cl. DT1: Dor 6D **50**
Rookery Cl. SP8: Gill 5K **5**
Rookery La. DT7: H Bot 1B **34**
Rook Hill Rd. BH23: F Clif 1F **97**
Rook La. DT11: W Whi 2H **45**
Roosevelt Cres. BH11: Bourn 7B **74**
Ropers La. BH16: Upt 7F **79**
BH20: W'ham 3H **113**
Rope Wlk. DT3: Abb 5D **46**
Rope Walks DT6: Brid 4C **38**
Ropley Rd. BH7: Bourn 7E **84**
Rosamond Av. DT6: Ship G 6K **39**
Rosamond Ct. DT6: Burt B 6H **37**
Rosamund Av. BH21: Merl 4C **72**
Roscrea Cl. BH6: Bourn 3K **95**
Roscrea Dr. BH6: Bourn 3K **95**
Rosebank La. DT11: B For 2E **30**
Roseberry Gdns. SP8: Gill 3H **5**
Rosebery Cl. BH31: Ver 5J **55**
Rosebery Rd. BH5: Bourn 2C **94**
Rosebud Av. BH9: Bourn 4G **83**
Rose Ct. SP8: Gill 5J **5**
Rose Cres. BH15: Pool 1D **90**
Rosecroft Rd. DT4: Wey 3D **106**
Rosedale Cl. BH23: Chris 1C **96**
Rose Farm Cl. BH22: Fern 2B **74**
Rosefields DT11: Blan 6C **30**
Rose Gdns. BH9: Bourn 4F **83**
Rosemary Ct. BH23: H'ffe 7J **97**
Rosemary Gdns. BH12: Pool 7F **81**
Rosemary La. DT3: Abb 5D **46**
Rosemary Rd. BH12: Pool 7F **81**
Rosemount Rd. BH4: Bourn 5B **92**
Roslin Gdns. BH3: Bourn 7D **82**
Roslin Rd. BH3: Bourn 7E **82**
Roslin Rd. Sth. BH3: Bourn 7D **82**
(not continuous)
Ross Cl. BH20: Bov 2C **110**
Ross Gdns. BH11: Bourn 1G **81**
Ross Glades BH3: Bourn 1E **92**
Rossiters Quay BH23: Chris 1A **96**
Rossley Cl. BH23: Chris 4J **87**
ROSSMORE .7K **81**
Rossmore Pde. BH12: Pool 6F **81**
Rossmore Rd. BH12: Pool 6F **81**
Rotary Cl. BH21: Coleh 5D **64**
Rotherfield Rd. BH5: Bourn 4D **94**
BH23: H'ffe 5H **97**
Rotherham Rd. DT5: Cast 3C **118**
Rothesay Dr. BH23: H'ffe 7J **87**
Rothesay Rd. BH4: Bourn 1C **92**
DT1: Dor 5F **51**
Rotterdam Dr. BH23: Chris 7B **86**
Rough Down La. DT6: C'outh 4J **35**
Rough Height BH19: Swan 6J **117**
Roumelia La. BH5: Bourn 3A **94**
ROUNDHAM 3B **122**
Roundham Gdns. DT4: Wey 2F **107**
DT6: Brid 7D **38**
Roundhaye Gdns. BH11: Bourn 7K **73**
Roundhaye Rd. BH11: Bourn 1K **81**
Roundhayes Cl. DT4: Wey 2E **106**
Roundways BH11: Bourn 3J **81**
ROUSDON .1A **126**
Rousiball La. DT2: Buck N 7F **27**
Row, The DT10: S New 5B **16**
Rowan Cl. BH20: Sandf 6C **112**
BH23: Chris 6H **87**
BH24: S Leo 7K **59**
DT4: S'hill 5E **102**
SP7: Shaf 2D **8**
Rowan Dr. BH17: Pool 5G **79**
BH23: Chris 6H **87**
BH31: Ver 6H **55**
Rowan Ho. DT1: Dor 4F **51**
Rowan Wlk. DT2: Char D 1H **49**
Rowbarrow Cl. BH17: Pool 4C **80**
Rowbarrow La. BH21: Mans 1G **33**
Rowden Mill La. DT10: S Cau 4K **15**
Rowe Gdns. BH12: Pool 7K **81**
Rowena Rd. BH6: Bourn 2H **95**
Rowland Av. BH15: Pool 2C **90**
Rowland Ct. DT4: Wey 5J **103**
ROWLANDS .7K **63**
Rowlands Cvn. Pk. DT3: Chick 7C **102**
Rowlands Hill BH21: Wim M 7A **64**
Rowlands Rd. DT11: Stour 2H **29**
Rowlands Wait Touring Pk.
BH20: Ber 4G **53**
Rownhams Rd. BH8: Bourn 3J **83**
Royal Arc. BH1: Bourn 3A **94**
Royal Belvidere Cres. *DT4: Wey . . .7J 103*
(off Crescent St.)
Royal Chase Rdbt. SP7: Shaf 4D **8**
Royal Cl. BH23: Chris 6H **85**
Royal M. DT1: Dor 3F **51**
Royal Motor Yacht Club 4F **99**
Royal Oak Rd. BH10: Bourn 1C **82**
Royal Signals Mus. 6J **31**
Royal Ter. DT4: Wey 1H **107**
Royal Victoria M. BH4: Bourn 4D **92**
Royster Cl. BH17: Pool 5A **80**
Royston Dr. BH21: Wim M 7B **64**
Rozelle Rd. BH14: Pool 3G **91**
Rozel Mnr. BH13: Pool 5B **92**
RSPB Cen. 7G **103**
Ruben Dr. BH15: Hamw 5F **89**
Rufford Gdns. BH6: Bourn 2G **95**
Rufus Castle (remains of) 2K **119**
Rufus Ct. SP8: Gill 5J **5**
Rufus Way DT5: East 7D **118**
Rugby Rd. BH17: Pool 5J **79**
Ruins La. DT6: Chid 5B **36**
RUISHTON .1A **122**
Rundlestone Ct. DT1: Poun 3A **50**
Runnymede Av. BH11: Bourn 7H **73**
Runton Rd. BH12: Pool 2K **91**
Runway, The BH23: Chris 7F **87**
Rushall La. BH16: Corf M, L Mat . . .2A **78**
RUSHCOMBE BOTTOM 6H **71**
Rushcombe Way BH21: Corf M 7G **71**
Rushetts Cl. DT5: S'well 4H **119**
Rushford Warren BH23: Mude 2D **96**
Rushmere Rd. BH6: Bourn 7E **84**
Rushton Cres. BH3: Bourn 1F **93**
Ruskin Av. BH9: Bourn 3H **83**
Russell Av. BH19: Swan 6J **117**
DT4: Wey 3F **107**
Russell Cotes Art Gallery & Mus. 6K **121** (5G **93**)
Russell Cotes Rd.
BH1: Bourn 6K **121** (5G **93**)
Russell Dr. BH19: Swan 6J **117**
BH23: Chris 1B **96**
Russell Gdns. BH16: Hamw 3E **88**
BH24: S Ive 6D **60**
Russel Rd. BH10: Bourn 7C **74**
Russet Cl. BH22: Fern 6D **66**
Russet Gdns. DT6: Brid 2F **39**
Rutland Mnr. BH13: Pool 3A **92**
Rutland Rd. BH9: Bourn 6H **83**
BH23: Chris 5H **85**
DT4: Wey 7F **103**
Rutter Cl. SP7: Shaf 4D **8**
Rutt La. Hollow BH20: Ber 1H **53**
RYALL 1J **35** (1B **126**)
Ryall Rd. BH17: Pool 5B **80**
DT6: Ryal, Whit C 1H **35**
Ryall's La. DT9: Bis C 7G **15**
Ryam La. DT2: Cors 7F **25**
Ryan Bus. Pk. BH20: W'ham 2H **113**
Ryan Cl. BH20: W'ham 2H **113**
BH22: Fern 5C **66**
Ryan Ct. DT11: B For 5B **30**
Ryan Gdns. BH11: Bourn 7B **74**
BH22: Fern 5C **66**
Rydal Cl. BH23: Chris 2F **85**
Ryecroft Av. BH11: Bourn 1J **81**
Rye Hill BH20: Ber 4H **53**
Rye Hill Cl. BH20: Ber 3H **53**
Ryemead La. DT4: W Reg 6E **106**
Ryland's La. DT4: Wey 4F **107**
Rymbury DT3: Pres 3C **104**
RYME INTRINSECA 2C **123**
Ryme Rd. DT9: Yet 7F **13**

S

Sackmore Grn. DT10: Marn 3H **9**
Sackmore La. DT10: Marn 3H **9**
Sackville St. DT11: W Kin 6H **45**
Sadborow La. TA20: T'ombe 7C **22**
Saddle Cl. BH21: Coleh 6G **65**
Saddle St. TA20: T'ombe 6D **22**
Saffron Ct. DT9: Sher 4D **12**
Saffron Dr. BH23: Chris 6F **87**
Saffron Way BH11: Bourn 3H **81**
St Albans Av. BH8: Bourn 7H **83**
St Albans Cres. BH8: Bourn 7H **83**
St Albans Rd. BH8: Bourn 7H **83**
St Alban St. DT4: Wey 2H **107**
St Aldhelms BH14: Pool 3K **91**
St Aldhelm's Cl. BH13: Pool 4K **91**
St Aldhelms Ct. BH19: Swan 4J **117**
St Aldhelm's Pl. BH13: Pool 3K **91**

St Aldhelm's Rd.—School Cl.

St Aldhelm's Rd. BH13: Pool 3K 91
DT9: Sher .2C 12
St Andrews BH23: Chris 1J 95
St Andrew's Av. DT3: Rad 4H 103
St Andrews Church (remains of) . . .2K 119
St Andrews Cl. DT1: Dor 5G 51
DT9: Leig 5D 14
St Andrews Dr. DT6: C'outh 6H 35
St Andrew's Gdns. *DT6: Bradp 2F 39*
(off Shoe La.)
St Andrews Ho. DT6: C'outh 6H 35
St Andrew's Ind. Est. DT6: Brid 2F 39
St Andrews Mdw. DT7: L Reg 4C 34
St Andrews Rd. BH18: B'tone 1J 79
DT6: Bradp, Brid 3D 38
St Andrew's Ter. DT6: Bradp 2F 39
St Andrew's Vw. DT11: M And 7B 44
SP7: Fon M 4C 10
ST ANDREW'S WELL 2F 39
St Andrew's Well DT6: Bradp 2F 39
St Anne's Av. BH6: Bourn 2G 95
St Anne's Rd. BH16: Upt 7D 78
DT4: Wey 5G 107
St Ann's Ct. BH1: Bourn 2A 94
St Anthony's Rd.
BH2: Bourn 1H 121 (2F 93)
St Antony's BH4: Bourn 5D 92
St Antonys Sq. DT9: Sher 5C 12
St Aubyns Ct. BH15: Pool. . .5A 120 (5K 89)
St Augustin's Rd. BH2: Bourn 2F 93
ST BARTHOLOMEW'S HILL 1C 125
St Brelades BH14: Pool 6G 91
St Brelades Av. BH12: Pool 4H 81
St Catherines BH21: Wim M 1A 72
St Catherine's Chapel 6C 46
St Catherine's Cres. DT9: Sher 5A 12
ST CATHERINE'S HILL 3G 85
St Catherine's Hill La.
BH23: Chris 4H 85
St Catherine's Pde. BH23: Chris . . .5H 85
St Catherine's Path BH6: Bourn 4G 95
St Catherine's Rd. BH6: Bourn 4G 95
St Catherine's Way BH23: Chris 3F 85
DT9: Sher 5A 12
St Cecilia's Gdns. DT6: Brid 2D 38
St Clair Rd. BH13: Pool 2J 99
St Cleeve Way BH22: Fern 2C 74
St Clements Gdns. BH1: Bourn 2K 93
St Clements La.
BH15: Pool 6A 120 (6K 89)
St Clements Rd. BH1: Bourn 2K 93
BH12: Pool 7E 80
BH15: Pool 7E 80
St Davids Cl. DT1: Dor 5G 51
St David's Ct. BH1: Bourn 2A 94
St David's Rd. BH16: Upt 6D 78
DT4: Wey 5F 107
St Edmund St. DT4: Wey 2H 107
St Edwards Cl. BH20: Corf C 3B 114
SP7: Shaf 3C 8
St Edwards Ct. SP7: Shaf 4C 8
St George's Almshouses
BH15: Pool 6A 120
St Georges Av. BH8: Bourn 6J 83
BH12: Pool 6F 81
DT4: Wey 5J 103
St Georges Cl. BH8: Bourn 6J 83
BH19: Lan M 5C 116
BH23: Chris 7H 87
DT1: Dor 4J 51
St Georges Ct. BH1: Bourn 2A 94
BH22: Fern 7E 66
St Georges Dr. BH11: Bourn 3H 81
BH22: Fern 1C 74
St George's Est. Rd. DT5: East 1H 119
St Georges Hill DT7: L Reg 4B 34
St Georges Rd. DT1: Dor 4H 51
DT5: East 1H 119
SP7: Shaf 4C 8
St Georges School Ct. *DT1: Dor 3G 51*
(off High St.)
St Giles Cl. DT6: Chid 4B 36
St Helen's La. DT2: Catt, Chilf 4F 41
St Helen's Rd. BH20: Sandf 6B 112
DT1: Dor 3E 50
DT4: Wey 2D 106
St Helier Av. DT3: B'wey 6F 101
St Helier Rd. BH12: Pool 5H 81
ST IVES 6C 60 (2A 130)
St Ives End La. BH24: S Ive 7C 60
St Ives Gdns. BH2: Bourn. . . 1J 121 (2F 93)
St Ives Pk. BH24: Ash H 6C 60
St Ives Wood BH24: S Ive 6D 60
ST JAMES 4A 8
St James BH5: Bourn 4A 94
DT8: Bea 2B 24
St James Cl. BH15: Pool . . .6A 120 (6K 89)
St James Ho. *BH15: Pool 3D 120*
(off Denmark Rd.)
St James Pk. DT6: Bradp 1G 39
St James Rd. BH22: Fern 6A 66
St James Rd. DT6: Neth 7A 24
St James's Sq. BH5: Bourn 2C 94
St James's St. SP7: Shaf 5A 8
ST JOHNS 1B 72
St John's Cl. BH21: Wim M 1B 72
DT5: Fort 5B 118
St John's Ct. *BH1: Bourn 2A 94*
(off Palmerston M.)
DT4: Wey 7J 103
(off William St.)
St Johns Gdns. BH9: Bourn 5F 83
St John's Hill BH20: W'ham 4H 113
BH21: Wim M 7B 64
SP7: Shaf 4A 8
St Johns Rd. BH5: Bourn 3A 94
BH15: Pool 1E 120 (3B 90)
BH23: Chris 1H 95
St Julien Cres. DT3: B'wey 7F 101
St Julien Rd. BH20: Bov 1A 110
St Just Cl. BH22: Fern 2B 74
St Juthware Cl. BA22: Hal 2H 25
St Katherine's Av. DT6: Brid 3E 38
St Katherine's Dr. DT6: Brid 2E 38
St Lawrence DT6: Burt B 6H 37
St Lawrence Cres. SP7: Shaf 2C 8
St Lawrence Rd. DT3: Upw 5G 101
St Ledger's Pl. BH8: Bourn 1K 93
St Ledger's Rd. BH8: Bourn 1K 93
ST LEONARDS 1A 68 (2A 130)
St Leonard's Av. DT11: B For 5D 30
St Leonards Ct. DT11: B For 5C 30
St Leonards Farm Cvn. Pk.
BH22: W Moo 5G 67
St Leonard's Rd. BH8: Bourn 1H 93
DT4: Wey 3H 107
St Leonard's Ter. DT11: B For 4D 30
St Leonards Way BH24: Ash H 6K 59
St Luke's Ct. DT6: Brid 2B 38
St Luke's Rd. BH3: Bourn 7F 83
St Maradox La. BH9: Bourn 4F 83
St Margarets
BH2: Bourn 1H 121 (2F 93)
St Margaret's Av. BH23: Chris 1J 95
St Margarets Cl. BH21: Wim M 7J 63
St Margaret's Hill BH21: Wim M 6J 63
St Margaret's Rd. BH10: Bourn 4B 82
BH15: Pool 1D 120 (3B 90)
St Marks Rd. BH11: Bourn 3B 82
St Martins Cl. BH20: W'ham 3H 113
DT2: Broad 6C 108
St Martins Fld. DT2: Mart 2J 47
St Martin's Hill BH16: Hol H 3D 112
St Martin's Ho. *BH20: W'ham 3H 113*
(off North St.)
St Martin's La. BH20: W'ham 3H 113
St Martin's Pl. BH20: Sandf 6B 112
St Martins Rd. BH16: Upt 7C 78
BH20: Sandf 6B 112
DT4: Wey 4G 107
DT5: Fort 5B 118
SP7: Shaf 4C 8
St Martin's Sq. SP8: Gill 4H 5
St Mary's Cl. BH20: W'ham 2F 113
DT11: W Whi 2G 45
SP5: Six H 2C 20
St Mary's Ct. BH6: Bourn 4G 95
SP5: Six H 2C 20
St Mary's Gdns. DT8: Bea 2B 24
St Mary's M. BH22: Fern 1D 74
St Mary's Pl. DT6: Brid 4D 38
St Mary's Rd. BH1: Bourn 1K 93
BH15: Pool 2E 120 (4B 90)
BH22: Fern 7D 66
DT9: Sher 5A 12
St Mary St. DT4: Wey 2H 107
St Mary Well St. DT8: Bea 3C 24
St Merrin's Cl. BH10: Bourn 2C 82
St Michaels *BH2: Bourn 4D 92*
(off Norwich Av.)
DT7: L Reg 4D 34
St Michaels Cl. BH15: Hamw 4G 89
BH31: Ver 5F 55
DT9: O Com 2H 11
St Michaels Ct. *BH2: Bourn 4D 92*
(off Poole Rd.)
DT4: Wey 3G 107
St Michael's La.
BH2: Bourn 5F 121 (4E 92)
DT6: Brid 4C 38
St Michael's M. BH2: Bourn 5F 121
St Michael's Pl. BH2: Bourn 5F 121
St Michael's Rd.
BH2: Bourn 5F 121 (4E 92)
BH20: W'ham 4H 113
BH31: Ver 5F 55
St Michael's Rdbt. BH2: Bourn 4D 92
St Michael's Trad. Est. DT6: Brid . . .4C 38
St Monicas Priory DT11: S'bury 6D 32
St Nicholas Ct. DT11: Chil O 2H 19
St Nicholas Gdns. DT11: Dur 4G 29
St Nicholas St. DT4: Wey 2H 107
St Osmund Cl. DT9: Yet 7G 13
St Osmund's Community Sports Cen.
. . . . .5G 51
St Osmunds Rd. BH14: Pool 3G 91
St Patricks Av. DT4: Wey 3D 106
St Patricks Ind. Est. DT11: Shil 4E 18
St Paul's Cl. DT9: Sher 2D 12
St Pauls Ct. DT4: Wey 1G 107
St Paul's Flats DT9: Sher 2D 12
St Paul's Grn. DT9: Sher 2D 12
St Paul's La. BH8: Bourn 3H 93
St Paul's Pl. BH8: Bourn 3G 93
St Paul's Rd. BH1: Bourn 3G 93
DT5: Fort 5B 118
St Peter's Cl. DT11: P'erne 2F 31
St Peter's Ct.
BH1: Bourn 4K 121 (4G 93)
St Peter's Ga.
BH1: Bourn 4J 121 (4F 93)
St Peter's Rd.
BH1: Bourn 5J 121 (4F 93)
BH14: Pool 3E 90
St Peter's Rdbt.
BH1: Bourn 5K 121 (4G 93)
St Peter's Wlk. BH1: Bourn 5H 121
St Rumbold's Rd. SP7: Shaf 4C 8
St Saviours Cl. BH7: Bourn 7E 84
Saints Cl. BH21: T Leg 3E 58
St Stephen's Ct. BH2: Bourn 3G 121
St Stephen's La. BH31: Ver 4G 55
St Stephen's Rd.
BH2: Bourn 3F 121 (3E 92)
St Stephen's Way
BH2: Bourn 4H 121 (4F 93)
St Swithins Av. DT6: Brid 3C 38
St Swithins Cl. DT9: Sher 4D 12
St Swithins Ct. DT6: Brid 3C 38
St Swithins Rd. DT6: Brid 3C 38
DT9: Sher 4D 12
St Swithun's Rd. BH1: Bourn 3H 93
St Swithun's Rd. Sth.
BH1: Bourn 3H 93
St Swithun's Rdbt. BH1: Bourn 4H 93
St Thomas Cl. BH10: Bourn 4D 82
St Thomas Rd. DT1: Dor 3E 50
St Thomas St. DT4: Wey 2H 107
St Valerie Rd.
BH2: Bourn 1H 121 (2F 93)
St Vasts Rd. BH19: Swan 6K 117
St Winifred's Rd.
BH2: Bourn 1H 121 (2F 93)
Salerno Pl. BH15: Hamw 5F 89
SALISBURY 1D 125
Salisbury Cres. DT11: B For 3D 30
Salisbury M. *DT1: Dor 3G 51*
(off High St.)
Salisbury Rd. BH1: Bourn 3A 94
BH14: Pool 2G 91
BH19: Swan 6K 117
BH23: Burt 2A 86
BH23: Sop 7K 77
BH24: Blas, Ring 3H 61
DT4: Wey 1G 107
DT11: B For, P'erne 2E 30
SP7: Shaf 4C 8
(not continuous)
Salisbury St. BH21: Cran 1G 21
DT1: Dor 3G 51
DT10: Marn 4K 9
DT11: B For 5B 30
SP7: Shaf 4C 8
Salisbury Ter. *DT1: Dor 3G 51*
(off Salisbury St.)
Salisbury Vs. *DT1: Dor 3G 51*
(off Salisbury St.)
Salisbury Wlk. DT1: Dor 3G 51
Sally King's La. SP7: Shaf 3A 8
Salterns Ct. BH14: Pool 7F 91
Salterns Point BH14: Pool 7F 91
Salterns Rd. BH14: Pool 4E 90
Salterns Way BH14: Pool 7F 91
Salter Rd. BH13: Sandb 5F 99
Saltings Rd. BH16: Upt 1D 88
SALWAYASH 1B 126
Samantha Cl. BH10: Bourn 3E 82
Samphire Cl. DT4: Wey 5H 103
Samples Way BH17: Pool 6D 80
Samson Rd. BH15: Hamw 4F 89
Sancreed Rd. BH12: Pool 7J 81
SANDBANKS 4G 99 (2D 129)
Sandbanks Bus. Cen.
BH13: Sandb 5F 99
Sandbanks Rd. BH14: Pool 4D 90
Sandbourne Av. DT11: B For 2D 30
Sandbourne Cl. BH19: Swan 5G 117
Sandbourne Rd. BH4: Bourn 6C 92
BH15: Pool 3B 90
DT3: Over 5B 104
Sandecotes Rd. BH14: Pool 3G 91
Sanderling Cl. DT3: B'wey 6G 101
Sanderling Ct. BH5: Bourn 4K 93
Sanders Grn. DT11: W Whi 2H 45
SANDFORD
Ringwood 2A 130
Wareham 6B 112 (2C 129)
Sandford Cl. BH9: Bourn 3J 83
Sandford Dr. BH20: Sandf 4C 112
Sandford Holiday Pk.
BH16: Sandf 4C 112
Sandford Ho. BH20: Sandf 4B 112
Sandford La. BH20: W'ham 2H 113
Sandford La. Ind. Est.
BH20: W'ham 1H 113
SANDFORD ORCAS 1D 123
Sandford Orcas Manor House 1D 123
Sandford Orcas Rd. DT9: Sher 1A 12
Sandford Rd.
BH20: Sandf, W'ham 2H 113
Sandford Ter. BH20: Sandf 6A 112
Sandford Way BH18: B'tone 4H 79
SANDFORD WOODS 6A 112
SANDHILLS
Sherborne 2D 123
Dorchester 1F 41
Sandhills Cvn. Pk. BH23: Mude 2F 97
Sandhills Cl. BH17: Pool 4B 80
Sandhills Cres. BH20: Wool 6B 110
Sandholes Cl. DT5: S'well 4G 119
Sandhurst Dr. BH21: T Leg 4G 59
Sandilands Cl. SP8: E Sto 1K 7
SANDLEHEATH 1A 130
Sandleheath Rd. SP6: Ald 5H 21
Sandon Ct. BH8: Bourn 7J 83
Sandown Rd. BH23: Chris 1C 96
Sandpiper Cl. BH17: Pool 5H 79
Sandpiper Way DT4: W Reg 6F 107
SANDPIT 3D 22
Sandpit La. BH15: Pool . . .3E 120 (4B 90)
Sandringham Cl. BH9: Bourn 2H 83
Sandringham Ct.
BH2: Bourn 6H 121 (5F 93)
BH8: Bourn 1J 93
BH19: Swan 5J 117
DT1: Dor 5H 51
Sandringham Gdns. BH9: Bourn 2H 83
Sandringham Rd. BH14: Pool 4F 91
Sandringham Sports Cen. 4G 51
Sandsfoot Castle (remains of) . . .5H 107
Sandsfoot Holiday Pk.
DT4: Wey 4G 107
Sandy Cl. BH21: Coleh 4E 64
Sandy Hill La.
BH20: Corf C, Woolg 2B 114
Sandyhurst Cl. BH17: Pool 5A 80
Sandy La. BH6: Bourn 2D 94
BH16: Upt 1C 88
BH21: Coleh 4E 64
BH21: Cow 6D 62
BH21: T Leg 1E 58
BH23: Chris 4G 85
BH24: S Ive 7B 60
BH31: Ver 4G 55
DT11: Chil O 1H 19
Sandy Mead Rd. BH8: Bourn 5B 84
Sandy Plot BH23: Burt 5A 86
Sandy Way BH10: Bourn 3E 82
(not continuous)
San Remo Towers BH5: Bourn 4A 94
Sarah Cl. BH7: Bourn 6D 84
Sarah Sands Cl. BH23: Chris 6B 86
Sark Rd. BH12: Pool 6H 81
Sarum DT9: T'ford 1K 13
Sarum Av. BH22: W Moo 7E 58
(not continuous)
Sarum Ct. BH14: Pool 3G 91
Sarum St. BH15: Pool 6A 120 (6K 89)
Saulfland Dr. BH23: Chris 6H 87
Saulfland Pl. BH23: Chris 6H 87
Saville Ct. BH21: Wim M 2B 72
Savoy Ct. SP7: Shaf 3B 8
Sawmills La. DT1: Dor 6E 50
Sawyers La. DT2: Strat 4C 48
Saxonbury Rd. BH6: Bourn 1G 95
Saxon Cen., The BH23: Chris 7K 85
Saxon Ct. BH20: W'ham 2H 113
Saxonford Rd. BH23: F Clif 7G 87
Saxonhurst Cl. BH10: Bourn 1E 82
Saxonhurst Gdns. BH10: Bourn 2E 82
Saxonhurst Rd. BH10: Bourn 2D 82
Saxon King Gdns. BH6: Bourn 3K 95
Saxon Mead Cl. SP8: Gill 3G 5
Saxon Ri. DT11: W Stic 5J 29
Saxon Spur SP7: Shaf 2C 8
Saxon Sq. Shop. Cen.
BH23: Chris 1K 95
Saxon Way SP6: Ald 7J 21
Scaplen's Court (Mus.) . . .6A 120 (6K 89)
Scarf Rd. BH17: Pool 6D 80
Schelin Way DT11: Shil 6F 19
School Cl. BH31: Ver 3G 55
DT1: Dor 3F 51
DT3: Chick 5B 102

Steppes—Talbot Rdbt.

Steppes BH19: Lan M 4D 116
Steppes Hill BH19: Lan M 5D 116
STERTE 1A 120 (3K 89)
Sterte Av. BH15: Pool 1A 120 (3K 89)
Sterte Av. W.
BH15: Pool 1A 120 (3K 89)
Sterte Cl. BH15: Pool 1A 120 (3K 89)
Sterte Ct. BH15: Pool 1B 120 (3A 90)
Sterte Esplanade
BH15: Pool 1B 120 (3A 90)
Sterte Ind. Est.
BH15: Pool 1A 120 (3K 89)
Sterte Rd. BH15: Pool 1B 120 (4A 90)
Stevens Cl. DT11: B For 3D 30
Stevenson Cres. BH14: Pool 4H 91
Stevenson Lodge BH4: Bourn 4C 92
Stevenson Rd. BH6: Bourn 4J 95
Stevensons Cl. BH21: Wim M 1A 72
Stevensons Ct. DT6: Brid 4D 38
Stevens Wlk. DT2: Buck N 6H 27
Stewart Cl. BH8: Bourn 2J 93
Stewart M. BH8: Bourn 2J 93
Stewart Rd. BH8: Bourn 1G 93
Stewarts Way BH22: Fern 5E 66
STEWLEY 2A 122
Stickland Ct. DT11: B For 5B 30
Stileham Bank DT11: M And 6B 44
Stile La. DT7: L Reg 5C 34
Stillmore Rd. BH11: Bourn 3H 81
Stillwater Pk. BH24: Poul 1K 61
STINSFORD 2K 51 (1A 128)
Stinsford Cl. BH9: Bourn 2H 83
Stinsford Cotts. DT2: Stin 2K 51
Stinsford Hill DT2: Stin 3H 51
Stinsford Rd. BH17: Pool 5B 80
Stinsford Vw. DT1: Dor 4H 51
Stirling Bus. Pk. BH21: Stap 5K 65
Stirling Rd. BH3: Bourn 7E 82
DT3: Red 3G 103
Stirling Way BH23: Mude 1F 97
Stirrup Cl. BH16: Upt 7F 79
BH21: Coleh 6G 65
STOBOROUGH 6H 113 (2C 129)
Stoborough Cl. DT3: Red 3F 103
Stoborough Dr. BH18: B'tone 4H 79
STOBOROUGH GREEN . . .7J 113 (2C 129)
Stoborough Grn. BH20: Stob 7J 113
Stoborough Mdw. BH20: Stob 7J 113
Stockbridge Cl. BH17: Pool 4F 81
Stockham La. DT8: Hurs 7F 23
STOCKLAND 3A 122
Stockley Rd. BH20: W'ham 1G 113
STOCKLINCH 2A 122
Stocks Farm Rd. BH22: W Par 4F 75
STOCKWOOD 3E 26
Stockwood Rd. DT9: Chet 7A 14
STOFORD 2C 123
STOKE ABBOTT 3B 122
STOKE FARTHING 1D 125
STOKEFORD 2B 128
Stokehouse St. DT1: Poun 4C 50
Stoke Rd. DT4: W Reg 5F 107
DT8: Bea 3B 24
STOKE ST GREGORY 1A 122
STOKE ST MARY 1A 122
Stokes Av. BH15: Pool 3A 90
STOKE SUB HAMDON 2B 122
STOKE TRISTER 1A 124
STOKE WAKE 3A 124
Stoke Water Ho. DT8: Bea 3A 24
Stokewood Leisure Cen. 7G 83
Stokewood Rd. BH3: Bourn 1F 93
STONE 6J 63
Stonebarrow La. DT6: C'outh 7K 35
Stonechat Cl. BH22: Fern 4B 66
DT3: B'wey 6G 101
Stonechat Ct. BH23: Chris 7D 86
Stonecrop Cl. BH18: B'tone 4H 79
Stonedene DT9: Sher 2C 12
Stone Gdns. BH8: Bourn 4C 84
Stonehill Ct. DT4: W Reg 5E 106
Stone Ho. *DT1: Dor 3G 51*
(off Pound La.)
Stone La. BH21: Wim M 6J 63
Stone La. Ind. Est. BH21: Wim M 6J 63
Stoneleigh BH13: Pool 7K 91
STONEY CROSS 1B 130
Stoney Lawn DT11: W Kin 6G 45
Stoneylawn DT10: Marn 4K 9
Stoney Path SP7: Shaf 4B 8
STONEY STOKE 1A 124
Stonyacres DT9: Yet 6G 13
Stony La. BH23: Burt 3K 85
BH23: Chris 7A 86
DT9: Bis C 5H 15
DT9: Holw 2G 27
DT10: K Stag 2G 27
Stony La. Sth. BH23: Chris 1A 96
Story La. BH18: B'tone 2K 79
Stottingway St. DT3: Upw 5F 101
Stourbank Rd. BH23: Chris 1J 95
Stourcastle Cl. SP8: Gill 2G 5
Stourcliffe Av. BH6: Bourn 3E 94
Stour Cl. BH21: L Can 1H 73
DT11: Shil 6G 19
SP8: E Sto 2J 7
Stour Ct. *BH12: Pool 3A 92*
(off Poole Rd.)
SP8: Gill .3G 5
Stourcroft Dr. BH23: Chris 4F 85
Stour Dr. BH20: W'ham 1H 113
Stourfield Rd. BH5: Bourn 3D 94
Stour Gdns. SP8: Gill 5G 5
Stour Hill SP8: W Stou 7D 4
Stour Hill Pk. SP8: W Stou 7E 4
Stour La. SP8: S Pro 4J 7
Stour Mdws. SP8: Gill 5G 5
STOURPAINE 2H 29 (3B 124)
Stourpaine Rd. BH17: Pool 4B 80
Stour Pk. BH10: Bourn 7E 74
DT11: Blan 6C 30
STOUR PROVOST 4H 7 (1A 124)
Stour Rd. BH8: Bourn 1J 93
BH23: Chris 2H 95
DT11: B For 5D 30
STOUR ROW 1B 124
STOURTON CAUNDLE 2A 124
Stourvale Av. BH23: Chris 6F 85
Stourvale M. BH6: Bourn 1E 94
Stourvale Pl. BH5: Bourn 2D 94
Stourvale Rd. BH5: Bourn 2D 94
Stour Valley Nature Reserve 1F 83
Stour Vw. Cl. DT10: S New 4C 16
Stour Vw. Gdns. BH21: Corf M 4G 71
Stour Wlk. BH8: Bourn 2K 83
BH21: Wim M 2B 72
Stour Way BH23: Chris 4F 85
Stourwood Av. BH6: Bourn 4E 94
Stourwood Rd. BH6: Bourn 3F 95
Stowcastle St. DT1: Poun 4C 50
STOWELL 1D 123
Stowell Cres. BH20: W'ham 4G 113
Stowey St. DT1: Poun 4B 50
Straits DT5: East 1J 119
Strand, The DT6: Brid 4C 38
Strand St. BH15: Pool 6A 120 (6K 89)
STRATFORD SUB CASTLE 1D 125
STRATFORD TONY 1D 125
Strathmore Dr. BH31: Ver 4G 55
Strathmore Rd. BH9: Bourn 2G 83
STRATTON 4C 48 (1D 127)
Stratton Rd. BH9: Bourn 2J 83
Streche Rd. BH19: Swan 2K 117
BH20: W'ham 4G 113
STREET .3A 122
Street, The DT6: C'outh 6H 35
DT11: S Wal 6A 10
SP7: Mot .2C 6
SP8: S Pro 4H 7
Street La. DT9: L'ton 3B 14
Streets La. BH24: Crow 7K 61
Strete Mt. BH23: Chris 7C 86
Stretton Ct. BH14: Pool 3F 91
Strides La. BH24: Ring 4H 61
Strode Gdns. BH24: S Ive 6D 60
Strodes La. DT2: Char D 2J 49
Stroud Cl. BH21: Coleh 6E 64
STROUD COMMON 3E 4
STROUDEN 5A 84
Strouden Av. BH8: Bourn 5H 83
Strouden Rd. BH9: Bourn 5G 83
Stroud Gdns. BH23: Chris 1C 96
Stroud La. BH23: Chris 1C 96
Stroudley Cres. DT3: Pres 3C 104
Stroud Pk. Av. BH23: Chris 1C 96
Struan Cl. BH24: Ash H 5B 60
Struan Ct. BH24: Ash H 5C 60
Struan Dr. BH24: Ash H 5C 60
Struan Gdns. BH24: Ash H 5B 60
Stuart Cl. BH16: Upt 7D 78
Stuart La. SP8: Gill 4F 5
Stuart Rd. BH23: H'ffe 6J 97
Stuart Way DT6: Brid 3F 39
Stubbings Mdw. Cvn. Pk.
BH24: Ring 4G 61
STUBHAMPTON 2C 125
STUCKTON 1A 130
Studcombe DT2: Ever 5B 26
STUDLAND 4K 115 (2D 129)
Studland Rd. BH4: Bourn 6C 92
BH20: Corf C 1B 114
Studland Way DT3: Red 3F 103
Studley Cl. BH23: H'ffe 6K 97
STURMINSTER MARSHALL
. . . . .6H 33 (3C 125)
STURMINSTER NEWTON
. . . . .5C 16 (2A 124)
Sturminster Newton &
Stalbridge Leisure Cen. 3C 16
Sturminster Newton Mus. & Mill
. . . . .4C 16
Sturminster Rd. BH9: Bourn 2H 83
Sturt La. BH8: Bourn 3D 84
BH20: Ber 2K 53
Stut La. DT10: F Nev 1E 28
Styles Cl. DT8: Bea 2C 24
Styles La. DT2: Pud 2C 52
Sudan Rd. DT4: Wey 4G 107
Suffolk Av. BH23: Chris 4H 85
Suffolk Cl. BH21: Coleh 6G 65
Suffolk Rd. BH2: Bourn . . .4F 121 (4D 92)
(not continuous)
Suffolk Rd. Sth. BH2: Bourn 3D 92
Summercroft Way BH22: W Moo . . .1E 66
Summerfield Cl. BH21: Hay 1F 73
BH23: Burt 4A 86
Summer Flds. BH31: Ver 6F 55
Summerfields BH7: Bourn 7B 84
Summerhill BH13: Sandb 5F 99
Summerhill Ho. *DT7: L Reg 4D 34*
(off Charmouth Rd.)
Summerhill Rd. DT7: L Reg 4D 34
Summer La. DT2: Ever 6B 26
Summers Av. BH11: Bourn 7B 74
Summer's La. BH23: Burt 5B 86
Sunbury Cl. BH11: Bourn 7A 74
Sunbury Ct. BH2: Bourn 4G 121
Suncliffe Ct. BH19: Swan 3K 117
Sunderland Dr. BH23: Chris 7F 87
Sundew Cl. BH23: Chris 5G 87
DT4: Wey 5J 103
Sundew Rd. BH18: B'tone 4G 79
Sun La. DT2: P'hide 4H 43
DT6: Morc 4J 35
Sunningdale BH15: Pool 4C 90
BH23: Chris 1H 95
Sunningdale Cres. BH10: Bourn 2C 82
Sunningdale Gdns. BH18: B'tone . . .1J 79
Sunningdale Ri. DT3: Over 5B 104
Sunnybank DT6: Brid 3C 38
Sunnybank Dr. BH21: Coleh 6F 65
Sunnybank Rd. BH21: Coleh 6F 65
Sunnybank Way BH21: Coleh 6F 65
Sunnydale Rd. BH19: Swan 7K 117
Sunnyfields DT3: S Poy 2C 104
Sunny Hill Ct. BH12: Pool 2H 91
Sunny Hill Rd. BH12: Pool 2H 91
Sunnyhill Rd. BH6: Bourn 2D 94
Sunnylands Av. BH6: Bourn 3H 95
Sunnymoor Rd. BH11: Bourn 5A 82
Sunnyside BH20: Rid 6K 113
BH20: W Lul 6G 111
Sunnyside Ct. DT9: Yet 7G 13
Sunnyside Pk. Cvn. Site
BH24: S Ive 6E 60
Sunnyside Rd. BH12: Pool 7H 81
DT4: W Reg 5E 106
Sunnyside Ter. BH20: W Lul 6G 111
DT9: Sher 4C 12
Sunridge Cl. BH12: Pool 1A 92
BH19: Swan 5J 117
Sunrise Bus. Pk. DT11: B For 1D 30
Sunset Lodge BH13: Pool 5A 92
Sunshine Wlk. BH19: Swan 5J 117
Super Bowl
Bournemouth 4K 121 (4G 93)
Surrey Cl. BH23: Chris 4H 85
DT4: Wey 7D 102
Surrey Gdns. BH4: Bourn 3C 92
Surrey Lodge BH4: Bourn 3D 92
Surrey Rd. BH2: Bourn 3D 92
BH4: Bourn 3C 92
BH12: Pool 2A 92
Surrey Rd. Sth. BH4: Bourn 3C 92
Sussex Cl. BH9: Bourn 2H 83
Sussex Farm Way DT9: Yet 7H 13
Sussex Rd. DT4: Wey 7F 103
Sutcliffe Av. DT4: S'hill 5E 102
Sutherland Av. BH18: B'tone 1G 79
Suttil Cres. DT6: Pym 1E 38
SUTTON
Castle Cary 1D 123
Wimborne 5E 20
SUTTON BINGHAM 2C 123
Sutton Cl. BH17: Pool 4F 81
DT3: S Poy 2C 104
SP8: Gill .5G 5
Sutton Ct. Lawns DT3: S Poy 2C 104
SUTTON MANDEVILLE 1C 125
SUTTON MONTIS 1D 123
Sutton Pk. DT3: Pres 3D 104
SUTTON POYNTZ 2D 104 (2A 128)
Sutton Rd. BH9: Bourn 5H 83
DT3: Pres 3D 104
SUTTON WALDRON 7B 10 (2B 124)
Swaffield Gdns. DT4: W Reg 4E 106
Swainson Rd.
DT11: B Cam, P'erne 1J 31
Swains Row DT6: W Bay 1H 37
SWALLOWCLIFFE 1C 125
Swallow Cl. BH17: Pool 6H 79
BH20: Wool 6C 110
Swallow Ct. DT4: Wey 1G 107
Swallowfields SP8: Gill 2H 5
Swallow Way BH21: Coleh 4E 64
SWANAGE 5J 117 (3D 129)
Swanage Bay Vw. Holiday Pk.
BH19: Swan 6H 117
Swanage Coastal Pk.
BH19: Swan 6G 117
Swanage Mus. 5K 117
Swanage Railway
Corfe Castle Station 2B 114
Harman's Cross Station 2A 116
Herston Halt Station 4G 117
Norden Station 1A 114
Swanage Station 5J 117
Swanage Rd. BH19: Stud 5H 115
Swanage Sailing Club 5K 117
Swanbridge Ct. DT1: Dor 3G 51
Swanbridge Mobile Home Pk.
DT1: Dor 3F 51
Swanbrook M. BH19: Swan 5J 117
Swan La. DT2: P'hide 5H 43
Swanmore Cl. BH7: Bourn 7D 84
Swanmore Rd. BH7: Bourn 1D 94
Swannery Bri. DT4: Wey 1H 107
Swannery Ct. DT4: Wey 1H 107
Swansbury Dr. BH8: Bourn 4D 84
Swan St. BH21: Cran 2G 21
Swans Yd. *SP7: Shaf 3B 8*
(off High St.)
Swan Yd. DT9: Sher 4C 12
SWAY 3B 130
Sway Gdns. BH8: Bourn 4K 83
Sweep, The BH24: Ring 4H 61
Sweetbrier Drove BH21: S Mar 5A 62
Sweet Hill La. DT5: S'well 4G 119
Sweethill M. DT5: S'well 4G 119
Sweet Hill Rd. DT5: S'well 5G 119
Sweetmans Rd. SP7: Shaf 3C 8
SWELL .1A 122
Swift Cl. BH17: Pool 6H 79
Swinton Av. BH20: Bov 1A 110
Swordfish Dr. BH23: Chris 7F 87
SWYRE 3B 46 (2C 127)
Swyre Rd. DT2: W Bex 3B 46
Sycamore Av. BH16: Sandf 3C 112
Sycamore Cl. BH17: Pool 5H 79
BH20: Sandf 6C 112
BH23: Chris 6F 85
SP5: Six H 2C 20
Sycamore Ct. BH24: Poul 1K 61
Sycamore Pl. BH21: Stap 7H 65
Sycamore Rd. DT4: S'hill 5E 102
Sycamores, The SP8: Bour 2D 4
Sycamore Way SP8: Gill 5F 5
Sydenham Cres. BH20: Wool 6C 110
Sydenham Rd. BH19: Swan 5F 117
Sydenham Way DT1: Dor 4G 51
Sydling Cl. BH17: Pool 4F 81
Sydling Rd. DT2: Cer A 4A 42
SYDLING ST NICHOLAS . . .7C 42 (1D 127)
Sydney Pl. SP8: Gill 5G 5
Sydney Rd. BH18: B'tone 3J 79
BH23: Chris 5G 85
Sydney St. DT4: Wey 1F 107
Sylmor Gdns. BH9: Bourn 4G 83
Sylvan Cl. BH24: S Leo 7K 59
SP8: Gill .3H 5
Sylvan Rd. BH12: Pool 1F 91
Sylvan Way SP8: Gill 3H 5
Symes Rd. BH15: Hamw 3G 89
SYMONDSBURY 1B 126
Symonds Cl. DT3: Rad 4H 103
Symonds Ct. DT2: C'ster 6J 49
SYNDERFORD 5D 22
Syward Cl. DT1: Dor 4J 51
Syward Rd. DT1: Dor 5H 51

T

Tabbit's Hill La.
BH20: H Cro, Woolg 2A 116
Tabernacle, The DT11: B For 5C 30
Tabernacle Ct. *DT11: B For 5C 30*
(off The Close)
TADDEN 5F 63
Tadden Wlk. BH18: B'tone 4H 79
Tait Cl. BH17: Pool 7C 80
Talbot Av. BH3: Bourn 6D 82
Talbot Ct. BH9: Bourn 5F 83
Talbot Dr. BH12: Pool 6B 82
BH23: Chris 4K 87
Talbothays Rd. DT1: Dor 5G 51
TALBOT HEATH 7C 82
Talbot Hill Rd. BH9: Bourn 6D 82
Talbot Mdws. BH12: Pool 6B 82
Talbot M. BH10: Bourn 5B 82
Talbot Ri. BH10: Bourn 4C 82
Talbot Rd. BH9: Bourn 6D 82
DT7: L Reg 4C 34
Talbot Rdbt. BH3: Bourn 7D 82

HOSPITALS and HOSPICES
covered by this atlas.

N.B. Where Hospitals and Hospices are not named on the map, the reference given is for the road in which they are situated.

ALDERNEY COMMUNITY HOSPITAL 5G **81**
Ringwood Road
POOLE
BH12 4NB
Tel: 01202 735537

BLANDFORD COMMUNITY HOSPITAL 4B **30**
Milldown Road
BLANDFORD FORUM
DT11 7DD
Tel: 01258 456541

BOURNEMOUTH NUFFIELD HOSPITAL
   (DERWENT SUITE) 5D **84**
Castle Lane East
BOURNEMOUTH
BH7 7DR
Tel: 01202 390999

BOURNEMOUTH NUFFIELD HOSPITAL, THE
   ....1K **121** (2G **93**)
67-71 Lansdowne Road
BOURNEMOUTH
BH1 1RW
Tel: 01202 291866

BRIDPORT COMMUNITY HOSPITAL 2B **38**
Hospital Lane
BRIDPORT
DT6 5DR
Tel: 01308 422371

CHRISTCHURCH HOSPITAL 6H **85**
Fairmile Road
CHRISTCHURCH
BH23 2JX
Tel: 01202 486361

DORSET COUNTY HOSPITAL 4E **50**
Williams Avenue
DORCHESTER
DT1 2JY
Tel: 01305 251150

FOREST HOLME HOSPICE 3E **120** (4B **90**)
5 Seldown Road
POOLE
BH15 1TS
Tel: 01202 448103

FORSTON CLINIC 1J **49**
Herrison Road
DORCHESTER
DT2 9TB
Tel: 01305 361300

HARBOUR BMI HOSPITAL, THE 2E **120** (4B **90**)
St. Mary's Road
POOLE
BH15 2BH
Tel: 01202 244200

HERBERT HOSPITAL 5B **92**
Alumhurst Road
BOURNEMOUTH
BH4 8EP
Tel: 01202 584300

JOSEPH WELD HOSPICE 6E **50**
Herrington Road
DORCHESTER
DT1 2SL
Tel: 01305 251052

KING'S PARK COMMUNITY HOSPITAL 2B **94**
Gloucester Rd.
BOURNEMOUTH
BH7 6JF
Tel: 01202 303757

LEWIS MANNING HOUSE HOSPICE 1G **99**
1 Crichel Mount Road
POOLE
BH14 8LT
Tel: 01202 708470

POOLE GENERAL HOSPITAL 2E **120** (4B **90**)
Longfleet Road
POOLE
BH15 2JB
Tel: 01202 665511

PORTLAND COMMUNITY HOSPITAL 3B **118**
Castle Road
PORTLAND
DT5 1AX
Tel: 01305 820341

ROYAL BOURNEMOUTH HOSPITAL 5D **84**
Castle La. E.
BOURNEMOUTH
BH7 7DW
Tel: 01202 303626

ST ANN'S HOSPITAL 2J **99**
69 Haven Road
POOLE
BH13 7LN
Tel: 01202 708881

ST LEONARD'S COMMUNITY HOSPITAL 4J **67**
Ringwood Road
Hampshire
RINGWOOD
BH24 2RR
Tel: 01202 584200

ST MARY'S MATERNITY HOSPITAL 2E **120** (4B **90**)
St. Mary's Road
POOLE
BH15 2JB
Tel: 01202 665511

SWANAGE COMMUNITY HOSPITAL 6J **117**
Queens Road
SWANAGE
BH19 2ES
Tel: 01929 422282

TRIMAR HOSPICE 6J **103**
9 Greenhill
WEYMOUTH
DT4 7SW
Tel: 01305 767527

VICTORIA HOSPITAL (WIIMBORNE) 7J **63**
Victoria Road
WIMBORNE
BH21 1ER
Tel: 01202 858200

WAREHAM COMMUNITY HOSPITAL 3G **113**
Streche Road
WAREHAM
BH20 4QQ
Tel: 01929 552433

WESTHAVEN HOSPITAL 7E **102**
Radipole Lane
WEYMOUTH
DT4 0QE
Tel: 01305 786116

WESTMINSTER MEMORIAL HOSPITAL 4B **8**
Magdalene Lane
SHAFTESBURY
SP7 8BD
Tel: 01747 851535 / 475200

WEYMOUTH COMMUNITY HOSPITAL 6J **103**
Melcombe Avenue
WEYMOUTH
DT4 7TB
Tel: 01305 760022

WINTERBOURNE BMI HOSPITAL, THE 6E **50**
Herrington Road
DORCHESTER
DT1 2DR
Tel: 01305 263252

YEATMAN HOSPITAL 4C **12**
Hospital Lane
SHERBORNE
DT9 3JU
Tel: 01935 813991

Printed and bound in the United Kingdom by Polestar Wheatons Ltd., Exeter.